SEX ROLES IN CHANGING SOCIETY

Random House
New York

SEX ROLES IN CHANGING SOCIETY

edited by GEORGENE H. SEWARD
UNIVERSITY OF SOUTHERN CALIFORNIA

and ROBERT C. WILLIAMSON
LEHIGH UNIVERSITY

 Published in the United States by Random House, Inc., New York, and simultaneously in Canada by Random House of Canada Limited, Toronto.

Library of Congress Catalog Card Number: 79-102391

Manufactured in the United States of America by The Kingsport Press, Inc., Kingsport, Tenn.

Typography by Jack Ribik.

FIRST PRINTING

ACKNOWLEDGMENTS

Both editors are indebted to Mrs. Margaret Fistner, Mrs. Pauline Groff, Mrs. Susan Karlyn, and Mrs. Ruth McGuire for the invaluable help given us by their manuscript typing. Special thanks are due Mrs. Alice Stowell of the University of Southern California Psychology Department for her expert suggestions and her continuous encouragement throughout the project. We are also grateful to our respective spouses for their editorial advice, understanding, and patience during the preparation of the manuscript.

As editors we acknowledge with gratitude the privilege generously granted us by authors and publishers involved, of reprinting excerpts from previously published material:

Acropolis Books: *Queen Sheba's Heirs* by Edith E. Lord, 1970.

George Allen & Unwin Ltd.: *A Study of Contemporary Ghana* by Walter Birmingham, I. Neustadt, and E. N. Omabee, 1967.

The Clarendon Press, Oxford: *Both Sides of Buka Passage* by Beatrice Blackwood, 1935, pp. 146–149.

The John Day Company, Inc.: *My Several Worlds* by Pearl S. Buck. Copyright 1954 by Pearl S. Buck. Permission granted for British Commonwealth by Methuen & Co. Ltd.

Faber and Faber Ltd.: *The Position of Women in Primitive Societies and other Essays in Social Anthropology* by E. E. Evans-Pritchard, 1965, pp. 45–46.

Francis L. K. Hsu: *Under the Ancestors' Shadow,* Columbia University Press, 1948.

H. A. Junod: *The Life of a South African Tribe,* Macmillan, 1927, pp. 177–178.

MacDonald & Evans Ltd.: *The Modern African* by Charles Obukar and John Williams, 1965.

McGraw-Hill: *Sex and the Social Order* by Georgene H. Seward, 1946, chapter 10.

Pantheon Books: *Report from a Chinese Village* by Jan Myrdal, 1965.

Penguin Books Ltd.: *African Outline* by Paul Bohannan, 1966.

Science: "The Generation Gap" by Margaret Mead, Vol. 164 (April 11, 1969), p. 134. Copyright 1969 by the American Association for the Advancement of Science. We express particular thanks to Dr. Margaret Mead for suggesting the selection used.

Stanford University Press: "Sex differences and cultural institutions" by Roy G.

D'Andrade, in *The Development of Sex Differences,* Eleanor E. Maccoby, ed., 1966, pp. 201–202.

Teachers College Press: "Worker, Mother, Housewife: Soviet Woman Today" by Mark G. Field and Karin I. Flynn. This article appeared in a slightly different form in *The Role and Status of Women in the Soviet Union,* edited by Donald R. Brown. Reprinted by permission of Teachers College Press. Copyright © 1968 by Teachers College, Columbia University.

Yale University Press: *The Role of the Aged in Primitive Society* by Leo Simmons, 1945, p. 81.

For Some Women and Men of the Twenty-first Century

HEATHER

LAUREL

LARRY

ERIC

MATTHEW

The Contributors

George A. De Vos: Anthropology, University of California, Berkeley.

Mark G. Field: Sociology, Boston University, and Harvard University Russian Research Center.

Karin I. Flynn: Sociology-Anthropology, Boston University, and Harvard University Russian Research Center.

Stanley L. M. Fong: Psychology, State University of New York, Buffalo.

Clellan S. Ford: Anthropology, Human Relations Area Files, Yale University.

Fred J. Goldstein: Clinical Psychology, Beverly Hills, California.

Ruth E. Hartley: Psychology, Growth and Development Program, University of Wisconsin, Green Bay.

Irene M. Josselyn: Psychiatry (Child), University of Southern California, School of Medicine, Los Angeles, California.

Alfred Katzenstein: Clinical Psychology, Institut für Kortiko-Viszerale Pathologie und Therapie; Deutsche Akademie der Wissenschaften zu Berlin, German Democratic Republic.

Ursula Lehr: Psychology, Psychologisches Institut der Universität Bonn, West Germany.

Rita Liljeström: Sociology, Sociologiska Institutionen, Goteborg, Sweden.

Edith E. Lord: Psychology, University of Miami, Florida.

Margaret Mead: Anthropology, American Museum of Natural History, New York, New York.

Albert I. Rabin: Psychology, Michigan State University, East Lansing, Michigan.

Hellgard Rauh: Psychology, Psychologisches Institut der Universität Bonn, West Germany.

S. N. Sinha: Psychology, Department of Philosophy and Psychology, University of Rajasthan, Jaipur, India.

C. D. Spinellis: Sociology, Athenian Institute of Anthropos, Athens, Greece.

George Vassiliou: Psychiatry, Athenian Institute of Anthropos, Athens, Greece.

Vasso Vassiliou: Psychology, Athenian Institute of Anthropos, Athens, Greece.

Hiroshi Wagatsuma: Sociology-Anthropology-Psychiatry, University of Pittsburgh, Pennsylvania.

The Editors

Georgene H. Seward: Psychology, The University of Southern California, Los Angeles, California.

Robert C. Williamson: Social Relations, Lehigh University, Bethlehem, Pennsylvania.

PREFACE

At the close of World War I, the senior editor presented an evaluation of the man-woman relationship in *Sex and the Social Order* [McGraw-Hill, 1946 (1954)]. Now the time has come for a fresh look at the roles of a new generation of men and women who have grown up under the influences of postwar changes. Rather than attempt direct comparison with the earlier, more limited work, the present editors have broadened the base of inquiry by enlisting as coauthors experts on, and often from, selected societies to report on the current situation in their respective areas. These areas sample Orient and Occident, Western and Eastern European blocs, and advanced industrialized as well as underdeveloped countries. Needless to say, the sociopolitical viewpoints of the contributors reflect the cultural diversity and are presented for the reader's evaluation without editorial comment.

A source of further variety in perspective and presentation is the professional affiliation of writers who cover a wide social-science spectrum. In treating such complex social orders as the USSR, Sweden, and the Germanies, sex-role behavior is viewed sociologically in terms of group norms, with heavy reliance on statistical comparisons. Primitive cultures, on the other hand, are for the most part limited to ethnological description and personal impression. A special case in point concerns the treatment of African societies written in the wake of the contributor's evacuation from Nigeria, ". . . in a rowboat, with my parrot in one hand, and my viola in the other." Under these circumstances, she had no alternative to relying on her own extensive experience in the Veld. Her anecdotal approach, however, makes up in immediacy and vividness for an excusable paucity of library documentation. When it comes to interpreting developmental or clinical material, neither statistical analysis nor description are appropriate; study in depth is needed to reveal the psychodynamics underlying role behavior. Varied as these approaches are, they share a common focus on social rather than biological sex-role behavior. Sexual behavior in the sense of erotic practices is beyond the scope of the present volume and is treated only insofar as it may throw light on social sex roles.

Although our primary concern is with the social sex roles of both men and women, disproportionate attention may often seem to be given the feminine role. Such apparently undue emphasis is a function of woman's fluctuant social status in many cultures. Although her *biological* role of childbearing is a constant, her social role has varied according to the success or failure of her civil rights struggles over the centuries against the repressive "minority" status in which she has been held. In the case of men, it has been the *social* role of "provider" that, with few exceptions, has remained constant, whether implemented by big game hunting in the primitive forest or on the modern stock market. Changes in male social sex roles for the most part have come about as accommodations to, or counterbalances for, the more drastic female social role changes.

The general plan of the book is first to trace the development of sex-role patterns in Western culture and then to present the contemporary scene in selected societies the world over. From an analysis of this cultural assortment are drawn implications for the future. The reader-target is identified as the educated person with a responsible concern for the particular problem of sex roles in relation to the more general social changes taking place today.

University of Southern California
Lehigh University
February 1970

GEORGENE H. SEWARD
ROBERT C. WILLIAMSON

CONTENTS

PROLOGUE

THE PROBLEM IN PERSPECTIVE

The Editors

part 1: Origins of Sex-Role Patterning

Prehuman Origins

Sex Roles in Changing Society obviously has a social focus; that focus is *human* society. Nevertheless, it is well to remind ourselves of the subhuman social organizations that set the stage for man and reveal the origins of social sex roles. From fish to man, gender is associated with specific behaviors. Below the mammals there are sex differences in dominance that are correlated with androgen function on the inside, and with certain types of stimulation on the outside. In higher forms, the increasing complexity of brain development means increasing capacity for modification through experience, learned modes of adaptation to the environment taking precedence over ready-made instinctual patterns [Seward, 1946 (1954)]. By the time the primate level is reached, social influences have become so intricate and compelling as to clearly foreshadow culture. The work of Harlow and his team (1962, 1965, 1966) on the rhesus monkey has supplied ample evidence in support of this point. At the same time, the results show certain sex differences that are unequivocally due to genetic factors. They include the forceful approach or "threat response" of the male and the passivity, withdrawal, and rigid posturing of the female. Out of these infantile sex-linked behavior patterns develop the affectional bonds and the social ordering of the mature monkey. According to Harlow (1962) :

> These secondary sex-behavior differences probably exist throughout the primate order, and, moreover, they are innately determined biological differences regardless of any culture overlap [pp. 4–5].

So impressed was Harlow with the biological basis of these behavior patterns that he does not hesitate to generalize his results to man and indeed finds parallel evidence in the aggressive play of preschool children (Sears, 1965) .

Some Primitive Societies

Bearing these considerations in mind, we may turn to the task in hand. Ford's comparative study of primitive societies led him to conclude that in spite of diversity from one group to another, social sex roles are influenced by biological heritage. Activities like fighting, hunting, and building were usually defined as "masculine," while those involving care of the young, cooking, handicrafts, and home occupations received the "feminine" label. Like Mead's (1949) "basic regularities," Ford finds men transculturally the more dominant, aggressive, and sexually active; women, the more emotionally expressive and nurturant. These sex-linked differences strongly suggest the genetic factors invoked by Harlow to explain male-female monkey behavior. Ford makes the point, however, that such cultural influences as economic and political controls may set the limits within which the presumably natural sex differences are permitted expression. In all cultures, maleness and femaleness are institutionalized as statuses and become the core of the psychological identities of most individuals.

Emergent Africa

Lord's approach to sex roles in *Emergent Africa* is based on a lengthy and intimate acquaintance with the peoples of this continent. Since Africa represents over a hundred major tribes, generalizations are risky, but there are some major themes that cut across most of the societies. Woman's status is generally inferior to man's, inevitably so in polygynous groups. Divorce is at the discretion of the male, a characteristic diffused in part by Arab culture that has contributed to female subjection throughout Africa. Not all the mores, however, are alien to Western culture. For instance, the bride price (now often paid in cash rather than cattle) is reminiscent of the dowry, which was long entrenched in many Western countries, and the significance of role played by women in the royal families is not unlike the monarchical system of Europe.

Native folkways are rationalized as universal in cultural behavior: Polygyny, for example, is defended because of the supposed surplus of women, yet census data show the sex ratio to be roughly equal to that in other parts of the world.

But Africa is on the move. The influence of missionary and commercial contacts with the West, the processes of urbanization, education, and political independence are disturbing the traditional patterns of male superiority. The extended kinship system has had to undergo a number of modifications as individuals and families migrate to the city (Aldous, 1965). Moreover, feelings of doubt and confusion about courtship and marriage are indicated by letters written to a West African newspaper (Jahoda, 1959). This process of Westernization and its impact on marriage and family institutions is possibly slower, or at least is in its incipient stages, compared with what is happening in parts of the Near East, southern Asia, and certainly Latin America, but it appears to be accelerating. Both men and women are acquiring new roles, and in the long run the latter will probably change the most. As women acquire an education and the right to vote, they also begin to enter a variety of new occupations. The state bureaucracy, the city, and the school all have their inevitable effects in extending the role expectations of both sexes.

Sexual Identity Crises in the Life Cycle

In all cultures, each individual must face the task of finding an ego identity (Erikson, 1959) and life goal (Bühler & Massarik, 1968). The problem of sex identity formation is approached in depth by Josselyn. Her psychoanalytic work with adolescents from Western core culture brings out the importance of biological factors in behavioral sex differences, as did Ford's cross-cultural comparisons among primitive peoples and Harlow's laboratory studies of monkeys. Josselyn defends the argument that ego development follows a different course in the two sexes—the girl passively receiving nurturance from her mother, while the boy breaks away from her to assert his aggressive masculinity. These innate trends are overlaid by cultural superstructures that may entrench or distort them. As Seward (1964) has pointed out elsewhere, in complex literate society the daily activities of men and women are often remote from the biological substrate that is much more in evidence in primitive life. Actually, the relevance of innate patterning is open to question in the urbanized, computerized society that demands neither greater muscular strength and aggressiveness of the male, nor exclusively childbearing and caring of the female. The blurring of social sex stereotypes is facilitated by the extension of the middle-class segment, the greater participation of women in the economic, political, and educational life of the community and, most significantly of all, by the trend toward smaller families with their greater role flexibility (Bernard, 1968; Rosenkrantz *et al.*, 1968). Under such complex circumstances as Josselyn reminds us, it is increasingly difficult to find "appropriate" sex-role models in parent or peer. In her opinion, sex-role confusion has become aggravated by the extreme youth-centering that has resulted in a Barbie-doll ideal of womanliness!

Skin color and sex identity conflict

Sex identity development is complicated in the various minority subcultures that often have atypical forms of family life. The difficulty of finding acceptable role models is compounded by the necessity to integrate the indigenous patterning with that of the prevailing core culture (Brody, 1968; Seward, 1956, 1958). Although detailed discussion of this issue is beyond the scope of the present volume, a few examples may serve to illustrate its nature.

In the case of the Negro American, confusion has resulted from discrepancies between core-culture role expectancies and insuperable obstacles in the way of fulfilling them (Erikson, 1968; Pettigrew, 1964). Throughout the three centuries of oppression and discrimination in America, the black man has been so effectively barred by white society from playing the protector-provider role prescribed for males by that society, that the black woman, however reluctantly, has had to assume it by accepting the uninviting types of work open to her. Under the circumstances, it is no wonder that mothers without partners often express their inner conflict by overprotecting or dominating their children with especially adverse effects on the masculine identity of the boys (Parker & Kleiner, 1966).

In Negro homes, even where there is a husband, the breadwinner-wife is the one who makes the major decisions for the family (Blood & Wolfe, 1960). So important is the mother in the poor black family that the idea of a "mother cult" as an ethnic folkway has grown up around her authority role. "Negro matriarchy" is a myth, however, based on the reality of class, not race. Oscar Lewis (1966), in his work with Puerto Ricans, has pointed out that it is characteristic of all "cultures of poverty." The partial sex-role reversal has had a castrating effect on the male Negro, resulting in serious identity disturbances (Kardiner & Ovesey, 1951; Seward, 1954; Seward, 1964). As Seward (1964) has described the situation:

> A father who has realistic doubts about his ability to support his family, coupled with ramifying doubts about his personal worth and masculinity, can hardly be a pillar of strength for his son to emulate [p. 133].

The weak masculine identity may account for the low interest in romance and marriage found in a group of blue-collar Negro boys in comparison with a corresponding group of whites (Broderick, 1965).

Brody (1968) sees the deficiency in the father-model as predisposing the Negro boy to a defensive homosexual orientation that may combine with the "normal" suspicious vigilance of the disfavored minority member to produce true paranoid sensitivity. With conflict built into the developing ego structure, the ground is prepared for the diverse forms of psychopathology that have been found in the black American (Grier & Cobbs, 1968). As equality of status and opportunity are achieved, the group differences erroneously ascribed to "race" may be expected to disappear.

For the "brown" American, the source of sex identity conflict is the *machismo* cult of Old Mexico, which makes a boastful masculinity the measure of a man's worth. Although some of the father's power was extended to his "grown sons," the prevalence of the "absentee father" forced the boys to develop reaction formations against the danger of feminine identification with the ever-present mother.

In the Mexican American family, the adolescent son as the link with the outside world acts as mentor and protector of the American outlook and practices for his younger siblings. The male role is colored by the image of the "macho" personality that includes sexual prowess, male dominance, physical strength, adventurousness, and courage—characteristics not easily understood by law enforcement officers! A very different upbringing is afforded the girl who, under the guidance of her mother and protection of her brother, is trained for the home where she will be a faithful wife and loving mother (Heller, 1966). According to a recent study of Mexican Americans in East Los Angeles, the incongruence between Mexican and Anglo male ideals caused severe identity conflict in the boys. For the girls, the problem was less stressful inasmuch as their role in reality was closer to that of the Anglo female whom they had set up as model (Derbyshire, 1968).

Looking toward the East, the newcomers from China and Japan at first settled in the Chinatowns and Little Tokyos of American cities, where they tried to preserve cultural and family bonds. Movement away from the ghetto, however, meant a loosening of ties to the old ways and greater acculturation pressure toward the new. An important source of stress concerned sex-role expectancies. In the case of Japanese Americans, the father's authority diminished concomitantly with the sons' becoming more assertive. Even more conspicuous were the frequent shifts in women's roles, accelerated by the war and relocation, from subservience to independent work outside the home (Yamamoto, 1968). Such reorientation was achieved at the cost of inner conflict as De Vos' studies over a decade ago demonstrated (1954, 1955). In the present volume, De Vos and Wagatsuma's chapter, *Status and Role Behavior in Changing Japan* reveals some parallel changes accompanying Westernizing trends in urban Japan.

The process of acculturation for Chinese Americans has followed an analogous course, with a new cycle recently initiated by refugees from the Communist mainland (Fong, 1968). One area that focuses the differential sex-role strain in Chinese culture is that of the student. Traditionally, education was reserved for men only, on the assumption that it would threaten the girl's feminine virtue of devotion to her future mother-in-law and the wish to bear many grandchildren for her. Fong and Peskin (1969) have reported evidence of a "masculine protest" style among China-born students in the United States on visas, supporting the theory that the female who adopts a student role is rebelling against tradition and feels alienated from the Chinese feminine ideal of modesty, patience, and reserve. Later, in

Fong's chapter on *Sex Roles in the Modern Fabric of China,* we shall have an opportunity to examine the situation in selected parts of China today.

Sex Identity Deviation and Inversion

Further variations from the core cultural main theme may be found in other ethnic subcultures but no "subculture" demonstrates the crucial importance of early socialization more dramatically than that of the sexual invert for whom in most cases cross-sex parental identification, especially in males, has replaced the usual identification with a same-sexed model. Recent evidence suggests that Lesbianism may bear little relationship to the establishment of feminine identity (Gundlach & Riess, 1968). Although biological factors may play a predisposing part, in the vast majority of cases it is experience, especially in early childhood though sometimes in adolescence, that precipitates the problem (Kinsey, Pomeroy & Martin, 1948). In his chapter, Goldstein analyzes the faulty learning that distorts the individual's development and leads to an assortment of deviant linkages between anatomy and role behavior. He shows how the sexual deviate has been forced by public sanctions into minority-group status and the development of a separate subculture. As a clinical psychologist, Goldstein examines the institutionalization of homosexuality and indicates some of the problems and methods of psychotherapy for this psychosocial disorder.

part 2: The Sexes in Western Culture

Sex Roles, Ancient to Modern

Turning to Part II, our chief concern is with the man-woman picture in contemporary Western culture. Seward's chapter, which reviews the course of sex-role and status fluctuations from Minoan days to the end of World War II, may serve as a baseline from which we may view the current scene.

Despite conspicuous value differences that separated the early peoples of Western culture, the assumption of male superiority provided a common denominator. Furthermore, despite the acceptance of monogamy as the marital norm, men were freer to experiment outside marriage. This ideology permeated the Middle Ages, and even the Renaissance failed to upset male dominance, even though both sexes of the upper class gained a richer experience during this period than they had known before. In the New World, frontier conditions and vague democratic notions provided a milieu in which the European mold was questioned, yet equality between the sexes was not seriously posed until the late nineteenth century.

American Core Culture

The struggle for equality has continued to the present, especially in the occupational world. Looking at United States core culture today we may note many changes since the Lynds' "Middletown" typified American life. Hartley indicates that between 1947 and 1962, 60 percent of the increase in the entire labor force represented women. In colleges, the 1960 census showed a trend in women's majors toward the basic and applied sciences and away from education and home economics.

These changes in female orientation are paralleled by the entry of men into the traditionally "feminine" occupations of primary school teaching, social work, library science, dietetics, and nursing, which suggests complementary shifts in masculine role and attitude.

Hartley draws attention to the inadequacies of our culture in preparing boys and girls during their childhood and adolescence for their adult sex roles. The traditional roles were not geared to meet the social expectations and tasks of postwar youth. They are even more inappropriate for the society that is currently evolving. These new roles must accommodate to the changes occurring in the occupational world and in the realm of sex experience, marriage, and family life. Appeals to develop woman power, like appeals to develop black power, are based on the assumption of unlimited opportunity (Lewis, 1968). There is serious question, however, as to whether the cultural lag, in fully utilizing the female resources, will catch up with the rapid social changes before overpopulation and automation will send the women once again back to the shelter of the home.

Marriage Roles, American Style

It is in the dynamics of marriage, to which Williamson turns, that sex roles assume special significance. His chapter is focused on American society where a revolutionary shift in equilibrium between the sexes took shape, largely under the impetus of the nineteenth century movements for women's rights. These movements and the employment of women went hand in hand with increasing industrialization and urbanization. In addition, a number of social changes were taking place, from the innovation of the automobile and the mass production of contraceptives to the diffusion of Freudian ideas and the concept that an unhappy marriage could be resolved by divorce. These changes were not unique to the United States, but they seemed to have their greatest vogue there. Their roots and implications were not well understood, either at home or abroad, but their effect on role behavior has been both deep and extensive, including dating practices, courtship, and mate selection. Even so, the woman still does not have equal bargaining power in her social interactions with the man.

The chapter deals with questions of role relationship in marriage: How does the individual resolve the "self esteem," the "I," and the "me," in the resocialization process of the early years of marriage (Brown, 1966)? How do two people in this intimate setting learn to perceive their needs and those of the spouse? How do they learn to communicate effectively with each other? How do they resolve their respective demands in decision-making? What function does conflict serve in marriage: a release from tension, a means of constructive self-examination, a ritualized expression of guilt and anxiety? The chapter suggests some answers to these questions, with no pretense that the complexity of marriage relationships can be understood in a limited examination of the research literature. The discussion is intended rather as an introduction to the problem.

Role Themes in Latin America

The cultural background of Latin America is heterogeneous, based on several ethnic strains, and essentially a "mix" of Spanish feudalism and the indigenous societies overwhelmed by the *conquistadores* and their descendants. Diversity in geographic settings and historical development, a rigid class structure, and rural-urban differentiation make impossible the description of a "typical" Latin American culture.

In this context, Williamson examines what to most Westerners is a unique configuration of male and female role relationships. Even the marital union has a style of its own. The insistence that the state and the church conduct separate ceremonies, usually a burdensome expense to the peasant and the urban lower class, results in the decision, on the part of many, to have no ritual at all. Consequently, the consensual union is the norm in several countries. Despite a history of common-law marriages on their own frontier, most North Americans do not understand that Mexicans in Los Angeles or Puerto Ricans in New York may not necessarily formalize their marriages, however enduring these unions may be.

Most disturbing to the visitor in Latin America is the markedly unbalanced relation he perceives between the two sexes. Women have a subordinate, almost masochistic role in marriage and in society generally, despite sharp regional and class differences. Although the middle-class wife enjoys a more permissive role than her lower-class sister, conformity demands may mean that the psychological strain is the greatest for the middle class. The *machismo* system is the most regressive aspect of sex differentiation. Maleness, especially as demonstrated in sexual adventures, is the norm for one sex, whereas virginity until marriage is stringently demanded for the other —a reminder of earlier Western history and of Spain's Arab past. The tenacity of these mores is evident from their persistence in the American Latin subcultures, as we have noted in the case of the Mexican American.

The Swedish Model

On the whole, Northwestern Europe has moved toward greater equality between the sexes. In Sweden, a dual role for women has evolved that has been the subject of intense debate over the past decade. Liljeström's chapter reports the controversy and supports the more radical solution presented in a recent United Nations report on the status of women that provides for a true equality between the sexes through "men's emancipation" for complete sharing with women of domestic as well as work roles. Since theory has not found acceptance in general practice, there remains an uneasy balance between men and women, and vocational roles are still demarcated along sex lines.

Greater equality in social sex roles in Sweden is correlated with relatively greater permissiveness in sexual behavior than in most Western countries. For more than a generation, the majority of men and women have entered marriage with sex experience, although not of a promiscuous type (Svalastoga, 1954). It is indeed the antithesis of what one encounters in Latin cultures. On the other hand, comparing North American with Scandinavian sex culture, Christensen (1960) finds that:

> The United States has more terminal petting, younger ages at marriage, more guilt associated with premarital coitus, a greater tendency to hurry the wedding when caught with pregnancy, a disproportionately higher divorce rate associated with premarital pregnancy, and so on [pp. 72–73].

It may well be that the United States and Western Europe are moving toward the Scandinavian model.

Several differences set off Scandinavian cultures from those we have discussed. For one, there is the homogeneity of the society. In contrast, Anglo-America and particularly Latin America have sharp regional, ethnic, and class differences even within a given nation. Although rural and urban differences in Sweden are pronounced and class differences are perceptible, relations between the sexes are not generally colored by the marked subcultural differences found in countries such as the United States or Brazil. Moreover, the minimal role of religion may be relevant to the rationalistic attitude mentioned by Liljeström. Perhaps more important than either of these attitudes is the influence of the *welfare state.* The social services available in Sweden make for individual security. Contraception, abortion, and financial assistance for illegitimate children as well as for those born in wedlock assure the woman of her dignity as a human being and make her independent of the man.

Male and Female in the Two Germanies

In Germany, the split since the Occupation ushered in changes in both Western and Eastern sectors—the newly constituted *Federal Republic* and *Democratic Republic.* In the West, according to Lehr and Rauh, the sex-role differential is less steep than previously and women have enjoyed greater access to education, politics, and the general economy. The effect of all these changes has been a "leveling of sex-role differences." The law of 1949, providing for equality between the sexes, set an ideal toward which West German society could move. While there has been no basic change in sixty years in the proportion (one-third) of women in the labor force, many new occupations have been opened to them, as Lehr and Rauh show. Yet, a number of managerial and professional roles are still forbidden territory.

Demographic as well as sociopolitical changes in Germany have affected sex and family roles. As with the Soviet Union in the vacuum left by the war, women became not only the more numerous sex and assumed far more importance occupationally, but they also became the sustaining force in the family. Under the circumstances, it is no wonder that the old patriarchal pattern gave way. In 1954, Schelsky (1954) pointed out that less than one-fourth of the families could be regarded as patricentric, the remainder falling in categories of transitional, equalitarian, or matricentric. Even in rural areas, roughly half have abandoned the traditional form. These changes do not mean that authoritarianism has disappeared; it is still there, only differently directed and administered. Recent research comparing West German with American family structure (Seward & Larson, 1968) indicates that the father, on the old European model, continues to exert more authority than is typical in the United States. In general, as Lehr and Rauh point out, there is more pressure in the German home for children to obey and be orderly, although it seldom reaches the "children should be seen and not heard" extreme. In the case of women, careers are still viewed as detrimental to the stability of the home, but at least the old-fashioned *Hausfrau* has been supplanted by the richer lover-companion role.

From the German Democratic Republic, Katzenstein reports that women are eagerly participating in social action, although marriage and motherhood remain central. Their dual role is eased by a state system of nurseries, day-care centers, special medical dispensations, and childbearing bonuses. The author contrasts the *Kinder-Kirche-Küche* attitudes of Nazi youth toward women with the German Democratic Republic boy's willingness to share the girl's interest in family and homemaking. While these changes suggest a more complete break with the past than has occurred in West Germany, Katzenstein makes the point that equalitarian status and rights between the sexes ". . . do not necessarily imply equal role playing."

It is too early to assess German society and the kind of stabilization of sex roles that is taking place. The debacle of Germany in World War II left the youth in both West and East isolated from the parents who had openly or tacitly supported the Nazi political system. Today, adolescents are turning to peer groups for new role models, with resulting greater equality between the sexes. New evidence indicates that the postwar generation in the two Germanies is taking a responsible part in rebuilding society. Sex-role changes seem to be moving at a more rapid pace in the East than in the West. In the German Democratic Republic, girls have been found to display greater activity than their counterparts in the Federal Republic, who adhere more closely to the tradition of feminine passivity (Seward & Larson, 1968). What the differential effect of these changes in the two Germanies will be on the relations between men and women, parents and children, will have to await another generation.

Soviet Woman Today

Traditionally, Russia was patriarchal in the extreme. In Czarist times, the husband's and father's will were unquestioned and wife-beatings a matter of course. The Revolution basically changed the social system, restructuring the pattern of family life, especially as regards the role relationships between husband and wife. The leaders of the Revolution preached a doctrine of sex equality which, according to Field and Flynn's chapter, has remained the official line through the past two decades in spite of ideological swings and great subcultural and regional differences among the sixteen nations making up the Soviet Union.

As may be noted, in the German Democratic Republic and in Sweden, sex "equality" has amounted to a new kind of "double standard," with the women accorded the dubious "privilege" of full participation in the world outside the home combined with full responsibility inside it. The four types of women outlined by Field and Flynn, the "comrades positive; willing; reluctant; and parasitic," point up the diversification of the feminine role that has emerged in Soviet Russia. Literature and the press have graphically pictured the dilemma facing women in their dual role (or triple if we include "loyal citizen" in addition to "wife-mother" and "worker").

In the case of the man, the idea of having a working wife has had to be accepted because of the inadequate income of the average breadwinner. The idea of sex equality, however, has not been gracefully assimilated. Signs of stress have been exhibited in alcoholism and other forms of escapism to which the confused husband has been found to resort. Furthermore, public and private behavior may not jibe: a man who may be equalitarian at work may be a bear at home, or the reverse situation may obtain (Geiger, 1968). In any case, there seems to be a continuum of decision-making and power structure in the Soviet home from the old-fashioned peasant authoritarianism to the partnership of the urban professional.

The Sexes: Ideology and Reality in the Israeli Kibbutz

The Kibbutz, as Rabin presents it in his chapter, is the most successful utopian venture in history. Its reorientation of the nuclear family and extension of kinship ties has provided a broad interpersonal base for socializing the child (Talmon, 1965). Nevertheless, the elimination of the usual sex division of labor by freeing women from domestic chores and basic child-training practices has proved too simplistic a solution to the "woman problem" which is reflected in higher neuroticism test scores of Kibbutz girls (Rabin, 1968). At first, female enthusiasm ran high and was expressed in such symptoms of reaction formation against their femininity as blue jeans, repudiation of lipstick and jewelry, and casual manners. More recently, women have become disenchanted with their new role. The physically too strenuous tractor-driving and harvesting led them back to their former service-oriented work. Moreover, they prefer to work in their own homes with their own children rather than in the Kibbutz.

With increasing cultural development and greater opportunity for both sexes to enter professions, the Kibbutz type of institution may take on new meaning. Meanwhile, the biosocial issue regarding sex roles that we introduced at the outset of this chapter is again pointed up. In light of the evidence for innate sex-linked behaviors, the question remains open as to whether occupations providing outlets for male force and female nurturing might not result in greater satisfaction for individual men and women even though they may be no longer crucial to the operation of the social system.

Milieu Development and Male-Female Roles in Contemporary Greece

In our survey of Western culture we have come full circle with the Spinellis, Vassiliou, and Vassiliou chapter on contemporary Greece. The authors, representing the Athenian Institute of Anthropos, present a picture for us of the archaic and modern role-blending that has its counterpart in the mingling of archaic and modern stones in the city of Athens. The old ways suited to the old milieu fail to meet the demands of the industrial age and are crumbling under its impact as surely as the ancient Acropolis is crumbling under the industrial smog that now surrounds it.

The "proper man" and "proper woman" of Greece put family obligation above self-realization and ingroup loyalty above getting along on the "outside" with the "strangers" of the business world. The authors point out that these homely values are no longer adequate for survival. Culture conflict between old and new has led to serious role strain in the behavior of men and women caught in the transition. The chapter emphasizes the need for new models to relieve the strain and allow free movement into the future.

part 3: The Sexes in the East

Between West and East

As we shift to the Eastern cultures, we are aware of the greater significance of traditional kinship systems and of more rigid sex-role differentiation and segregation. Eastern cultures are rural in character, and the communal pattern remains dominant. At the same time, much of Eastern culture is feeling the impact of Western technology. Incipient urbanization based on industrialization stands in contrast to the imperial cities of ancient times. Breaks are appearing in the feudal structure. Literacy, nationalization, political and social liberation have been among the rallying cries among the societies undergoing transformation, all of which are evolving at different rates under the influences of regional, ethnic, and religious loyalties.

Turkey [1]

Seward's chapter calls attention to the transformations brought about in the Soviet East under pressures of the communist system. In Turkey, even more dramatic changes were brought in by the downfall of the Ottoman Empire and the emergence of a republic half a century ago. The historical basis of Turkish culture was a group of Central Asian peoples driven west by advancing Mongols. Moslem rule gained supremacy and superimposed its types of family life, including a polygynous marriage system, over the classical patriarchism that had prevailed. In addition to introducing polygyny, Islamic culture permitted divorce, but it is not certain as to how widespread the Moslem marriage system was diffused.

Basically, the pattern did not change during the several centuries of Islamic rule and the expansion of the Turkish empire, although some Western influence was felt in the cities because of contact with foreigners. By 1900, polygyny was on the decline. After World War I, the policies of Kemal Ataturk radically transformed the country. Adoption of the Swiss Civil Code in 1926 markedly altered the way of life for women. They were assured of civil rights, the end of polygamy, and either party could, in theory at least, initiate divorce. By 1930, women were given the right to vote. All these legal gains involved deepseated changes in the mores, such as removal of the veil and leaving mate selection to the individual.

Occupationally, women have assumed a number of roles originally ascribed to men. They now constitute an increasing proportion of the medical, legal, academic, and engineering professions, a remarkable change in view of the fact that even as recently as a decade ago only 14 percent of females and 35 percent of males could read and write (Lerner, 1958).

In Turkey today, social relations between the sexes are highly variable, depending on the educational level of the parents and other subcultural conditions. The range of behavior varies from the "approval of participation in a mixed excursion to a public beach in bikini bathing suits, to the prohibition of greeting classmates of the opposite sex in a small coeducational Anatolian high school." When the controls are too tight, frustration and consequent emotional problems occur, as indicated by a nationwide attitude survey among high school students (Abadan, 1967). When, on the other hand, social change proceeds faster than the individual's preparation to cope with it, other emotional problems occur, as in the "epidemic" anomic suicides among married women. Deprived of the pseudosecurity of the paternalistic regime and suddenly forced by the reform movement to assume unfamiliar responsibilities as part of the new emancipation, many resorted in desperation to suicide as the only way out.

The situation in the hinterland is quite a different story. Life has always been traditional at the village level where adherence to Moslem values remains strong. Depreciation of the female, whose fidelity and subjection to the male are deeply rooted, is taken for granted. Virginity before marriage is even more emphasized by these rural Turkish communities than in Latin America, and after marriage the wife is restricted to household routines and expected to defer all family decisions to her husband.

Although the pace varies from city to country, the old order all over Turkey is gradually yielding to new sex roles in work and social relationships.

The Arab World

What Turkey accomplished in the 1920s, the Arab world has been doing in the 1950s and 1960s, especially in those areas where contact with the West has been maximal. The need to involve the total population in the nationalist movement has benefitted women's status. Egypt under Nasser adopted a number of reforms, and the Tunisian code outlaws the veil, permits the wife as well as the husband to sue for divorce, and allows women access to certain occupations previously outlawed to them. Woman's suffrage has come to most Arab countries, education is now possible and, at least in the cities, family planning has taken root.

Industrialization, the revolution in transportation, and mass media communication have been the basic change agents. It is impossible for women to see Western movies, observe tourists from abroad, and act as key-punch operators in Damascus or Aleppo, without questioning their submerged position. Reluctantly, the male is accepting these changes. For instance, in a survey of Arab and Christian students in the Middle East (Iraq, Egypt and Lebanon), 97 percent of the male students accepted the idea of women's working before marriage, but 41 percent objected to it after marriage (Goode, 1963). Although this sample represents an elite group, it is nevertheless a harbinger of change in these countries. Freer marriage choice, relinquishing the bride price, entrance of women into "male" occupations at nearly equal rates of pay, are all among the changes that Europe and North America underwent during the Industrial Revolution of the nineteenth and early twentieth centuries.

The Far East

Men and Women of India Today

In the Indian subcontinent, family traditions and the rigidity of sex roles have been only slightly changed for most of its half billion people despite independence from colonial rule for approximately a generation. One reason, as Sinha points out in his chapter, *Men and Women of India Today,* is the nature of ethnic, religious, and caste belongingness, which more than anywhere else in the world, structures lifeways here. The relationship of the sexes is determined by these more demanding subcultures. Legal norms have been adopted to reduce both sex inequality and discrimination based on caste, but the difference between the ideal and the real continues, and except for cosmopolitan centers, progress on these fronts is difficult. In marriage, a woman is still clearly subordinate to her husband, and her entry into education and the employment world is little more secure than it was two decades ago. It is this deep contrast between past traditions and present ideals that made it possible for India to elect a woman prime minister and at the same time to deny women any identity outside their family setting. Perhaps the most crucial test case, both for the advancement of the nation and for the liberation of women, will be the degree to which birth control methods can be diffused beyond the urban middle class.

Status and Role Behavior in Changing Japan

Japan, the most Westernized Asian country with the highest standard of living, has been undergoing enormous transformation beginning with the industrialization of the last century and the democratization after the defeat in World War II. As De Vos and Wagatsuma show in their chapter, the roles of men and women must be seen in the perspective of a highly traditional culture that is focused on deference to status based on family lineage, age, and sex.

Sex roles are still sharply differentiated but not to the degree that they were before the war. As the authors point out, many of the stereotypes of the aggressive, self-indulging male and the subservient female must be revised. Marriages are no longer arranged exclusively from the standpoint of family aims, but the affectional needs of the young partners have been increasingly recognized. In other words, while role commitment still has top priority in the marriage system, companionship is increasing in importance. The shift in norms and values has produced role strain. As in Turkey, anomie has arisen because of the conflict between tradition and Western influences (Dore, 1958). The individual is now confronted with so many role alternatives that he finds himself, like the contemporary Greek, in the dilemma of having to choose between family loyalty and personal goals. In this connection, the compulsion felt by the modern Japanese wife to support family unity and at the same time to efface her own needs is a frequent source of marital struggle. This point is documented by Ezra Vogel's (1963) studies of familial relations, also cited by Norbeck and De Vos (1961). The most common pattern of conflict concerns the wife, caught between conformity to the old behavioral styles and desire for the new freedom. She feels tension, on the one hand, toward her mother-in-law who in the past could exert unquestioned authority over her, and, on the other, toward her husband because of his habit of seeking gratifications, including sexual relations, outside the home.

Westernizing is creating many of the same problems for the Japanese in the homeland that we have noted in the acculturating Japanese minority in the United States.

Sex Roles in the Modern Fabric of China

Fong's chapter suggests that the impact of Westernization on China has run much the same course as in Japan and is creating many of the same problems already noted among acculturating nationals from these countries in the United States.

The "winds of change," shifting from the clan system and the hierarchical family of the agrarian Old China, to the democratic form of the industrialized New China, have stirred up much culture conflict between the generations and the sexes. Progress toward Western-type dating and marriage patterns with improved status and more meaningful roles for women has been slow and painful. These trends that began more than half a century before the Communist regime, are still going on in Taiwan and Hong Kong today.

Communism has pushed the trend toward modernization further, undermining the traditional family system. Although still remaining a basic social unit, the former position of authority and economic power that the family once enjoyed has been greatly curtailed, and much of the loyalty to father and ancestors has been transferred to the state. As in Soviet Russia and the Democratic Republic of Germany, social sex roles have been altered only to the point of permitting women to *add* outside work to their domestic chores. A single sex-role standard, dictated by individual inclination rather than by politics or gender, remains to be evolved.

Our overview of the problem to which the present volume is addressed has demonstrated Murphy and Leighton's (1965) point that cultural change as it affects individuals is mediated through the role-structure of the system. In most contemporary societies, change in response to the expanding urban sprawl of industrialization has necessitated accommodation in the roles of men and women. The rate of change has varied with cultural heterogeneity, mass media, global transportation, and effective birth control. The change in itself may be beneficial insofar as it mobilizes creative potential. However, if the tempo is too rapid to permit integration of new values or learning of new skills, stress is inevitable and is likely to be reflected in increased tension between the sexes. A case in point is the marital discord between acculturating couples where husband and wife are moving at different speeds.

Change in social sex roles, whether fast or slow, and however fluctuant, has been uniformly in the direction of equalizing the status of women with that of men. Nevertheless, beneath the status battle of the sexes there still lurk the neglected vestiges of a biological polarity of roles: the male—dominant, intrusive, instrumental, and achieving; the female—submissive, receptive, expressive, and nurturing. Owing to the plasticity of human response mechanisms, cultures have been able to play the biological sex differences up or down, with little regard for the subtleties of "role affinity." Equal status has usually been interpreted to mean performing the same roles, while in fact a wide variety of roles may express equivalent statuses. Those representing the basic biological tendencies would presumably yield greater comfort and satisfaction than those that run counter to them. Thus, for women, roles in which nurturing functions outweigh power manipulations would be preferable while the converse situation would hold for men.

In evaluating the problem of sex roles in the changing societies examined in the following chapters, the reader will do well to keep in mind not only the question of status equality but also the less recognized question of role affinity.

Note

[1] This section was based in part on unpublished material contributed by Professor Nezahat Arkun of the University of Istanbul.

References

Abadan, Nermin. "Turkey." In *Women in the Modern World,* R. Patai, ed. New York: Free Press, 1967, pp. 82–105.

Aldous, Joan. "Urbanization, the Extended Family, and Kinship Ties in West Africa." In *Africa: Social Problems of Change and Conflict,* P. L. Van den Berghe, ed. San Francisco: Chandler, 1965, pp. 107–16.

Bernard, Jessie. *The Sex Game.* Englewood, N.J.: Prentice-Hall, 1968.

Blood, Robert O. Jr., and Donald M. Wolfe. *Husbands and Wives: The Dynamics of Married Living.* New York: Free Press, 1960.

Broderick, Carlfred B. "Social Heterosexual Development among Urban Negroes and Whites." *Journal of Marriage and the Family,* 27 (May 1965), 200–12.

Brody, E. B., ed. *Minority Group Adolescents in the United States.* Baltimore: Williams & Wilkins, 1968.

Brody, Eugene B. "Minority Group Status and Behavioral Disorganization." In *Minority Group Adolescents in the United States,* E. B. Brody, ed. Baltimore: Williams & Wilkins, 1968, pp. 227–43.

Brown, William D. "A Social-Psychological Conceptual Framework of the Family." In *Emerging Conceptual Frameworks in Family Analysis,* F. Nye & F. M. Berardo, eds. New York: Macmillan, 1966, pp. 176–97.

Bühler, Charlotte, and Fred Massarik, eds. *The Course of Human Life.* New York: Springer, 1968.

Christensen, Harold T. "Scandinavian and American Sex Norms: Some Comparisons with Sociological Implications." *Journal of Social Issues,* 22 (April 1966), 60–75.

Derbyshire, Robert L. "Adolescent Identity Crisis in Urban Mexican Americans in East Los Angeles." In *Minority Group Adolescents in the United States, op. cit.* Baltimore: Williams & Wilkins, 1968, pp. 73–110.

Dore, R. P. *City Life in Japan: A Study of a Tokyo Ward.* Berkeley: University of California Press, 1958.

De Vos, George. "A Comparison of the Personality Differences in Two Generations of Japanese Americans by Means of the Rorschach Test." *Nagoya Journal of Medical Science,* 173 (1954), 153–265.

———. "A Quantitative Rorschach Assessment of Maladjustment and Rigidity in Acculturating Japanese Americans." *Genetic Psychology Monographs,* 52 (1955), 51–87.

Erikson, Erik H. *Identity and the Life Cycle.* International Universities Press, 1959.

———. *Identity: Youth in Crisis.* New York: Norton, 1968.

Fong, Stanley L. M. "Identity Conflicts of Chinese Adolescents in San Francisco." In *Minority Group Adolescents in the United States, op. cit.* Baltimore: Williams & Wilkins, 1968, 111–32.

——— and H. Peskin. "Sex-role Strain and Personality Adjustment of Chinese-born

Students in America: A Pilot Study." *Journal of Abnormal Psychology,* 74 (1969) 563–67.

Geiger, Kent. *The Family in Soviet Russia.* Cambridge: Harvard University Press, 1968.

Goode, William J. *World Revolution and Family Patterns.* New York: Free Press, 1963.

Grier, William H., and Price M. Cobbs. *Black Rage.* New York: Basic Books, 1968.

Gundlach, Ralph, and Bernard F. Riess. "Self and Sexual Identity in the Female: A Study of Female Homosexuals." In *New Directions in Mental Health,* B. F. Riess, ed., New York: Grune & Stratton, 1968, 205–31.

Harlow, Harry F. "The Heterosexual Affectional System in Monkeys." *American Psychologist,* 17, 1 (1962), 1–9.

———. "Sexual Behavior in the Rhesus Monkey." In *Sex and Behavior,* F. A. Beach, ed. New York: Wiley, 1965, pp. 234–65.

———. W. Danforth Joslyn, Monte Senko, and Aileen Dopp. "Behavioral Aspects of Reproduction in Primates." *Journal of Animal Science,* 25 (Supplement), (1966), 49–67.

Heller, Celia S. *Mexican American Youth: Forgotten Youth at the Crossroads.* New York: Random House, 1966.

Jahoda, Gustav. "Love, Marriage and Social Change: Letters to the Advice Column of a West African Newspaper." *Africa,* 29 (1959), 177–89.

Kardiner, Abraham, and Lionel Ovesey. *The Mark of Oppression: A Psychosocial Study of the American Negro.* New York: Norton, 1951.

Kinsey, Alfred C., Wardell B. Pomeroy, and Clyde E. Martin. *Sexual Behavior in the Human Male.* Philadelphia: Saunders, 1948.

Lerner, Daniel. *The Passing of Traditional Society.* New York: Free Press, 1958.

Lewis, Edwin C. *Developing Woman's Potential.* Ames, Iowa: Iowa State University Press, 1968.

Lewis, Oscar. *La Vida: A Puerto Rican Family in a Culture of Poverty in San Juan and New York.* New York: Random House, 1966.

Mead, Margaret. *Male and Female.* New York: Morrow, 1949.

Murphy, Jane M., and A. H. Leighton, eds. *Approaches to Cross-cultural Psychiatry.* Ithaca, N.Y.: Cornell University Press, 1965.

Norbeck, Edward, and George De Vos. "Japan." In *Psychological Anthropology,* F. L. K. Hsu, ed. Homewood, Ill.: Dorsey Press, 1961, pp. 19–47.

Parker, Seymour, and Robert J. Kleiner. "Characteristics of Negro Mothers in Single-headed Households." *Journal of Marriage and the Family,* 28 (November 1966), 507–13.

Pettigrew, T. F. *A Profile of the Negro American.* Princeton, N.J.: Van Nostrand, 1964.

Rabin, A. I. "Some sex differences in the attitudes of Kibbutz adolescents." *Israel Annals of Psychiatry and Related Disciplines,* 6–1 (1968), 62–69.

Rosenkrantz, Paul, Helen Bee, Susan Vogel, Inge Broverman, and Donald Broverman. "Sex-role Stereotype, and Self-Concepts in College Students." *Journal of Consulting and Clinical Psychology,* 32, 3 (1968), 287–95.

Schelsky, Helmut. "The Family in Germany." *Marriage and Family Living,* 16 (November 1954), 331–35.

Sears, Robert R. "Development of Gender Role." In *Sex and Behavior, op. cit.* New York: Wiley, 1965, pp. 133–63.

Seward, Georgene H. *Sex and the Social Order.* New York: McGraw-Hill, 1946 (Out of Print); Harmondsworth, Middlesex: Pelican Books, 1954.

———. "Learning Theory and Identification. V. Some Cultural Aspects of Identification." *Journal of Genetic Psychology,* 84 (1954), 229–36.

———. *Psychotherapy and Culture Conflict.* New York: Ronald Press, 1956.

———, ed. *Clinical Studies in Culture Conflict.* New York: Ronald Press, 1958.

Seward, Georgene H. "Sex Identity and the Social Order." *Journal of Nervous and Mental Disease.* 139, 2 (1964), 126–36.

——— and William R. Larson. "Adolescent Concepts of Social Sex Roles in the United States and the Two Germanies." *Human Development,* 11 (1968), 217–48.

Svalastoga, Kaare. "The Family in Scandinavia." *Marriage and Family Living,* 16 (November, 1954), 374–80.

Talmon, Yonina. "The Family in a Revolutionary Movement—The Case of the Kibbutz." In *Comparative Family Systems,* M. M. Nimkoff, ed. Boston: Houghton Mifflin, 1965, pp. 259–86.

Vogel, Ezra F. *Japan's New Middle Class.* Berkeley: University of California Press, 1963.

Yamamoto, Joe. "Japanese American Identity Crisis." In *Minority Group Adolescents in the United States, op. cit.* Baltimore: Williams and Wilkins, 1968, pp. 133–56.

PART ONE

ORIGINS of SEX-ROLE PATTERNING

1 SOME PRIMITIVE SOCIETIES[1]

Clellan S. Ford

In recent decades we have seen in the United States, in Europe, and elsewhere in the literate world a so-called emancipation of women. They now have rights and privileges that were customarily denied them only a century ago. How this came about and the conditions that made this transformation possible are a part of recent history. In the assessment of the changes that have taken place it may be useful to bear in mind the perspective provided by the ethnographic literature on the age-old roles of male and female in primitive societies.

By primitive societies we mean those societies that were not industrialized at the time of ethnographic description. They are generally not literate and might be termed uncivilized. This does not imply that their ways of life are in any way to be thought inferior. Their social life may be extraordinarily complex and their technology undeveloped, but in every instance their customs embody the wisdom of countless generations. Many of the problems they have faced and solved in their own way have been challenging to human beings all over the world in whatever era they may have lived.

Diversity of lifeways

As one examines the literature on primitive peoples, he is confronted with a bewildering diversity of lifeways. Some people obtain their food by foraging and hunting small game. Some live predominantly off the sea, supplemented by limited gardening. Others are pastoral people and still others practice intensive agriculture. Some people live a nomadic life; others are sedentary. Some people wear little if any clothing; in other groups both men and women are fully clothed. For some, premarital sex is a must; for others it is so strictly forbidden that death punishes the offenders who are caught. There is such tremendous variation as one moves from one society to another that it seems impossible to support any valid generalization about the lifeways of primitive people.

On the other hand, people everywhere face the same basic problems. In order to survive they must somehow obtain food and drink, find shelter from extremes of heat and cold, defend themselves against enemies, produce young and train them in those ways of life essential to their survival. Clearly there is no existing society, primitive or otherwise, that has not solved these basic problems and continued to do so with success. However, environs differ and present different obstacles and opportunities. Some people rarely need to cope with intense heat or intense cold; whereas for others, finding a means of protection is an absolute necessity. Even in similar environments, there are alternative solutions to basic problems of survival that in turn present other problems demanding solution. They also dictate to a considerable extent the amount of time remaining to a people for relaxation and creativity. Furthermore, each society has had its own unique history and learning experiences. The net result is that each society is in many ways different from any other and exhibits lifeways that seem strange and foreign to people brought up under different cultural conditions.

Variation in ways of life, in speech, and in patterns of thought from one people to another has given rise to the notion of cultural relativity. Each society is considered to be a little universe all its own, with its own rights and wrongs, its values, and its ways of living. Furthermore, individuals growing up in different societies are, because of that fact, totally unalike: they see the world differently and react to common stimuli in different ways —in short, they live utterly different lives. At the same time, no matter how unlike they may be, there are common aspects to human social life whatever the culture. Regularities beneath the facade of diversity are continuously being uncovered.

Predictability of behavior

When one visits another society, one which is entirely alien to one's own, first impressions lead to the conclusion that the people being visited act in a most peculiar fashion and appear to live without regularity or reason. There seems to be no accounting for when they do what they do. With further acquaintance, however, what may first have seemed bizarre and chaotic becomes more comprehensible. What the people do and say seems to exhibit an understandable patterning. In fact, upon examination, the behavior of people in every society becomes to a considerable degree predictable. That is to say, each member of a society can tell in advance what his fellow members are likely to do. Just as we can predict what our neighbors will do under various conditions with fair accuracy, so can those who live in primitive societies. And ethnographic descriptions are predominantly statements concerning the patterns of a people's behavior and thought and the conditions under which certain types of activity can be expected. The fact that human behavior is predictable within the framework of any primitive society seems at the outset to be quite remarkable. But upon reflection, it will not seem so strange. Within our own society we make the assumption in daily life that we can tell in advance how people are going to act under varying circumstances. We stake our lives in traffic on being able to predict the behavior of other drivers. While in primitive societies there may not be the same dangers attendant upon failing to anticipate what others will do as those accompanying us on the roads, there are tremendous advantages to a regulated social life, and in all societies this has been learned. There is no society, no matter how primitive, in which members do not for the most part behave in predictable fashion, whether or not the rules governing their activities are explicitly stated by them.

Classification by sex

Although there are some predictable patterns of behavior common to all the members of a given society—language, for example—by far the greater number of these patterns are characteristic of particular categories or segments of the population. In every society, people are classified in accordance with customary usage and are trained to behave in ways appropriate to their status. One such categorization, which is universal, is that which differentiates male and female. No primitive society fails to make this distinction. There is no social group where the roles of the two sexes are not expected to be different and consciously recognized to be so. Boys and girls are trained from an early age to behave in ways held appropriate to their sex. In adult life, certain activities are performed by the women; others are allocated to the men. Also specified by the culture are the proper attitudes of men and women and the moralities of their behavior.

The dichotomy between male and female is everywhere recognized, but in some societies individuals who, despite their biological endowment, desire to adopt the status of the opposite sex are permitted to do so. In a cross-cultural study, Ford and Beach (1951) found that in 64 percent of 76 primitive societies, homosexual behavior of some sort was regarded as acceptable for some members of the community. A relatively common situation is one in which young men decide to adopt female attire and to perform women's tasks. This may or may not involve adopting a female role in sexual activities. Less frequently, women may dress like men and attempt to play a masculine role. These patterns of behavior, though acceptable to the society for the individuals involved, do not indicate a lack of cultural distinction between male and female. The social group makes the basic distinction, but permits some of their members to behave as men or women irrespective of their biologically determined sex.

Biosocial sex differences

Anatomical and physiological sex differences separate male and female in a number of ways in addition to those directly related to reproductive function. Though these secondary sex differences are well known, it may be useful to keep them in mind when examining ethnographic data on the roles played by men and women in primitive societies. As will be seen, they help to explain a large part of the differentiation in sex-typed activities that may be observed cross-culturally. The following is a brief summary of some of the biological differences between male and female that seem to have cultural significance and that might be overlooked.

While more male infants are likely to be in any human population, they show a higher mortality rate than female infants during the first few years. Infant boys are less resistant to disease than infant girls, and they have less chance for survival into adulthood. In a biological sense, girls mature more rapidly than boys, arriving at puberty at an earlier age. Until the time of puberty, physical differences between the sexes are less pronounced than in adulthood. Differences in height, size of skeletal structure, and weight begin to show up markedly in early adulthood. Men are taller, larger, and heavier than women. They are stronger and more powerful in the sense of physical capabilities. They can lift heavier weights and throw things harder and farther. They also can run faster and for longer periods of time. Although physically able to do more arduous tasks, men are less durable and tend to die at an earlier age than women.

Secondary sex differences in aptitude and temperament are still in good measure a matter of speculation. These are aspects which seem more likely to be related to cultural conditioning, and it is preferable to assume at this point in our understanding that differences between men and women in these respects reflect primarily differential exposure and training. Too little evidence is available to us from the ethnographic literature to enable us to make assured judgments at this time. We cannot state unequivocally, for example, that men are innately more aggressive than women or that women have fundamentally more patience than men. Margaret Mead (1935, 1949) has been concerned specifically with the problem of determining how effectively training and conditioning can shape male and female aptitudes and temperaments. Her conclusion, briefly, is that cultural pressures are of tremendous significance and can under certain circumstances nearly negate such innate predispositions as there may be. Many more studies such as these must be undertaken, however, before we will have a definitive understanding of how differences in aptitude and temperament are brought about.

Sex roles and reproduction

For primitive peoples, the single most important biological fact in determining how men and women live is the differential part they play in reproduction. Men are necessary for conception, and this is recognized to be the case everywhere with a few possible exceptions. But it is the women who become pregnant, bear the children, and are equipped to nurse them. The role of the female in primitive societies pivots around her reproductive function. She is there primarily to conceive, bear, and care for her offspring. Women who for one reason or another fail to carry out this function are almost universally scorned and despised. Only rarely is the barren woman greeted with sympathetic understanding for her misfortune. In every culture there are medicines or rituals to which she can resort in her attempts to become fertile. In some societies a man will not marry a woman until she has demonstrated her ability to bear children. Childlessness in many societies is grounds for automatic divorce. To be a woman is to be a mother. Whatever else she may do in the way of routine activities, and however else she may participate in social life, her primary function is to reproduce.

Evans-Pritchard (1965) has stated the case very well:

> Now, I suppose that among those things that first strike a visitor to a primitive people is that there are no unmarried adult women. Every girl finds a husband, and she is usually married at what seems to us a rather early age. This fact, taken together with the further fact that in a society with a primitive technology and economy, running the home is a whole-time occupation, to which is added the care of small children, tells us, without our having to consider other matters, what is one important difference between modern civilized woman and her savage sister. Women among ourselves can choose to marry or not to marry, and if they choose not to marry they can devote their lives to teaching, research, administration, charity, or whatever it may be; or they can combine married life with a profession or job and with all sorts of interests outside the home. The primitive woman has no choice, and, given the duties that go with marriage, is therefore seldom able to take much part in public life. But if she can be regarded as being at a disadvantage in this respect from our point of view, she does not regard herself as being at a disadvantage, and she does not envy her menfolk what we describe as their privileges. She does not desire, in this respect, things to be other than they are; and it would greatly puzzle her if she knew that in our society many women are unmarried and childless [p. 45].

It is, of course, possible for every woman to have a husband in primitive societies only because in these societies polygamy is almost always permitted and in varying degrees practiced. Consequently, every women can be married, and custom also enables widows to remarry without difficulty. Usually, though by no means always, the new husband is a close kinsman of the deceased. The possibility of marriage for all women is another obvious difference between these societies and our own since women in our monogamous culture may choose to refuse marriage, and those who wish to marry cannot be certain of finding partners. In this connection it should be pointed out that the most telling feminist arguments, at least in the middle classes, favored allowing women greater opportunities in professional and public life to compensate for the possible lack of opportunity for marriage.

The physiology of woman's reproductive role has a significance in many societies that reaches far beyond the matter of giving birth to young and suckling them. Parturition is an event which is rarely taken lightly. Bearing a child is painful and replete with potential danger. The baby, the mother, or both may not survive the ordeal. Normal deliveries are always bloody, and there are inevitably lacerations of the genitalia, which provide exposure to potential infection. The entire process of giving birth constitutes a rather frightening experience, both for the woman herself and for those who may be with her.

It is often taken for granted that childbirth in primitive societies is easy and painless. There are only a few accounts of childbirth reported by ethnographers who have actually witnessed a delivery. One such account comes from Beatrice Blackwood (1935), who described a birth that she witnessed in a Solomon Island village. She leaves us no doubt as to the difficulties that were involved:

> Sanasi's first instructions to Manev were to come and sit close to the central pole of the hut, and hang on to it. This she did, raising her arms as far as possible above her head, clasping the post, which was immediately behind her, pulling on it, as Sanasi showed her. Presently a short log was brought, about 3 inches thick and about 2½ feet long. She was told to leave the pole and sit on this log, in a posture with her knees bent and her legs separated. Sanasi knelt behind her on one knee, pressing the other knee into her back, and clasping both arms around her body just below the armpits, the clasped hands resting on the protuberant abdomen and pressing it downwards. Another woman sat in front and held her knees wide apart.
>
> As the pains grew more severe, Manev shrieked and cried, and tried to get up. At one time there were four women holding her, one behind her, as described above, one holding each knee and pressing it outwards, and one standing behind with her hands pressing on Manev's shoulders, to keep her from springing up. At long intervals she was allowed a short respite, during which she lay on her side on the floor, but after a minute or two she was called back on to the log, and told that she must think of the child. Twice she vomited, but not violently.
>
> . . . This went on for five or six hours.
>
> . . . Then another four or five hours passed, the women still holding Manev as previously described. She appeared to be in great distress, and called repeatedly: "Atsat pio, atsat tagala!" ("Woe is me," in the two dialects current in this village.) . . . No notice was taken by the women of any of her cries.
>
> Once in a while the woman kneeling behind moved her clasping hands from the top of the protuberant abdomen to the bottom and shook it violently. This caused fresh cries and groans. Tears were streaming down Manev's face, she begged continually to be let alone and to be allowed to lie down. Once they let her lie on the ground for a minute or two, and once they helped her to her feet, and she stood for a few seconds,

> supported by two women. But most of the time she sat on the log, with knees drawn up and pressed wide apart.
>
> Towards morning they all came and sat in front of her, anxiously watching for the first sight of the child. As soon as the first glimmer of daylight appeared through the chinks in the walls of the hut, they put out the hurricane lantern I had brought with me, which up till then had faintly illuminated the scene, so that when the top of the child's head at last appeared it was distinguished with difficulty in the dim light of dawn. It was an occipito-anterior presentation, and apparently normal. Sighs of relief and smiles of pleasant anticipation came from all women [pp. 146–49].

Among primitive peoples, men do not generally attend the birth of a child, but there are exceptions. In some societies the woman's husband is present, and in others a male doctor may be called in to assist if complications arise. For the most part, whatever assistance is given to the mother is in the hands of elderly women or midwives. After the baby is born the mother and child usually remain in seclusion for a period of time that may last only a few days but may be as long as a month or more. This relative isolation during childbirth and for some time thereafter is adaptive, since it reduces the probability of infection for both the mother and the newborn infant. The importance of this procedure was really not appreciated by us until the development of modern hospitals. The markedly increased number of fatal infections due to new crowded conditions forced the development of aseptic techniques without which the custom of hospitalization could not have survived.

Although men do not participate in assisting the actual delivery of the child in most societies, the husband may have specific duties to perform that interrupt his routine. During the latter part of his wife's pregnancy, for instance, he may be restricted from engaging in hunting or fishing. Similarly, for a period of time after the baby is born he may be prohibited from performing various tasks. But even in those societies where restrictions are severe and he is obligated to stay in bed for a day or two, the interruption of his routine tasks does not last for long.

Nursing her child imposes still further limitations on the activities in which a woman can participate in routine fashion. Although the nursing period may (rarely) be less than six months, far more frequently it is for about two to three years. And by the time one child is weaned, the mother is likely to be pregnant again, and the cycle recommences. Not until the menopause is she free from her reproductive role.

Sex roles and social sanctions

Most of the restrictions imposed by primitive societies upon a woman's freedom stem directly from one or another aspect of her reproductive role.

Restrictions connected with pregnancy have been noted, as well as those imposed during the period after childbirth and during lactation. Among many peoples, limitations are placed upon the activities of women during their menstrual periods as well. Societies vary markedly, however, in the degree to which they curtail a menstruating woman's participation in social life. In a few societies, the only restriction placed upon her activities is that she may not engage in sexual intercourse. In a few other societies, menstruation involves strict seclusion and isolation. The majority of primitive peoples surround the woman with specific restrictions, leaving her free to move about with certain exceptions. Always she is forbidden sexual intercourse, frequently she may not go into the gardens, may not cook for a man or touch his hunting or fishing gear, and may not participate in religious ceremonies.

With respect to restrictions imposed upon women during menstruation, Stephens (1961) marshalls considerable cross-cultural evidence linking the prevalence and intensity of menstrual taboos to various child-rearing practices. His conclusion is that those practices that tend to produce male castration anxiety are associated with placing more severe restrictions on women during menstruation. In a parallel cross-cultural study, Young and Bacadayan (1965) present evidence in support of a different hypothesis, namely that menstrual taboos are institutionalized ways for men to discriminate against women and that they are most severe in societies where males are dominant and tightly organized. Whatever the reason may be for differential treatment of menstruating women, it appears that where modern hygiene has been introduced the tendency is for the restrictions to become minimal. Menstrual taboos disappear except for the restriction on sexual activity, and the period of confinement after childbirth is abbreviated. It seems clear that modern technology is making it possible to do away with some of the more stringent restrictions imposed upon women that are associated with their reproductive cycle. Even under optimum conditions, however, woman's reproductive role cannot help but interfere with many activities that men are relatively free to perform.

The fact that women bear children and men do not has apparently had other consequences with respect to their sex-typed roles. In a number of primitive societies, children and adolescents are permitted free or relatively unrestricted sexual activity provided that they respect the local incest regulations. But in those societies where adults attempt to control their young in sexual activities, a double standard appears to be the rule, with the female being the most strictly controlled. This seems to be directly related to the fact that she is the one who might become pregnant. Young men do not run the same risks that young women do and are generally permitted more freedom.

In adult life, many societies permit men to have more than one mate while at the same time women are forbidden to live with or to have liaisons with more than one man. There are few monogamous societies where only one man may be mated to one woman at a time. In most of these cases the pressures against adultery are generally more stringent for the woman than for the man. It seems fair to generalize that in the realm of sexual behavior, where restrictions are in force, men are in general permitted more freedom than are women.

It may be that modern technology will tend to eliminate this double standard with respect to sexual behavior. As contraception becomes perfected and permitted, social controls over sexual behavior, insofar as they are directed against unwanted pregnancies, will become unnecessary. Birth control will also permit women to space their children without interfering with their sexual behavior, thus leaving them free to engage in activities that would otherwise be periodically interrupted by unwanted pregnancies and childbirth.

Childhood and adolescence

In primitive societies, the training of children for their roles in adult life begins at an early age. In some, the training is casual, informalized, and apparently undirected. In some, too, little boys and girls spend most of their early life playing together. But even in such instances, it appears that much of childhood play involves imitative elements corresponding to the roles the children will be playing in their adult lives, including sexual roles. Where boys and girls are separated from each other early in life, there is more direct training and supervision. The girls help their older sisters and mothers with daily tasks, while the boys accompany the older boys and men and participate in masculine activities.

For girls, the menarche is a relatively obvious developmental event, and among many peoples this occasion is recognized in ceremonial elaboration. Common features of such ceremonies include seclusion, special instruction by older women in matters of sex, marriage, and proper feminine behavior, and, in many societies, the subjection of the girl to genital or other bodily mutilation. At the end of the seclusion period there is generally a feast that appears to have a function similar to the "coming-out" party in our own society.

A good descriptive account of a puberty ceremony for Thonga girls in Mosambique, Africa, is provided by Junod (1927):

> They will begin a seclusion period for one month. Three or four girls receive the initiation together. They are shut up in a hut, and when they come out, must always wear over their face a veil consisting of a very dirty grease cloth. Every morning they are led to the pool, and their whole body is immersed in the water as far as the neck. Other initiated girls or women accompany them singing obscene songs, and drive away with sticks any man who happens to be on the road, as no man is allowed to see a girl

> during this period. If a man happens to come near the group, the women ask him the secret formulae of the circumcision school, not the long ones but the short ones, probably those which contain licentious words. Should he be unable to answer, they beat him. It is said that a man who sees a girl during this month becomes blind! When the cortege of women accompanying the initiated has returned home, the nubile girls are imprisoned in the hut. They are teased, pinched, scratched by the adoptive mothers or by other women; they must also listen to the licentious songs which are sung to them. Though they are trembling from cold, being still wet, they are not allowed to come near the fire. They are also instructed in sexual matters, and told that they must never reveal anything about the blood of menses to a man. They are also exhorted to be very polite to every grown up person, and must salute everybody entering the hut, even those passing before the door, by clapping their hands. Sometimes the wind moves some dead leaves; they mistake this noise for the sound of steps and salute reverently!
>
> At the end of the month the adoptive mother brings the girl home to her true mother. She also presents her with a pot of beer. A feast takes place on this occasion [I, 177–78].

Though boys mature without any abrupt physiological change comparable to the onset of the menses in girls, there are gradual differences in appearance, speech, and the like that indicate approaching manhood. At some point along the line of this gradual maturation, many societies force their young males to undergo initiation rites that, like the puberty ceremonial for girls, seem to perform the task of instructing boys how to behave like men. More frequently than for girls, male initiation ceremonies involve a group of boys who undergo the ceremonial at the same time. Male initiation ceremonies for the most part last longer than girls' puberty rites.

As in the case of girls, boys are generally secluded during the period of their initiation. During this period they are subjected to a series of ordeals that may involve genital or other bodily mutilation. Invariably, the boys are given detailed instructions on matters pertaining to sex, marriage, and manhood.

Clothing and adornment

There seems to be a general tendency for people everywhere to seek some way of modifying their appearance. This may be accomplished by actually distorting the natural features of the body: elongating the neck, filing or removing teeth, stretching the earlobes or lips, scarifying or tattooing the skin, or deforming the head or feet. Face and body painting, cutting and depilating the hair or dyeing it—all are widespread. Ornaments may be appended to the nose or ears; bracelets, necklaces, and anklets may be worn. And all these are in addition to the customary clothing, for there are very few primitive societies in which women and men go completely nude.

Clothing, adornment, and the modification of bodily features seem to serve several functions. Concealment of the genital region is certainly a very common use of clothing, although in rare instances the mode of garb seems deliberately designed to direct attention to the male genitals. For many peoples, clothing is a protection from the sun's rays, or from cold and inclement weather. The use of oils and ointments smeared over the body may also be primarily an insulating device. Still other functions may be detected, but the most significant one here is the role that clothing and other modifications of one's appearance play in identifying one's status and position in the society. The appearance of an individual is utilized universally as a means of recognition and identification; appearance is one basic way of proclaiming one's position in social life.

Customary styles of dress generally differentiate male from female in primitive societies, and also provide criteria for differentiating according to age and other statuses. In early childhood there tends to be less emphasis upon the distinction between male and female. As adolescence approaches, the sex-typing of appearance becomes more marked. Quite commonly, the way in which a pubescent girl dresses and adorns herself proclaims the fact that she is an eligible but unmarried woman. She may also alter her clothing style after becoming a mother. Should she be widowed, she may change her appearance again. Similarly, a boy may adopt a different garb or adorn himself in new fashion after he has undergone initiation rites or has performed those feats which according to the values of his society permit him to proclaim himself an adult man.

Sex partners and marriage

In ethnographic perspective, by far the great majority of societies permit polygynous marriages, with one man allowed to marry more than one woman. Strictly monogamous marriages are rare among primitive peoples, and even in some of these the men are permitted to have additional consorts or concubines. Still rarer is the form of marriage known as polyandry, in which one woman may be married simultaneously to more than one man. Rarest of all is the case where two or more men are simultaneously married to two or more women.

A polygynous marriage in societies where women are producers of food and other goods permits the man who has several wives to collect surpluses and enhance his prestige. Another effect of such marriages probably is a reduction in the frequency of pregnancy for each wife, thus exerting a limiting effect upon population increase. However, in considering the matter of polygynous marriages, it should be borne in mind that although the society may permit a man to have more than one wife, he may in fact be unable for various reasons to acquire more than one. In a relatively large percentage of those societies that permit multiple wives, most men, in fact, live with only one at a time.

The selection of marriage partners is in all societies governed by cultural regulations. Primary incest, the mating of parent and child, is universally forbidden, and brother-sister marriages are likewise condemned with but very rare exception. In primitive societies, incest regulations extend beyond the primary family unit to prohibit marriage with certain other relatives. The extent of these prohibitions and the direction that they have taken varies from one society to another, depending primarily upon the traditional rules of descent and residence. In some societies, incest regulations are extended so widely that a large proportion of the members of each community are forbidden to marry. At the same time, many primitive societies limit the circle within which marriage can take place, insisting that the bride and groom come from the same locale, kin, or status group. Murdock (1949) provides a detailed analysis of these and related matters in his volume *Social Structure*.

The surroundings in which married people live is to a considerable degree determined by the residence rules characterizing the society. In a large number of primitive groups, it is customary for a woman to go with her husband and live the rest of her life with or near his parents. In many of these societies, this involves leaving the community in which she was born and raised, thus forcing her to live with comparative strangers. She is relatively unprotected by her own kin group, while her husband is surrounded by relatives and lifelong friends and acquaintances. In some patrilocal societies, newlyweds spend a period of one or two years with the bride's parents before taking up permanent residence with those of the groom. Presumably, such a custom assists the bride in making her adjustment to married life until she has borne a child. In a lesser number of societies, residence is regularly and permanently with the bride's family. This adds to the wife's security, since she is the one to stay at home in familiar surroundings. The groom is then put at somewhat of a disadvantage, since he has to leave his parents' home. But in most instances of matrilocal residence, the parental homes of both bride and groom are close to each other and therefore the husband is not very far removed from his own kinsmen. There are other rules of residence, but they appear rather infrequently in primitive societies. There are some peoples, for example, who permit married partners to choose between living with the parents of either, and there are some who permit, and even insist, that newlyweds establish an independent residence.

Daily lives of men and women

In primitive societies while there is always a division of labor between the sexes, it does not amount to a clear-cut dichotomy. Some tasks are exclusively performed by the men of the society and others by the women. Among none of these people are all tasks interchangeable, although the number of sex-typed activities may be fewer in some societies than in others. The division of labor by sex may be very clear-cut and sharply defined for many activities in some groups and for relatively few activities in others.

Sex roles vary markedly from one primitive society to another. Men perform tasks in some social groups that women habitually perform in others. Except for biologically determined activities and behavior closely associated with them, there seem to be many tasks that can be performed equally well by men and women. And in fact there are some activities that are exclusively male in some societies and performed only by women in others. Weaving often serves as a case in point. Among the Navaho Indians, the making of blankets is exclusively women's work; whereas among their neighbors, the Hopi, weaving is done only by the men.

At the outset, one would expect the role of male and female to be in large measure strongly influenced by biological heritage. Men are physically equipped to do many tasks much better than women can do them. If a division of labor is advantageous to the survival of the group, one would expect that a man would perform those tasks for which he is better physically prepared than women. By and large, this assumption seems to hold. Men fight, hunt, and build the houses and boats, for example. Men also perform auxiliary activities connected with these tasks. They make the weapons and tools. They engage in religious ceremonies believed to aid them in these affairs. And the men train the boys as soon as they are old enough to participate in adult activities.

Since women bear the children, it seems only natural that they should take care of them while they are young. In so doing, they often find themselves confined to the vicinity of the home and the performance of sedentary tasks. For the most part, women do spend much of their time taking care of their young, doing household chores, cooking, and engaging in handicrafts such as basketry, mat making, pottery, and the like. And although at a fairly early age boys may take off with the older men to hunt and fish, women continue to care for their girls and to teach them feminine skills. Older girls, remaining at home, frequently share the burden of caring for their younger siblings.

In an early comparative study Murdock (1937) provided data on the division of labor by sex for 224 primitive people from all parts of the world. While some objections may be made to the method used for classifying activities, the picture obtained from this survey is most interesting and is in close accord with what emerges from a general examination of the ethnographic literature. Murdock's study showed the following classification of activities:

Masculine: metal working, weapon making, pursuit of sea mammals, hunting, boat building, mining and quarrying, wood working, stone working, trapping, working in bone, shell, or horn, herding, house building, and clearing of land for agriculture.

Feminine: grinding of grain, water carrying, cooking, gathering of herbs, roots, and seeds, manufacture and repair of clothing, preservation of meat and fish, pottery making, fuel gathering, gathering of fruits, nuts, and berries, weaving, mat making, basket making, manufacture of thread and cordage, and the preparation of drinks and narcotics.

Non Sex-Typed: the manufacture of ceremonial objects and ornaments, trading, agricultural pursuits, body mutilation (e.g. tattooing), fire making and tending, and burden carrying.

Clearly such generalized statements do not imply any hard and fast rule as to the tasks that men and women perform in particular societies. It may be useful to give a brief summary of how the division of labor between the sexes works out in practice in at least one primitive group.[2] On the island of Naviti in the Yasawas, western Fiji, the men clear the land for gardens, plant the root crops of taro and yams, and after harvesting the crops carry them to the village. Moreover, they build the houses, and formerly at least, they built the canoes. In the matter of house building, however, they are to some degree assisted by women, who may prepare the bundles of thatch the men secure to the rafters. The men do whatever fishing may be done outside the reef, while on the reef it is mostly the women and children who hunt for shellfish and octopus, though occasionally men may seek out the latter. Men dive into holes on the reef and spear small fish. Women do the cooking as a general practice. However, when an earth oven is prepared for feasts, most of the work is done by the men, and it is they who see to the problems involved in roasting pigs just as they did in the case of roasting people during the time of cannibalistic practice.

In the matter of mat making, basket making, and the manufacture of twine, cord, and braid, there seems to be no fixed division of labor although mats and the more complicated baskets are mostly made by women, whereas cordage is more often made by the men. The manufacture of tapa, bark cloth, is exclusively a woman's task. Although women are generally involved in the upkeep of the house, men do assist them at times, and it is the men who for the most part tend to the cleanliness of the village grounds. This does not seem to reflect a preference for one type of work or another by either male or female, but rather it seems to be the natural result of the fact that the men spend more of their time away from the house, either house building, gardening, fishing, or meeting with the other men to talk about village problems and to plan future activities.

The possibility that the division of labor between the sexes can automatically regulate the amount of time that men and women are in proximity to one another is of considerable interest. In some societies this situation becomes elaborated and formalized to the point that conscious rules govern when males and females can be together. Such a situation is reported for a group of Melanesians. Davenport (1965), who studied them, reported that the fundamental division of labor provides that men do the fishing while the women garden. He writes:

> . . . the village is laid out so that along the front are located one or more men's houses where unmarried men spend much of their time during the day. Ranged behind the men's house or row of men's houses, sometimes at a considerable distance, are the family dwellings in which women and girls spend most of their time while they are in the village. Leading away from the dwelling side of the village are paths to the gardens, so that women may come and go between their houses and subsistence plots without passing the men's side of the village. Men's houses are normally located close to the sea, or, in inland villages, at the outskirts where the main path leads off to other villages. Hence men may come and go to the sea to fish, or travel from village to village with few encounters with women.
>
> Within the village, men's latrine areas are adjacent to the men's houses alongside the canoe passages and landings. Women's latrine areas are always located some distance away behind a high stone wall that screens the entire area from view. Paths to these screened women's areas are never traversed by men. A man caught anywhere near these paths or areas is assumed to be a Peeping Tom, . . . and is treated exactly as if he has been apprehended in illicit intercourse. In addition, women are allocated a portion of each beach area in full sight of the men's part of the beach where they may go to prepare roots and tubers for cooking and to dump household trash. Men avoid these areas as studiously as women avoid the men's beach area. . . .
>
> Within the village each dwelling is oriented with respect to the sex-designated areas and directions. Each house has at least two doors, one opens toward the men's house and is used only by men, another opens towards the back of the village and the gardens and is used only by women and children. Inside the house . . . is a kind of men's area where the husband, the head of the household, eats, sleeps, and, when he has visitors, talks with his men friends. Opposite or adjacent to the men's floor space, . . . is the area where women sit, eat, and sleep. Here the earth oven and other cooking facilities are located. . . . With working and living areas, as well as access paths and daily tasks allocated in this manner, men and women may go about their everyday activities with a minimum of face-to-face encounters [pp. 164–207].

The sexes in old age

In most primitive societies old age is a relatively minor problem, for people do not as a general rule live into the senium. Nevertheless, every society makes some provision for the fate of the elderly. Considerable prestige may be accorded them under certain circumstances and for a limited age period rarely extending into decrepitude. In many cultures, the infirm and incapacitated oldsters are helped into the afterworld, a custom widely approved even by the victims themselves.

As regards sex differences, a review of 250 preliterate societies led Simmons (1945) to the following conclusions:

> Sexual differences have been significant. The more favorable cultural milieu for aged men has been found to be within a patriarchal type of family organization where herding or agriculture has been the chief means of maintenance; where there have been more or less permanent residence, a constant food supply, and a well-regulated political system; and where property rights in land, crops, herds, goods, and even women have been deeply entrenched.
>
> Aged women seem to have gained relatively more prestige in simpler societies characterized by collection, hunting, and fishing; and particularly in matriarchal forms of family organization. Their position also seems to have been better among farmers than herders. Aged men have been able to achieve considerable prestige even under circumstances normally conducive to elevating the rights of women; but old women have often been at very great disadvantage where cultural factors have been weighted in favor of aged men. Wherever aged women have been respected, old men have rarely been without honor; but prestige for aged men has offered no assurance of the same status for women. If either sex has lost respect in old age, it has been more likely to be the women than the men [p. 81].

Elderly men who are no longer able to help actively in the more strenuous tasks often take on supervisory roles. Their accumulated knowledge is frequently respected, and they are often leaders of religious rituals and ceremonies. They are often valued as story tellers, particularly as transmitters of ancient lore and legend. Among some peoples, it is the aged men who are regarded as the most powerful makers of magic, healers of disease, exorcizors of enemies, controllers of the weather, and diviners of the future. Although elderly women in a few societies perform some of these roles, they are more likely to be engaged in taking care of their grandchildren and doing small chores around the home. Among many peoples, women after the menopause function as midwives and are constantly in demand to assist in childbirth within the community.

Thus, in most preliterate societies, the differential sex typing that characterized the previous phases of the life cycle is carried on into old age, with the ascription of the higher status roles to men.

Sex roles in cross-cultural perspective

After reviewing much of the cross-cultural literature on the division of labor by sex, Roy D'Andrade (1966) provides us with an interesting summary of his conclusions:

> The division of labor by sex involved in subsistence and other activities is strongly influenced by primary and secondary sex characteristics: generally males tend to perform those activities that are physically strenuous, dangerous, involve long periods of travel, and demand a high level of cooperation.
>
> Specialization by sex activities generalized from those activities that are differentially conditioned by physical differences to activities which are anticipatory or similar to the more directly conditioned activities. These sex differences can be seen in the division of labor, in the manufacture of various objects, in sex differences in socialization, and perhaps even in fantasy.
>
> Sex bias in forms of social organization, such as rules of residence and types of descent groups, is related to subsistence activities and the division of labor by sex; the sex which performs or initiates the basic subsistence activities is more likely to control the property that is involved in these activities, and more likely to reside together and to form a descent group.
>
> The cross-cultural mode is that males are more sexually active, more dominant, more deferred to, more aggressive, less responsible, less nurturant, and less emotionally expressive than females. The extent of these differences varies by culture. And in some cultures some of these differences do not exist (and occasionally the trend is actually reversed). These differences are related to and presumably influenced by which sex controls economic capital, the extent and kind of division of labor by sex, the degree of political "authoritarianism," and family composition.
>
> Maleness and femaleness are institutionalized as statuses in all cultures. Such statuses become psychological identities for most individuals. Usually individuals learn to want to occupy the sex status they are assigned; however, special cultural conditions can affect the degree to which one sex envies the status of the other. Male envy of female status appears to be increased by paternal absence, and is culturally institutionalized in rites such as the couvade and male initiation ceremonies or in special transvestite statuses.
>
> In fantasy dreams male and female differences can be seen as expressions of body imagery or as reflections of culturally institutionalized differences in activities and their reinforcement contingencies [pp. 201–202].

One might hypothesize that the development of technology would tend to narrow the gap between the sexes with respect to their physical capabilities. With machines available that utilize other than human energy, it would appear that the fact that one sex is stronger and larger than the other would begin to make little difference in the activities in which they might engage. Indeed, this point of view is not uncommonly believed by those who seek to establish complete equality of men and women.

Theory, however, does not always provide for all contingencies. An especially pertinent series of observations in this connection are provided by Spiro's (1956) study of a Kibbutz in Israel. He tells us that a fundamental problem in the community he studied was that of "the women." In the founding of the Kibbutz community, a major goal was the complete emancipation of women and an equality of the sexes in all respects. Women were no longer to be tied to the home and family, as it was believed that they were in bourgeois society. There was to be no sexual division of labor. Men and women both worked in the fields driving tractors, planting, and harvesting. Communal dining rooms and nurseries were provided to eliminate much of the burden of cooking and childcare. But things did not work out as they had been planned. Women simply could not perform the same tasks as the men. They found tractor driving and harvesting too arduous. Pregnancy made even less difficult tasks, such as gardening, too difficult. What happened was that before long women were finding themselves back in the age-old roles of cooking, housekeeping, laundering, teaching, and caring for children.

It does not seem likely that changes in technology or conscious striving for an equality of the sexes with respect to the roles they play will make any really fundamental changes in the forseeable future. Many theorists are prone to overestimate the relativity of culture and the malleability of human behavior. They tend to underestimate biological factors and their implications for social life. Men are male and women are female in their basic capacities and characteristics. The differences arising from their reproductive roles alone impose a basic cleavage between the sexes with respect to the kinds of lives they can live, and there are limits to the modification that can be tolerated if the social group is to survive. If women were somehow persuaded to forsake their basic biologic functions, there would soon be no society. The development of technology, with its major influence in reducing some of the differences between men and women, appears to have its limitations in equalizing the roles that each sex will play in social life and the statuses they will occupy in society.

Notes

[1] The evidence on which this chapter is based, unless specified to the contrary, is available in the Human Relations Area Files. These files contain detailed information on approximately 250 primitive societies representing the major geographical-cultural regions of the world. The societies covered are among those whose ethnographic coverage has been the most thorough and comprehensive. Even so, there are some aspects of the lives of these people that are not as well documented as one would wish. At the same time, the perspective that this cross-cultural evidence provides may be of some significance and may provide some insight into the variables involved in the shaping of sex roles in human societies.

[2] Personal observation, 1935–36, 1961, 1962.

References

Blackwood, Beatrice. *Both Sides of Buka Passage*. Oxford: Clarendon Press, 1935.

D'Andrade, Roy G. "Sex Differences and Cultural Institutions." In *The Development of Sex Differences,* E. E. Maccoby, ed. Stanford: Stanford University Press, 1966, pp. 174–204.

Davenport, William. "Sexual Patterns and their Regulation in a Society of the Southwest Pacific." In *Conference on Sex and Behavior,* F. A. Beach, ed. New York: Wiley, 1965, pp. 164–207.

Evans-Pritchard, E. E. *The Position of Women in Primitive Societies and other Essays in Social Anthropology*. London: Faber and Faber, 1965.

Ford, Clellan S., and Frank A. Beach. *Patterns of Sexual Behavior*. New York: Harper, 1951.

Junod, H. A. *The Life of a South African Tribe*. London: Macmillan, 1927.

Mead, Margaret. *Sex and Temperament in these Primitive Societies*. New York: William Morrow, 1935.

———. *Male and Female*. New York: William Morrow, 1949.

Murdock, George P. "Comparative Data on the Division of Labor by Sex." *Social Forces,* 15 (1937), 551–53.

———. *Social Structure*. New York: Macmillan, 1949.

Simmons, Leo. *The Role of the Aged in Primitive Society*. New Haven: Yale University Press, 1945.

Spiro, Melford E. *Kibbutz: Venture in Utopia*. Cambridge: Harvard University Press, 1956.

Stephens, William N. "A Cross-Cultural Study of Menstrual Taboos." *Genetic Psychology Monographs,* 64 (1961), 385–416.

Young, F., and A. Bacadayan. "Menstrual Taboos and Social Rigidity." *Ethnology,* 4 (1965), 225–40.

2 EMERGENT AFRICA

Edith Elizabeth Lord [1]

Most works on Africa begin with the statement that generalizations about the continent are dangerous or impossible. This is particularly true about cultural facets, including the social roles of men, women, children, and the aged. The number of different ethnic groups in Africa has been variously estimated from 800 to over 2,000, each with different languages, or dialects, and social customs.

Another problem confounding those who wish to understand Africa is that many Africans—as individuals, as tribes, and as nations—do not wish to be fully known or understood by non-Africans at this point in time. Foreign traders, colonizers, and missionaries began long ago to bring to the attention of Africans the manners, morals, and machinery of non-African cultures. Bohannan (1966) has observed that:

> Africans, when they were living a tribal life, were not deprived people. Lives of tremendous dignity and valued rewards can be lived away from the trappings of Western civilization. But once the consciousness of those trappings seeps into awareness, a new day has arrived, and a new struggle must ensue [p. 21].

However, many traditions from over a thousand years ago have resisted the pressures of mere centuries and exist little-changed today. Social sex roles are among the patterns that have proved highly resistant to change.

Even African adaptations of nonindigenous customs tend to become appropriated and resistant to change. For instance, in 1965 the writer asked a Liberian employee of the United States government in Monrovia, who spoke a barely comprehensible dialect of English, what he thought of providing American-English language training for local employees to enhance communications and understanding between Americans and Liberians. His response: "Better the Americans learn to hear Liberian English; we understand one another." Also, by the time the University of Nigeria was three years old, practically everything that had been done, even once, had become a "sacred tradition" resistant to change.

The writer made a study in 1965, of Nigerian attitudes toward tradition and change. The subjects belonged to the upper echelon of Nigerians employed by the United States government to assist in the implementation of binational development programs. Of thirty variables explored, the highest degree of unanimity (100 percent) was found to be the belief that change was desirable *only* if it did not interfere with traditions.

Americans and Europeans sometimes have difficulty understanding the political, legislative, and judicial systems of African nations because they tend to overlook the vital role religion has played, both traditionally and in the present. Many political activities were, and some still are, the responsibility of families or villages. The Oni (King) of Ife (a village in Western Nigeria) is traditionally the temporal, as well as the spiritual, ruler and head of the Yoruba people. Although his temporal power is somewhat diminished today, one of his more than thirty sons told the writer that he still receives tribute, as spiritual leader, from members of Yoruba tribes scattered from the Cameroons to the Ivory Coast. On this point Bohannan (1966) comments:

> On the surface, African institutions are changing very rapidly, but the quickening ideas, moulded by experience and language, have deep roots in African tradition and history. . . . Whatever trouble Africans and Europeans may have in discussing matters with one another in the post-colonial world, much at least is attributable to the fact that they make different political assumptions [p. 190].

The goods, living standards, and services developed by non-African societies are very attractive to Africans. In an effort to have the best of two worlds—the preservation of traditions and the acquisition of worldly goods and world-wide status—many African tribes and nations have constructed elaborate facades designed to present to the outside world a picture of a modern continent. Behind the facade, however, in the villages of Africa where the vast majority of Africans live and where the loyalties of most urban-dwellers remain, social roles persist largely unchanged. Africans usually feel a sense of primary responsibility and obligation toward certain people or groups rather than toward general ideas, principles, or sociopolitical systems. In exchange for the loyalty he gives to his kinship group, the African receives the equivalent of such welfare benefits as insured subsistence for life and care in his old age.

Africans have an authoritarian orientation toward practically all facets of human organization. An African joke goes as follows: "If two men were shipwrecked on a deserted island, what is the first thing they would do?" Answer: "If they were Englishmen, they would start a club; if they were Americans, they would organize a work-committee; if they were Africans, they would elect a chief." Rigid authoritarianism forms the basic structure of African rule, religion, and social and family patterns; the chief authority is male.

Male supremacy

In polygynous families, which predominate in Africa, it is possible for a boy to have a half-brother who is his senior by one day or less. Within the family and the village, this twenty-four-hour seniority can have great power; in fact, even the "elder" of identical twins takes precedence over the first-born, who is believed to be the second formed. And in the majority of ethnic groups, all males are considered superior to all females.

The authors of *The Modern African* (Obukar and Williams, 1965) devote four pages to "The women in modern Africa." Included in their discussion is the comment:

> Up to now African women had a clearly defined—and limited—part in our society. It started by their being a disappointment in most cases to their parents, who had almost invariably hoped for a boy! Having got over the shock, father usually reconciled himself by working out how much he would get as bride price when the time came. . . . It is only since our girls and women have been given more education and training facilities that we all realize the importance of women's contribution to the progress of our nation [p. 8].

In a later chapter on "Education, Training, and Employment," the authors list forty-one job areas for consideration by men, but only eleven for women (pp. 29–31). And in the introduction to their volume, they make the following crucial observation:

> One of the most far-reaching changes will have to come in our attitude towards women. This will by no means be easy nor will it be implemented as quickly as we would wish in the more backward regions . . . life in towns generally is easier for women. On the other hand the peasant people cannot rapidly change their way of life so that the women's lot is made easier. And this is where the real problem lies. It is not just a matter of some of our people stubbornly clinging to the tradition that a woman is the main beast of burden; unless they get some real practical help, women will just have to continue to carry water from far-off rivers, heavy loads of firewood from long distances, dig a meagre living from some exhausted patch of land, then carry the crops in crushing loads to faraway markets over country with few roads [p. 4].

Any possible source of this "real practical help" for easing the African woman's lot is not mentioned. Traditional attitudes toward sex roles in the division of labor militate against utilizing surplus male labor—freed from the traditional roles of warrior and hunter—in any activity relegated by custom to the female "beast of burden."

In the 1950s the writer, with the help of an Ethiopian artist, developed a set of drawings designed to illustrate the psychodynamic concepts incorporated in the Thematic Apperception Test (Morgan and Murray, 1935), as adapted to Ethiopian culture. The artist drew a number of pictures to illustrate each concept. The writer's Ethiopian colleagues then helped to select the final set of pictures. To illustrate a male and a female in ludicrous sex roles, the Ethiopians unanimously chose a picture of a woman playing a musical instrument and a man carrying a heavy water jug.

The University College of Addis Ababa, in the late fifties, offered an extension course entitled "Masculine and Feminine Psychology"; the course outline reads, in part, as follows: "Man's Vocation: to rule—in the family, in the society. Therefore he has the following characteristics: strength, reasoning, procreative and protective love. . . . Woman's Vocation: motherhood—Characteristics: gentleness, intuition, devotedness." It should be noted that at the time this course was offered, the curriculum for the University College was dominated by a dedicated group of Jesuits from Canada. However, the ultimate authority at the University was H.I.M. Haile Selassie I. Additional aspects of masculine and feminine psychology are presented in the course outline as follows:

> From the point of view of entirely sexual love, *man,* representing the *aggressive* generative element will engage in a daring, venturesome love. He will take the initiative. He will seek the conquest of the opposite sex. He will seek to possess the female. His will be an aggressive love which will lead him to act.
> *Woman's* role is to *receive*. Her love, therefore, will be the receptive type. Woman will show her love by seeking and accepting the marks of affection, whereas man will show his love by giving them to her. She will want to be conquered; but, more or less knowingly, she will play "hard to get" in order to excite his interest. She will avoid him, but only inasmuch as it will make her seem unattainable and consequently more desirable in his eyes.

With the only university in Ethiopia propounding the foregoing as "psychology," it is not surprising that merchants, at the same time, advertised the product NU-SWIFT as "A modern scientific discovery which instantly extinguishes any fire. So simple in action a girl can use it." This rash statement was quickly modified to read, "So simple that any intelligent girl can use it."

Roles of women

Among the Yorubas of Western Nigeria, wives not only feed and clothe themselves, but are also responsible for feeding, clothing, and educating their children. In some groups, the wives are also responsible for providing food for their husband. One modern, young Yoruba woman told the writer that she would be too humiliated to face her family if she ever had to ask her husband for support.

In the opinion of one American social anthropologist (Bohannan, 1966), the work load of the African male is even more strenuous than that of the female:

> A woman's day is taken up with farming, grinding the meal, cooking the porridge and the sauce. Yet most African women find time to attend markets, visit relatives and even sometimes to rest. Men's work is more strenuous, more varied, and . . . like farmers' work everywhere—seasonal. . . . They carry out the political and judicial affairs of the country, which in most African societies takes a lot of time on the part of many of the men [p. 133].

With the usual exception of baby care, most paid domestic services in Africa are performed by men. Proposed inclusion of training of women for domestic services—a proposal made by the writer in both Ethiopia and Nigeria—was met with strong resistance from representatives of the male labor force. At a conference of African women held in Lagos, Nigeria, in 1963,[2] a delegate from an industrializing Central African country assured conference members that as soon as higher-paid jobs in business and industry were available for men in African countries, the lower-paid employment as domestic servants would begin to be available for women.

Education and change

The education of women is probably the greatest single source of present and potential change in social sex roles in Africa; however, changes seem to be endorsed by a relatively small number of women and resisted by a relatively large number of men. Traditional education and modern, formal education of women are quite different. By custom, a female child may be betrothed at, or even before, birth, and at least part of the bride price may be collected within a few years after the child's birth. Not infrequently, the child "bride" is actually reared in the future husband's home, on the theory that the mother-in-law can better train the girl to please her husband when the marriage is consummated, at postpubescence. Related to this concept of training is a practice found among the market women of Nigeria, who place their young daughters with female relatives to learn the arts of trading, childcare, homemaking, and so on. The theory behind this practice is that the mother loves the child too much to provide the discipline required for effective training.

Formal education of women is introducing changes of many kinds. A case in point is the unofficial bride price among the Ibos of Biafra (formerly Eastern Nigeria), which escalates according to a fixed schedule related to the years of modern schooling acquired by a girl. Following World War II, the market for wives was so inflated by soldiers returning to their villages with severance pay that a law was passed providing for a bride-price ceiling of approximately 85 dollars. However, in practice, this legal ceiling is usually disregarded in favor of the illegally high scale based on years of education. A number of persons have seriously told the writer that a university degree almost prices a woman out of the market!

Nevertheless, the attitude toward women as inferior beings prevails. At the University of Nigeria in 1967, the writer participated in a lively faculty-student debate on the proposition that marriage to an educated woman seriously impairs a man's chances for happiness or success in marriage. The outcome of the debate, by audience vote, was in favor of the proposition, but the debaters and audience alike were quite surprised that the negative side actually won some votes, indicating a slight erosion of traditional attitudes toward women. Incidentally, the debate chairman, the Dean of Students, spoke forcefully *against* a man's chances for happiness in marriage to an educated woman rather than to a village maiden reared in the traditional ways.

In a 1944 Declaration of Government Policy, Haile Selassie I stated, "The education of girls is regarded as being at least as important as that of boys," and in 1955 a Government Notice Declaring the Necessity for Universal Fundamental Education included the statement, "It is required that all young persons, male and female, shall receive instruction in elementary education." In 1959, His Imperial Majesty decreed that girls should take priority in filling the inadequate number of seats available in elementary school classrooms, a decree that was quite widely ignored by the male school administrators. Also, the writer knows of more than one case where an Ethiopian father inquired about how much the government would pay him if he permitted his daughter to attend school; it should be noted that this same question was occasionally asked with reference to sons. Questioning of parents revealed that a few thought the government should compensate a man for the lost services and labor of his children if he complied with the government's request that they attend school.

Chains from the past

In those African cultures that have a form of ancestor worship there is a great respect for age, since nearness to the ancestor is believed to give a person greater wisdom and power. Within the community, children may be grouped in from four to as many as eight grades, depending on age. Each age-grade has its defined responsibilities and tasks; the groups and the tasks are separate for boys and for girls. While each age-grade is subservient to, and must show respect for, all members of older age-grades, females, regardless of age-grade, are considered inferior to males, as noted earlier in another context.

There is some evidence that changes are occurring more rapidly in the breakdown of male-female distinctions than in age-grade attitudes. For example, two Nigerian employees, a male and a female, both educated in England, were working in a United States government office in Lagos, Nigeria. The woman had seniority in terms of experience but was younger than the man who, at the time of his employment, insisted that he could work comfortably under the young woman's supervision. The arrangement failed, however, when the man discovered, and honestly admitted, that he could not tolerate the indignity of being in a subordinate position to a person in a younger age-grade than his own. The supervisor of both, a considerably older woman, elicited no such resistance in the young man.

All members of an extended family, indeed, of a clan, trace their origin to a single ancestor, and this ancestor is almost always a male. The writer has known few Africans, literate or illiterate, who were unfamiliar with the story of *the* ancestor who founded the family. Some of the accounts are highly dramatic and include worldly episodes of battles, flights, and perilous escapes as well as supernatural episodes that account for the place and incident of the founding of the family. In a village in the southeastern part of Ethiopia, the writer once witnessed a youth of about eight being drilled by a male relative in the history of his ancestry from his immediate family back to the original ancestor; reportedly, the lad would have to be letter-perfect in the recital of his heritage when the time came for him to pass from boyhood into manhood. Such stringent training was not traditionally given to girls; however, informants have reported that as the memory ritual for boys is decreasing, there is increasing emphasis on teaching girls to have knowledge of, and pride in, their ancestry.

Black Skin and Sex Roles

Ethiopia provides an interesting example of a people who trace their ancestry back to two women. Many versions of the story of King Solomon and Queen Saba (Sheba) are widely known. Less well known is the oft-told tale that all light-skinned Ethiopians are descendants of Solomon and Saba, while all dark-skinned Ethiopians are descendants of Solomon and Saba's black maidservant (Lord, 1970). While there is probably less prejudice against women among the Ethiopian élite than that in most other African countries, there is a quite strong, and apparently traditional, prejudice against blackness. A survey conducted by the writer in the late 1950s, with the assistance of university students of various tribal backgrounds, included a question concerning the desirable attributes of a wife; many of the male respondents, in a tribal cross section, stated that, "She must not be black."

Since the surging of independence among black African states during the last few decades, Ethiopia has increasingly identified itself as a part of black Africa, playing a major leadership role in that arena. And there are some indications that as the prejudice against blackness is declining, the rather special place of women in Ethiopia may also be decreasing, perhaps to conform to the more general antifemale patterns found among most other black African peoples. This is especially interesting when one remembers not only the role of Queen Saba as founder of Ethiopia, but also that the immediate predecessor of Haile Selassie I was a woman, Her Imperial Majesty Empress Zauditu.

The previously mentioned 1963 conference of African women in Nigeria had, as its Ethiopian delegate, *not* the Ethiopian woman invited and expected by the planning committee, but rather a Malagassay woman married to an American expatriate, both residents of Ethiopia only since the 1940s.

At this same conference, there was some discussion of the need for African women to reject their tradition-imposed conviction of inferiority in order to improve their status. As one delegate put it, "For thousands of years African men have been telling us African women that we are inferior to them, and we have come to believe them, despite all the evidence of science to the contrary." There was also much discussion among delegates of the need to urge women to vote and run for elective office in government. A delegate from predominantly Islamic Northern Nigeria was shocked to discover that she was the *only* representative from a region where women are denied the vote; she had thought this status was true of women throughout Muslim countries.

Speaking on a "Brains Trust" panel in Addis Ababa, an Ethiopian faculty member of Haile Selassie I University, with a Ph.D. from an American Ivy League university, prefaced her remarks with the request that no one in the audience misconstrue anything she said to assume the equality of women with men. "Because," she said, "I know we are inferior." Perhaps such an abject disclaimer may have contributed to the marital harmony of one family, but it probably contributes less than a little to a change in the social sex roles of African women. A much less educated woman friend of the writer, seated beside her in the audience, muttered, "Treason, treason to our sex." The latter remark would seem to be the more progressive of the two.

Changes in the Wind

An international women's organization recently invited an affiliated group in an East African country to select a delegate to attend a conference of African women. A member of the group told the writer that the all-male government of the country had usurped the selection privilege and appointed the wife of a politician, a socially and organizationally inactive woman who, presumably, was considered "safe" to speak for the women of the country outside the borders of that state. The organization, under pressure, reportedly agreed to the appointment of the "outsider" provided they could prepare the preconference agenda for the delegate and would be given the postconference report for review prior to its local release. As of January 1968, months after the termination of the conference, the women's organization in the East African country had not received any information concerning the conference nor any report from "their" delegate. Presumably, the leaders of the international organization were unaware of the façade. According to the informant, the educated women of the country are simmering over this incident. In fact, one tends to get the impression that informed women of the African continent are, quite generally, beginning to simmer. The twenty-first century might see some rather dramatic social changes in sex roles; possibly there may be prologues during the remaining decades of the current century.

Mrs. Annie Jiagge, Ghanaian High Court judge, was elected in 1967 as Chairman of the United Nations Committee on the Status of Women. The February 23, 1968 issue of the Accra *Daily Graphic* quotes Mrs. Jiagge as having urged the United Nations to concentrate its attention on how to eliminate discrimination against women on national and local levels. Mrs. Jiagge also commented that slavery exists in some countries.

The *Ghanaian Times* of February 5, 1968, quoted the Netherlands delegate to the same U.N. Committee on the Status of Women as stating that between two and four million women were still subjected to slavery in various countries. The Tunisian delegate, Mrs. Souad Chater, was quoted as referring to polygamy as "camouflaged or disguised slavery."

Shortly after Lieutenant Colonel Chukwuemeka Ojukuwu declared Eastern Nigeria to be the Independent Republic of Biafra on May 30, 1967, he promulgated a series of regulations affecting the employment status and rights of women that many women, especially those who were married, interpreted as reactionary. The proposals were resented by many women, and a delegation of protesters was received by the colonel. One delegate, a university faculty member, reported to the writer that logical arguments seemed to be making little impression on the military governor. Thereupon, reportedly, an aged market woman approached the colonel and simply said, in a local tongue, "Son, you are engaged in a war (with Nigeria) which, God willing, you will win; do not engage in a war you cannot win, do not fight the women of this country." Again, reportedly, Colonel Ojukuwu replied, "Thank you, mother. I shall heed your advice." And the conference ended. From that day to the present writing, Biafra has been engaged in a war for survival, so it is not possible to know whether or not the discriminatory vocational regulations were enforced or abandoned. But it is a matter of record that the women of Africa, old and young, literate and illiterate, are breathing the winds of change.

According to radio reports from Lagos, the federal capital of Nigeria, women are engaged in the actual fighting in the break-away state of Biafra. This is particularly interesting when one remembers that during England's conquest of Eastern Nigeria, the unforgotten and unforgiven battle was the one in which the Ibos of Eastern Nigeria sent their women to talk and negotiate with the advancing English armies, attributing to the English their own value system that included the prohibition of harm to women. But the English fired on the women. This destruction of the source of life was incredible to the nineteenth century Africans who became the twentieth century Eastern Nigerians. In 1968, the women of Biafra, reportedly, were not merely talking, they were firing as well as being fired upon, an interesting change in social sex roles as humanity approaches the twenty-first century.

Old Women as Witches

While African men are resisting the changing roles of African women or giving them only token support to impress the non-African world, there are interesting exceptions. An organization of young men's clubs in Nigeria includes working for social change as a policy and a goal. One of the affiliated clubs in Eastern Nigeria, in 1967, began working on a program to alter attitudes toward elderly women in a group of villages. While age is generally respected, there is widespread belief that a woman can attain an age much beyond normal life expectancy only through witchcraft. To reduce the danger from witches, the group of villages had established a special village where irritable old women, confessed witches, from all of the villages could be confined and isolated. The writer, in her fifties, was approached by an officer of the young men's club with the request that she visit the villages and talk with the people to demonstrate that all old women are not necessarily witches and to bear witness to the constructive use made by other countries, such as the United States, of their old women. Another part of the plan was for the writer to visit the village of witches to discuss with them their confessions of witchery—reportedly obtained under torture—and to show them that a woman could become very old without being a witch. Also, she was asked to introduce them to some handicraft activities, and to prove to the people of the other villages that one could safely visit the witches' village. Young men of Nigeria devised this rather elaborate plan to alter the social status of aged women in Eastern Nigeria. Unfortunately, civil unrest in Nigeria interrupted the project in the planning stage.

Dr. Thomas Lambo, psychiatrist with the University of Ibadan Teaching Hospital, has reported that male schizophrenics quite often attribute their disturbances to the fact that their mother is a witch, while emotionally disturbed women most frequently credit their physical and emotional ills to one or more of their husband's other wives. Dr. Lambo has also reported that patients in the university's very modern hospital acquiesce to all modern treatments, but invariably also accept the magic curatives brought by relatives on visiting days from the witch doctor in the village; also, he reports, students in London who have difficulty with classes, examinations, or living problems frequently write home to request that relatives discover who in the village is exerting malign influences on them.

An Ethiopian friend of the writer, apprenticed in his youth to a witch doctor, reported that the greatest number of customers were women and the largest number of requests were for love potions and death potions. There is the belief in Africa that none but the very aged ever die of natural causes. All other deaths are presumed to be caused by the evil machinations of relatives or neighbors. The way in which this belief affects social action is illustrated by an incident that occurred in a village near Lagos in the late 1960s. A tree fell and killed three children. The elders of the village appointed a committee to investigate. The committee did not check other old and rotten trees in the village but, rather, tried to discover which villagers had caused the tree to fall. In other words, a witch hunt.

Changing social roles

Traditional social roles of African women include not only the training of children but also, among elder women, the functions of listening to marital and family disputes, counseling and advising young married people, and judging the merits of women's complaints. The modern, educated African woman steps somewhat naturally into similar roles as education officer, teacher, professor, lawyer, and even judge. A marked change in roles for African women, however, is found in the political arena.

By custom and tradition, African men have exclusive control of the legislative and executive functions of government, be they tribal or national. But, increasingly, women are looking toward the vote, toward active participation in politics as a way of bringing about changes in their status. Several male politicians in Western Nigeria have told the writer that no candidate for public office had a chance of election without the support of the market women, and the women are just, just barely beginning to sense the power they wield. In 1968, the writer was invited to meet with a group of Ghanaian women university graduates planning to organize educated women nationally and regionally in order to exert a greater impact on social and political progress in Ghana.

The role of African women in politics offers an illustration of the impossibility of generalizing about Africa. As an example of diversity within one country, Nigeria provides an interesting case in point. Coincidental with the achievement of that country's full independence in 1960, each of the three regions elected a government. In the largely Christian Eastern Region, three women were elected to the legislature; in the Western Region, no women were elected to office, but reportedly voting by women was heavy; in the predominantly Muslim Northern Region, women did not have, and still do not have, the right to vote.

In the writer's experience, African males who practice polygyny, regardless of their socioeconomic or educational status, invariably protest that the female population of Africa is at least four times that of males, and that the only alternative to polygyny for women is prostitution. Most Africans, both men and women, believe that females, by nature, have an overwhelming need for sexual intercourse that must be satisfied in one way or another. A rather pathetic example of this belief is illustrated by one man in a group of four rapists who could not understand why the victim of their attack was crying. As reported to the writer, the man said, "But we only did it because we love you."

The foregoing attitudes regarding surplus women and the choice between polygyny and prostitution were publicly made most forcibly in 1963 by a Nigerian federal minister in a welcoming address to a conference attended by women from a large number of African nations. The speech was not well received; it was not openly criticized, but it led to indignant coffee-and-corridor criticisms among the delegates, many of whom equated polygyny with slavery.

Census figures in African countries are not reliable but, such as they are, they show sex ratios similar to those of other countries where the ratio has not been seriously disturbed by wars. One study (Kimble, 1961) reported a slight difference in sex ratios between tropical and nontropical Africa, with the former areas estimated at 95.6 males per 100 females and the latter areas with 107.2 males per 100 females (p. 108).

Available evidence suggests that prostitution is quite rare in the rural villages of Africa but quite common in urban centers. A Lagos newspaper, in 1967, carried a report of a judge who gave a group of convicted prostitutes a choice of jail sentences or returning to their villages to find husbands.

Marriage, Religion, and the Law

Extramarital sex relationships would seem to be the traditional norm among both men and women in many African societies (Fortes, 1962). This is perhaps understandable in polygynous societies where the one-man-one-woman ethic of modern Christianity is not universally valued, and in societies where marriages are usually arranged between families, often with little or no regard for mutual attraction or affection between the bride and groom.

Zelleke (1970) reports that in Keren, Eritrea, Ethiopia:

> The young bride spends the daylight hours with her mother-in-law and the other female members of the household. She approaches the bedroom of her husband only after dark and leaves early in the morning before daylight comes. This routine continues until such time as the wife, by the help of nature, produces her first-born child. Then, and only then, may the husband look upon the face of his wife, or the wife look upon the face of her husband [p. 62].

American citizens are familiar with marriage by a religious practitioner or a justice of the peace, and some states recognize common-law marriage. At sea, a ship's captain may perform a binding ceremony. Abroad, one of the official responsibilities of the United States Embassy consular officer is "to consummate" marriages between American citizens living in a foreign country. Marriage in African countries can be much more complicated.

Valid marriages in Ghana may be contracted in a variety of ways other than a Christian or Muslim ceremony. There is a marriage ordinance in the laws of Ghana that provides for a monogamous union that can be terminated only by a legal divorce. Customary marriage is based on tradition and varies in detail from tribe to tribe. Among urban couples, particularly if they have wealth or social status, a customary marriage may be followed by an ordinance marriage or a church wedding, sometimes by a combination of the latter two.

Although Ethiopia is the oldest continuously Christian country in the world, very few persons outside of the royal family actually marry within church buildings because there is no provision for divorce from such a marriage. Christian marriage services conducted outside the church may be dissolved by divorce, and often are.

In Ghana, especially in a population center such as Accra where exceedingly permissive attitudes toward religion prevail, it is not at all rare to find, within a single nuclear family, adherents of Roman Catholicism, Protestantism, Islamism, and animism. Among the author's Yoruba acquaintances in Lagos, Nigeria, are several persons who profess to be both Christian and Muslim. One explained that in this way he pleased the families of his Christian father and Muslim mother. Another admitted that he was not sure which was right so he was playing it safe by following the practices of both Christianity and Islam as far as possible. An Ethiopian acquaintance, whose Christian father had died, carried on a running argument with his Muslim mother because he refused to leave Addis Ababa and return to his village to marry the girl she had betrothed him to when they were both four years old. It is interesting to note here that in Zanzibar, now part of Tanzania, a Muslim man may marry a Christian or Jewish woman, but a Muslim woman may marry only a Muslim.

Most traditional African religions—usually some form of animism—condone polygyny as practiced in Old Testament times; in other words, they approve of having wives and concubines in unlimited numbers. In the case of a high-ranking chief or an important religious or political official, the number of wives may run into the hundreds. In Swaziland—the last of Britain's African colonies—King Sobhuze II, who led his people to full independence in 1968, is reported to have acquired fifty wives by 1933, the last time an official count was made, and has acquired unknown numbers of additional wives since that time. An African family may seek to improve its status by presenting a chief or a king with a free bride, thus attaining relationship with a big man and, especially if there are children, with his family.

Islamism, with many followers throughout the African continent, allows polygyny but limits the number of wives to four at any one time. It makes divorce easy for males. Christianity, with its contemporary taboo on polygyny, counts quite a few Africans among its membership, especially in Africa south of the Sahara. Most African countries have laws regulating marriages and divorces under all of these various religious belief patterns, and the patterns contain quite different attitudes toward women and the roles they must or may play as betrothed or married persons. Variations exist as well in regulations concerning children resulting from the unions. For example, one tribe in Eastern Nigeria distinguishes between big bride price and little bride price. In the event of divorce, the children belong to the father's family if the father paid a big price, but to the mother's family if he paid a little price.

Ownership of children varies from tribe to tribe throughout Africa and is usually determined by values other than the size of the bride price. For example, among the Nuers in the southern part of the Sudan, all children belong to a woman's husband, whether or not that husband is the father of the children. A Nuer widow, on the death of her husband, journeys from her home village to the village of her deceased husband, there to become the concubine of his male relatives; however, all of her children, conceived before or after her husband's death, "belong" to her husband. Gluckman (1963) reports other interesting details of attitudes of the Nuer toward women and children; for example, the frequent within-group tribal raids never include capture or killing of women and children, but raids of non-Nuer groups include them as fair trophies.

Bride price appears to be an increasingly difficult economic problem in Africa as the education of women increases. As late as October 1968, young Kenyans were protesting the burden of paying installments on an average bride price of $550, noting that ". . . as more young girls go to school, bride price is rising. Unashamedly parents declare the increased educational expenditure will be recovered—with interest—when they sell their daughter." The protest followed the report of an eighteen months' study by a commission on marriage and divorce formed by Attorney General Charles Njonjo and composed of men and women from the judiciary, the legal profession, and important civic posts. Concluding that elimination of the bride price would be impractical, the commission stated, "We believe there will never be equality between man and woman."

Economic factors are not among the most important, and in some ethnic groups are of little or no importance. Among the Guarages of Ethiopia, for example,

> Betrothal is entirely limited to persons of the same social standard. If a person of a very poor family suddenly attained a very high standard of living and consequently desired to marry into an already noble and wealthy family, he is, no doubt, risking a ceaseless controversy. The Guarages make a great effort to trace the lineage of a family before any step is taken toward marriage. Marital unions between persons of different social standing, even when motivated by psychological or economic reasons, rarely take place. Inter-marriage within the fifteenth degree of relationship is not permissible [*The Guarages and their Social Life,* p. 21. Prepared by "a Committee composed of tribal chiefs, elders, and educated young men from all the different parts of Guarage"].

Much confusion may result if a man shifts religious affiliation or undertakes a church marriage before or after a marriage by native law and custom. A Nigerian acquaintance of the writer had five wives. Through the influence of his American employer, he decided to become a Christian. This necessitated his marrying one of his wives in the church and sending the others back to their families. He chose to marry the most junior of the wives. This created serious trouble for him, especially with the family of his senior (first) wife. In some cases the courts of law recognize a marriage but the family does not; in other cases the family recognizes a marriage but the courts do not. Newspapers often report court cases involving an attempt to determine which wife is the legal wife or the senior wife.

Article 616 of The Penal Code of the Empire of Ethiopia (1957) makes bigamy "punishable with simple imprisonment, or, in grave cases, and especially where the offender has knowingly misled his partner in the second union as to his true state, with rigorous imprisonment not exceeding five years." However, Article 617 provides the following exemption: "The preceding Article shall not apply in cases where polygamy is recognized under civil law in conformity with tradition or moral usage."

A research project conducted by the present writer (1958) included a questionnaire that called for the Ethiopian subjects to state their religion early in the interview. The majority classified themselves as Ethiopian Orthodox Christians. A question later in the interview asked under what circumstances it would be permissible for a man to have more than one wife. A large number of self-identified Christians endorsed polygyny under a variety of circumstances, regardless of a man's religion; for example, polygyny is permissible, "If the first wife bears no children," or "If his wife gives him no sons," or "If more workers are needed in the fields," and so on.

An illustrated human-interest story in an African journal extolled the

Christian virtues of a wealthy and socially prominent pre-civil war Nigerian politician. One of the photographs showed him at his home organ surrounded by his family, and, according to the caption, playing Christian hymns to accompany the singing of his four wives.

Roman Catholicism is widespread among the Christians of the southern part of Nigeria. A Nigerian teacher reported to the writer that on returning from advanced study abroad, he was shocked to discover that his father had taken a second wife and pleaded to know how a devout Catholic could do such a thing. "But," explained the father, "I'm not an Irish Catholic; I'm a Nigerian Catholic."

Sex Practices

Traditional attitudes toward virginity and premarital sexual relationships vary widely among ethnic groups in both east and west tropical Africa. Changing attitudes toward female virginity are most marked in urban centers and among educated Africans.

Among some ethnic groups of Ethiopia, a member of the wedding party observes the consummation of the marriage and carries a blood-stained cloth from the bridal chamber outside to the waiting members of the wedding. Vulgar jokes concerning sacrificial chickens in the bridal chamber abound. Among the Amharas, according to Wodajo (1970), early in the morning following a wedding:

> The three best men, with some ten other men friends, go to the girl's home and tell her parents, in the time-honoured way, that their daughter has lived up to their expectations of her virginity. This is indicated by the presentation of a rose and a loaf of bread with Maria Teresa or Menelik silver coins in it.

Abdurahman (1970) describes a similar ceremony among the Ethiopians in which:

> Early in the morning after the consummation of the marriage, a calf is sent to the bride's house to announce the virginity of the girl. . . . The scared animal is pushed to the kitchen where it is daubed with butter in appreciation of its breaking the good news.

Virginity

Ghana provides an interesting example of varied attitudes toward virginity among ethnic or geographical groups within one nation (Birmingham, *et al.,* 1967):

> In the past girls were not expected to have sexual relations before their puberty rites were performed. . . . Since girls were usually married shortly

after this ceremony many entered their first conjugal unions as virgins. This was particularly so among the ethnic groups of the south where pre-nuptial chastity was valued. . . . [Today] the practice [of pre-marital sexual relations] has become very common although it is frowned upon. This increase in sexual freedom is not always confined to the urban areas but is also sometimes found in the rural areas. In Ashanti, for example, puberty rites are now performed in very few cases even in the rural areas. As soon as a girl menstruates for the first time her mother informs the Queen-mother of her community about the event, and from that time the girl is free to have sexual affairs with members of the opposite sex. Since, in a matrilineal society, the offspring of the girl will belong to *her* family, the girl's mother does not always discourage her daughter in her sexual adventures. The older women are anxious to have many grandchildren to increase the size of their matrilineage, and the early pregnancy of their daughters helps to achieve this [pp. 203–4].

Illustrative of the difference in attitudes toward virginity of some of the ethnic groups in northern Ghana is the fact that many women among the Konkembas have experienced pregnancy prior to their first marriage or are pregnant at the time of marriage. Reportedly (Tait, 1961), among the Konkembas, the ". . . husbands show not the slightest sign of displeasure at the pregnancy of a bride [p. 204]." Likewise, a study of the Tallensi (Fortes, 1949) revealed an indifferent attitude toward virginity in a bride, for they reportedly hold the conviction that, ". . . copulation and marriage are not the same thing [p. 101]."

Fertility vs. Infertility

University of Nigeria students of the writer identified two small, geographically separated ethnic groups in Eastern Nigeria that believe a woman is not suitable for marriage until she has borne a child as evidence of her fertility. In Ethiopia, sterility is a cause for much grief, as is evidenced by a special song sung by childless women as part of the birth customs in Jimma. Addressed to Mare, the spirit that helps women through pregnancy and childbirth, some of the lines are as follows (Adem, 1970):

Oh Mare, Oh Marami, eternal Mistress of the have-nots, have pity.
What did the cat sacrifice for thee that begets eight?
What did the sterile do that walks in continuous tears?
Oh Mare, grandest child of powerful nature,
Come and witness the great dance held in your favour.
A small loaf is better than a big, broken one;
Begetting a female is better than no baby at all.
Oh, Mare, take me to your favour.
Say: "You sterile, beget a baby and suckle it."
The husband hates the sterile—she lacks perfume, makes bad broth.
The sterile is looked down upon by relatives—she discontinues the race.
The mother of five, her death is observed as if she died in the palace;

Thousands will accompany her coffin and hundreds carry her to the grave.
On the other hand, who likes the unfortunate sterile?
Her death is as if in woods and slaves accompany her to her rest.

Twin Status

Among many African groups, the birth of twins has particular significance ranging from perception of the event as a curse to considering it a great blessing. Among some Nigerian ethnic groups, the belief is held that every person is dual; that one part of the duality exists on earth as a living being while the other part exists beneath the earth as a spirit, mingling with ancestors and with both good and bad spirits. If properly propitiated, the spirit twin is capable of interceding in the spirit world on behalf of its dual self existing among the living. A similar belief has been encountered in Ethiopia. That both manifestations of the dual self should exist in living form on earth simultaneously is untenable. In some cases, both twins are thrown into the bush to die at birth; in other cases, one of the twins is "permitted" to die as soon as possible, thereby enabling its return to the spirit world to function properly in behalf of the earth-side aspect of the self.

In Lagos, the writer talked with a European-educated African mother of three-year-old identical twins, who explained that her family in her home-village was unaware of the multiple birth. On periodic visits to her home, she had taken first one then the other of the twins since, she explained, her family would arrange the death of one of them if their coexistence on earth were known. At age three, the children were too bright to make alternate visits without risking discovery; the mother's quandary was to decide which one to take with her regularly and which to deprive of acquaintanceship with the ancestral family. She expressed no fear concerning the visiting twin's talking to his grandparents and other relatives about his twin brother, explaining that this would merely suggest a close, perhaps even precocious, relationship with his other self in the spirit world.

In neighboring Ghana, the treatment of twins, by a number of tribal groups, reflects quite different attitudes. Twins, male or female, are believed to be especially blessed by God, and their parents are considered particularly fortunate. The one exception is that a young man is considered unlucky if his first offspring is a set of twins. Identical twins are considered to be "perfect twins." A shrine is built by the people for the twins, and it is the site of a weekly ceremony with the twins dressed in special white cloth and adorned with arm and neck jewelry. The harvest is observed annually by offering the first fruits of the earth to the shrine; next, the twins enjoy a special luxury meal, and then everyone celebrates the harvest with thanksgiving and feasting. In parades, as well as in other situations, the secondborn twin takes precedence over the firstborn since he is believed to have been conceived first and, hence, is the elder.

The traditions and customs pertaining to twins prevail regardless of the religious affiliation of the parents. This is not surprising in a country where religious freedom is so broad that, as mentioned earlier, within one family there may be followers of Christianity, Islamism, and animism, and where one person may follow more than one belief. However, there is one custom that is on the decline: Traditionally, twins are given to the chief of the village, boys as favored servants and girls as wives; the chief, in turn, may offer girl twins in marriage to any of his village elders of sufficient status and wealth to provide properly for such precious wives. This practice is dying. The changing custom is believed by some to conflict with the unpardonable crime a man commits if he flirts with his wife's sister, behavior particularly unbecoming in a chief.

Queen Mother Status

Another position of high status for women in Ghana, both traditionally and in modern times, is that of the Queen Mother. This position may be hereditary, appointive, or elective, and the incumbent may be very old or a mere child. During the writer's most recent visit to Ghana, in 1968, much newspaper publicity was given to the investiture as Queen Mother of a little girl of eight. The Queen Mother is the center of female activities within the group; she is the intermediary between the chief and those women with problems or grievances. Also, the chief relays through her to the women his wishes and orders—how many women are needed for this or that work activity, for example. In ceremonies and parades, her position is second only to that of the chief; and riding with her in her palanquin is a little girl representing her Soul, just as a little boy rides with the chief to represent his Soul. The Queen Mother has a special place of honor in the extended family and is entitled to a servant from each major family in the clan.

One may wonder how a woman can attain such status in a predominantly male authoritarian culture. The "real" family in Ghana is matrilineal, with power and leadership extending from the eldest woman of a clan to her children and their offspring. The chief of the clan is the eldest son of the eldest woman. The smallest unit, or immediate family, includes a husband as head of the household, a wife, and their children. Traditionally, one husband may head several such units; however, this practice is limited today primarily to nonurban residents, farmers, and fishermen. The will of the husband is final in all matters, and the position of the family exists only during his lifetime. In most, but not all, clans, neither the wife nor the children of a family unit inherits whatever has been accumulated by the husband; control of dependents and properties reverts to the extended or "real" (matrilineal) family on the death of the husband.

In Ghana today, one can see an increase in the role of women as forces to be reckoned with in the society, both through the continuing power of the traditional Queen Mother and the emerging power of the embryonic Ghanaian Association of University Women. Change is in the air. A Ghanaian proverb states, "It is the snail that says, 'Let me be where I am; I am content.' " And another proverb from this traditionally highly authoritarian culture states, "Authority is an egg in a man's hand."

Clothes as Symbols

If we remember earlier comments about the facade some African groups present to the world to create a desired appearance, the subject of clothing becomes interesting. Dr. Thomas Lambo, a psychiatrist from Nigeria, stated in a symposium at the American Psychological Association's 1965 meetings in Chicago, that an African's sense of self is something that he puts on like a garment. At an informal gathering following his speech, the writer's name-badge fell to the floor and she said, "In Nigerian terms, I have lost my identity." He responded, "You understand exactly what I was trying to say."

Shortly after Nigeria became independent in 1960, there was a national surge throughout Nigeria to forego modern Western dress and return to traditional tribal costumes. Despite the hazards of wearing flowing robes on a motorcycle in traffic-jammed Lagos, postcolonial urban Nigeria proudly shifted back to precolonial garb, possibly a symbol of clothing newly-won independent statehood with the dignity of the past.

Within twenty-four hours after Biafra declared its independence from Nigeria, students and faculty of the University of Nigeria shed traditional clothes and appeared, with very few exceptions, in modern Western garb. Symbolically, this seemed to be an off-with-the-old and on-with-the-new, goodbye-yesterday-and-hello-tomorrow sort of behavior.

In early 1968, Tanzania passed some rather stringent regulations designed to force a group of rural citizens to forego their traditional dress, which left one buttock bare, and to don Western-style trousers. Reportedly, strong government measures are being required to enforce the shift in dress.

In Nigeria, Ghana, Ethiopia, and the Sudan, the writer met a number of men in Western dress whose female relatives wore only traditional costumes. Not infrequently a man whose position brings him into social contact with non-Africans will, with or without marriage, acquire a "parlor wife" who is familiar with European and American social manners, who wears modern non-African clothes, and who accompanies him to culturally mixed affairs and serves as his hostess.

These are but a few examples of the way in which some Africans apparently tend to take on the roles they wish to portray by a mere change of costume, almost as if they were to say, "That which I appear to be, I am."

Impediments to change

Without doubt, as heretofore noted, one of the greatest forces for change in social sex roles in Africa is education. However, a study of Ethiopian superstitions (Lord, 1958) revealed that 61 percent of the teachers in the sample, 60 percent of the students, and 54 percent of the medical auxiliaries (nurses and aides) believe that, "Too much learning results in madness."

In 1957, the writer discussed with a Libyan government official the problems of female education in a Muslim culture. He said one faction wanted to require girl students to forego purdah, the lifting of their veils, as a condition for admission to public schools. But he reported that he was among the group that convinced education officials that if they could merely get parents to permit their daughters to attend school, these girls would discover other cultural patterns and would not only break free of purdah, but would also be a force for educating the female adults in their families to look on today's world with uncovered faces.

The traditional role of the African girl is work, work, and more work. She helps her mother with the housework and with the care of the younger children, often carrying a baby more than half her size on her back; she is expected to help with the preparation of land for planting, with digging, weeding, and harvesting; in some countries she also shares with her brothers the responsibility for herding the sheep, goats, or cattle. But today in Africa thousands upon thousands of girls are in modern day schools or boarding schools. These girls will become the educated mothers of the next generation of Africans, and they will be the grandmothers and female tribal elders of the first generation of the twenty-first century. And that is when the number of educated African women may be large enough, and their status high enough and strong enough, to bring about truly significant changes in the status and the social roles of the masses of women on the African continent.

Aside from witchcraft, demons, spirits, juju, the evil eye, ancestors, and other supernatural forces that play such powerful roles in African cultures, the strongest forces are traditionalism—the *old* ways—and tribalism—*our* ways. Both of these forces are blocking modernization and national unification of an estimated 220,000,000 Africans. And they are impeding changes in the social roles of women. Shortly before the Federation of Nigeria fell apart, a member of the faculty of the University of Ibadan, formerly a College of the University of London and one of the most prestigious universities in Africa, had the following to say on this subject (Tugbiyele, 1967):

Whether we like it or not and whether we accept it or not, over 95% of our "educated" men and women are still tribalists, and jingoists, including academically reputable university professors, university students and very top executives. We pretend to be detribalised but, in actuality, we are more tribalistic than the ordinary run of people.

If this Federation collapsed, it would be because of tribalism, sectionalism and nepotism *in the hearts* of at least 98% of the people of Nigeria. It would be due to mutual prejudices, stereotypes and myths of nationality and tribal groups about other nationality and tribal groups. It would be due to the vigorous—though sometimes subtle—attempts of Regions and tribes to dominate other Regions and tribes be it in the church, market, shop, education, employment, and other spheres of national life.

At the time the preceding statement was made by a scholar of Western Nigeria, the Ibos of Eastern Nigeria had already suffered losses of from 30,000 to 50,000 of their members through the 1966 and 1967 massacres of their people in Northern Nigeria by civilians and military personnel of other Nigerian tribes. The Ibos, perhaps the most rapidly modernizing ethnic group, having elected three women to their regional legislature, having given Nigeria and the world poets, playwrights, and novelists of great talent, having in large numbers shed traditional tribal dress, having left tribal villages to work for progress and unity throughout Nigeria, having supplied most of prewar Nigeria's skilled technicians and at least 40 percent of her civil servants—these Ibos were driven back to a small area of their original homeland as part of a tribalistic conflict that is still raging as these words are written and which may have reduced the Ibos of Nigeria/Biafra to impotence by the time these words go to press. What price progress?

The present crisis in Nigeria is itself symbolic of the painful changes taking place in Africa. It is significant that this nation, the most populous in Africa, is rich not only in tribal custom and folklore but in art and literature. Indeed, one of the catastrophes of the war is that the distinguished writers of the Ibo tribe—most of the best-known novelists and playwrights in English-speaking Africa—have lost contact with the Western world, or at least with their usual publishing house (Heinemann) in London.

Finally, we are reminded again that all Africa is in transition. The relations between the sexes, as well as marital and family norms, will continue to change for all these nations, and the tragic situation in Nigeria may bring on change even more rapidly there than among its neighbors.[3]

Notes

[1] In June of 1968, the writer terminated fourteen years of service in the African Bureau of the foreign aid program of the Department of State.

The original draft of this chapter on Africa was written while the author was on assignment from the United States Department of State's Agency for International

Development to the Department of Psychology of the University of Nigeria. That draft, and all related documentation, were last known to be among the writer's personal effects in a warehouse in Port Harcourt, Biafra (formerly Eastern Nigeria), presumably among the losses of the tragic civil war that has raged in Nigeria since the spring of 1967. As a substitute for the lost manuscript, this essay reports impressions gleaned from the writer's eleven years of working in Africa and visiting twenty-one African countries. Most of the material relates to Ethiopia, Ghana, and Nigeria, the countries with which the author is most familiar.

[2] The Role of African Women in Urban Development, sponsored by the United Nations Educational, Social, and Cultural Organization.

[3] Since this chapter was written word has come of the fall of Biafra, defeat of a proud people's struggle for human dignity and freedom (G.H.S., ed.).

References

Abdurahman, Mohamed. "The Harrari Wedding Customs." In *Queen Sheba's Heirs,* Edith Lord, ed., Washington, D.C.: Acropolis Books, 1970.

Adem, Awal. "Birth Customs in Jimma." In *Queen Sheba's Heirs,* Edith Lord, ed., Washington, D.C.: Acropolis Books, 1970.

Birmingham, Walter, I. Neustadt, and E. N. Omabee. *A Study of Contemporary Ghana,* Vol. II. London: George Allen & Unwin, 1967.

Bohannan, Paul. *African Outline.* Middlesex, England: Penguin, 1966.

Daily Graphic, Accra, Ghana (January 13, 1968).

Daily Graphic, Accra, Ghana (February 23, 1968).

Fortes, M. *The Web of Kinship among the Tallensi.* London: Oxford University Press, 1949.

——— (ed.) *Marriage in Tribal Societies.* London: Cambridge University Press, 1962.

Gluckman, Max. *Custom and Conflict in Africa.* Oxford: Basil Blakewall, 1963.

The Guarages and their Social Life. Addis Ababa: Commercial Printing Press, no date.

Kimble, George H. T. *Tropical Africa,* Vol. I. New York: Foreign Policy Association, 1961.

Lord, Edith, ed., *Queen Sheba's Heirs,* Washington, D.C.: Acropolis Books, 1970.

———. "The Impact of Education on Non-Scientific Beliefs in Ethiopia." *Journal of Social Psychology,* 47 (1958), 339–53.

Morgan, Christiana D., and Henry A. Murray. "A Method for Investigating Fantasies: the Thematic Apperception Test." *Archives of Neurology & Psychiatry,* 34 (1935), 289–306.

Penal Code of the Empire of Ethiopia. Addis Ababa: Negarit Gazeta, Extraordinary Issue, 1957.

Obukar, Charles, and John Williams. *The Modern African.* London: Macdonald & Evans, 1965.

Tait, David, *The Konkemba of Northern Ghana.* London: Oxford University Press, 1961.

Tugbiyele, E. E. Quoted in *The Sketch,* Nigeria (May 21, 1967).

Wodajo, Kifle. "Wedding Customs Among Amharas." In *Queen Sheba's Heirs,* Edith Lord, ed., Washington, D.C.: Acropolis Books, 1970.

Zelleke, Tadesse. "Betrothal and Marriage in Koren, Eritrea." In *Queen Sheba's Heirs,* Edith Lord, ed., Washington, D.C.: Acropolis Books, 1970.

3 SEXUAL IDENTITY CRISES IN THE LIFE CYCLE

Irene M. Josselyn, M.D.

Sexuality and the human species

The human species is one of the very few forms of animal life in which sexuality has a dual role. As it does for all complex organisms, sexuality serves to insure the continuity of the species. When other considerations do not interfere, it also provides a unique form of pleasure, irrespective of whether or not the goal of reproducing the species is sought or attainable. This species-related phenomenon intensifies and broadens the scope of sexual pleasure, but at the same time creates complex situations that may lead to crises in sexual identity. Once a biological function encompasses emotional as well as physical factors, the individual's psychological drives, needs, and frustrations create a potential for richer experience in the fulfillment of the originally biological need. The capacity to fuse sustained, multifaceted love with sexual impulses indicates emotional health and maturity.

For whatever reason, man is a social animal. He seeks interrelationships with others of his kind, and in so doing creates a social group. At times the resultant social structure transcends the particular drives of the individual (Josselyn, 1968b). This is true of other animal forms that instinctively remain members of a group, but the human being does not react solely on instinct. He is aware of his social affiliation and is, to a degree, selective and self-directed in his participation.

The individual's capacity for affective experience, and particularly the interplay between the individual and his society, deepen the fulfillment of his biological needs. Both the self-oriented and the socially oriented aspects of his psychological gestalt may create confusion—a confusion resulting both from internal conflicts, which may be idiosyncratic to the individual, and from conflicts between internal needs and external demands of the society (Freud, 1933).

Sexual Behavior and Social Demands

As is true of all socially acceptable or unacceptable behavior, human sexual patterns are influenced by the particular culture. When a culture has sharply defined sanctions and limits, there is usually less conflict created for the individual; he complies without sharp awareness of alternative behavior (Mead, 1928). When the socially imposed framework has fewer guidelines (and often these are hazy), the individual is more exposed to his own internal conflicts. Since these conflicts are not solved through the restraints of taboos or effectively channeled by sanctions defined by group cultural patterns, the individual has greater responsibility for establishing his own guidelines. Even when the mores of a society are flexible, however, there are definite but not always clearly formulated limits beyond which the individual cannot go without exposing himself to recriminations.

Social Demands and Western Culture

In present-day Western culture, the complexity of life is so great that flexibility is often necessary in dealing with problems. Superficially, the culture does not offer many directives. A son, for example, is not usually expected to follow in his father's footsteps. He is free to choose a career compatible with his own interests—interests that may have originated in his exploration of many fields his father never cultivated. On the other hand, freedom and flexibility have limits. The social mores say, in effect, "You are free, but . . ." The boy choosing a career different from that of his father is expected to make a choice of one that is, if not superior to his father's in status, at least the equal of his father's. In so doing, he is expected to achieve a financial reward that will provide a buying power at least equal to that of his father's. He may be confronted with a conflictive situation where the internal and self-focused interests lead to one form of gratification, while the wish to experience the gratification of social acceptance creates an opposing goal.

Unless the biological urge for fulfillment is in accord with cultural mores, sexual conflict is unavoidable. Internal desires and externally imposed standards must, if conflict is to be minimized, be fused—a fusion that will lead to the individual's sexual identity. On the basis of this fusion, a man can say that whatever else he is, he is both physically and psychosocially a man; a woman can equally identify herself as a physical and psychosocial woman.

Psychosocial sexual identity is not easily attained in a flexible society. There are certain obvious examples of this truth. For instance, on the basis of the biologically determined sex of the individual, it is impossible to differentiate sharply the social role that the man or the woman will fulfill. Any definition of the socially determined function of a male in current Western society can immediately be destroyed by statistical evidence that women can and do fulfill the same role, even when it is economically unnecessary for them to do so. Any definition of the social function of a woman can readily be disproved by evidence that men can function as adequately in that role (Williamson, 1966, pp. 88–93). Because there is no culturally formulated differentiation or any direct demand for such a differentiation, biological sexuality may lead to an expression of the individual's direct needs that are often, but not always, primarily sexual.

For example, a woman may, for some nonsexual need, be concerned with the gratification of utilizing her business acumen. She dresses in tailored clothes and, for convenience, wears her hair extremely short. This does not necessarily mean that she is pretending to be a male; she may be primarily interested in her talents as expressed through her business activity. Her tailored appearance may represent her identity as a businesswoman; it may or may not represent denial of her sexual self-concept.

Increasingly in Western culture, the individual determines his own behavior patterns, formulated neither on the basis of his biologically determined sex, nor on arbitrary social mores. Because the milieu so vaguely defines his identity in the multiple roles he strives to fulfill, he experiences an identity crisis whenever the role he has accepted proves to be unsatisfactory, beyond his ability, vulnerable to the impact of other roles he has or wishes to assume, or unexpectedly questioned by his society. It is not surprising that crises in sexual identity may occur as a part of, or as the sole component of, any transient or sustained choice.

In addition to the above-mentioned causes of confusion in social roles, there are more basic reasons for sexual identity crises in Western culture. They fall into two broad, interrelated categories. First, there are those that are primarily determined by social mores. Mores impose responsibilities and offer gratifications that transcend physical, sexual discharge. They determine the accepted paths that extend beyond physical sexual fulfillment, encompassing the total social structure of the current society. Second, there are those related to conflicts concerning the direct and/or sublimated sexual gratification of the individual. The two categories interrelate but equally give a basis for crises in sexual identity.

Family Orientation Aspects of Sexual Identity

Contemporary Western culture is a family-oriented culture (Williamson, 1966, pp. 5–22). The family is conceptualized as the optimal medium for the sexual expression of its adult members; the fundamental core of the family being the father, the mother, and the child. In the past, the core family was supported by other members—grandparents, aunts, uncles, and cousins (the extended family). While the father and mother were the center, they formed an inherent part of a larger unit. As a result, the father and mother gained emotional support, could be relieved of certain responsibilities, and were guided by the mores of the larger family unit.

The central role of the family in Western culture has been weakened by an increasing tendency for the immediate family to separate from the larger extended family. This has been attributed to the shift from rural to urban living. An extended family group was often needed as a labor force on the farm. In urban areas the extended family is not needed and, in fact, often becomes an economic disadvantage. Also, mobility itself is crippled by an extended family. When the family depends on income from only one of its members, relocation is easier than if the family contained several wage earners who would have to give up their jobs and be ready to move. Western culture is mobile, either as a cause or a result of the diminution in the importance of the extended family.

There has also been a philosophical change based upon the psychological conceptualization of maturity. The philosophy of the culture is that an adult manifests maturity by severing the strong bonds with his extended and childhood family and by establishing himself as the independent nucleus of a new unit, whether that unit be his own family, his peer group, or his geographically defined identity.

The shift from the large family unit to the more circumscribed one is primarily true of the mobile, middle- and upper-class families. Among the lower economic and minority groups, broader family relationships have remained more intact, possibly for economic reasons. However, even the members of the lower economic group are increasingly less dependent upon the extended family. Financial aid for dependent children, the unemployed, the acutely ill, and the aged is becoming the responsibility of society rather than the sole responsibility of the individual's family. The government is rapidly replacing the extended family.

The extended family is not and probably will not become a thing of the past. But what were once bonds of iron are now gossamer threads, the strength of the latter depending upon the emotional meaning of the tie. Undoubtedly, the family ties that persist in low income groups and minority groups are not solely for practical reasons. The anxiety created by insecurities that are, or seem to be, overwhelming reactivates the need to feel close to those of primary significance.

This precarious tie may create a crisis in identity. Currently, it is quite acceptable for an adult son to have real affection for his father, *if* that affection does not carry an implication of a child-father relationship. Maturity, whether in a male or a female, today implies that all childhood bonds must be severed. But an emotional carry-over from childhood is an integral part of the individual. Many segments of society believe this tie should be hidden or disguised if it cannot be erased; if none of these possibilities is effectively accomplished, the individual has failed to achieve truly adult masculinity or femininity. The effect of this cultural shift and psychological definition of maturity creates painful confusion, due possibly to guilt, shame, or a deadening of all positive, interpersonal affects in order to avoid the supposed dangers of a resurgence of feelings attributable to childhood relationships. A person's capacity to love, an important part of mature sexuality, may be self-consciously inhibited because of uncertainty as to its roots.

Paralleling, perhaps coincidentally, the cultural phenomenon of the breakdown of the extended family into smaller units is the increasing interest in the study of the psychology of the individual from birth to death. On the basis of observations, many conceive parenthood to be the final step in individual maturation (Benedek, 1952; Deutsch, 1945). The hypothesis is that the gratification of the biological sexual drive is increased through parenthood. Through the child-parent relationship, the new indivdual is protected for a longer period, thus enhancing personal development. Moreover, the cultural mores have a broader continuity than instinctual behavior alone would provide.

"The Parents"

The child-parent relationship is not unique to humans; there are many other animal species that have a degree of parental orientation. The human species expresses this biological heritage in a more multifaceted form with a progressively confusing lack of role differentiation based upon biological differences. When newspapers, popular magazines, and "scientific" articles decry juvenile delinquency, school dropouts, and other social maladjustments, there are "parents," with no sexual differentiation, who are seen as responsible.

"Parents" are supposed to provide security (usually implying emotional security), stimulation (usually implying stimulation so that academic work will be done), and controls (usually implying that the controls be such that the child does not bother the neighbors but at the same time is allowed freedom of self-expression). "Parents" are supposed to be gentle, understanding, and consistent. Above all else, they must present a picture of two people who are as one, never irritated at each other, and always, as far as the basic philosophy is concerned, agreeing. There should be no personal differences and no manifest differences between the two sexes as each becomes a parent (Ackerman, 1958).

The concept of parents without clearly differentiated sex roles can lead to confusion, both for the child and the adults. While the idea that parents should present a united front to the child is a valid rationale in most instances, it does not lead to individualization of the parents in the mind of the young child, or often in that of the adult. "Father knows best," a phrase now relatively unknown in home life, must have aided, for better or worse, the clarification of sexual contrasts in the family!

Quite aside from the lack of distinction between male and female in the composite term "parent," the shift from the large family unit of the country to the smaller unit of the city has complicated the parental roles of the mother and father. This is well illustrated by contrasting parental experience during pioneer days with the current parental experience. The child of that earlier period learned "at his mother's knee," and from his father in the field. Contact with a peer group beyond the family constellation was typically on those rare social occasions when many families gathered together. Harvesting, barn-raising, and church gatherings were total family activities. These events assured that the child would be under close supervision and would participate in the work of an adult of the same sex.

Today a child is encouraged, as soon as he is able to show a modicum of judgment, to play in the neighborhood; in the absence of readily available social contacts with his peer group, he is sent to nursery school. From the time he enters kindergarten or first grade, the direct teaching he has received from his parents is markedly diluted by those not as emotionally meaningful to him—his teacher or his peer group. Soon, homework and social activities outside of the home limit his time with his parents. In urban areas parents often do not know, except perhaps as mere acquaintances, the parents of their children's friends. They know their child's friends on the basis of their company manners, or lack of such. At the same time, parents are urged to accept responsibility for all the behavior of their child.

If parenthood is sublimation and/or the most mature stage of the sexual drive, then this achievement has many more limitations than the more immature or unsublimated drive. It is not always easy to bear the burden of family responsibility and simultaneously to experience the pleasure of psychological fulfillment idealized parenthood is supposed to provide. The vague definition of the role of each sex in childrearing, the complexity of the demands upon each individual as parent, and the impossibility of fulfilling all those demands create an identity crisis situation for both male and female. This crisis understandably stimulates some to escape from those socially defined roles that have been superimposed upon their biological heritage.

The Individual

In addition to the emphasis upon the family, Western culture has another tenet, one potentially in conflict with a family-focused orientation. This tenet stresses the rights of the individual; the dignity of the individual should be inviolate and the pursuit of happiness is an inalienable right. These concepts have been concretized in the political and social philosophy.

Our social structure, based upon the family yet guided by the philosophy of the sacredness of the individual, requires the individual to function well within the family unit and, simultaneously, to sustain a sense of self-uniqueness. These elements, which have the potential to be either incompatible or compatible, manifest themselves most dramatically in the sexual patterns of the members of Western society. Increasing knowledge of the components that foster the mental health of individuals in the social structure leads to the conclusion that the family provides the soil for psychological development; at the same time, however, the divorce rate is climbing in Western culture.

Factors Contributing to Identity Crises

As was stressed earlier, it is impossible to describe why an individual or a group functions in a certain way by placing biological facts, social pressures, and psychological ramifications in distinct categories. In perhaps no study of human behavior is this more apparent than in the study of sexual goals and the pattern by which one attains these goals. The unmarried adolescent mother or father provides a simple example of this. Physically, sexual maturation is attained during the teens (Josselyn, 1952). The clinical manifestation of this is when a teenage girl becomes impregnated by a boy of her own peer group.

Physical maturation does not necessarily imply psychological maturation. Studies of unmarried teenage girls who are pregnant indicate that they have many psychologically immature reasons for their pregnancy. There is present in most an unconscious, if not conscious, wish to be pregnant, to give birth to a child, and to succor it. The immaturity becomes apparent when the symbolic meaning of the pregnancy is ferreted out (Josselyn, 1965; Young, 1954). It becomes a significant factor if the girl attempts to assume the role of mother in rearing the child. A complex society requires maturity in the fulfillment of many roles. Interrelated with the subtle demands of the social structure are the economic demands. The young father is not in a position to support a family; he is not "man" enough.

Economic pressure as a factor in sexual identity is not limited to the teenage group. Men conceptualize themselves, and are conceptualized by others, as adequate males if they fulfill their designated role of provider. Women conceptualize themselves, and are conceptualized by others, as truly women if they have husbands who are adequate in their roles. At this point the psychological aspects of sexual identity become clearly related to its social formulation. The social and psychological demands that the teenager cannot meet impinge upon the self-concept of the psychologically immature male or female irrespective of age.

Biological Sex Differences

That for the purpose of reproduction there is an inherent, biologically determined difference in sexual roles for the male and female is self-evident. The female carries the ovum and the foetus and can feed the newborn. The male provides the sperm that makes the development of a new life possible. This is only one facet of a broader differentiation illustrated by the dissimilar body structure of the male and female that enables each sex to play a basically different role in the service of the continuity of the species. These physical differences between the male and female are sexually and genetically, rather than culturally, determined (Scheinfeld, 1943, pp. 145–154). Some recent work on genetic factors is of interest in this regard. The reports of Telfer *et al.* (1967), Wiener *et al.* (1968), and Casey *et al.* (1966) suggest that when a chromosome anomaly occurs in which a male has one *x* and two *y* chromosomes instead of the normal one *x* and one *y* chromosome he is, at least among a prison population, in the taller group of inmates and unmanageably aggressive and belligerent. The implications of these findings for normal masculinity are still speculative.

Most animals act in a fashion that would seem to justify the assumption that their responses are determined by their sexual identity; the role of that identity is reproduction. While it is true that many animals seem to evidence homosexual rather than heterosexual responses, they typically have no difficulty in functioning in a heterosexual role when stimulation for such behavior occurs. For the male, stimulation occurs externally, and for the female, internal hormonal stimulation makes for responsiveness. There is no reason to assume that the human animal differs biologically. Humans are more sensitive to the impact of external events, and the problem of sexual identity, in spite of physical evidence that would seem to make it self-evident, is solved, if at all, by a more circuitous route.

In general, the destiny of the male and the female, though basically determined by anatomy, has been somewhat modified by reality demands, learned expectations, or even chance selectivity. It is possible that the anatomical-biological-psychological basic differences of the sexes are dependent primarily upon the male's sexual capacity to intrude—anatomically, through use of the penis (Josselyn, 1968a). Erikson (1968) has approached the problem more broadly and more definitively, pointing out the possible psychological significance of the woman's internal space (the uterus) as opposed to man's primary psychological orientation to external space. A valid generalization would be that upon the primary physical difference between the male and female is built the further differentiation of their roles—some biological, such as pregnancy, others psychological, such as sexual and nonsexual inherent drives and the influence of the social milieu.

Psychological Stress

In order to find expression in a culture demanding complicated adaptive patterns, biologically determined sexual drives are subjected to many possibly crippling overt and covert pressures. Inadequate sexual identity may be the result of an inadequate childhood environment; the individual may not have observed behavior in adults by which he could determine his own goals for adult interpersonal relationships. There are some who believe that developmental distortions and lacks manifested in adult behavior originated in the psychological struggles of the individual during maturation (Buxbaum, 1959; Freud, 1965; Josselyn, 1955; Saul, 1960). There are also those who disclaim the deep psychological effect of childhood experiences (Baldwin, 1968). If the question is ever to be answered, various points of view should be subjected to imaginative exploration. The material in this chapter is based upon the assumption that the adult individual is a product of biologically given characteristics modified by: (1) his potential for affective experience, memory of symbols, and extrapolating from experience through learning, and (2) his social milieu. His childhood provided the pillars, well cemented into the biological foundation, around which the adult character and personality has been built.

Conflicts in Masculine Identity

Perhaps the male has the greatest conflict in establishing a sexual identity. Western culture has evolved a philosophy concerning interpersonal relationships; interpersonal relationships are apparently initiated and strengthened if a close emotional bond between the infant and mother is fostered at early infancy. A father, in relation to an infant, is assured of a place in the sun if he acts as a mother surrogate. As the infant matures to a stage of awareness of himself as separate from others, he first mimics and then identifies with those most significant in his world; the first steps in identification are conditioned by those who care for him.[1] Optimally, they represent tender, responsive, primarily nonhostile people. They are the ones who soothe pain, relieve stress, and protect.

Mother as First Identification Object

The infant's first step in self-conceptualization is not determined by his own sex or the sex of the person with whom he identifies; it is determined by the significance of a particular person to him. It would seem inevitable that in a society that stresses the importance of gentle, tender, loving care by a mothering person or persons, the infant's first tenuous identification would be with such people, irrespective of their sex. It has been recognized that this early identification with a mother figure plays a significant role in the female child's capacity to accept her own maternal fulfillment as an adult (Benedek, 1959). However, it can create early confusion for the male child.

How the male child comes to identify himself as a male is related to multiple factors. It would seem likely that the biological determinants of his sex would lead him to a vague awareness of his gender. This is suggested by the insistence of many infant nurses that the guesses infants make as to whether a dressed neonate is male or female are correct beyond statistical chance. There are many old wives' tales that suggest boy and girl infants behave differently; these tales are proving to be based on observable differences. There are children who, affected by parents who wish them to be a different sex, superficially accept the parentally desired sex rather than their actual sex. However, they do not really resemble the sex they are supposed to be; no effeminate male reflects true femininity; no masculine girl reflects true masculinity (Dicks & Childers, 1934, 1944).

A little boy's awareness of his sex is intensified by his observation of physical differences between his own body and that of a girl, and his similarity to his father and dissimilarity to his mother. Certainly, the culture fosters sexual differentiation through verbal instructions and responses to the boy. It utilizes the boy's awareness of his sex identity by urging him toward a concept of masculinity that involves being a "real boy." He must not turn to his mother for succor or he will be taunted as being a baby or like a girl. The father helps him to break away from identifying with his mother by emphasizing the desirability of a masculine identity. If he is interested in his son, the father will say, "Women do this, but we *Men* do this" (Mead, 1949, pp. 265–280).

The little boy considers himself correctly identified as a boy during the second year of life. Equally so, the little girl, irrespective of any conflict she may have over the absence of a penis, accepts for better or worse that she is a girl. The resolution of the oedipal conflict, as conceptualized by certain schools of psychology, intensifies the identification of the boy with the father; it is not, in the opinion of the author, the original source of that identification, at least in the current culture.

Shift in Models

Undoubtedly, this shift from an identification with a tender, caring person (usually the mother), to an identification with a more aggressive, brave, masculine figure was, as has been pointed out, pragmatically fostered in the early history of the culture. People survived because men could hunt, till the soil with crude instruments, and effectively participate in wars of protection or conquest. The physical strength of the male complemented the female role of caring for the helpless infant and the home; the male could have an image of himself as a man of strength, bravery, and skill in areas that were his unique territory. He did not relinquish his desire to be tender, but directed it toward the helpless—a response he did not see as being weak or effeminate because his total role was one of strength, bravery, and aggressiveness. Women valued these male characteristics because they assured her's and her child's survival. Her image of the true male was determined by those functions that women ordinarily could not fulfill.

As the male child grows up, confusion begins. The urban male of today has no greater fight than with crowded transportation, the dishonesty of business associates, the struggle as a union member or as an opponent of unions, the fight against disease if he is a doctor, or the mind of an opponent if he is a lawyer; these are all areas in which the opponent or colleague may be a female. In the agricultural world, progress in the field of machinery has lessened the need for strength, and greater knowledge of productivity has resulted in the fact that farming increasingly is becoming an intellectual pursuit. Organized business does not demand severe tests of man's physical skills and strength. The purveyor of food is now the corner supermarket; hunting has become a sport, not a necessary source for nourishment. For the most part, the battle for survival is intellectual, not based upon physical strength or physical courage and not necessarily based on the sex of the opponent. Unskilled laborers are perhaps the only men who continue to have ways to express their masculinity within the framework of their essential work; there is for them the essentialness of their physical strength.

Cultural Changes and Confusion

In contemporary Western civilization, the hero-warrior is considered uncivilized rather than the epitome of masculine superiority. Present pacifist attitudes toward war and heroism formerly represented the feminine approach to life. Women opposed war in part because it deprived them of the security of the home that peace provided. Furthermore, because they did not actively participate in the battles themselves, war placed them in the role of the helpless victim rather than the aggressor. Most importantly, it involved a destruction of that which they created—their children. Only when women became convinced that war would protect them, lead to aggrandizement of their men, or provide greater resources to meet the needs of their family or the expanded family, the nation, did a warlike attitude become aroused in them. The pacifist attitude of women is possibly a biological heritage (Lorenz, 1966). It may, however, reflect the human being's ability to adapt to and ultimately modify reality. After all, the League of Nations and the United Nations, as limited in effectiveness as they have proved to be, were at least the dream of men who were statesmen, not "weak pseudo-women."

The social philosophy of protection for those unable to protect themselves, again a "feminine" point of view, has increasingly become the social philosophy of the culture. Regardless of the pros and cons concerning the method employed, civilized men of Western culture do not believe that a family should starve because the man of the household does not hunt. If tender care is a feminine prerogative, men have always been contaminated by their *x* chromosomes.

As a result of these cultural changes, society's attempt to preserve an archaic image of the male prototype has little validity. Except in sports and the "uncivilized" role war provides, there are few tasks requiring heroic physical self-denial and strength. Even war only abstractly makes a provision for such emotional discharge; hand-to-hand combat is practically nonexistent. "The enemy," except in guerilla warfare, is a distant, often unseen machine or airborne bomb. Furthermore, as suggested above, even those areas formerly the prerogative of men are rapidly being encroached upon by progress or modified so that women as well as men can perform the work involved. The male is pressed to play the role of being manneristically strong —to sound like the fighter, cool in the face of danger, unswayed by gentle feelings, able by sheer strength (perhaps now of voice rather than muscle) to conquer windmills—a role that has little or no pragmatic value.

Role Expectancies and Impotence

The male's biologically determined sexual role in the service of reproduction has remained intact. However, it has not led to complete confidence in his masculinity. Prior to the more modern attitude toward feminine sexuality, particularly during the Victorian era, a game was played between men and women. Regardless of whether it was complimentary to the man or not, at least the game assured him of his dominance over the woman. Many women were quite vocal in expressing their belief that sexuality, except for purposes of reproduction, was a residual of "animal nature" in the male. The woman saw herself as a "pure" member of the superior species. The "pure" woman either accepted her sexual role as a duty to a loved person who had not yet evolved from the state of being an animal, or she rejected the sexual role. In some instances, wives felt complimented when their husbands turned to mistresses or a prostitute because they believed their husbands did not want to violate their purity.

While on the surface this concept of masculinity would seem a rather untenable position for a man, he was able to show his strength by "raping" his wife, an assertion of himself that gave him confidence. The fact that many women enjoyed being so "raped" was a secret of the bedroom and perhaps resulted in the idea that women are masochistic because they derive sexual pleasure from the fantasy of being "raped" (Josselyn, 1968a).

The modern study of female psychology reveals what many women knew in the privacy of their own thoughts but had hidden; women, like men, are a form of animal life (Kinsey *et al.,* 1953). As a form of animal comparable to the male, they also can enjoy their sexuality. This has created a very serious problem for women. On the other hand, looking at it from the man's standpoint, it has created a dual problem for him. His masculine assertiveness is now threatened by woman's willingness to seek sexual pleasure; he can no longer feel that it is his male strength that makes it possible for him to assert himself in marital rape. His wife may actively approach him if her desires are more aroused than his at the moment. He can no longer determine "when" without consideration of her wishes. He has lost the sole prerogative of calling the tune, finding himself often responding to hers when she calls.

It would seem that this has resulted in the increased frequency of impotency among young men. When the man alone determined the sexual life in a marital relationship, he sought it only when he felt a strong desire, a desire at times intensified by his wish to prove his masculinity. Now a man may find that due to fatigue or other considerations, he does not respond sexually to his wife's overtures. He fears that he will be impotent and thereby reveal that he is not the man he has tried to make her believe he is. It is an anxious situation for a young man and at times results in severe feelings of inadequacy due to the inability to perform sexually as he fantasies true men of the past could.[2]

There is a second problem with which the man may be confronted. In spite of the general applicability of feminine enjoyment of sexuality, it is true that many women have problems that are related to frigidity (Benedek, 1952, pp. 394–95; Bonaparte, 1953). These women do not completely fulfill their sexual desires. This would seem to be particularly true when a woman has become convinced that intercourse should result in a climactic orgasm if she is a true woman. This concept will probably undergo modifications as more is learned of feminine psychology. There are indications that many women who do not experience a climactic orgasm do experience a rise in sexual tension and then a pleasing, gratifying relaxation of it, without the orgastic experience that textbooks describe. Whether this response is the result of conflicts or whether it is a normal response in certain women is still open to question (Benedek, 1952; Deutsch, 1944). Irrespective of the final answer, there is a tendency for the woman to place the blame for her failure to reach a sexually orgastic climax on the man. It is easy to see why the woman does this; she does not wish to face her own inadequacy and, therefore, she says that the man must be failing her. The resultant anxiety this creates for him lessens his sexual expressiveness so that he finds himself deprived of full gratification.

Conflict in Feminine Identity

Aside from the biological aspects of feminine sexual identity, the culture, as it does for the male, introduces many hurdles. Cultural patterns are passed from one generation to the next primarily through the child's experiences with, and observations of, the parents. This occurs not only because the parents demand acceptance of culturally determined standards, but more basically because of the small child's identification with the parent image of love, protection, and childcare. The parent most frequently identified with this image is the mother. A little girl's initial identification with her mother continues, and theoretically the mother is the prototype of the feminine role that the little girl will strive to emulate as she gradually structures her sexual identity.

Short-term Mothering

There are two patterns in family planning that limit the girl's opportunity to identify with the feminine maternal role. There is a tendency to encourage smaller families and a tendency to have the children close together rather than to space them over the reproductive period. It is possible that these phenomena have resulted in a girl child's having less experience with a mothering mother in her own childhood than was true when families were large and the reproductive period was limited only by physiology. The girl in a large family frequently not only saw the mothering pattern of her own mother, but she herself played a mothering role to the younger children in the family, or was mothered by an older child. Today the little girl is frequently away from her mother a good part of the time—in nursery school and in play groups—and does not experience mothering by an older sister or mothering of a younger sister at the time when the memory patterns that will have bearing on her future adjustment are beginning to be established. In fact, she is often sent to nursery school so that she will not see the mothering of her infant sibling.

"Barbie Doll" Model

There is another problem for the young girl in her identification with her mother. Whether it is significant or not, an interesting phenomenon at present is the doll choice of little girls. The enthusiasm for the "Barbie doll" has been rather baffling to clinicians. Six and seven year old girls prefer to play with these dolls, obviously adolescent representations, than play with the cuddly dolls they can mother. Is this a passing fad on the part of little girls, or is it an indication of something more basic in our culture that is related to the conceptualization of the female? Little girls would seem to be less interested in emulating their mother's motherliness; they are more interested in identifying with her sexual role, and that role is formulated by the adolescent, not by the mature woman.

As indicated earlier, the realization of female sexual enjoyment did not necessarily free women from the impact of the prior cultural patterns. Women are now theoretically able to enjoy sexual relationships, but many find that they, as individuals, cannot do so. As a result, some women feel inadequate as women and struggle to find some proof of their adequacy. In doing so they wage a continuous war against the outward signs of their maturation; they strive to look "young," to act "young," and to be considered "young." They try to be the Barbie doll with which their daughters play. In contrast to the man's desire to emulate the image of the men of past generations, the woman struggles against the image of the women who defined her sex role. In so doing she does not provide a clear-cut image of the mature woman to her daughter or, incidentally, her son.

The Masculinized Mother

There is possibly another reason why mothers provide a limited object of identification for their daughters. They consider their normal passive, receptive longings as evidence of their own inadequacy rather than as a valuable biological heritage that enables the family to exist. Their answer to the dilemma is to strive to remain, at least superficially, the adolescently seductive, sexual female. Thus, they deny themselves the gratification that maturation in a feminine role could offer, in which they would allow themselves openly to be protected as they fulfill their maternal function. An alternative is sometimes chosen. They not only fulfill the mother and housekeeping roles, but also those of plumber, carpenter, electrician and family accountant. They seem to imply that the only valid reason for the existence of a man is the unfortunate handicap of the woman that she was not born an effective hermaphrodite.

Feminine Role Ambiguities and Conflict

Modern Western culture has also had its impact on woman's conceptualization of her place in the world. She still retains her importance as the one who cares for the unborn child. Typically, she also continues this care during the early infancy period. Whatever her social status, with the possible exception of those who are members of the upper economic group, she must serve as chauffeur for children who are preoccupied with activities that they share not with her but with their peer group members for whom she is also a chauffeur. She must have meals on time that do not conflict with TV shows. She must be a good mother to her confiding children while she is a good wife to her exhausted or frustrated husband and, if her husband and she aspire to the former's being a junior executive, she must fulfill the role of a supporting, calm, socially adept, but self-effacing wife.

The woman's childcare period is much shorter in many instances than it was in the past. With the enthusiasm for nursery schools, a woman finds herself in a situation where her role of the past is in part taken over by others. There is an exception to this. If her child manifests characteristics that result in poor adaptation to the environment beyond the home, the responsibility to correct the behavior is often placed upon her. In many instances, she is blamed for the difficulty rather than encouraged to feel she can be a creative part of the team to correct it.

Concern about the "population explosion" and the social encouragement that family size be limited to the economic capacity of the wage earner are understandable reasons for the shortened or infrequent periods of child-bearing. These considerations, however, may create for the woman a psycho-social conflict, particularly during the years of fertility. She is sharply restricted in the fulfillment of her primary biological role, a role that unconsciously is firmly woven into her psychological totality.

At the same time, the roles of mother, wife, and homemaker are, for many women, no longer self-fulfilling. Many of the creative tasks that were essential for the woman in a less mechanized society are now supposedly done by others or are made available through stores and through mechanical devices in the home. Her deprivation, however, is to a large extent the dream of the advertisers who have, by implication, denied the creativity of her work in the home. They have not necessarily made her tasks easier; they have just made them different. She still has strenuous work to perform as a housewife. The eight-hour day does not exist for her. The decrease in availability of domestic help has intensified the burden of keeping the home clean. As she struggles with an awkward vacuum cleaner, a recalcitrant washer and dryer, and an ineffectual dishwasher she wonders why machinery for the home does not function to decrease labor to the degree that machinery in the factory, in construction work, and in the doctor's office appears to have done. She does not always remember that dictating machines, electric typewriters, and even computers also break down. Nor does she take into consideration the number of hours her husband spends in dull, routine activities in order to bring forth evidence of productiveness. But in the eyes of too many men and women, much of the woman's responsibility in the home is seen as the occupation of a second-class, nonproductive member of the human race.

The former belief that women were intellectually inferior and unable to do the tasks and assume the responsibilities of men led to a eulogizing of the masculine prerogatives and to a depreciation of the woman's role in the home and in society. It is therefore not surprising that women find themselves restless, with a desire to do something to prove their worth when the home and the children no longer need them (Friedan, 1963; Komarovsky, 1953; Lundberg & Farnham, 1947; Mead, 1949). As a woman turns to outside activities she is faced with certain choices; whatever choice she makes appears to be either alien to her sexual heritage or a depreciation of her importance as a person. The social structure gives her conflicting answers.

As one possibility, she can turn to volunteer work. Women find it satisfactory to invest themselves in it as real and serious work. Unfortunately, as is reflected in the volunteer's attitude, there is a tendency to minimize the validity of volunteer work. If she has an important committee meeting and an appointment with her hairdresser, the hairdresser is apt to win out. This is an interesting commentary on the culture in general. The implication is that what is paid for is of value; what is not paid for does not give status or impose obligations. As an additional aspect, monotonous or routine tasks that will lead ultimately to a desired goal are considered intolerable if there is no financial compensation. Volunteer work is, therefore, either considered as "busy work" to fill in time not more excitingly occupied, or too boring to compete with an afternoon tea.

As a second alternative, a woman can seek an outlet in one of the professions that in the past has been considered the province of women—for example, nursing or teaching. These professions are gradually being invaded by men, though many women still feel they have particular competence in these areas. If a married woman's premarital training was based upon the anticipation of such a role, she may look forward to identification in that previous training only to find that progress in her chosen field has been such that what she learned in the past has become archaic and she must be retrained.

A third possibility open to women is entrance into the technical, business, and professional worlds, areas previously considered the prerogative of men. Competence in such areas prove to some that women are the equal of men. This choice rarely solves her problem satisfactorily. A creative area of work is demanding of time, energy, and thought. The demands it makes may collide head-on with the biosocial role of the married woman. A married woman who is as skilled as a man is not as free to function in many situations. Her biological role of childcare, preserved as it has been in Western culture, creates occupational difficulties for her that the man does not have. If, for example, a child of ten years develops a sudden high fever while attending school, our culture decrees that the mother, not the father, leave work so that the child can have what is defined as adequate care. Providing time off for mothers so that they can fulfill their maternal role and still be gainfully employed does not make her the same as a man; it only indicates that she can perform certain tasks a man can. Her unique role in the culture is not as an "equal" of man, but as a mother. This attitude will continue until the role of the mother of children is abdicated. If such a change occurs the culture, for better or worse, will change. A culture cannot, any more than a person, have its cake and eat it too.

Adolescence and identity crisis

For both the male and the female in our society, the adolescent sexual phase creates sexual confusion and the most acute sexual identity crises (Blos, 1962; Erikson, 1950; Josselyn, 1952). Toward the end of the last century, educators and others, aware of the future difficulties children would have in entering an adult world and accepting their sexual role in that world, stressed that education should include instruction for living, specifically for acceptance of a sexual function. They recognized the significance of sexual ignorance in the maladjustment of adults in the society into which the child was born. The result was the formulation of what seemed to provide an answer. Children should not be deprived of knowledge in return for their sexual curiosity, nor should the answers include any negative aspects regarding the human sexual role. A directive was given: Children should be told of the sexual aspects of life, and told in such a way that previously instilled ideas of its impropriety were to be avoided. Sex was to be presented in the framework of its meaningful beauty. However, having so glamourized it, was considered important that the child be told that sex was not to be enjoyed except in the sanctioned citadel of marriage. This has become the "modern" approach to sex education.

At the same time, children are exposed to the self-centered rights of adults to be happy and to abandon marriage if happiness is not found there. Mass media always reflect a significant aspect of the culture. The mass media present to adolescents a picture of life in which sexuality is not, as they have been told, the frosting on the marriage cake, but is in reality a candy that could, if the cake is good, be used as frosting but that is equally good as candy instead of frosting.

The Meaning of Teenage Sex Behavior

There are considerable contradictions in the reports of investigators concerning the sexual behavior of the unmarried adolescent girl or boy (GAP, 1966; Williamson, 1966, pp. 204–211). Clinical experience suggests that there is growing sexual freedom in the teenage group. Whether or not this is indicative of changes in the mores of the culture, it has implications concerning the future concepts of the male-female role in society. The goal of some young people of the present is not that of biological survival of the species, but quite the contrary, it is "sexual gratification" regardless of the continuity of the species, of permanent relationships, and of all that the family represents to the culture. Frequently, adolescents seek not sexual gratification, but closeness with another to ease the aloneness experienced as the ties to childhood dissolve; their sexual behavior is simply a tool that, at least transiently, obliterates the aloneness. "Love-ins" are not necessarily sexual orgies; they are attempts by young people, alienated from their milieu, to experience closeness. The young people, under these conditions, are typically not promiscuous. They experience a deep love for each other, and although their sexual behavior is an expression of love, the problem is that the love does not mean mature heterosexuality. On the other hand, to many adolescents sexual availability has become a way to be "popular" and to be a part of the group. It is also, in many instances, an attempt to prove adequacy in a sex-defined role (Deutsch, 1967).

Many adolescents find themselves sexually inadequate, an inadequacy they deny and attempt to correct by compulsively repeating the act in which they have previously failed. It is not surprising that the adolescent frequently experiences sexual failure. As indicated in the preceding discussion, Western culture has woven sexuality into its philosophy as the symbolic expression of the family-oriented structure; this philosophy is not readily ignored since it is basic to the cultural format. Furthermore, because of the female's need to be protected in the fulfillment of her role as a woman, it is not surprising that she experiences failure of real sexual fulfillment more often than a boy in these early sexual explorations; they are experiences that offer her no protection.

The tragedy of the birth of a child as the result of sexual experimentation is self-evident. As indicated above, neither the biological father or mother is, in most cases, sufficiently mature to function in a socially complex parental role. An interesting double standard becomes apparent when a young, unmarried girl becomes pregnant as the result of intercourse with a boy of approximately her own age. As long as she will renounce the boy and hopefully give up the child when it is born, society in most instances does everything possible to protect her and support her. The hostility that a social group typically feels toward someone who has violated its mores is turned toward the father of the unborn child. If he attempts to express his concern and his accompanying confusion he is often told, "You should have thought of that sooner." He is either forbidden to see the girl or, if allowed to, is confronted with the attitude of others that resembles the dog trainer who housebreaks a dog by rubbing the dog's nose in the "accident." It is not surprising that the boy often meets this social rebuff by denying any concern about the situation. This defense, however, does not solve the internal turmoil many of the "unmarried fathers" experience, particularly when the relationship between the girl and himself, while undoubtedly not that of a mature man and woman, was extremely meaningful to both.

The current adolescent age group may be giving us a message that we are not adequately hearing. As one observes the new patterns of dancing, it is possible to interpret them as such a message. The bodily movements are suggestive of a discharge of sexual tension; however, that discharge is only exhibitionistically related to another person. As a sexual object, the dancer of the opposite sex appears to have no meaning as a person to whom to relate. The individuals look off into space, with little or no synchronization of movement. The pattern appears to be similar to masturbatory discharge rather than indicative of approaching heterosexual relatedness.

Western culture fosters heterosexuality by defining the sexes as complementary to each other. By providing premature sexual excitation that the young person cannot handle appropriately, has it actually blocked the achievement of true heterosexual relationships? As a result, it is possible that the family, as the foundation of Western culture, will increasingly cease to be a secure base. This would seem a potential solution to the current sexual identity crisis. If it occurs, not only will the culture undergo a radical change, but possibly women, and certainly men, will have to find a different means of discharging the human impulse to love and care for the helpless and defenseless child. In the meantime, the human capacity to fuse sexuality and love may be expressing itself in a form alien to the family-oriented culture.

The fantasy of male-female dichotomy

Historical Source

The present confusion of individuals in regard to their sexual identity and society's confusion concerning the role identification of both sexes are possibly related to our failure to relegate that which is history to history, resulting in the retention of the belief that the historical manifestation of an inherent drive is the drive itself. Did the current culture preserve an archaic concept of sexual differentiation while abandoning the Stone Age by a progressive refinement of tools to deal with reality? Men and women live in a sexual Stone Age while they feed an inventory of their material life into a computer. The basic differences between male and female are a reality. In Western culture, fantasy has defined our concept of *Man* and *Woman,* and we are thus left with a caricature of *Homo sapiens.* According to that fantasy, *Man* is physically strong, courageous, objective, and unswayed by emotions other than anger; tenderness is permissible only within the framework of husbandry. Personal physical or emotional pain must be borne by him with stoicism and without the support of others; meaningful relationships with others can be tolerated only if disguised by superficial social relationships and bravely abandoned without evidence of remorse. *Man* must always be as independent of others as was the lone hunter of the past, caught in a blizzard many miles from his camping site. When *Man* weeps at the new grave of his beloved wife or child, others accept his right to do so but shyly turn away as if to acknowledge that *even Man* can be weak, although he deserves privacy when his strength fails.

Woman, in this stereotype, is quite different. She is helpless, except in her role as a mother and housewife; she is swayed by feelings and incapable of thinking objectively. She is frightened, and thus needs strong, courageous *Man.* If she does manifest bravery under unusual circumstances, she is complimented in a somewhat dubious way; it is said she is as brave as a *"Man."* Because she is emotional rather than objective, she comforts *Man* in whom she has blind faith. She accepts the rejection of her solicitude, realizing that once *Man* is comforted, his "weakness" is vanquished; he becomes again the epitome of the image *Man.*

In the interrelationship of the sexes in this fantasy *Man* is the dominant, controlling force, never manifesting weakness by sharing with *Woman* the exploration that leads to decisions. *Woman* is a passive, submissive parasite who, through her capacity for sentimentality, soothes the wounds of the fallen hero, *Man.*

In prehistoric and early historic times this dichotomy undoubtedly had validity or the fantasy would not have evolved; the mother and child needed the protection of the male against other animals and the forces of nature. The male focused his protective interests upon mother and child. This fantasy has remained intact to a surprising extent, stressed by the culture, imposed upon *Man,* and ambivalently worshiped by *Woman.*

Was this particular dichotomy of roles based upon inherent differences, or was it related to the capacity of the human species to adapt to its environment and thus selectively control it? Whether this fantasy has validity in our present culture is a question, since the protective role of the cave man, as well as his heroic battle with the forces of nature to obtain food for his family, have to a large extent been taken over by social forces represented in law enforcement officers and supermarkets.

Contemporary Refutation

That our conception of male and female roles is unsatisfactory is made manifest by the number of books and articles that are published refuting it. Some, particularly those for popular consumption, are so vitriolic that the question of whether the protestors protest too much arises (Frieden, 1963; Lundberg & Farnham, 1947). Increasingly, scientific contributions, though not always free of emotional overtones, are correcting the implications of the fantasy (Horney, 1937; Kelman, 1967; Mead, 1949; Montagu, 1953). Most of these studies stress the fallacy of our definition of femininity. Masculinity more often remains defined as a state of relatively sterile or easily abandoned emotional interrelationships; the male role in the intimate primary relationship of the family is conceptualized as protective, but that protectiveness is essentially the protection that his earnings can bring.

The lack of empathy for the human side of the male is poignantly illustrated in the cultural attitude toward divorce. Unless the wife is flagrantly unsuited for motherhood, the children are awarded to her. There are valid reasons for this, but the assumption is that the father, if he is a proper father, is a peripheral person and a provider of support. What it means to him to give up the more intimate role of father is ignored. Even he himself usually assumes that he should not feel any intensity of emotional pain as long as he has planned a college education for his offspring. Deep psychotherapy of divorced fathers often reveals a repressed mourning for the type of relationship he had with his children before his divorce.

The battle of the sexes

With evolution, *Homo sapiens* has progressively utilized the brain to create a more complicated environment. Apparently, there has been a relative increase in the complexity of the psychic structure. Owing to these developments, as indicated earlier, differentiation of the sexes has become obscure. If one compares the elementary biological functions of man and woman with their social ramifications, it appears that the "battle of the sexes" in our culture is really a panic-induced struggle to determine who a person really is.

A lack of clear-cut identity leads to confused behavior that is frequently expressed through a struggle against others. The struggle enables the individual to feel separate, and thus a self-identifiable individual. This response is a recapitulation of the past. The negativism of the two-year-old serves to establish his boundaries of an "I" different from the "other" who would mold him. The rebellion of the adolescent is in part a struggle to establish separation from the person he was of the past, whom he sees as a mirror image of his parents and others, not as a person (Erikson, 1950).

Men at one time undoubtedly felt secure in their identity because nonmales brought out the contrast. When women found their identity undermined by changes introduced by the machine age, and found themselves with no identity they could admire, they sought a new identity. As a model, they accepted that which they had always admired; they would be the equal of men. This undermined the security of the male and the battle was on. Behind the battle are psychological conflicts.

It is a major characteristic of human beings to wish to achieve self-respect and the respect of others. Unless emotionally crippled by an overwhelming sense of defeat, they find gratification in working toward this goal and experience pleasure from the rewards (Hendrick, 1943; White, 1959, 1960). Women are human enough to wish to have pride in themselves, pride that is partially rooted in the willingness of others to admire what they do; they do not enjoy being self-depreciating or depreciated by others.

The complaint of women that modern methods have deprived them of the real meaningfulness of their role as homemaker is possibly overstressed. Enthusiasm over the discovered capabilities of women has had a more significant impact. In many instances, she can do the same type of work as men. Men certainly are threatened by this invasion of their territory, and women feel challenged to prove they can invade. This struggle undoubtedly occurs in part because woman's role in the past was depreciated. Men have striven to perpetuate their superiority to women, a striving that is based in part upon their need to abandon the infantile mother-child relationship that offered perpetual dependency, and the need to deny a sex-alien person with whom to identify. It is also based upon the human need to be respected. When women prove to be competent in what was previously a man's territory, there is too often an implied or direct assault on the man that can be summarized by the statement, "See, you are not so good; I can do it too."

On the other hand, women in their role as childcaring individuals have wished to see men as strong and capable of protecting them. Even in the modern world she does, during her childbearing and childcaring period, long for a protective person. If she is emotionally mature she longs for protection from a husband, not a mother and/or father. The mature man wishes to be the protector when protection is needed or desired.

Superiority in the Sexual Identity Crisis

If one considers all of the sexually determined physical attributes and limitations and wishes to establish superiority of one sex over the other, the starting point should be carefully appraised. Montagu (1953), for example, has to his own satisfaction established the superiority of the female. Through the centuries the contrary point of view has been taken [Seward, 1946 (1954)]. Superiority and inferiority actually reflect the area chosen for comparison rather than a true criterion for comparing and contrasting the two sexes. An orange and a banana have certain similarities, certain differences, certain advantages, and certain disadvantages when compared and contrasted. It is the value system of the individual consumer that determines whether, for that person, one type of fruit is superior or inferior to the other.

The so-called battle of the sexes is a token battle; the basic problem concerns who the individual is in terms of his or her sexual identity in the current world. As indicated earlier, many of the areas that women have invaded were considered men's before. Many of the areas that men had invaded previously were considered women's. In actuality, they were in all instances areas that were not dedicated to one or the other sex, but rather, areas that were claimed by squatter's right; originally the areas were open range! A man can be as good a teacher as a woman; a woman can be as adequate a doctor. This does not create a sexual identity crisis if, in both instances, the individual accepts and is comfortable in his/her own sexual identity so he/she does not see the role he/she is playing as a description of whether he/she is a man or a woman, but rather as roles to be adapted to the biological sexual identity. Because this attitude toward the sexes has not been established in our shifting culture, either by individuals or the group, the struggle between one's self-concept and the relationship of that self-concept to others has been chaotic.

Equality vs. Sameness

The battle of the sexes, if it were won, would result in Western culture's making men and women "its," irrespective of who the victor might be. Equality in the developing culture has, in many instances, been defined as being "the same" rather than as complementary parts of a whole. As long as sexual identity involves the capacity to care emotionally for each other and to find expression of the sexual bond in the broader experience of parenthood, equality cannot mean sameness.

The human species has evolved into an organism with an inherent capacity to be tender, to understand others, to master forces alien to survival, and to find gratification in living. Erikson (1968) makes a strong plea for utilizing that which he conceives as femininity to solve world problems. The characteristics involved, however, are not male or female; they are human characteristics. They are also characteristics that are attributable to heritage from both the male and female. The rapidly changing nature of the culture has resulted in a lag of adaptation of this inherent human characteristic to sexual identity.

Men and women have many similarities; this is self-evident, since they are both human beings. They have definite differences; one is male and one is female. It would seem that it should be possible for the battle of the sexes to end not in victory for either side, but through an awareness that the similarities should not be confused with the differences, and that both the similarities and the differences form a basic foundation of any culture to assure preservation of the species.

Notes

[1] The term "identification" is used with a variety of meanings (Axelrad & Maury, 1951). The above use of it is defined by the context.

[2] This is based upon the author's clinical impression. The actual numbers responding in this way may be statistically insignificant. As a clinician for forty years, the author is impressed by the shift in the etiology of problems of impotency. Whether what is seen in the psychiatrist's office is a forerunner of a more general problem of the future, only time will tell.

References

Ackerman, N. W. *The Psychodynamics of Family Life.* New York: Basic Books, 1958, pp. 159–87.

Axelrad, S., and L. M. Maury. "Identification as a Mechanism of Adaptation." In *Psychoanalysis and Culture,* G. B. Wilbur and W. Münsterberger, eds. New York: International Universities Press, 1951.

Baldwin, A. L. *Theories of Child Development.* New York: Wiley, 1968.

Benedek, T. *Studies in Psychosomatic Medicine: Psychosexual Functions in Women.* New York: Ronald Press, 1952.

———. "Parenthood as a Developmental Phase: A Contribution to the Libido Theory." *Journal of the American Psychoanalytic Association,* 8 (1959), 389–417.

Blos, P. *On Adolescence: A Psychoanalytic Interpretation.* New York: Free Press of Glencoe, 1962.

Bonaparte, M. *Female Sexuality.* New York: International Universities Press, 1953.

Buxbaum, E. "Psychosexual Development." In *Readings in Psychoanalytic Psychology,* M. Levitt, ed. New York: Appleton-Century-Croft, 1959.

Casey, M. D., *et al.* "XYZ Chromosomes and Antisocial Behavior." *Lancet,* 2 (October 15, 1966), 859–60.

Deutsch, H. *The Psychology of Women. Vol. I: Girlhood.* New York: Grune & Stratton, 1944.

———. *The Psychology of Women. Vol. II: Motherhood.* New York: Grune & Stratton, 1945.

———. *Selected Problems of Adolescence.* (Monograph series of The Psychoanalytic Study of the Child No. 3.) New York: International Universities Press, 1967.

Dicks, G. H., and A. T. Childers, "The Social Transformation of a Boy Who Had Lived His First Fourteen Years as a Girl. A Case History." *American Journal of Orthopsychiatry,* 4 (1934), 480–517.

———. "The Social Transformation of a Boy Who Had Lived His First Fourteen Years as a Girl. II: Fourteen Years Later." *American Journal of Orthopsychiatry,* 14 (1944), 448–52.

Erikson, E. H. *Childhood and Society.* New York: Norton, 1950.

———. *Identity: Youth and Crisis.* New York: Norton, 1968.

Freud, A. *Normality and Pathology in Childhood: Assessments of Development.* New York: International Universities Press, 1965.

Freud, S. *New Introductory Lectures on Psycho-Analysis.* Trans. W. J. H. Sprotts. New York: Norton, 1933.

Friedan, B. *The Feminine Mystique.* New York: Norton, 1963.

Group for the Advancement of Psychiatry. *Sex and the College Student.* New York: Atheneum, 1966, pp. 43–50.

Hendrick, I. "The Discussion of the Instinct to Master." *Psychoanalytic Quarterly,* 12 (1943), 561–65.

Horney, K. *The Neurotic Personality of Our Time.* New York: Norton, 1937.

Josselyn, I. M. *The Adolescent and His World.* New York: Family Service Association of America, 1952.

———. *The Happy Child.* New York: Random House, 1955.

———. "The Unmarried Mother." In *Sexual Behavior and the Law,* R. Slovenko, ed. Springfield, Ill.: Thomas, 1965, pp. 356–78. Series of selected papers prepared by Tulane University School of Law.

———. "Passivity." *Journal of the American Academy of Child Psychiatry.* 7 (1968a), 569–88.

———. "How Many Basic Drives?" *Smith College Studies in Social Work.* 39 (1968b), 1–19.

Kelman, H. "Karen Horney on Feminine Psychology." *American Journal of Psychoanalysis,* 27–2 (1967), 163–83.

Kinsey, A., C. E. Martin, W. B. Pomeroy, and P. H. Gebhard. *Sexual Behavior in the Human Female.* Philadelphia: Saunders, 1953.

Komarovsky, M. *Women in the Modern World.* Boston: Little, Brown, 1953.

Lorenz, K. *On Aggression.* M. K. Wilson, trans. New York: Harcourt, Brace & World, 1966.

Lundberg, F., and M. F. Farnham. *Modern Woman: The Lost Sex.* New York: Harper, 1947.

Mead, M. "Coming of Age in Somoa." In *From the South Seas.* New York: Morrow, 1928 (1940).

———. *Male and Female.* New York: Morrow, 1949.

Montagu, M. F. A. *The Natural Superiority of Women.* New York: Macmillan, 1953.

Saul, L. J. *Emotional Maturity.* Philadelphia: Lippincott, 1947 (1960).

Scheinfeld, A. *Women and Men.* New York: Harcourt, Brace, 1943.

Seward, G. H. *Sex and the Social Order.* New York: McGraw-Hill, 1946.

Telfer, M., D. Baker, G. Clark, and C. Richardson. "Incidence of Gross Chromosomal Errors Among Tall Criminal American Males." *Nature* (December 17, 1967), 1249–50.

White, R. W. "Motivation Reconsidered: The Concept of Competence." *Psychological Review,* 66 (1959), 297–333.

———. "Competence and the Psychosexual Stages of Development." In *Nebraska Symposium on Motivation,* M. Jones, ed. Lincoln: University of Nebraska Press, 1960.

Wiener, S., G. Sutherland, A. Bartholomew, and B. Hudson. "XYZ Males in a Melbourne Prison." *Lancet* (January 20, 1968), 150.

Williamson, R. C. *Marriage and Family Relations.* New York: Wiley, 1966.

Young, L. *Out of Wedlock.* New York: McGraw-Hill, 1954.

4 SEX IDENTITY DEVIATION AND INVERSION

Fred J. Goldstein

The dynamics of behavior are rooted in the primary group to which an individual belongs, and his historical development is predicated upon the sociocultural attitudes of that group. The patterned behavior of the societal fabric is woven of expectation, rewards, and punishments; sexual norms evolve from the same patterning that determines other behavior. The fact that millions of our population at some time experience homosexual urges and acts testifies to the confused and contradictory nature of our sexual mores.

Initially, the choice of an object for sexual satisfaction is undirected. It is not biologically or instinctively determined, but it is molded by the primary group and the larger social environment that group represents.

This chapter will be confined to a succinct discussion of homosexual drives and acts occurring in the postpuberty period, the genesis of sexual inversion and correlated sex role deviation, past and present clinical approaches, and basic theoretical concepts necessary for an understanding of the invert.

Problems of definition

Incidence of Inversion

Contrary to the layman's misconception, homosexuality is neither a rare nor a modern phenomenon. References to homosexual practices occur in the Bible, the Koran, the Talmud, and in all periods of recorded history. At times, such sexual conduct was associated with religious rites. Judeo-Christian teachings established the principle that sex relations were for the purpose of procreation and, therefore, like-sex overt acts were a profanation and violation of moral law, punishable as a capital crime. This occasionally may have served as a deterrent to some, but more probably it imposed upon inverts a need for greater secrecy and deception in order to survive.

It was not until the late nineteenth century that any attempt was made to discover the incidence of inversion. Beginning in 1899, Hirschfeld (1914), in Germany, made the first professional study and arrived at an estimate of 2 to 5 percent. Influenced by this research, Havelock Ellis (1901), working along the same lines in England, came up with a figure of 2 to 5 percent for males and—for reasons unknown—double that figure for females. It is not known that he ever conducted a systematic survey. Others guessed that homosexuals represented 6 percent of the total population.

The Kinsey Reports (1948, 1953) on male and female sexual behavior disputed the idea that men and women were either heterosexual or homosexual or represented opposite poles of sexual response. The scale employed in this study ran from 0–6, permitting a graduated classification of sexual responses from the totally heterosexual at one extreme to the totally homosexual at the other. A study of approximately 20,000 subjects showed that 28 percent of the females had responded homosexually to some degree as had 50 percent of the males interviewed. The disparity between earlier estimates of incidence and those of the Kinsey Reports does not represent a spectacular increase in the number of homosexuals in proportion to the total population. Previous studies were influenced by varying definitions of the term, by an understandable reluctance on the part of the inverts to discuss their sex experiences, and by conclusions drawn from atypical or inadequate samplings.

The Homosexual as a "Minority"

Taking into account that the Kinsey figures quoted in this chapter rule out adolescent sex play (engaged in by 70 percent of boys and about 14 percent of girls), and that the categories 0, 1, and 2 cover persons who have had no homosexual experience or only casual contacts, the inescapable fact remains that these people represent one of the largest minority groups. Because of the fear of being recognized and stigmatized, they do not speak for themselves but rely upon a hard core of "organized" homosexuals who fight for acceptance as equals in a hostile society. No schizophrenic confined to a hospital suffers as much or is subjected to so much scorn, ridicule, and ostracism as the alleged homosexual who, in most cases, is living with a sexual orientation and drive over which he has little or no control.

Like members of other minority groups, he is finding increasing tolerance on the part of his peers but his future still is in severe jeopardy. He faces a life in which discrimination, contumely, family censure, and police surveillance (including registration in some states) create a sense of such total rejection that he becomes not only a social alienation problem but a mental health problem as well.

Manifestations of the sexual drive

The sexual drive in man once was believed to be an instinct focused on a particular type of partner and, if normal development ensued, a heterosexual conclusion could be anticipated. Freud (1905) postulated a bisexual constitution in which all individuals went through a latent homosexual stage. Currently, knowledge of human sexuality suggests that the human organism is sexually undifferentiated at birth, and that the psychosocial demand for being masculine or feminine is not innate but acquired through the learning process. This is supported by Klinefelter's and Turner's Syndromes where even hermaphroditic confusions regarding a subject's sexuality do not lead to inversion but reflect his (or her) rearing.

Such training often determines which of several alternate routes the sexual impulse will take. It may be directed toward oneself (autoerotic), toward others of the same sex (homosexual), toward those of the opposite sex (heterosexual), or it may represent any combination of these three (polysexual). Alternatively, the individual may renounce the drive by sublimation, repression, and/or inhibiting its expression. Inhibition is an attempt to avoid or control sexual urges, whereas sublimation and repression represent recognition of the need and a commitment to finding an outlet for it. Both heterosexuals and homosexuals may eschew all sex activity for religious or other reasons.

From the viewpoint of the clinician, *the individual who is inverted is one who moves toward, feels for, and fantasies about like-sexed partners and actively retreats from involvement with opposite-sexed partners.* This sexual patterning is dependent upon identifications made in early life.

Identification is a result of part-object introjections and projections that occur throughout the developmental period. There is no total or complete incorporation in any person. The patterning of human behavior takes place by introjecting various aspects of those basic figures in the child's environment who provide love and protection and serve as a defense against a threatening world. In the homosexual individual, a fundamental misdirection in the identification pattern causes the sexual drive to run counter to what society considers normal. In such cases, social sex role behavior will also be deviant inasmuch as it follows the sex identity.

Normal identification is established when the parents provide adequate introjects of what male and female adults are. They accept the child's growth and impulses, recognize and accept his basic sexuality and needs, and establish for him their "rightness" and his. As typical "models," they will give the child a social introduction that will also be sex-appropriate, thereby training him in the socially expected sex role behavior.

Truncated identification is established when the child is reared by the opposite-sexed parent and identifies with the only sex available. The person assuming the parental role often maligns the absent figure and fosters a negative image of masculinity or femininity, as the case may be, in the mind of the child. Ordinarily, there is no experience to fill the void created by the absence of the same-sexed adult until the individual is far past the stage where identification could be made. A child growing up in such a situation is doubly handicapped, having neither an appropriate sex identification model nor a reciprocal social sex-role partner.

Rejective identification may occur when one parent is held in contempt by the other, and the child is dominated and made an ally of the opposite-sexed parent. Sullivan (1956) uses the expression "bad me" to describe the reaction of the child who is determined to avoid the humiliating rejection experienced by his same-sexed parent. This often takes the form of a vengeful turning away from masculine aggressiveness or feminine passivity; to *not* be like Father or *not* be like Mother. The introject exists, but in its negative form.

Overidentification may coexist with other types that have been discussed. It results from overcloseness, dependence, and stimulation by one parent at the expense of the other. The child cannot grow up or move in directions that would threaten the relationship with the "close" parent.

For many inverts, life is a relentless search for the felt deficit in their early environment and may constitute a kind of identification patterning in which they are drawn toward, or try to find and immediately become involved with, a prototype of the person lost or absent in their past. A good part of developmental anomalies found in the histories of inverted persons is based upon such gaps and distortions originating within the family configuration. The search for significant introjects during critical phases of development is germane to an understanding of inverts. Many who have gaps in available introjects revert spontaneously to heterosexuality without "obvious" emotional distress. Homophile organizations and some clinicians deny such shifts, but evidence seen and shared leaves little doubt that they do occur.

It is unfortunate that the less sophisticated still choose to recognize a cultural stereotype in which the world is divided categorically into men and women, and deviation from this stereotypic image renders a person suspect. The behavioral referent for inversion is one of the least reliable bases for discrimination. It is only in the *meaning* of such behavior that one begins to understand the behavior itself.

On the surface, referent persons dress like and mimic the conduct of those they reject or those with whom they wish to identify. Among these cross-sexed individuals may be counted the transvestites and Eonists. Such manifestations often occur in men and women having no inverted sexual yearnings, and some referred to by Ellis (1901) had no sexual encounters with either sex. A few transsexuals are so determined to make full identification with the other sex that they subject themselves to castration or operational procedures.

What is significant is that there are many types of inversion, and no single definition does justice to inverts as individuals. To categorize them collectively is to encourage the ready stereotype, to dehumanize them, to set them apart, and to allow society to react to them prejudicially.

The dynamic school of psychology and psychoanalysis has contributed greatly to an understanding of the internal referent that is often hidden in everyday relationships and runs counter to surface behavior. There are many people who live what appears to be a normal heterosexual life, while being aware that in dreams and fantasies there are impulses that suggest they are inverted. Also, it is clinically known that this is confluent with other drives, and that sexual activity often denotes the existence of some paramount drive that has been subsumed in the sexual act. This may be a need for independence, dominance, power, submission to a strong force that threatens, punishment, rebellion, or avoidance of greater threats. Any of these can occasion homosexual thoughts, interests, and activities in men and women who essentially are heterosexual.

The writer differentiates between three types of relationships that can occur between two persons of the same sex. There is the *homophilic* response that has no sexual connotation but covers the many situations in which an individual finds greater pleasure in sharing certain experiences with members of his own sex: men enjoy fishing, hunting, golfing, and playing poker with other men; women like to shop or discuss their children and other home-oriented interests with other women. A second type of relatedness is that in which the emphasis is on sexual-genital contact with no meaningful or enduring contact beyond the gratification of the sex drive. This category embraces *homosexual* relatedness in the commonly accepted usage of the term. Finally, there are those who seek to relate in the full sense of sharing love and companionship as well as sex, and hope to establish a union equivalent to the heterosexual marriage. This can be referred to as *homoerotic* relatedness. Society's concern and prohibitions are based on the distorted notion that these latter two categories are equivalent.

Long experience with inverts has led the author to the following conclusions regarding homosexual orientation and subsequent overt acts:

1. *Initially the sexual drive is undirected.* Depending upon the social forces brought to bear, it can be directed toward the opposite sex, the same sex, or both sexes. It can also be sublimated or inhibited.
2. *Homosexuality is learned.* It is best understood in psychodynamic or internal frames of reference and is rooted in patterns of relationship within the family or family surrogates.
3. *Effective interaction of three persons within the family is usually required to direct the sexual drive toward deviancy.* When one parent is absent, the recognition of this parental void can affect the sexual orientation of the child. The interaction of types of parents, type of child, and situations that contravene his or her learning to look for emotional satisfaction with the alternate sex are contributory to inversion.
4. *There is no single pattern of identification that explains all, or even most, inverted development.* For a sexually adult individual, the pattern of

identification is central to the precipitate character and introjected image of self which can make one's role as male or female inverted or heteroverted.
5. *An antisexual bias within the family or nuclear group is a common cause for the sex drives being diverted.* This is an attitude stemming from the Judeo-Christian heritage that causes children to feel guilty about, and refrain from discussing with members of their family, their normal sex impulses. The frequency with which parents admonish their sons and daughters about succumbing to the wiles of the opposite sex, while ignoring the potential danger of intimacy with members of the same sex, continues to puzzle this analyst.

Varieties of sexual inversion

When the varieties of sexual behavior and the preferences exhibited by the homosexually oriented are considered, it is found that they fall into several classifications. There is the *incidental homosexuality* of adolescence and preadolescence. This is part of the maturation process and signifies a not uncommon curiosity about sex. It should be anticipated by parents and usually can be treated unemotionally as part of an exploratory period. Also, there is the *chaotic homosexuality* of impulse-ridden character disorders and schizophrenics who were not aware of their homosexuality prior to their emotional illness. Rado (1956) makes a classification that he terms *reparative homosexuality,* which occurs when neurotics have been traumatized by heterosexual contacts. Much could be written (and has been) about each of these behavioral manifestations, but this section is, of necessity, limited to common practices of postadolescent or adult individuals who are drawn to the same sex for sexual gratification. The problem is more extensively treated in Marmor (1965).

Dress and Mannerisms

The public has a stereotype of how the invert looks and acts. It sees the "obvious" male homosexual as one who is effeminate in his manner of walking, speaking, and gesticulating. In fact, the man may have been mother-dominated, have a so-called "artistic temperament," or characteristics that are physiological or acquired, but any or all of these can place him within the commonly held stereotypic pattern. The female homosexual is less suspect since wearing slacks, having short hair, and smoking in public are generally acceptable. In the case of either sex, there is a pronounced tendency to assume the attire of the opposite sex. Eonists and transvestites may go so far as to adopt the undergarments and/or outer habiliments of the sex with which they identify. A man may elect to appear hypermasculine (weight lifters, wrestlers, truckdrivers), or a woman may choose to appear hyperfeminine (dancers, models, "charm school" products) in order to avoid any hint of an inverted sex object choice. Their sexual contacts may or may not be homosexual—and many are not—but identification problems are implicit.

Those who frequent bars and clubs catering to perverts wear what amounts to a uniform to make themselves easily identifiable: tight pants, the wide belt, boots and bulky jackets are characteristic costume. The "hippies" have introduced certain variations on this pattern. When both males and females affect long hair, hiphuggers, beads, and medallions, sex role characteristics are erased and gender alone represents basic sexuality; however, it is not erotic and exhibits a lesser regard for the sex object.

Choices and Methods of Sexual Gratification

Sexual activity exhibits a wide range of preferences. Under specific circumstances, there are those who engage in homosexual acts because there is no other outlet for their sexual needs. This is frequently a transitory stage and occurs most often in prisons, the armed services, and at all-male or all-female schools. While those participating must be counted among that part of the population that has had homosexual experience, a life pattern of homosexuality is not the necessary outcome. Once released from their enforced contact with same-sexed associates, most adapt to, even welcome, heterosexuality.

A great many homosexuals seek their contacts in public restrooms, motion picture theaters, and "health clubs." These represent three degrees of what could be called "economic opportunity" and promiscuity. In a restroom, two men may enter adjoining cubicles to indulge in mutual masturbation or to perform fellatically through a "glory hole," a pelvis-high aperture cut through the wall. Usually there is little verbal communication, identities are not revealed, and the men may leave as they arrived, separately, after obtaining sexual gratification. Less frequently the act takes place in a single cubicle, but fear of entrapment by the law is a deterrent.

In a theater, contact is made by the touching of arms and legs and a single or mutual masturbatory experience can take place under cover of a coat; or, having found a likely partner, they may retire to the restroom or elsewhere. Health clubs, steam rooms, and saunas offer a wider range of contacts and are meeting places for men of means. Here the clientele have passed the age for, or are reluctant to, or need not search for partners in restrooms and bars. They are more mature and represent a higher socioeconomic order. "Masseurs" are available to provide not only massages but masturbation and other forms of sexual release for the affluent homosexual.

Certain streets in major cities have procurers who are usually young heterosexuals who feel they perform a legitimate function since the customers they pick up are not for their own enjoyment. Many male prostitutes can be had only through the services of these procurers because police interception is not applicable in these cases (Rechy, 1963; Reiss, 1961).

In their intimate relations, the gamut is run from mutual masturbation to anolinctus. Many refuse to penetrate or be penetrated, while others refuse fellatic activities either actively or passively. However, as they grow more experienced, many acts formerly forbidden or considered "disgusting" become acceptable. Many avoid anolinctus because of the fit of the phallus and anus, which can be extremely painful and damaging.

Promiscuity is commonplace and not given the importance it has in the heterosexual world. Few male partners stay together exclusively for any length of time. Whatever emotional content the relationship may have had is eroded by lack of confidence in one's potency and ability to satisfy, and the relationships typically are subjected to extreme jealousy and stifling possessiveness.

Lesbians make contact through bars and clubs, but they are more selective and their unions last longer. Their methods of gratification include such practices as embracing, all-over kissing, breast fondling, stimulation of the clitoris singly or mutually, oral-genital stimulation (cunnilingus), tribadic practices (the women lying face to face and deriving satisfaction from the rhythmic friction of the touching clitorides), or the use of a dildo (a simulation of the male penis strapped around the loins and worn by the aggressor or "male" partner). They also make use of the *soixante-neuf* position, vibrators, or combinations of any of the above-mentioned practices. Many women have elongated clitorides that can be inserted in the vaginal orifice to approximate heterosexual intercourse. Finger practices may imitate the phallus. Lesbian relationships tend to be more meaningful and enduring than male homosexual relationships. A large percentage of them have children from a former marriage or have a homosexual life distinct from their heterosexual families. Like men, some seek group-sex experiences, and sadomasochistic variations are not unknown.

In many homosexual relationships there is an initial revulsion on the part of the passive member who submits rather than participates. There are aggressors who instigate the action but will not play the passive role (the man who will penetrate but refuses to be penetrated), but for the most part either acts as "male" or "female." The interchangeability of the parts played is characteristic of couples who have attained a homoerotic union that promises hope of continuing mutual satisfaction. When this stage is reached, inverts not only reject the advances of promiscuous homosexuals but avoid the places they frequent and try to establish a quasi-heterosexual respectability.

The extreme of transsexual identification is found in men who alter their morphology in order to become the females they wish to be. Since it is impossible to affix a phallus surgically, these changes solely involve men because male genitals can be removed and replaced by an artificial vagina. By substitutive chemical treatment, it is possible for them to acquire the feminine contour and the adipose deposits that allow them to look like women, as well as to have sex with men as women. This writer considers this group emotionally disturbed to the point of psychosis.

Bisexuality

Because society has decreed that homosexuality is an all or nothing matter, it is difficult to accept the gray area noted in Kinsey's data. There are many who are not so fearful of the opposite sex or so unable to meet the expectations of our culture that they totally avoid sexual activity with the opposite sex. It is possible to have such feelings, dreams, and attractions and to accept these impulses as part of the life pattern without acting them out, as is evidenced by the conduct of priests and nuns.

Others have learned or devised, consciously or unconsciously, various tricks that enable them to meet the demands of the world in which they live. Men and women, who by accepted standards may be happily married, will fantasy a like-sexed partner, or perform satisfactorily by blotting out the partner with whom the act is taking place. One husband fantasied young boys and then readily could become erect and engage in coitus with his wife. These individuals could be called pseudoheterosexuals or latent homosexuals, but it is doubtful if such terms contribute anything toward clarifying the problem.

The word "latent" has a history in psychoanalysis based on a theoretical assumption of bisexuality in all persons. This was mentioned earlier in this chapter and has been soundly criticized in one of the Rado articles to which reference was made. Clinical experience indicates that such individuals are, in the main, homosexuals who do not panic in their relations with the other sex. Many can indulge sexually with either sex while relating more intimately with one of the same sex. Call girls can make a living part of the day with little or no feeling for the opposite-sexed partner but become passionately involved with another woman. It is the writer's observation that in such unions the performing member usually is homosexually oriented but not totally aversive to the opposite sex.

Some Lesbians seek marriage in order to have children and then promptly separate from their spouses or obtain a divorce. The marriage may continue, however, if one of the partners is absent a great deal or totally undemanding, thus permitting either partner to enjoy relationships where the real emotional involvement is homosexual and satisfaction occurs outside the marital union.

In many troilistic or group situations where men and women perform at the same time, a pairing-off in one of several patterns is common to those involved: one may be voyeuristically excited, another homosexually excited, and the other emotionally involved heterosexually with one person. Many can enjoy homosexual excitement or voyeurism under the protective guard of the group's activity. If they had to singly and openly acknowledge such perverse inclinations they would find the admission far too threatening to their self-image.

The word "latent" to describe sexual urges is misleading and often vicious in its intent as it is used currently. It would be helpful if it could be dropped from discussions of homosexuality. Bieber *et al.* (1962) data support the theory that those who have experienced some intimate and sexual acts with the opposite sex without panicking are better able to respond to the clinician's efforts to effect exclusively heterosexual orientation.

The role of the clinician

Theoretical Approaches

Early studies of homosexuality and perversion left little hope for changing the sexual pattern of the deviate. Holdovers from the 1800s were genetically and biologically oriented and spoke often of "genetic deviation," "congenital illness," and "errors of nature" (Kallmann, 1952) . It is obvious that such orientation would militate against the clinician's attempts to understand, reach, and/or alter an individual's sexuality.

Freud assumed that homosexuality was irreversible; that homosexuals obtained so much satisfaction that few would seek treatment, or once having begun it, would not persevere in analysis or be motivated to change. Stekel (1950) , as well as Freud, offered the theory that all persons were bisexual and that the neuroses of homosexuals were the result of their struggle to repress their heterosexuality. Homophilic behavior was considered a sign of the same conflict. Functioning within the framework of such dicta, the therapist typically gave diagnoses of "oedipal rivalry," "fear of the mother," "castration anxiety," and other choice concepts that were supposed to apply to everyone. These practitioners presented case after case—the total small by comparison with modern methods of research—of involved dynamics in which various equations abounded: breast-penis, oral incorporation, anal-vaginal equivalence, and similar pairings are a few examples. There was, and is, considerable validity to such explanations, but the proliferation of these elegant linkages that came so glibly from the lips of the therapist had little effect upon the patients with whom he dealt. Such interpretations were intended to lead to insight and then to understanding and change, which they failed to do. Very often insight and understanding are handed to the analyst by the patient at the first interview because the invert who seeks aid is highly sophisticated and well-read in the literature of homosexuality. Changes in values, attitudes, and conduct, however, depend upon more factors than comprehension of the problem. A definitive review of much of this material has been covered by Ellis (1963). The genetic, hormonal, and body-build hypotheses clearly have been discredited.

Homosexuality as an acquired condition is generally accepted and has formed the basis of treatment modalities for inversion. A modern version of Freud's bisexual theory is expressed in the Rational-Emotive therapeutic approach where emphasis is placed on the antisexual bias inherent in society. The goal of the clinician is to help the homosexual alter his prejudiced attitude toward heterosexuality. The analyst who accepts Harper's (1963) statement that the ideal state of affairs would be one in which "no one was rigidly opposed to any form of sexuality" can avoid stigmatizing his patient and relate to him without being influenced by social mores.

Currently, a number of psychoanalysts and other psychotherapists view the deviate as having a basic ego defect that masks a psychotic process. Bychowski (1956) emphasizes the approach whereby the patient is helped to adjust to his inversion without feeling that it is necessary to alter his object choice. Conversely, Sullivan (1956) feels that those who manifest homosexual inclinations should not be told that they are homosexuals or taught to live with their inversion, because they already feel sufficiently different from their peers. Rather, the problem should be approached obliquely and they should be encouraged to believe that these tendencies have other psychic significance. To label them, he feels, is one of the "most vicious miscarriages" of therapy. Bergler (1956) offered his theoretical position and such concepts as the "injustice collector," oral masochism, and the need for punishment, which have become part of the vocabulary of analysis. His claims of success in altering inverts are not taken seriously because of his obvious contempt for homosexuals. Only an extreme masochist could stay in treatment and be subjected to the verbal abuse he describes.

Over the last century there has been a progression from pronouncements that offered little hope for change, through an attempt to help the homosexual to adapt as best he could to a hostile environment, and finally to a much more optimistic approach to the problem. Today's successful analyst utilizes the best of several techniques garnered from the failures, as well as the successes, of the past.

One study gave treatment results for a group of 106 homosexuals with the following results: 27 percent became exclusively heterosexual; of those who began as wholly homosexual, 10 percent became heterosexual; and 50 percent of the bisexuals became heterosexual (Bieber *et al.*, 1962).

Other research substantiates the belief that transfer of the sex object can be effected in many instances and, in many more, the subject can accept himself as a different but no less worthy member of society. Ironically, some of the strongest opposition comes from the organized and militant minority of inverts who cling to the theory that "they were born that way," that they are "normal" and not disturbed by their inversion, and that treatment for the "genuine" homosexual is never successful. On this hypothesis, they tend to denigrate analysts and to discourage others from engaging in therapy.

Practical Approaches

All of this suggests the need for serious consideration of the clinician's approach.

1. He must accept the patient without moralizing and without deriding inversion or attempting conversion to heterosexuality. To be guilty of any of these is for the analyst to place himself in a position analogous to that of a white racist treating a Negro.
2. The patient must be allowed to set the goals to be attained rather than having them set for him. It is too easy to label a patient by some diagnostic entity and try to effect a "cure." Many patients enter analysis to avoid persecution, to get over a compulsive self-destructive search that offers no hope of intimacy, or through fear of becoming emotionally involved in intimacy that goes beyond the casual sexual encounter. None of these suggests a wish to change the sex-object choice, but each is a legitimate objective that the clinician can help his patient to realize.
3. The clinician should comprehend clearly the sociogenic problems created by society's attitude toward atypical sexual behavior. Apart from the inversion, he can find any or all diagnostic entities coexistent with homosexuality but not necessarily resulting from the inversion. He must recognize the fact that those deviates who do no harm to others or attempt to "corrupt" others still are subject to archaic laws and taboos that can create serious mental problems. Knowledge of their sexual orientation occasions hostility in others and this in turn makes them fearful, self-demeaning, guilt-laden and withdrawn. As long as mores predicated on irrational and primitive attitudes toward nonconformity exist, *treatment makes sense only if the patient wishes to adapt to the accepted social pattern*. That decision is his, not the clinician's.
4. Compulsive behavior, phobic avoidance, and insulation from others are no different in the homosexual population than the schizoid mechanisms manifested by nondeviates, and they should receive comparable treatment.
5. Details of the patient's sexual life are critical elements in making an evaluation of his therapeutic needs. His reluctance to furnish such information frequently leads the therapist to assume and/or create "a fit" with his learned theories. Such a priori conclusions are a disservice to the patient who will, when rapport is established, volunteer such information as he wishes to give regarding details of preference, mode of behavior in sexual contact, and the types of partners sought.
6. The most common reason for a patient to leave his therapist is because the latter fails adequately to handle the mounting sexual anxiety, panic, and guilt that brought the homosexual to him. Seeking casual sexual part-

ners frequently is an unrecognized expression of loneliness, impotence, and depression—an inability to relate to people as a whole. When the patient recognizes that his conduct is a symptom, and his analyst regards it as such, the foundation has been laid for a sound therapeutic relationship and true communication.

Summary

Behavior patterns of homosexuals, as well as those of heterosexuals, are the result of early experience in the primary groups to which they belong. They make certain identifications that determine the direction their initially undirected drives will take. The homosexual is the product of a childhood environment that has resulted in a faulty identification.

Society rejects the atypical individual, distrusting that which it does not understand. As a result, the large segment of the population that is inverted is subjected to discrimination, ostracism, and harassment. Unfortunately, circumstances over which no one may have control often determine the familial pattern that creates a climate for homosexuality, or the nuclear unit unwittingly contributes to misdirecting the child's sexual expression. In any case, the end result is the same, and every invert is a lonely and frustrated person searching for an unrealized identification.

Inversion takes many forms ranging from fantasies and suppressed yearnings to promiscuity. Between these extremes are gradations of sexual expression.

The clinician who elects to work in the field of homosexuality must accept each patient without bias and permit him to set his own goals. This sounds deceptively simple: prejudice is not set aside readily, nor is it easy to accept a compromise instead of a "cure," even when it is in the best interest of the patient. By making use of existing techniques, together with his own, it is probable that a competent analyst will bring the homosexual to the point where he recognizes his problem, alters or accepts his condition (as he chooses), and makes the necessary adaptations. To free him from guilt and self-destructive impulses is to give him an opportunity to survive in a hostile world.

Conclusions

Society needs to be educated to a more realistic attitude toward sex. Old concepts must be abandoned and new mores established. Premarital, extramarital, and atypical sexual experiences are commonplace, whether or not one wishes to acknowledge the fact. Youth is displaying a refreshing candor, but the "generation gap" will widen progressively unless the older members of the social structure bridge it with tolerance and compassion. As far as inverts are concerned, a positive contribution can be made by encouraging legal reforms that would permit those who do not hurt others or seek to "corrupt" to enjoy the rights of first-class citizens.

References

Bieber, I., *et al. Homosexuality.* New York: Basic Books, 1962.

Bergler, E. *Homosexuality: Disease or Way of Life.* New York: Hill & Wang, 1956.

Bychowski, C. "Homosexuality and Psychosis." In *Perversions,* S. Lorand and M. Balint, eds. New York: Random House, 1956.

Ellis, A. "Constitutional Factors in Homosexuality: A Reexamination of the Evidence." In *Advances in Sex Research,* H. G. Beigel, ed. New York: Hoeber Medical Division, 1963.

Ellis, H. *Studies in the Psychology of Sex.* Vol. 2, Part 2. *Eonism and Other Supplementary Studies,* pp. 161–86. Philadelphia: F. A. Davis (1901–1910) 1928.

Freud, S. *Three Essays on the Theory of Sexuality* (1905). First English ed., London: Imago Publishing Co., 1949.

Harper, R. A. "Psychological Aspects of Homosexuality." In *Advances in Sex Research,* H. G. Beigel, ed. New York: Hoeber Medical Division, 1963, pp. 187–97.

Hirschfeld, M. *Die Homosexualität des Mannes und des Weibes.* Berlin: L. Magnus, 1914.

Kallmann, F. J. "Comparative Twin Study on the Genetic Aspects of Male Homosexuality." *Journal of Nervous and Mental Disease,* 115 (1952), 283–98.

Kinsey, A. C., W. B. Pomeroy, and C. E. Martin. *Sexual Behavior in the Human Male.* Philadelphia: Saunders, 1948.

——— and P. H. Gebhard. *Sexual Behavior in the Human Female.* Philadelphia: Saunders, 1953.

Marmor, J., ed. *Sexual Inversion.* New York: Basic Books, 1965.

Rado, S. "An Adaptational View of Sexual Behavior." In *Psychoanalysis of Behavior,* S. Rado, ed. New York: Grune & Stratton, 1956. Collected papers.

Rechy, J. *City of Night.* New York: Grove Press, 1963.

Reiss, A. J., Jr. "Queers and Peers." *Social Problems,* 9, 2 (1961), 102–20.

Stekel, W. *The Homosexual Neurosis.* New York: Emerson Books, 1950.

Sullivan, H. S. *Clinical Studies in Psychiatry.* New York: Norton, 1956.

PART TWO

THE SEXES in WESTERN CULTURE

5 SEX ROLES, ANCIENT TO MODERN

Georgene H. Seward

Sex roles as an index of social change may be misleading if considered apart from the total social context. Their relationship to the overall pattern determines their meaning at a particular time and place. Thus, woman's low status may mean respectability in classical Athens or republican Rome, degradation in Nazi Germany, and sex repression in rural America. Conversely, her high status may reflect Minoan flexibility in goddess-nurtured Crete, social disruption in imperial Rome, romance in the High Renaissance, and necessity in Soviet Russia. In any case, social sex roles can be evaluated only in light of the social whole [Seward, 1946 (1954)].

Beginnings in antiquity

Minoans and Mycenaeans

As the first link in the European chain, ancient Minoan civilization surprises us by its unmistakable air of modernity (Durant, 1939). Here women could hold their own with the most advanced of our times. We find them mingling freely, unveiled and bare-breasted, with men at the theater, the bull dances, and other public events. The feminine role included working in the fields beside men as well as the more homely arts of weaving and making bread or pottery (Glasgow, 1923). Indeed, the women of Crete who still echoed an earlier mother cult were accorded a level of esteem and privilege comparable with the goddess-worshiping high civilizations of Mesopotamia and Egypt (Seltman, 1962).

Among the Mycenaeans on mainland Greece, the center of family authority was the father. It was he who arranged marriages for his daughters —and love after rather than before the nuptials became the order of the day. Education for girls and boys was differentiated, with girls trained for a domestic role, and boys for the more strenuous life of fighting and hunting. Achaean women were still free, however, to move without restraint among men and, on occasion, they seem to have engaged in serious discourses with them (Durant, 1939; Seltman, 1962).

Ancient Sparta

After the Dorian conquest, a military state was set up in ancient Sparta. Here the women retained many of the freedoms they had enjoyed during Mycenaean times, but these freedoms were now preempted for developing supermen of their sons rather than for enriching their own personalities. Wrestling, boxing, racing, quoits, darts, and other athletic activities were used to build strong bodies of girls as well as boys. In military schools that boys attended after the age of seven, special attention was given to the control of pain, hardship, and misfortune (Durant, 1939). Whether love was crushed by these stern measures and the cold baths that accompanied them (Langdon-Davies, 1927), we cannot be sure; but we do know that social and sexual intercourse were freer than in other parts of the Greek world of the time (Seltman, 1962). Even after marriage, which was still by arrangement rather than choice, the girl like the boy retained her freedom to go about at will and was permitted bold, outspoken, and often overbearing behavior that might appear masculine to us. Marriage was held in high esteem, and divorce, illegitimacy, and prostitution were minimal. In spite of the prevailing idealization of male friendship based on aesthetic appreciation and religious sacrifice to Eros as a safeguard in battle, homosexuality in the narrow sense of sexual inversion was not a problem (Licht, 1932; Seltman, 1962).

Classical Athens

It is one of the paradoxes of history that when Greek culture was at its peak, the position of women was the lowest (Tucker, 1922). Authorities differ in their interpretation of this situation, but one important factor seems to have been social class. Athens, under the democracy with its middle-class standards, deprived the former aristocrats of the privileges enjoyed in Minoan-Mycenaean or Spartan society with which it has so often been erroneously compared (Lacey, 1968). In an effort to protect their children's citizenship under Pericles' stiff new laws, Attic men overprotected their women with an Oriental vigilance made familiar to them through trade and war contacts with the Persians.[1]

With the exception of poor women, who, like their men, had to go out to work and share in all aspects of the bitter struggle for subsistence, Athenian females were wards of some male relative from birth to death. On leaving her father's guardianship at marriage, the girl was at the mercy of her husband who had absolute power over her property and person. Within her own home she was confined to *gynaecia,* special quarters at the rear of the house where she was safely hidden from the impertinent gaze of male visitors. Outside the home her rare appearances, aside from neighborly contacts, were made under strict surveillance and heavy veiling and limited to such occasions as family weddings and funerals, or attendance at special religious and theatrical events (Durant, 1939).

The women were not alone in having their freedom curtailed, for the men also had to obey certain social sanctions concerning family matters: They were legally responsible for their parents and sons and had to choose their brides from daughters of citizens (Lacey, 1968).

Differences in sex typing began in childhood. After six, the little boy was taken from the women's quarters for a carefully planned course in morals, manners, and sports. Meanwhile, the little girl was left at home to receive instruction in the practical domestic skills of cooking and weaving that would enable her to look after her future family's physical needs (Durant, 1939). Such training was hardly conducive to stimulating the mind or cultivating the personality. Having grown up sheltered from men and society, the little maid of Athens could hardly emerge at fifteen or sixteen years as a congenial companion for the man of the world her father expected her to marry. Indeed, for feminine companionship men of high rank depended on the *hetairai,* those charming courtesans who fled from the seclusion of the conventional role and lived in their own "bachelor apartments." Aspasia, mistress of Pericles, set the style of the salon in Athens for centuries to come. For the man in the street, entertainment and sexual relaxation could be found among prostitutes of lower orders.

Lack of communication between the Athenian man and his bored and boring wife often led the man to an emotional attachment to boys with whom he could share his friendship and feelings (Durant, 1939). Male homosexuality gained prestige by Plato's extolment of it as superior to sex relations between men and women (Seltman, 1962).

The double sex standard in the Periclean Age failed to reflect the clear light of Hellas and was soon to be condemned in tragedy and satirized in comedy by the best playwrights of the time. In our own time, Kitto's (1951) tortured rationalizations, designed to show the Attic gentleman's high regard for the lady whose civil rights he denied, do no more than reveal the old-fashioned British gentleman's paternalistic gallantry toward a "weaker sex."

Roman Sex Roles and Politics

Shifting the scene to Rome, we may trace changes in sex roles to changes in political structure. The stoic republic presents much the same picture of male dominance as does Athenian democracy. The *paterfamilias* also possessed absolute legal power over his family, including that of exposing or selling his children and of condemning his wife to death for a variety of offenses ranging from adultery to stealing the keys to his wine cellar

(Durant, 1944). In this setup too, women at every stage of life found themselves under the tutelage of men: first, the father or brother; then, the husband, who in old Roman law was "father"; and finally, the son or male guardian became the mentor whose consent was needed to validate her property rights as well as marital contracts (Langdon-Davies, 1927). In spite of this legal subordination, the woman of the Roman Republic actually enjoyed more latitude than did her classical Greek sister, for she was allowed to join her husband at table and altar and to go out without his permission. Within her home she became the honored "madame"—*mea domina*—rather than the slave of her household. Her education included elementary school in addition to the routine domestic training in spinning, weaving, and cooking. Poor women, however, virtually were slaves.

During the period of imperial expansion, while the men were away conquering the world, the Roman woman's increased responsibilities added to her status *de facto* if not *de jure*. Marriage came to rest wholly on the formal consent, if not romance, of the partners, and the wife was practically independent of her husband who had no actual power over her. Patrician matrons could afford slaves to perform the household chores, while they were at liberty to attend circuses, theaters, and banquets, to beautify their bodies, or to cultivate their minds. In the early empire, education of upper-class women often extended to the "finishing" schools where such cultural interests as painting, singing, and playing the lyre might be pursued (Friedländer, 1928). Before the end of the empire, women were entering all the professions. Many became noted verse writers, literary critics, or students of Greek and Roman poetry, while others devoted themselves to science, to becoming leaders in medicine or law, to philanthropy, religion, or even to politics. Those who had the temerity to challenge age-old male prerogatives brought down on themselves a storm of protest from such guardians of the Establishment as Cicero, Cato, and Juvenal.

At lower economic levels where a vigorous equality invariably prevails of necessity, women found their way into shops and the newly industrialized factories of the textile and other trades. In pointing up the improved female status, Goodsell (1934) commented that the women of the Roman Empire had more in common with those of twentieth century America than with their own countrywomen under the republic.

Along with greater freedom for women, which reflected the breakdown of traditional family structure, went the less favorable symptoms of easier divorce, childlessness, celibacy, legalized prostitution, and homosexuality. In broader perspective, the common denominator of all these changes may be found in the military state that gradually eroded all the basic institutions of Roman life. Unfortunately, the culture did not endure long enough to witness the reconstruction of a greater society through the joint effort of women and men in a time of peace.

The Middle Ages

The Middle Ages ushered in a new phase in the evolution of social sex roles. The freedom won at great cost by the women of imperial Rome was denounced by the early Christian fathers. Under the influence of St. Paul, women were irrationally hated, feared, and degraded. The evil picture of woman contrasting with the ideal of sexual asceticism was personified by the devil-possessed witch (Langdon-Davies, 1927). Only in rural areas such as central Sicily, far from the beaten path, did girls remain gay, happy, and natural, true "pagani." As for the rest, the downgraded women became rehabilitated to a degree through the worship of the Virgin, which counterbalanced the sick male notion of Eve, the Temptress. The Virgin Mary took over much of the earlier cult of the mother goddess, Artemis. Through docile obedience to the Son, the Virgin Mother became a mediator of salvation of sinful women (Seltman, 1962).

The Lady

The Virgin in heaven had her earthly counterpart in the *lady,* who shared honors in the age of chivalry with the crusading knight's most valued companion, the horse. Tutored to read, recite stories, and play the harp, women were better educated than men of the times and in a position to influence their manners (Langdon-Davies, 1927). The developing "code of courtly love" made the lady an object of male adoration for pure friendship's sake (de Rougemont, 1940). According to the new convention, it was quite proper for the emotionally starved wife in a marriage of convenience to have a knight in shining armor who wore her colors and devoted himself to her service. Romantic love became an independent principle of worth and offered norms of conduct that helped to transform the warrior into the gentleman. Moreover, emphasis on the personal factors in the relationship between the sexes, though at the time considered relevant only to extramarital affairs, contributed to the ultimate love-marriage ideal (Durant, 1950).

Through arranged marriage, women came under the control of their husbands who in theory and law had authority to force their obedience by physical means if necessary. In practice, however, the wives enjoyed high prestige because their domestic domain was the center of industry. This was especially true during the long wars when, as in Roman times, much responsibility fell on their shoulders. During the protracted absences of their husbands, wives were in full charge of the estates, having to attend the sick, fight lawsuits, and at times stand siege. Increased self-esteem, combined with new wealth derived by widows from rich fiefs, elevated the married woman once again to a position of power. Indeed, when the men returned from battle, it was they who became dependent. Miscast for the domestic scene, they wasted their time drinking and sleeping until the war cry sounded again (Putnam, 1940).

The ladies of the evolving feudal aristocracy enjoyed many privileges denied those of humbler status. Continued prejudice appeared in sex inequities within the craft guilds as well as in the professions, many of which kept their doors barred to women (Durant, 1950).

The Nun

For the gifted woman—maiden or widow—who wished to escape a life of trivia, the convent paradoxically became a haven. In the seclusion provided her as a "bride of Christ," opportunities were available for interesting work denied by the world at large. Here the nun could copy and illuminate manuscripts, teach children who were boarded at the convent, and even serve as nurse in hospitals (Durant, 1950). Moreover, initiative and leadership were permitted expression in administrative functions. The lady abbess was virtually a baron—an overlord of an immense property that she held directly from the king (Putnam, 1940).

The Renaissance

Universal Man and Woman

With the rebirth of the classic spirit, the *joie de vivre* so long buried beneath the weight of the medieval Church burst forth with renewed vigor. Its infectious vitality added new zest to the relations between the sexes no less than to other areas of living. Although the romantic love introduced during the Middle Ages continued to be idealized in song by the troubadours (Rowbotham, 1895) and extolled by the Neoplatonists (de Rougemont, 1940), other dimensions were added. As the feminine role, especially in upper-class society, became enriched through the participation of women in the revival of learning and the art of living, a new intellectual comradeship between men and women developed (Langdon-Davies, 1927; Seltman, 1962). The self-actualized "universal man," bold in boudoir and battlefield, knowledgeable in art, letters, and philosophy, found his female match. The energy, beauty, and courage of the Renaissance woman have been immortalized by such heroines as Caterina Sforza, for her defense of Forli, and Bianca Visconti, for governing Milan (Burkhardt, 1937; Durant, 1953). Women of the period acted not only for themselves but, like their Roman predecessors in antiquity, exerted important influences on the men who still retained legal authority over them. Even the average woman, trained for a domestic role and closely guarded before marriage, was familiar with the classics, literature, philosophy, and the arts (Durant, 1953).

Court and Salon

The spiritual love that had been set on a pedestal during the Crusades took on a more frankly sensual cast in the new era. Since marriage as an important economic contract between families could not be entrusted to the caprices of desire, other outlets were recognized. Adultery was widespread and unofficially condoned. Prostitution on a variety of levels again flourished, including in its ranks a class of genteel courtesans who graced the Renaissance salons in Rome and Venice and were reminiscent of the Athenian *hetairai*. Homosexuality, associated with Greek revival rather than cultural degeneration, also became popular in Italy at this time.

The Renaissance radiance beginning in Italy gradually spread over Europe. Spain, under Moorish influence where women were kept in Arabic seclusion, was alone impervious to the new brightness. In France, the salon of the Marquise de Rambouillet could have challenged in brilliance and taste the court of Pericles. Here might be found Richelieu, Balzac, Condé, La Rochefoucauld, and other distinguished frequenters. England under the Great Queen also scintillated. Elizabethan Man, like *l'uomo universale* of Italy, was vital and vibrant, sensitive to literature, apt to be violent in speech and action, but saved by a never-failing humor. Women were free to develop their talents and tenderness, and contributed beauty, charm, and wit to the stimulating scene (Durant, 1953).

On all fronts, the Renaissance showed life being lived intensely with both men and women eagerly making the most they could of themselves and of one another.

Modern times

Puritan Forces of Reaction

The creative spell of the High Renaissance was broken by the turbulence of the Reformation and the Industrial Revolution. The Puritans revived the medieval fear of woman as a temptress, which provided the rationalization for the brutal witch hunts of the period.

Changes in the work relations between men and women also adversely affected woman's social identity. For people of the emerging middle classes, the struggle for existence at first produced the rough and ready kind of equality usually characteristic of hard times. The women no less than the men were trained in some skill that served as an economic asset and were allowed to display courage, initiative, resourcefulness, and wit in practicing it. In turn, the tradesman considered it his duty to be well-informed on domestic affairs. Marriage took on the air of partnership even though wives were still technically subject to their husbands (Stern, 1939). With the rise of capitalism and the ensuing competition for jobs, however, women no longer shared directly in production and had nothing to offer in exchange for their support. Many functions were taken out of the home without allowing the women to follow them. The new order even failed to recognize their age-old priority in the fields of healing and teaching. Increased professional standards depending on the higher education they were denied, put occupation in these areas beyond their reach and left them captive within the four walls of their homes as in the Athenian *gynaecia* twenty-two centuries earlier. Under these circumstances, it is no wonder that their physiques and personalities took on a prison pallor in comparison with those of their robust grandmothers.

As in all eras, class lines cut across sex lines with the result that women of the aristocracy enjoyed privileges shared by neither the men nor the women at the poverty level. The lot of the poor working woman was disastrous under the new factory system that exploited her as cheap labor for the profit of the wealthy whose puritan hostility added insult to her injury. Her only compensation was the improved status she gained at home as a result of her economic help and of hardships equally shared with the family (Stern, c. 1934).

By the time of "the Enlightenment," the deterioration of women's status was complete. The ideal of feminine charm centered on passive docility and clinging dependence on men. The practice of female parasitism spread through all but the lowest classes until work came to be a misfortune and disgrace instead of a source of dignity and personal worth. The opening of educational and professional opportunities to members of both sexes who had the means and interest to take advantage of them at least pointed the way to a more enlightened future (Seltman, 1962).

The Pioneers

An exception to the pervasive deterioration of women's status appeared in the American colonies where the frontier served as a leveling influence that gradually altered the patriarchal tradition of the continent and raised the status of wife and child in the evolving democratic family. The individualism that was in the air eventually penetrated the stuffy atmosphere of Victorian drawing rooms and paved the way for the Lucy Stoners of more recent times.

Between world wars

A review of the changes in social sex roles throughout the development of Western culture reveals their dependence on the prevailing social climate

[Seward, 1946 (1954)]. Within the framework of the patriarchal family the position of women above the poverty line has fluctuated. In periods of stress they have been appreciated as persons and have shared equally with the men. In more usual times, they have been treated like other disadvantaged "minorities" and denied the rewards of the status symbols jealously hoarded by the male majority. Under such circumstances power is vested in men, and women together with children and animals become subjugated (Fromm, 1936) . These trends are nowhere more beautifully illustrated than in contemporary society. A study of striking contrasts is afforded by comparing Germany, the Soviet Union, and the United States as they appeared between World Wars.

The German Reichs

Germany itself has witnessed a double pendulum swing from right to left, and back and forth again within a generation. The authoritarian tradition of the *Kaiserreich,* according to which the *Kinder-Küche-Kirche* slogan defined the role of women, was demolished by the vigorous *Frauenbewegung* of the Weimar Republic, resulting in a complete transformation of social sex roles. During this brief awakening, women participated with men in every phase of life: the universities welcomed them and in turn opened up all professions (Puckett, 1930) . So firmly entrenched did their new status become that none but the upcoming National Socialists dared to challenge it (Villard, 1933) .

The *Third Reich* witnessed an extreme regression to the right. Reaction in the social structure as a whole undermined the progress women had previously achieved and led to a baser degradation than they had ever experienced in the history of Western civilization. The female's world as defined by Hitler (1941) was restricted to, "her husband, her family, her children, and her house" (pp. 287–88) . All women were to be fitted into a single mold on the assumption of a universal maternal feeling and unlimited wifely docility (Kirkpatrick, 1939) . Her primary function in the new order was to breed potential soldiers. In accordance with this principle, her education was slanted and differentiated from that of boys. As in ancient Sparta, this involved a maximum of physical, combined with a minimum of intellectual, training. At the same time anticontraception measures were adopted.

Women were seen as the source of nourishment not only in their capacity as breeders of German youth but also as tillers of German soil. They were to be strong peasants as well as strong mothers. As part of the double training for the role of housewife and peasant, compulsory labor camps were instituted. Young girls were sent out to help with heavy work on the farm in the belief that folk-centered labor service would teach girls the true mission and place of woman based on the blessings of work in close relationship to children, animals, and nature (Kesserlring, 1941) . This amounted to putting all German women in the position of the virtual slavery that had applied to the domestic servants of an earlier era.

For the unmarried woman, only those occupations were open which were deemed appropriate to the Nazi conception of "female nature" (Brady, 1937). During the Depression, professional women suffered heavily through loss of position and opportunity. The economically deprived were allowed to work insofar as they provided the cheapest source of labor (Kirkpatrick, 1937). With the onset of war, wholesale discharges had to be checked and the movement reversed for the duration. The war, however, was no more than an armistice in the fight against women. Even under the emergency conditions the employer was not allowed to forget sex differences in social roles. He was advised to bear constantly in mind that, while employment of women was indispensable, they were not naturally adapted to life of that sort. For this reason, they were to be given only simple and mechanical work and were to be placed under male supervision because of their readiness to take orders from a man. Demobilization was seen as putting an end to the employment of female workers who had been engaged only to replace the men in the armed services (Anonymous, 1941).

Another trend that emerged during the Nazi regime, symptomatic of steep status differences between the sexes, was the romanticizing of male friendship. The glorious role of man in contrast to the ignominious role of woman was that of a warrior like the mythical Siegfried, hero of the *Niebelungen.* The cult of the Führer was instilled in the youth through the *Hitler-Jugend.* According to this doctrine, the state is founded on a male league in which warriors are linked together by loyalties nobler than the emotions men feel for women and more nearly resembling the worship of the gods. These emotions were often expressed in frank, unsublimated homosexuality that was not discouraged. Decadence, on the other hand, was seen as the inevitable result of participating with women (Von Shirach, 1934; Viereck, 1941).

The Soviets

In sharp contrast with Nazi Germany, the Soviet Union during the same period broke down the social role dichotomy between the sexes. Through the socialization of industry, power was shifted from the owners of the means of production to all workers, female as well as male (Van Kleek, 1935). Women were to share equally in the privileges and responsibilities of production. They were to have the same education, work opportunities, wages, time off, rest periods, and social insurance. Moreover, since childbearing was regarded as a functional expense in the performance of public duty, married women were granted special compensations in the form of maternity leaves with guaranteed reinstatement after delivery. Proper care was assured for babies through nurseries provided by the industrial plants where mothers could take regular "nursing breaks" to feed them (Webb & Webb, 1936). Despite a long tradition of subjugation and much resistance even from the women themselves, the main objectives were achieved. The new freedom was attained not through a feminist movement fighting against men, but in the course of a struggle of both men and women for a new way of life. The men supported the women and spurred them on until they not only became a vital part of the system but rose to the highest positions within it (Fairchild, 1937).

Even more important than the elevation of women in political, cultural, and economic status was their new personal independence and dignity as human beings. In no sphere were men accorded greater liberties or advantages than women. Even in the most intimate domain of sex relations, women were treated as adults whose behavior was left entirely to their own discretion. In the new morality there was but a single standard. Sex was neither sacred nor profane but, quite simply, natural. From the child's earliest days, sex was familiar to him as a positive value without a special mystique surrounding it. Contrary to societies where it has attained an exaggerated importance through repression, sex in the early days of the USSR did not exert a disproportionate influence on art, literature, theater, or cinema (Eddy, 1931). The healthier attitude was evident in the reduction of such social pathology as prostitution, venereal disease, and pornography (Barash, 1926). The new Russian family benefitted from the changed relationship between men and women. Far from approving promiscuity, the new order held up monogamous marriage as the ideal, based on love and companionship and freed from traditional economic complications. No longer was there a patriarch whose word was law. No longer were children to be seen and not heard. Instead, the family became a little group of people of assorted ages and sexes bound together by ties of personal intimacy. The socialization of many of the physical functions previously performed in the home left more time for cultivating the more important psychological values (Grunfield, 1942; Makarenko, 1967).

Among the Moslems of the Soviet East, women had been regarded as scarcely human. They were sold to their husbands in childhood and forced to work as slaves. On the husband's death the widow legally became the property of the nearest relative along with the domestic utensils, livestock, and other possessions (Webb & Webb, 1936). Against this background, progress was necessarily uphill work. The story of reforms in the eastern soviets is dramatic (Halle, 1938). New institutions had to be devised as media for the dissemination of new ideas. The early workers had to veil themselves to gain the confidence of the Oriental women. At first they made their contacts in public baths and in the streets. Later, the women's clubs provided a means of overcoming timidity and encouraging unveiling in one another's presence. Little by little, resistance to change yielded to the persistent efforts of the Soviet underground. So revolutionary were the reforms of the newly alerted Eastern women that they have leaned over backwards in some cases. An example of a reversal of Western prejudice is the case of the political executive in Uzbekistan who was dissatisfied with her male physician not because he had *proved* to be incompetent in any way, but because he was *expected* to be incompetent on account of his sex.

American "Gothic"

"Middletown." Meanwhile, in the United States the Lynds (1929) presented a picture of the American scene in their study of the "typical" Midwestern city of Middletown. Here, as late as 1924, traditional authoritarian family forms were retained, although their content was gradually yielding to democratic influences. Marriage was a blend of contract and romance originating in an "unanalyzable mystery" but guided by the invisible hands of designing parents. On entering the state of matrimony, the young couple were expected to make a home of their own. The patriarchal mold survived in the wife's exchanging the name of her father for the name of her husband, a custom reverting to the marriage *cum manu* of the Roman Republic when the girl passed from the hand of her father to the hand of her husband. More reminiscent of those ancient times were the lack of community of interest and companionship between the partners. The divergence of social roles became apparent in mixed social gatherings where the men and women tended to gravitate apart, or the men did most of the talking while the women lent their respectful ears. The social distance reflected the role differentiation, the husband providing a good living, and the wife a good home to live in. The masculine and feminine worlds really amounted to two subcultures in Middletown: the woman's lay within the household and involved the care and teaching of small children, always with male authority in the background; the man's by contrast was part of the larger world of affairs outside the home.

The marked cleavage in sex roles led to a discounting of the broad socializing values of education for women. As one Middletowner expressed the typical attitude: "The thing girls get from high school is the ability to know how to choose a 'real one' from a 'near one.'" It also led to the assumption that men and women must be very different kinds of people. Men were considered stronger, bolder, more logical, and more reasonable, but at the same time to need the coddling and reassurance as in *Life with Father*. Women, on the other hand, though more delicate physically, were presumed to be stronger morally, purer, more refined, more sympathetic, and more sensitive. The prevailing attitude accepted by women as well as by men is beautifully summed up in the motto of the local federated women's club: "Men are God's trees; women are His flowers."

A decade after the original study, a sequel (Lynd & Lynd, 1937) showed Middletown still following Dorothy Dix's daily column extolling woman's subordination. But the Depression was seriously threatening the old tradition by preventing many men from providing for their families, thus making it necessary for wives, especially among the working class, to help. Under these circumstances, the rigid sex-role caste could not be maintained. As a consequence, more participation of men in the home and of women outside it became commonplace. Gradually, women's place was less exclusively confined to the home and careers began to open up alternative choices. Significant of this trend was the growing talk among high school girls of working after graduation rather than "just marrying and settling down."

In spite of the shift in emphasis, the basic pattern of social sex roles remained unaltered. Until World War II, the male was still being trained to dominate while the female was oriented toward domestic and service functions.

"Plainville, U.S.A." The rural counterpart of Middletown may be found in Plainville (West, 1945), another Midwest community but closer to the pioneer pattern according to which a man occupied a frontier with his sons, the family was a tight-knit unit to which each member contributed according to his assigned obligations. Within the rigorous patriarchal clanlike structure, different roles were ascribed to the sexes, each with clearly defined sets of duties and privileges. The husband owed his wife a good living off the farm and was expected to be kind and true to her, while the wife was responsible for household matters as well as for the personal care of her children and the sexual needs of her husband. Just as the husband was not to meddle with the home, the wife was not to meddle with the farm. The man's world involved a money economy including ownership of land, livestock, farm implements, the family car, etc., while the woman's domain was bounded by the house, poultry yard, garden, and all the accoutrements of a subsistence economy. Territorial rights were defended by public opinion and female transgressions into male areas resulted in the lowering of a man's status. Sex role differentiation was conspicuous at the harvest. During this season, gangs of men worked together year after year for mutual help in threshing, butchering hogs, and sawing wood, while the women cooked the harvest feast for their hungry men. The whole provided a gay social ritual that repeatedly validated the group identity.

Training for social roles began before birth with the parents' admitted preference for boys because of their greater usefulness on the farm. Boy babies were regarded as "little men" who were "naturally stronger." A father's delight was to see his little son dressed in blue denim overalls as soon as he could walk. Little girls, on the contrary, were seen as "dolls," passive and malleable to social demands. This differential treatment reinforced the submissiveness in girls and the domination in boys that were to characterize lifelong attitudes between the sexes. Toward parental authority both boys and girls were expected to show unquestioned obedience which, if not spontaneous, was enforced by "breaking the spirit" of the recalcitrant. Children were brought in line with the mores by a system of teasing, kidding, shaming, and threats of the "bugger man." While the mother had the task of administering routine discipline, it was as an obedient and dutiful delegate of the father who, as "lord and master," was always the final judge whose punishment would be swift and sure.

Brought up in subordination to the father, the boy needed to break away from home ties in order to develop sufficient independent aggressiveness to perpetuate the patriarchal model when he was ready to establish his own family. From his age peers he learned such "outlaw" activities as fighting, drinking, and sexual behavior. By late adolescence the youth might move away to "see the world" and "sow some wild oats."

For girls there was less conflict between home and society since the submissive role of child to parent could be carried over intact to that of wife to husband. An intrinsic aspect of the feminine role was sexual frigidity, with "mother" idealized as a nonsexual object. Although chastity until monogamous marriage was the official line for both sexes, there was an unofficial double sex standard inasmuch as less sexual restraint was expected of boys than of girls. Dating with parentally approved partners was frequently followed by a conventional courtship and brief, top-secret engagement culminating in a marriage to the death. A formidable array of social and religious sanctions supported this act.

The social subordination and sexual prudery of females combined effectively to stifle their personal growth and to degrade their status as adults. In spite of this handicap, Plainville girls had got the idea that women were supposed to be men's equals, and many expressed their preference for the role of beautician, stenographer, or teacher compared with that of the lackluster farmer's wife.

A follow-up study of the same community fifteen years later (Gallaher, 1961) showed Plainville caught up in the widespread process of urbanization, government subsidies, and technological changes that were gradually transforming the old family farm system. So deeply rooted was tradition, however, that at that time the effects had apparently not yet trickled down to the grass-roots level of social sex roles. Husbands still prided themselves on being the breadwinners, while wives were still restricted to the nonmoney subsistence economy.

The pictures of American life afforded by these "typical" urban and rural communities exhibit a family resemblance to each other in the patriarchial pattern of father domination and mother subordination. Thus, old ways become entrenched because of the models parents provide for the upcoming generations. In each subculture the "good" paternalistic parents develop "good" obedient children who may be counted on to perpetuate the cycle as long as there are no major social or economic upheavals to render it maladaptative. In Middletown, the Depression was the social force that threatened the old forms; in Plainville, it was the urbanization trend and change in farm economy. In either case, and in all analogous cases throughout the country where obedience is bought at the expense of personal growth, communication between the sexes and the generations becomes role ritual instead of meaningful dialogue. The frustrations lurking in such a system carry high explosive potential in the resentments and rigidities they foster (Kardiner *et al.,* 1945). In the face of the revolutionary trends of the present, such compensatory outlets as old-time religion can hardly be expected to maintain the relatively contained setup of the past in the face of the revolutionary trends of the present.

Contemporary Scene: Preview

The decades that have spanned the period since the world wars have witnessed striking changes in the three variants of Western culture just reviewed. A divided Germany has moved rapidly away from the status quo in diverging directions, the West trying to maintain a middle-of-the-road democracy as reflected in the less patriarchal family (Baumert and Hüninger, 1954; Schelsky, 1955), and the East following the Soviet line. Russia, meanwhile, in an effort to accommodate to changing pressures from all sides, has shifted emphasis in many social areas including that of sex and family (Geiger, 1968). In the United States, old ways have been challenged by youth who are seeking answers to social problems from their peers rather than elders. This new youth culture stands for equality between sexes and freedom to choose social role or sexual behavior according to personal need rather than social stereotype.

Evaluation of the world changes over the past generation in the social sex roles of boys and girls growing up during the period depends on research at the cross-national level, which has been meager because of formidable obstacles to communication and comparison. A recent effort in this direction is a study of youth groups from American communities, including the noteworthy Middletown, and from the two Germanies (Seward and Larson, 1968). Concepts of masculine and feminine models were rated on a dozen objective scales. While many significant differences among the groups appeared, the most conspicuous finding was the generation gap within each group that separated adolescents from their parents. Within the limits of this study, contemporary youth, regardless of sex or nationality, appeared to be moving away from the old models and toward the adoption of new social identities involving more action, leadership, cooperation, and wisdom.

In a sequel to the study reported, the editors of the present volume (Seward and Williamson, 1969) examined the professional goals of the original subjects and also those of comparable groups from Chile, Poland, and Turkey. The analysis showed that the Germans, from both East and

West, were the most ambitious of all. Within each of the countries included, however, striking differences were found between the sexes, the boys consistently expressing higher vocational aims than the girls. Further investigation is needed to clarify the extraordinary persistence of such traditional sex-role typing in the special area of work on the part of the same boys and girls who eagerly sought to share responsibility in general for the society of the future.

Note

[1] Personal Communication, Dr. Edward Phinney, Jr., Classics Department, University of Southern California.

References

Anonymous. "The Employment of Women in Germany under the National-Socialist Regime." *International Labor Review,* 44 (1941), 617–59.

Barash, M. "Sex Life of the Workers of Moscow." *Journal of Social Hygiene,* 12 (1926), 274–88.

Baumert, G., and E. Hüninger. *Deutsche Familien nach dem Kriege.* Darmstadt: Roether, 1954.

Brady, R. A *The Spirit and Structure of German Fascism.* New York: Macmillan, 1937.

Burckhardt, J. *The Civilization of the Renaissance in Italy.* Middlemore, trans. New York: Oxford University Press, 1937.

De Rougemont, D. *Love in the Western World.* M. Belgion, trans. New York: Harcourt, 1940.

Dillon, E. J. *Russia Today and Yesterday.* New York: Doubleday, 1930.

Durant, W. *The Story of Civilization: The Life of Greece.* New York: Simon & Schuster, 1939.

———. *The Story of Civilization: Caesar and Christ.* New York: Simon & Schuster, 1944.

———. *The Story of Civilization: The Age of Faith.* New York: Simon & Schuster, 1950.

———. *The Story of Civilization: Part V, The Renaissance.* New York: Simon & Schuster, 1953.

Eddy, S. *The Challenge of Russia.* New York: Farrar, 1931.

Fairchild, M. "The Russian Family Today." *Journal of the American Association of University Women,* 30 (1937), 142–48.

Friedländer, L. *Roman Life and Manners under the Early Empire.* Magnus, trans. London: Routledge, 1928. 4 Vols.

Fromm, E. *Studien über Autorität und Familie.* Paris: Felix Alcan, 1936. Sozial-psychologische Teil, pp. 77–135.

Gallaher, A. *Plainville: Fifteen Years Later.* New York: Columbia University Press, 1961.

Geiger, K. H. *The Family in Soviet Russia.* Cambridge: Harvard University Press, 1968.

Glasgow, G. *The Minoans.* London: Jonathan Cape, 1923.

Goodsell, W. *A History of Marriage and the Family.* New York: Macmillan, 1934.

Grunfield, J. "Women's Work in Russia's Planned Economy." *Social Research,* 9 (1942), 22–45.

Halle, F. W. *Women in the Soviet East.* New York: Dutton, 1938.

Hitler, A. *My New Order.* New York: Reynal, 1941.

Kardiner, A., *et al. The Psychological Frontiers of Society.* New York: Columbia University Press, 1945.

Kesserlring, M. "Formende Kräfte im Weiblichen Arbeitsdienst: Ein untersuchender Beitrag zur volkischen Jugendkunde." *Zeitschrift für Pädagogische Psychologie und Jugendkunde,* 42 (1941), 49–68.

Kirkpatrick, C. "Recent Changes in the Status of Women and the Family in Germany." *American Sociological Review,* 2 (1937), 650–58.

———. *Woman in Nazi Germany.* London: Jarrolds, 1939.

Kitto, H. D. F. *The Greeks.* Harmondsworth, Middlesex: Pelican Books, 1951.

Lacey, W. K. *The Family in Classical Greece.* London: Camelot Press, 1968.

Langdon-Davies, J. *A Short History of Women.* New York: Literary Guild of America, 1927.

"Licht, H." (Paul Brandt). *Sexual Life in Ancient Greece.* London: Routledge, 1932.

Lynd, R. S., and H. M. Lynd. *Middletown.* New York: Harcourt, 1929.

———. *Middletown in Transition.* New York: Harcourt, 1937.

Makarenko, A. S. *The Collective Family: A Handbook for Russian Parents.* R. Daglish, trans. New York: Doubleday, 1967.

Puckett, H. W. *Germany's Women Go Forward.* New York: Columbia University Press, 1930.

Putman, E. J. *The Lady.* New York: Sturgis & Walton, 1940.

Rowbotham, J. *The Troubadours and Courts of Love.* New York: Macmillan, 1895.

Schelsky, H. *Wandlungen der deutschen Familie in der Gegenwart.* 3rd ed. Stuttgart: Enke, 1955.

Seltman, C. *Women in Antiquity.* New York: Collier, 1962.

Seward, G. H. *Sex and the Social Order.* New York: McGraw-Hill, 1946 (Out of Print); Harmondsworth, Middlesex: Pelican Books, 1954.

———. "Sex Identity and the Social Order." *The Journal of Nervous and Mental Disease,* 139 (1964), 126–36.

——— and W. R. Larson. "A Comparative Study of Social Sex Roles in the United States and the Two Germanies." *Human Development,* 11, 4 (1968), 217–48.

Seward, G. H., and R. C. Williamson. "A Cross-national Study of Adolescent Professional Goals." *Human Development,* 12 (1969), 248–54.

Stern, B. J. "Women, position of, in historical societies." *Encyclopedia of the Social Sciences,* 15 (1935), 442–50.

———. "The Family and Cultural Change." *American Sociological Review,* 4 (1939), 199–208.

Tucker, T. G. *Life in Ancient Athens.* London: Macmillan, 1922.

Van Kleek, M. "Women in Industry." *Encyclopedia of the Social Sciences,* 15 (1935), 451–59.

Viereck, P. R. E. *Metapolitics, from the Romantics to Hitler.* New York: Knopf, 1941.

Villard, O. G. *The German Phoenix.* New York: H. Smith, 1933.

Von Shirach, B. *Die Hitler-Jugend.* Leipzig: Kohler & Amelang, 1934.

Webb, S., and B. Webb. *Soviet Communism: A New Civilization?* New York: Scribner, 1936. 2 Vols.

"West, J." (Withers, C.). *Plainville, U.S.A.* New York: Columbia University Press, 1945. Reprinted in *The Psychological Frontiers of Society,* A. Kardiner, *et al.* New York: Columbia University Press, 1945, pp. 259–412.

6 AMERICAN CORE CULTURE: CHANGES AND CONTINUITIES

Ruth E. Hartley [1]

Sex role and role-culture interaction

At least one sociologist has called the social transition currently in process "a cultural mutation." [2] He was referring to the relentless shift of population from rural areas to urban complexes and the accompanying change in dominance from agriculture to industry. These changes have special significance for sex roles. To the extent that they affect the cultural complexity of life in the United States, they affect the specification of sex behavior peculiar to the nation.

Sex roles, as particular instances of social behavior, must conform in general to cultural pressures influencing the society. As a social role—a pattern of expected behaviors reinforced by socially instituted rewards and penalities—the sex role has been traditionally one of the most basic (Banton, 1965). It has been a highly generalized role, determining and limiting the other roles an individual might pursue.

Highly generalized roles, however, are most suitable to simple social organizations. Complexity in social organization requires flexibility and diversification in its role systems. More complex systems, composed of more specialized roles, tend to particularize role behaviors and to limit the implications of a given status or position. Hence, as societies grow more complex, the number of roles increases and the segment of living subtended by any given role decreases. The sex role is no exception.

Technological advance tends to usher in economic advances. Economic advance is accompanied by role specialization and differentiation. These latter processes lead to flexibility in the definition of basic roles and to diffuseness in their content.

Technological advance leads also to increasing industrialization. Industrial societies tend to be rational, pragmatic, and future-oriented. They tend to legitimate role patterns less by reference to tradition than by reference to expediency and utility. Rapid growth and intensification of industrialization set the stage for and create the demand for adjustments in role patterns. Within recent decades, the accelerated rate of industrial development in the United States is so clearly attested by its position in world trade as to need no further comment.

Increasing industrialization brings increasing urbanization. Improved technology releases farm labor and industrial expansion lures it to concentrated population centers around the new sources of work. Role definitions change swiftly when people simultaneously must adjust to the demands of new situations and lose the traditional support of old associations. Moreover, living in a city means exposure to a variety of ways of doing things. The force of tradition is further weakened by losing the support of homogeneity of experience. Cities are logical nexus for change.

In recent years, the flow of population in the United States from rural areas to cities has become a rushing stream. At present, only a small minority of people still live in farming sections while the majority reside in urban areas. With such marked change in population balance, it would be illogical to expect sex role definitions to remain the same as when most people lived on farms.

Signs of change

The Patriarchal Pattern

At this point we might reasonably ask, "What specific signs of change are perceptible?" To make a judgment about change we need a frame of reference, or a base line. The base line we shall measure the current picture against is the patriarchal, male-dominant, role-segregated pattern characteristic of most of Western culture before World War I. According to this pattern, women were limited to domestic duties after marriage and men earned the money to support the family. Women were considered inferior to men intellectually, physically, and emotionally. Men were strong, women were weak. Women were dependent, men were self-reliant and commanding. Men gave orders, women obeyed. Women were timid, men were bold. Women were fearful; men, courageous. The qualities of one sex were the antitheses of the other, and no overlapping was acceptable. Similarly, also, the activities of each sex were strictly delineated and exclusive.

The most dramatic changes from the above pattern took place in women's roles. Degler (1964), evaluating the impact of World War I on women, states: "By the close of the twenties the ordinary woman in America was closer to a man in the social behavior expected of her, in the economic opportunities open to her, and in the intellectual freedom enjoyed by her than at any time in history" (p. 659).

Women and Work

Changes in the male role seem to have been adjustive rather than innovative at first, made in response to female role changes. Among women, the most notable change is signalled by the increasing proportion of married women entering the labor market. Contrary to the traditional assumption that woman's place is in the home and only in the home, women have, for the moment at least, broken out of the boundaries of domesticity. In the period of 1947 to 1962, three-fifths of the entire labor force increase was made up of women. Those contributing the most to this trend were married women living with their husbands. They comprised more than half of the total female work force (Peterson, 1964). This dramatic evidence of the entry of wives into the work world suggests that some shifts have occurred in the content of wife and mother roles, lending them greater diversity and diminishing their power to command total areas of an individual's life. Choice in the style of fulfilling one's sex role rather than economic need alone would seem to be responsible for the increase in working mothers inasmuch as they come for the most part from the well-heeled social strata. They work because work fills an achievement need not met in other ways (Sobol, 1963).

The age distribution of working women suggests another change in the female role. Since 1940, a rapid increase in the number of women over thirty-five in the labor force has occurred. In the twenty-five years from 1940 to 1965, the rate of labor force participation of women forty-five to fifty-four years old doubled. This was the age range accounting for the highest proportion of working wives (Hilton, 1965). With most women completing their childbearing by about the age of thirty, these figures suggest that the grandmother role has also changed. At an age when formerly women were settling down to rocking chairs and knitting, currently almost half are moving out to take up new responsibilities in the work world. Of this trend, college-trained women were in the lead. In March 1964, 74 percent of women who had completed five years or more of college were in the labor force, while the comparable figure for those with an eighth grade education was only 31 percent. Of married college-educated women living with their husbands, 63.4 percent were employed. Rates went steadily up from age twenty-five to age sixty-four, especially for wives with five or more years of college. A peak of 85.5 percent occurred in the forty-five to fifty-four year bracket.

If we accept the proposition that increasing participation in the labor force after marriage signifies a basic change in female sex role definition, it is obvious that educational progress among women would compound this change. To estimate the extent of such sex role transformation, we need to look at some statistics on women's higher education (Hilton, 1965). Between 1950 and 1964, the proportion of women twenty to twenty-four years of age enrolled in school more than doubled. In the case of those between twenty-five and thirty-four years of age, the increase was more than fivefold. Moreover, in 1964, women earned about 40 percent of all bachelor and first professional degrees conferred, compared with only 24 percent in 1950. For all masters or second level degrees, the comparable percentages were 32 and

29, less change from previous achievement but in the same direction. The upward trend of these figures would lead one to expect more and more women to combine marriage, motherhood, and paid employment as time goes on.

As increasing numbers of women successfully combine families and work, they become more visible on the social horizon, and the pattern they embody becomes less unusual, hence more easily accepted. When more than half the members of any group implement a course of action, that course is likely to become a norm for the group, and group norms are likely to generate coercive powers. For the college-educated women, to combine work with motherhood will no longer mark her an oddball, but rather, a conformist. There are indications that this is already happening. Ruth Useem (1963) reports, for example, that housebound nonemployed wives and mothers are becoming defensive about their positions.

As girls and boys grow up in households where mothers as well as fathers work, work will become part of the normal definition of the female sex role—the girls incorporating it as part of their own self-concept, and the boys accepting it as the usual thing. In a study conducted by the writer (Hartley, 1959–1960 a) on concepts of female roles, daughters of working mothers significantly more often than daughters of nonworking mothers spontaneously mentioned holding a job as one of the things a woman should be able to do. More also planned on a vocation for themselves other than that of housewife.

Growing acceptance of job-holding wives is indicated in several reports of men's attitudes. In 1964, the Women's Bureau surveyed the work status of women who had graduated from college seven years earlier (Wells, 1966). Among married women with children under six, and those with no children, the proportions in the labor force were 90 percent and 80 percent respectively. Questioning the employed married graduates about their husbands' attitudes revealed opposition to their working on the part of only 4 percent. In the total sample of married graduates, including those not working, 17 percent of the husbands were reported to be opposed to their wives' working. There was relatively little difference in the response of those with or without children.

As part of her research on sex roles, the writer (Hartley, 1959–1960 b) investigated the attitudes of the subjects' husbands concerning their wives' working. In no instance was resentment expressed. The sample contained subjects from upper middle-class and lower middle-class backgrounds. The attitude of upper middle-class husbands could best be described as indulgent. "I gave her everything else she wants," said one, a successful physician. "If she wants this [to hold a job], let her have it."

Lower middle-class husbands, on the other hand, seemed appreciative of their wives' working as a sign of their willingness to help out with the family finances. As they perceived the situation, the economic picture left a family no choice if they wished to maintain a satisfactory standard of living. "Who can live on one salary these days?" is the way one husband put it.

In a study of the marital adjustment of families in which wives worked, Nye (1963) gathered data in three Washington towns, from 1,993 mothers of whom 32.1 percent were employed. The sample contained subjects from a wide range of economic and educational levels. Nye reports that of the husbands of the women employed full time, nine out of ten approved of the arrangement.

Research by Nolan (1963) on a rural sample of families with working mothers revealed similar results. Again, 90 percent of husbands said it was worthwhile for their wives to work. Nolan's couples also contained subjects from all levels of socioeconomic status.

These data suggest that acceptance of outside work combined with marriage and motherhood is not limited by geographical area or economic level. The samples mentioned came from the East and the West, from a large city, from towns of 10,000 to 20,000 population, from rural areas. The subjects spanned a socioeconomic range from professionals to laborers, and an equally wide educational range. We can expect this acceptance to grow as more wives enter the labor force and more husbands discover the values of the arrangement.

Changes in Male Roles

The change in female sex-role definition represented by the massive entry of wives and mothers into the labor force was inevitably paralleled by a related change in the role of the husbands. Two traditional aspects of male role definition had to shift to accommodate to the new role of women. One was the expectation that the male would carry the complete responsibility for the economic well-being of the family. With contributions to the finances of the family from the wife's earnings taking on increasing significance, the exclusive responsibility of the male could now be relaxed.

The second aspect related to the customary rejection of male participation in domestic affairs, with the latter designated as "woman's work." A study of 324 intact white families with children of school age in Detroit, reported by Hoffman (1960), demonstrated that the employment of mothers was associated with the increased participation of fathers in routine household tasks. Husbands of working mothers also made more decisions about household affairs than did husbands of nonworking mothers. Working wives expected more participation of husbands and rejected the traditional sex-role ideology that excluded the male from household and childrearing activities. However, the concomitant of male dominance was not rejected by the working wives. Although the two-job families showed a less differentiated sex-role activity picture, the traditional power structure was not implicated in any simple fashion. Some working wives endorsed the dominant position of the male; others did not. Work status of the wife seemed neither a relevant nor a determining factor in relation to this attitude.

Nolan's (1963) study of rural families with working wives showed husbands of these women participating to a greater extent in homemaking activities than husbands of full-time housewives. However, even the latter helped with housekeeping tasks. Only full-time farmers with nonworking wives seemed to maintain the traditional rejection of housework.

It is interesting to note that the greatest difference between the nonfarm husbands of working wives and of full-time homemakers was the relative degree of participation in childrearing, husbands of working wives more often assuming total responsibility for assistance with school work.

In a recent study, Wilkening and Bharadwaj (1967) indicated that even in farm families the sex-role dichotomy was softening. According to their findings:

> The division of labor within the family area between husband and wife suggests that responsibility for family tasks follows the interests and availability of the spouses rather than following the traditional role expectations [p. 711].

Since children are sensitive to the sex-role models their parents present, we may logically expect more overlapping in domestic sex-role involvements as the current generation of children grows up. In the writer's study of sex-role concepts (Hartley, 1959–1960 a), boys showed more awareness of male participation in domestic work than did girls, mentioned more often men's performance of domestic tasks, and indicated that they thought men as well as women took care of children. Girls were inclined to view these activities as more exclusively female. This would suggest that in their own definitions of male-appropriate sex-role activities, domestic routines and childcare would have a legitimate place.

Evidence that this is already happening comes from the Texas Cooperative Youth Study of teenagers. In the Texas sample, *both* boys and girls revealed a keen concern for the family, for family living, and for the home (Moore and Holtzman, 1966). This finding is not surprising if we take note of other studies that reveal that sons as well as fathers share in the traditionally feminine household tasks when mothers work (Blood, 1965).

It is not only in the *work* of the household that changes are taking place. Perceptible changes in attitude are also occurring in broad segments of the population, not only in husbands of working mothers. Lopata (1965), for example, reports nonworking wives as perceiving a shift in the man's role that involves a change in the direction of partnership or companionship with his wife.

Other Trends toward Equalitarianism

In the wake of the freeing of women from the restrictions of the home, several other bastions of traditional sex-role patterns have begun to yield. One is the notion of sex-connected intellectual abilities and another, the general superiority of the male. The limitation of women to domestic affairs was supported by an elaborate system of beliefs leading to the conclusion that females were not capable of dealing with anything more demanding. Women were supposed to be too dull mentally and too undisciplined emotionally, too weak physically and too helpless morally, to be trusted to take care of themselves, or of anything else of importance. The woman could not live away from the protected stronghold of the family, which would have as its protector some male, endowed, along with his sex, with mental alertness, physical strength, self-control, objectivity, and moral discrimination. If one accepted these sets of assumptions with their implications that the qualities specified were unchangeably and inevitably sex connected, it followed that in worldly matters men were superior to women.

When they first began to take their place in the world outside the home, women did little to contradict these beliefs. Their work was largely concentrated on those activities that were projections of what had been female domestic responsibilities—the teaching of children, the care of the sick, and various kinds of service occupations. As they had served family members, so they emerged to serve outside the family in offices, in factories, in shops. Typically, the jobs in which they were concentrated were low-paying and of low status. Even those attaining college training supported the stereotype by staying with the "feminine" subjects—education, home economics, humanities, and the arts. Mathematics and the sciences were considered too demanding for female brains, and the girls accepted this opinion.

The relentless push of technology combined with a labor shortage has provided grounds for questioning the traditional assumptions about women's abilities. The 1960 census showed that there were some women workers in each of the 479 individual occupations listed. There has also been a shift in college majors, away from education and home economics, toward basic and applied sciences. By 1965, the number of professional and technical women reached 313 million— a rise of 1.4 million over the previous quarter century (Hilton, 1965).

Publications of the Women's Bureau of the U.S. Department of Labor repeatedly urge girls and counselors of girls to consider the fields of physics, engineering, mathematics, and chemistry, implying that these fields would welcome women and pay them fair salaries (Terlin, 1967). Official sources report growing success for women in attaining top government jobs. During the period 1964–1965, the President appointed 120 women to "top jobs." In the 26 largest federal agencies, 889 women were appointed in the top grades, and about 2,698 promotions of women were made at this level during the same period (Women's Bureau, 1966, p. 4).

Parallel to this movement of women into occupations and statuses that had been regarded as male reserves has been a migration of men into what had been regarded as women's occupations. Since the end of World War II, teaching in primary as well as in secondary schools has had an increase in males. Young men are coming in constantly greater numbers into social work, library science, dietetics and nutrition, and nursing (Alpenfels, 1962). According to one placement agency with offices in twenty-four cities, employment of males as clerks and typists rose 30 percent during the years 1965–67. During the same period, employment of male secretaries climbed 50 percent; male calculator and adding machine operators advanced 75 percent. The agency reported that the men applied for the work in response to advertisements placed in the female help wanted columns (Porter, 1967).

The reasons for this development may be temporary—a combination of increasing disorder in our cities and an expanding economy that requires work beyond the usual daylight hours. Whatever the reasons, the effects seem to be in the direction of a dedifferentiating sex role picture.

It is important, however, to estimate accurately the strength of the apparent trend toward equalitarianism. Contrary to popular belief, men are seemingly more willing than women to cross traditional sex barriers—or are finding it easier to do so. Although some women are engineers, they make up only 1 percent of the profession; only 3 percent of lawyers are women, 6 percent of doctors, 7 percent of chemists, 3 percent of dentists. The myth of women's inferiority to men continues to be bolstered by the lower salaries paid for the same work as men. The median annual wage for the full-time working woman in 1965 was $4,859 compared with $6,497 for men (Brody, 1968). The median annual salary for women college professors was almost $1500 less than the median for men (Hilton, 1965). Women averaged less than men in salaries paid for five out of six office jobs in a survey reported in 1962 (Wells, 1962).

The Civil Rights Act of 1964 casually included the word "sex" in the list of characteristics that were not to be used as grounds for discrimination in employment, and in a short time 40 percent of the claims of discrimination before the Equal Employment Opportunity Commission were on behalf of women. Yet a full year after the Civil Rights Bill was law, the Attorney General had failed to initiate action in a single case involving sex discrimination (Brody, 1968).

On the other hand, some signs of progress toward equality status can be discerned in post-1964 changes in the personnel policy of some companies. Maternity leave was given to pregnant employees; women were allowed to include husbands as dependents under group life or medical insurance policies; male-female retirement ages and male-female wages were equalized. Jobs formerly restricted to men were opened to women—jobs such as public utilities inspectors, warehouse inventory persons, and supervisors in factories. Concurrent with these actions, about 6 percent of the plants and 3 percent of the offices opened up certain jobs to men for the first time (*Report on Progress,* 1967).

A 1968 presidential directive to the Federal Civil Service Commission to provide equal employment opportunities for women in government, both in appointments and in promotions, has had some interesting effects. For the first time, volunteer services in civic and social projects, medical programs, Parent-Teacher Association projects, and other frequent recipients of women's unpaid labor will be given credit toward employment placement and salary determination (Young, 1968). This move tacitly recognizes the special disadvantages under which women have been operating in filling traditional female roles, and it offers means for converting previously unvalued experiences into equivalents of more directly vocation-directed experiences customarily open to men.

With the completion of childbearing, large numbers of women wish to return to school in their thirties to qualify for the jobs they will be free to take a few years hence. In response to this growing educational need of mature women, special programs have been developing and were reported for forty-four states and the District of Columbia by January 1968. These programs should help mitigate the disadvantage in vocational advancement women have been under if they chose to give priority to their traditional roles as wives and mothers (Wells, 1968).

Two fairly long-term trends are continuing to create conditions likely to encourage the entrance of still more women into the labor force. One is the shortage of labor that makes their contribution of pressing importance. This leads managements to offer concessions that will make possible the participation of mothers of young children who would otherwise not be free to leave their homes.

The other facilitator is the continuing revolution in the kitchen. The introduction of a variety of labor-saving devices reduces work and increases time available for use outside the home. In addition to decreasing the amount of time needed for activities that had formerly been labeled specifically female, the development of factory-prepared foods removes the need for any degree of specialization in previous training and puts food preparation into the category of unskilled labor that anyone, including children, can perform. This tends to reduce any ego-boosting value the activity might have, so that females are less tempted to claim it exclusively. For the same reason, males need not feel awkward because of lack of experience. Thus, the kitchen revolution has the effect of desexualizing the preparation of food.

Other domestic chores follow much the same pattern as they become mechanized. They are released from the traditional definitions as they are depersonalized. With an automatic dishwasher, neither woman nor man "does" the dishes—the machine does. So, too, are clothes consigned to the machine. With the removal of personal contact, the activity becomes one no longer defined by role expectations, but becomes psychologically available to either sex. Since men are by custom identified with machinery, the more domestic chores are committed to machines, the more they are masculinized.

Sexuality and Equalitarianism

A side effect of the blurring of sex-role specific behavior may be an intensification of the enjoyment of sexual relations. Rainwater (1966) has reported that the degree of gratification in sexual relations indicated by a sample of married couples he studied seems to be related to the degree of segregation that characterizes their conjugal roles. When these are jointly organized, sexual interest and enjoyment is highest. When these are highly segregated, sexual relations are least satisfying. With the blurring of rigidly defined demarcations between role-assigned conjugal activities, we might logically expect more conjoint activity, more mutuality in general, and more sexual satisfaction. It is noteworthy that the conjugal roles of middle-class husbands and wives are jointly organized to a higher degree than those of lower-class couples and their enjoyment of sexual relations is also higher. As more women go out to work and the middle-class pattern of conjoint organization spreads, a resultant improvement in intimate relations can be expected to follow. Instead of sundering married couples, as has been predicted, the wife's working may bring them closer together.

The key to the association between enjoyment of sex and the nature of sex-role implementation seems to be the fact that the wife's interest in sex is heavily dependent upon a sense of interpersonal closeness and gratification in her total relationship with her husband. Husbands in segregated relationships consistently overestimate the amount of satisfaction their wives find in sex, and show little concern for mutual gratification. Since segregated role relationships are characteristic of lower-class marriage (Komarovsky, 1962), it is not strange that the longer a lower-class couple is married, the less interest and enjoyment they find in sexual relations with each other (Rainwater, 1966).

One of the most significant changes in sex-role concepts has taken place in the area of female sexuality and sexual morality. Parelleling women's movement in the direction of equality with men in education and in the labor market, sentiment also developed for sexual equality for women. This encompassed two areas: women's sexual responsiveness and women's right to bestow their sexual favors. In reaction against the Victorian assumption that women had neither sexual needs nor sexual response came the current attitude that women could and should experience orgastic pleasure in the sex act. In contradiction to the previous acceptance of the "double standard" that permitted men access to sexual adventure outside the marriage state while denying it to women, contemporary opinion holds that women should have the same rights as men, either to abstain or to indulge, as they see fit. Those who do not condone premarital sexual experience condemn it for males as well as females. If it is accepted at all, the tendency is towards accepting it for woman as well as for men. In large cities, at any rate, the sex relations of mature unmarried women appear to be less and less matters of public concern. That this is also so on many college campuses is indicated by the decision on several campuses that college women may have access to contraceptives at the discretion of the college physician (Bernard, 1966).

This revolution in relation to female sexuality has inevitable impact on the style with which men are expected to fill their roles as lovers. Since wives are no longer required or expected to "submit" to their husbands in marital relations, it becomes incumbent on the husband to learn how to make intercourse sufficiently gratifying for his wife so that it does not have to be "imposed" on her. Similarly, with every woman persuaded that orgastic pleasure is her right—indeed, almost her duty—she is given justification for demanding that her husband develop skill as a lover. It is possible, also, that in seeking the sexual fulfillment she feels she has a right to, a woman can demand more than a man can respond to. Because women have briefer refractory periods, their orgastic capacities can be greater than men's. Vis-à-vis a female who wants to be sure she is experiencing her sexuality as fully as she is supposed to, a male's confidence in his own sexual powers can be undermined (Brenton, 1966). This can be a particularly uncomfortable situation for the American male because he grows up in a culture that neither acknowledges the need for nor arranges systematic channels for learning loverlike skills. A culture where the double standard was characteristic, and where males were expected to get premarital sexual experience with prostitutes who had no right to demand any kind of skill of their partners, is not a culture that is likely to have developed any accommodation to the new state of affairs.

Such accommodation may, however, be currently developing, at least in the upper middle class. There is little doubt that a generally permissive attitude toward premarital sex relations is developing among college youth. The greatest change in attitude seems to have come about in the liberal segments of the middle-class and upper-class white unmarried females. Although there are no statistics that indicate *more* premarital coital experience in college youth in the last two decades, there is evidence of a profound change of attitude toward such experience. What the deviant individual might have done thirty years ago, the conformist does today. Acceptance of sexual indulgence, however, is closely associated with affection and responsibility by both males and females. This transforms the sex act from one leading to egocentric pleasure to one that elaborates a total relationship and deeply involves the psychological interaction of both participants. For the male, this expectation makes the prostitute no longer a suitable sex partner.

For the female, it takes coital participation out of an exclusively marital context (Reiss, 1966).

Although it is asserted that statistics do not support the contention that premarital sex relations have become more frequent in the last twenty years, at least one study gives us pause. Dr. Sylvia Herz is cited by Goodman Ace (1968) as reporting an investigation of sex relations on three college campuses in the New York-New Jersey region that showed that 42 percent of the students questioned admitted having had relations "often"; 19 percent, "very often"; 31 percent, "a few times"; and only 8 percent, "never." A total of 92 percent of a college sample avowing sexual experiences raises questions of possible underestimation of premarital indulgence by other investigators.

It is true that the Herz data may not be characteristic of the country as a whole. Reiss (1966) warns us that sex standards are far from monolithic in a nation as complex as the United States. He points out that upper, middle, and lower social classes have different patterns of sexual permissiveness, and that each class contains groups that hold opposed positions on this issue. He says:

> If one took a sample of upper, middle and lower social classes, but limited it to only those who were generally conservative, then the lower social classes would fit the stereotyped view and would be the most permissive sexually. However, if one took a sample of all three classes but limited it to only those who were generally liberal, then the *upper* class would be the most permissive and the lower class the least permissive [p. 125].

Most recent findings indicate that premarital sexual permissiveness is being supported by those who are generally liberal. It is acknowledged that a liberal group setting is generally more susceptible to social change than a conservative one. That may be why the impetus for another new democratic surge in relation to sex-role tolerance is discernible on college campuses. This one has to do with the issue of homosexuality. As the current climate is receptive to demands for equality by females, it is equally encouraging to others who have been assigned the position of "low man" on the basis of their sexual preferences. Discriminated against in the past in relation to jobs, service in bars and restaurants, and the right to hold public meetings, as well as being liable to arrest for their sex practices, homosexuals are beginning to make a public stand for their rights. Increasingly they are taking their grievances to the courts, openly acknowledging their sexual identification and insisting on being judged by their public demeanor and skill qualifications rather than by their private sexual practices. Their stance received support when, in 1961, Illinois adopted a penal code that took private sexual acts between consenting adults out of the province of the law. They are receiving growing support from the heterosexual world, from heterosexual lawyers who volunteer to represent them, from Protestant clergymen who assert that, "The sex act is morally neutral." Supporting groups forming on college campuses are composed of heterosexuals as well as homosexuals, with the former lending their support much in the manner that liberal whites supported civil rights activities on behalf of nonwhites before the latter developed strength and activist leaders of their own (Alverson, 1968).

Continuity amid change

Persistence and Regression

In our effort to do justice to recent developments we may have overemphasized the changes that are visible. Much remains of the traditional, male-dominant role patterning. Most women are still exclusively homemakers. In the United States at least, they have failed to fulfill their bright and shining promise of the thirties. Instead, they seem to have regressed to an acceptance of their earlier, more limited domestic role, inspiring Betty Friedan's (1963) diatribe in *The Feminine Mystique* that makes an appeal for their reemergence. The dilemma of women lies not only in continued prejudice against them in the outer world but also in their continued acceptance of an inferior stereotype of themselves that is no longer either valid or even congruent with current conditions.

Acceptance for the self of a stereotype that implies inferiority and social undesirability is illustrated in a study reported by Paul Rosenkrantz and his coworkers (1968). On a questionnaire consisting of 122 bipolar items describing personal characteristics, 74 males and 80 female college students indicated what they thought typical adult males, adult females, and they themselves were like. Results showed more frequent high evaluation of stereotypically masculine than feminine characteristics by both sexes. The feminine characteristics, designated as such by the subjects, were judged to be less socially desirable. Yet the female subjects in their self-evaluations assigned to themselves the very characteristics they had judged to be less desirable but stereotypically feminine. Among the items designated as "feminine" and assimilated to the females' self-concepts were the following:

1. not at all resourceful
2. not at all intellectual
3. feels very inferior
4. very immature
5. not at all intelligent
6. not at all competent
7. not at all realistic
8. very subjective
9. very submissive
10. very easily influenced.

Males and females agreed closely on assigning the items to the masculine and the feminine stereotypes. The girls' incorporation of the undesirable stereotypic qualities into their self-concept is so manifestly disadvantageous that one wonders what they gained by it. It is understandable if they perceived the identification as having social advantages, which might be the case if they saw the socially less desirable qualities as desirable for themselves because these qualities were coveted by people they admired. If, for example, the girls believed they would gain acceptance by males if they showed the stereotypic inferior "feminine" qualities, their assimilation of those qualities might make sense. However, the accuracy of such an assumption is thrown into doubt by a series of studies by Steinmann and Fox. In the study most relevant to our concerns, the investigators interviewed 837 American women and 423 American men, seeking to find out whether male and female perceptions of the female role in the United States were congruent. The subjects were college students, professionals, businessmen, and businesswomen. The instrument used for this study was an *Inventory of Feminine Values.* Half the items delineated family-oriented values and half delineated self-achieving values. The women responded in terms of themselves, the ideal woman, and male ideas of the ideal women. The men responded in terms of their ideal woman.

Results indicated that the ideal attributed to males and their expressed ideal coincided in only nineteen out of the thirty-four items. The disagreement mainly developed out of the women's assumption that men would desire a completely subservient female, while the male subjects took a relatively liberal position opposed to obsequiousness. One surprising finding was that the men saw their ideal woman as rearing children to believe in the equality of the sexes. Other items not anticipated correctly by the female subjects were that the men thought a capable woman had the duty to be active, that the ideal woman would like to create something important, and that a wife's opinion is as important as a husband's opinion. At least half the men, however, also thought that marriage and children should be the most important aspects of a woman's life (Steinmann & Fox, 1966).

With the ambivalence of men from the most liberal social milieu, highly educated and upper-middle class, it is perhaps not surprising that the female college subjects of Rosenkrantz *et al.* (1968) should still be going by the old rules. Those might well have been the rules they perceived when they were growing up. Both the limitations of a child's eye view and the human tendency to assimilate the new to the old would tend to minimize perception of differences in departures from customary patterns. Some results from the writer's investigation of the development of sex-role concepts illustrate this point (Hartley, 1959–60 a). Boys and girls, eight and eleven years old, were asked to tell what men and women, respectively, needed to know and what they should be able to do. A completely conservative picture emerged despite the fact that half our subjects had working mothers. The children saw the woman as responsible for the care of the children and the home, the man as the breadwinner. Although male participation in domestic activities was mentioned, this was seen as "helping" the mother, with the implication that the major responsibility was hers. The mother's outside work was perceived as "helping" the father provide for the family. When the mothers who held jobs were interviewed (Hartley, 1959–1960 b), they described themselves as occupying the same roles their children saw for them—that of "helping" persons. Their husbands were still seen as the major and responsible breadwinners. The mothers considered their work an aspect of their nurturant function. It was not a substitute for family obligations, but an addition to the traditional roster of womanly duties.

It is not surprising that persistence of the old stereotypes becloud current realities. The mass media deliberately promote this situation. For example, the editors of *Harper's* Magazine (1962), in a foreword to the October 1962 issue said:

> . . . beneath the eye shadow, the black leopard, or the wig—the American woman today is not very different from her mother or grandmother. She is equally attached to the classic, feminine values—sexual attractiveness, motherly devotion, and the nurturing role in home and community affairs. *She is no* great figure in public life or the professions [p. 16; Italics ours].

Examination of any "woman's" magazine would reveal other blatant examples, frequently cleverly worded, of slanted writing persistently ridiculing the active and self-actualizing woman. There seems to be a persistent effort to stem the tide of change, to persuade girls and women that it is best for them to "stay in their place."

For many women and men no change has taken place. These people belong mainly to the blue collar group. As Komarovsky (1962) describes them, sex roles largely remain segregated and male dominant. It may be significant that these working-class couples are less satisfied with life in general than those of middle-class status.

Growing up feminine or masculine

Differential Emphases for the Sexes

It is not surprising that girls and women seem unprepared to utilize maximally current opportunities for self-realization. They have, after all, received very little relevant preparation. There is little in a girl's training to emphasize instrumental competence or achievement in mastery of the impersonal aspects of the environment. From infancy, small females are valued in terms of the attractiveness of their persons and the appropriateness of their interpersonal responses. They are directed toward the manipulation of persons as the means of obtaining gratification. Little is demanded of them in the way of competitive or autonomous achievement. The stress is not on proving one's prowess, but rather on avoiding the objectionable. Girls gain approval by not rocking the boat, by doing the rather undemanding things that are expected of them, and by accommodating themselves to the adult members of the family in which they are firmly ensconced. A girl need not be bright if she is docile and attractive. Brightness is often regarded as a hazard, and girls are made to feel they should disguise such unseemly tendencies.[3] This kind of treatment is likely to produce rather timid, unventuresome, unoriginal, conformist types. Obviously, such types are neither eager nor equipped to seize opportunities to strike off in new directions. This inference is substantiated by the small proportion of girls who graduate from college. In 1965, only 16 percent of female students continued to graduate from college (Women's Bureau, 1967). A 1955 study by the *Educational Testing Service* found that of the brightest high school graduates not going on to college, two-thirds were girls (Stice, *et al.,* 1956)—perhaps no longer so.

The training of the male of the species is quite different. Apparently a somewhat less mature organism at birth,[4] his more frequent and less rewarding demands for attention bring increasingly diminishing returns in contrast to the experience of girl infants whose needs are increasingly attended to.[5] Almost from birth, the boy has more problems to solve autonomously. In addition, he is required to limit his interests at a very early age to sex-appropriate objects and activities, while girls are permitted to amble their way to a similar status at a more gradual and natural pace (Hartley, 1959). The male is faced early with establishing a sex identity different from that of the most constantly present person in his life, his mother or his nurse. Moreover, the manner in which he is influenced to do this compels him constantly to solve problems. He is not told, "Do thus and so." Rather, he is challenged to discover what he should do by being told what he should *not* do, as in the most frequently employed negative sanction, "Don't be a sissy!" This manner of induction surrounds the early process of sex role formation with a degree of anxiety for the boy that is lacking in the girl's smoother experience. The girl does not have to change her primary sex-role identification, since her first one is the correct one for her. She is not required to limit her interests and activities abruptly before she is ready to do so of her own desire, because parents have no anxiety about her eventual sex-role attainment. Interest in "boyish" things is an acceptable and approved aspect of American girlhood (Hartley, 1964). Interest in "girlish" things is generally forbidden and anxiety-provoking in American boyhood.

Beyond early childhood, during the school years, the boy is constantly open to challenge to prove his masculinity. He must perform, adequately and publicly, a variety of physical feats that will have very little utility in most cases in adulthood. He is constantly under pressure to demonstrate mastery over the environment and, concomitantly, to suppress expression of emotions. "Don't be a sissy," is accompanied by, "Big boys don't cry." He gets little sympathy for his hurts; instead he hears demands that he hurt others in retaliation. There is little schooling in the softer virtues in the training of most boys.

Consistencies and Inconsistencies

In some ways the boy's training in sex-role behavior is consistent. He is early and steadily pushed into dependence on and competition with his peers. He is forced into autonomous problem solving and demonstrated achievement. To this extent, he is encouraged to develop characteristics that would stand him in good stead in an all-masculine world of work.

In other ways, the boy is not adequately socialized for adulthood. Many of the demands made on him are inconsistent with the requirements of adulthood. Intellectual performance is subordinated to physical prowess in childhood and adolescence; increasingly complex technology demands more and more intensive training in abstract concepts in adulthood. The values must be reversed. The boy is conditioned to live in an all masculine society, defining his own self-image by rejecting whatever smacks of femininity. In adulthood he will have to adjust to a heterosexual work world, perhaps even take orders from a female, a species he has been taught to despise as inferior. Finally, the emphasis on repression of emotions, the high value of stoicism, leaves the boy wholly unprepared for the emotional closeness and intimate personal interaction now more and more expected of a lover and a spouse.

The girl is no more fortunate. The progression of roles through which she must pass is no more congruent in succession than the boy's. In middle childhood she, too, is expected to develop physical skills. They are the coin with which regard is acquired in childhood. The boyish girl is the admired model. Suddenly, in adulthood, she must transform herself into the feminine, physically attractive, not too capable figure of nineteenth century fantasies. This requires a good deal of egocentric attention to her person. If she is successful, both her presence and her attention are removed from the home. Marriage, the objective of these efforts, plunges her into a new role for which she is most unprepared, that of the housewife. The skills of the housewife are less and less frequently taught in schools, and the adolescent's outside directedness effectively prevents much direct learning in the home.[6] The next role, motherhood, is one for which the girl is least well prepared. She must deny her egocentricity in order to become a self-giving being completely absorbed in the welfare of others. After a relatively short span of time granted her to develop these emotion-oriented skills, she is precipitated into a new situation as the children grow, a situation in which too great an absorption in children becomes an embarrassment. She is now told to look beyond the home for her self-fulfillment and is expected to come up with a repertoire of instrumental skills that will be valued in the marketplace.

In the last act, a final set of reversals is demanded of both men and women. In later maturity, retirement looms for them both. For the woman it is perhaps the lesser threat—a return to the home center, the insideness of living with which she had once before come to terms. For the man, a true reversal of a lifelong orientation is demanded. From being outside-directed by long training and performance, the man must somehow turn inside, into the home and into himself, for direction and sustenance for his terminal years.

It is not strange that the individuals who have been less conformist and who have somewhat deviated from the traditional sex-role values in their development seem to sustain the succession of inconsistent sex-role demands most successfully. It is the young woman who manages to develop an achievement orientation and the skills to satisfy it who can most smoothly take her place outside the home, in the competition of the marketplace, when her children no longer need all her time. It is the man who manages to develop personal interests apart from absorption in his breadwinner role who continues zestful living after retirement. Effective living at each stage seems to require individual and idiosyncratic emendations of the broad sex-role categories of training and activity society establishes.

Problems, hindrances, and some suggested solutions

Cultural Lag in Childrearing

Changes in social conditions always result in some dislocations and discomfort for some individuals. Behavior is likely to change to some extent in response to the immediate demand of altered circumstance, but old attitudes tend to linger on, to serve as impediments to both the speed and efficiency of transformations in custom. The effect of such impediments to changes in sex role functioning are different for men and for women.

As already indicated, the continuing attempt to inculcate into boys some of the outgrown qualities of the frontiersman and the primitive warrior do them a disservice for the more urban kind of life that will characterize most of their adulthood. These qualities, subsumed in the "stiff upper lip," "strong, silent," "big boys don't cry" stereotype of masculinity, prevent the development of sensitivity to or respect for emotions in others, inhibit ability to communicate or reveal inner states of feeling, and are responsible for alienation from the deepest wellsprings of motivation in the self. The methods used to coerce boys into this single socially approved pattern, regardless of whether it suits their individual gifts, bring in their wake anxiety and self-doubt, fear and rejection of the opposite sex, and alienation from the one person with whom identification is essential for comfort, the father (Hartley, 1959). Moreover, in the course of persuading its victims to accept its stringent and often painful demands, this system of rearing males implants compensatory expectations of superiority in ability and position, usually over females, which are becoming more and more unrealistic. When the adult male reared under this system finds that his experiences are not congruent with the responses he has been led to expect, and that his interpersonal skills are inadequate to the requirements of both his marital and his vocational situation, he is understandably unhappy (Hacker, 1957; Brenton, 1966).

In an era of swift technological change, a source of particular discomfort for the male in the obsolescent patriarchal model is its insistence on rigidly segregated role patterns and its specification of the role of breadwinner as the only acceptable validation of masculine worth. Technical developments, while offering new opportunities to many, also hold threats for the man whose skills do not keep up with them. Unfortunately, the men most likely to be threatened with loss of jobs by technological progress are those who cling most strongly to the patriarchal model—the less well educated blue-collar workers whose base for both vocational and personal validation is least flexible.

Compulsory retirement, as we have indicated earlier, is an aspect of modern industrial organization for which the traditional masculine values do not prepare the individual to function effectively. To the man who judges himself by his ability as a breadwinner and has concentrated exclusively on implementing this image of himself, retirement can be, and often is, little short of tragedy. The frequency of difficulty in adjusting to retirement is indicated by the swift growth of professional retirement counselors ("Corporate Baby Sitters," 1968).

Obviously, a broad-based and flexible view of what constitutes masculinity would stand both the prospective retiree and prospective retrainee in good stead. However, it is not enough that such a change in self-concept be arranged for the man. His wife must also endorse it. Unfortunately, the female view of male utility seems also to be confined to his role as worker and earner (Lopata, 1965). If women desire more freedom in choosing the bases of their own valuation, they must somehow learn to extend the same liberty to men.

The dimensions of feminine discomfort with the current scene are somewhat different from those of men. They also are finding that they were prepared for a world that does not exist. Asked what they consider their most important role, they unhesitatingly answer "motherhood" (Lopata, 1965). Yet, asked what changes motherhood brings to a woman, four out of five answers are in negatives: "It ties her down" (Hoffman, 1963). Little girls, observing adult women, perceive limitations and frustration in the female role (Hartley, 1961). Although research data indicate that women find vocational activities sources of great satisfaction (Hoffman, 1963), young girls are encouraged to think only up to the day of their wedding, ignoring for all serious thought and planning the thirty to forty years they will have available for self-fulfillment in work outside the family. Although official publications from the Women's Bureau declare repeatedly, "The entire world of work is open to women," school counselors and parents continue to diminish girls by discouraging intellectual effort. Colleges have disadvantageous quota systems, and graduate schools regard women with suspicion. Female applicants are discriminated against in the award of both fellowships and educational loans. To achieve "equality" a female still has to demonstrate that she is "more equal" on all fronts—ability, stability, and determination (Women's Bureau, 1960).

As an additional drag, a mother who works from choice frequently carries a load of socially fostered guilt (Hartley 1959–60b). Despite the fact that research has failed to establish any direct connection between a mother's working status and detriment to her children (Siegal, 1961), the attitude of society remains hostile and accusatory toward the working mother. Research data have indicated that a mother's working seems to have some very desirable effects on her children: daughters have more of the self-determination and spunk needed for modern living, take a less passive approach to the world outside the home (Blood, 1965), and assume a more positive attitude toward the woman's role (Hartley, 1961). Despite these findings, critics of the working mother retain their suspicious attitudes and continue to press for flaws in her family life, adding a burden of defensiveness to the unavoidable complexities of maintaining simultaneously several equally demanding roles. One result of this enforced defensiveness and guilt is that children perceive the whole work situation as one that is disliked and to be rejected by both men and women (Hartley, 1959–60a). How this type of perception during childhood influences attitudes toward work in adulthood deserves consideration.

Stereotypes and Social Structure

The battle for freedom from coercion in traditional sex-role patterns is far from won for males or for females. Stereotypes tend to be self-perpetuating. The patriarchal model is locked into the very structure of society. For example, the full-day work unit, developed when the husband was generally the sole breadwinner and the wife devoted herself completely to domestic affairs, has become institutionalized and so encysted in the rigidities of contracts and union agreements as well as custom as to be virtually unassailable in ordinary times. Combined with a lack of public childcare facilities, this situation effectually prevents a mother from competing with males on equal terms, from an economic as well as a skill point of view. It also prevents a father from being a full partner in his children's rearing while he maintains the customary role of breadwinner. Availability of part-time work at all skill levels, or access to adequate, affordable childcare facilities for all who want it would be minimal essentials before real equality in sex roles could be approached and before real choice for the individual would validly exist.

The expectation that the man of the house would be the breadwinner has resulted in the related valuation that a husband's career has primary priority and his wife's only secondary value. This has the effect of limiting a wife's geographical mobility and making it virtually impossible for her to follow opportunities in her professional field freely. In turn, this situation subjects the woman to vocational exploitation, since she cannot bring to bear the autonomous force of competition in her labor market. Even when a woman is as well prepared and effective as the men in her field, she cannot expect to advance as steadily as they if she also accepts maternity. Each time she leaves the labor force to give birth to a child or to raise a family she loses in competitive impact and in job seniority. All these disadvantages that a woman faces in vocational competition make it uneconomic in most families to give her career top priority over her husband's. Hence, even if the individuals involved held convictions supporting complete sex-role equality, the conditions of the work world are rigged so that the implementation of such convictions seem inexpedient.

Social Engineering for the Future

Full expression in the work situation of the traditional patriarchal expectations is proving no longer viable. When the employer expects to have complete priority in the life of the male employee, as occurs frequently with rising young executives in large firms, havoc often ensues in his private life (Barnett, 1967) . The mismatch between the traditional patriarchal assumptions under which big business operates and the current climate of expectation of interpersonal functioning between wives and husbands leads to insoluble marital conflicts. These, in turn, interfere with the efficiency of the man in his work role, the very item the company attitude was presumed to enhance. Situations of this kind are characteristic of transitional periods. Awareness of this probably influenced Ruth Useem's (1963) description of the course of sex roles in the near future when she said:

> The Sixties will bring conflicts, controversies and personal discomfiture; those who cling to traditional patterns of sex-related roles will find themselves in positions which bring fewer traditional rewards, and those who create new patterns and roles will enjoy only partial success. But, despite difficulties, the desexing of roles is going on and, indeed, must go on if our society is to meet the challenge of filling roles essential to our civilization [p. 7].

Individuals alone, however, cannot meet the challenges of new social needs without help from organized structural units of the community. If employment outside the home is to be a fully accepted and fully rewarding aspect of a woman's role, new and expanded community services will be necessary in relation to childcare, health, education, safety, recreation, counseling, and homemaker services. The concept of education as a continuing experience for both men and women will have to be implemented by training planned for and accessible to adults. Sophistication about childrearing and family relationships, based on knowledge of human development, is as necessary for the modern man as technological training may be for the modern woman, if both are to live comfortably and perform effectively in modern society. The quality of sex role development in the United States in the future will depend as much on social engineering as on individual attitude. The direction is clear, but the effectiveness in functioning and the cost in human happiness will depend on the speed with which relevant governmental bodies and existing organizations can be geared to recognize the new realities.

Notes

[1] Formerly, University of Hawaii. Part of the work involved in writing this chapter was supported by the Division of Human Development, Department of Home Economics and the Agricultural Experiment Station, College of Tropical Agriculture, University of Hawaii.

[2] Mace, D. Unpublished address presented at the Minister's Institute on Mental Health, Athens, Georgia, February 27, 1964.

[3] Neugarten, Bernice L. "Women's Changing Roles Through the Life Cycle." Paper presented at the Convention of the National Association of Women Deans and Counselors, Denver, Colorado, March, 1961.

[4] Bell, Richard. Chief, Child Research Branch, National Institute of Mental Health. Personal Communication.

[5] Moss, Howard. Child Research Branch, National Institute of Mental Health. Personal Communication.

[6] Lopata, Helena Znaniecki. "The Life Cycle of Social Role of Housewife." Paper presented at the Midwest Meetings of the American Sociological Association, Spring 1965.

References

Ace, Goodman. "Sex, A Drug on the Market." *Saturday Review,* 12 (January 6, 1968).

Alpenfels, Ethel J. "Women in the Professional World." In *American Women: The Changing Image,* B. B. Cassara, ed. Boston: Beacon Press, 1962, pp. 73–89.

Alverson, Charles. "U.S. Homosexuals Gain in Trying to Persuade Society to Accept Them." *Wall Street Journal,* 172 (July 17, 1968).

Banton, Michael P. *Roles: An Introduction to the Study of Social Relations.* London: Tavistock Press, 1965.

Barnett, John. "Growing Job Demands Shatter the Marriages of More Executives." *Wall Street Journal,* 1 (May 10, 1967).

Bernard, Jessie. "The Fourth Revolution." *Journal of Social Issues,* 22 (April 1966), 76–87.

Blood, Robert O. "Long-Range Causes and Consequences of the Employment of Married Women." *Journal of Marriage and the Family,* 28 (February 28, 1965), 43–47.

Brenton, Myron. *The American Male.* New York: Howard-McCann, 1966.

Brody, Jane E. "Sex and the College Girl." *Honolulu Star Bulletin,* B–2 (January 9, 1968).

"Corporate Baby Sisters." *Wall Street Journal,* 1 (June 11, 1968).

Degler, Carl H. "Revolution without Ideology: The Changing Place of Women in America." *Daedalus,* 92 (Spring 1964), 653–70.

Editorial. Harpers Magazine, 16 (October, 1962).

Friedan, Betty. *The Feminine Mystique.* New York: Norton, 1963.

Hacker, Helen M. "The New Burdens of Masculinity." *Marriage and Family Living,* 19 (August 1957), 227–33.

Hartley, Ruth E. "Sex-Role Pressures and the Socialization of the Male Child." *Psychological Reports,* 5 (1959), 457–68.

———. "Children's Concepts of Male and Female Roles." *Merrill-Palmer Quarterly of Behavior and Development,* 6 (1959–60), 83–91a.

———. "Some Implications of Current Changes in Sex Role Patterns." *Merrill-Palmer Quarterly of Behavior and Development,* 6 (1959–60), 153–64b.

———. "Current Patterns in Sex Roles; Children's Perspectives." *Journal of the National Association of Women Deans and Counselors,* 25 (1961), 3–13.

———. "A Developmental View of Female Sex-Role Definition and Identification." *Merrill-Palmer Quarterly of Behavior and Development,* 10 (1964), 3–16.

Hilton, Mary H. *1965 Handbook on Women Workers.* Washington, D.C.: U.S. Government Printing Office, 1965.

Hoffman, Lois W. "Parental Power Relations and the Division of Household Tasks." *Marriage and Family Living,* 22 (February 1960), 27–35.

———. "The Decision to Work." In *The Employed Mother in America,* F. Ivan Nye and Lois W. Hoffman, eds. Chicago: Rand McNally, 1963, pp. 18–39.

Komarovsky, Mirra. *Blue Collar Marriage.* New York: Random House, 1962.

Lopata, Helena Z. "The Secondary Features of a Primary Relationship." *Human Organization,* 24 (Summer 1965), 116–23.

Moore, Bernice M., and Wayne H. Holtzman. *Tomorrow's Parents.* University of Texas Press, 1966.

Nolan, Francena L. "Rural Employment and Husbands and Wives." In *The Employed Mother in America, op. cit.,* pp. 241–50.

Nye, F. Ivan, "Marital Interaction." In *The Employed Mother in America, op. cit.,* pp. 263–81.

Peterson, Esther. "Working Women." *Daedalus,* 92 (Spring 1964), 671–99.

Porter, Sylvia. "Your Money's Worth." *Honolulu Advertiser.* A–9 (June 16, 1967).

Rainwater, Lee. "Some Aspects of Lower Class Sexual Behavior." *Journal of Social Issues,* 22 (April 1966), 96–108.

Reiss, Ira L. "The Sexual Renaissance: A Summary and Analysis." *Journal of Social Issues,* 22 (April 1966), 123–37.

Report on Progress in 1966 on the Status of Women. Washington, D.C.: U.S. Government Printing Office, 1967.

Rosenkrantz, Paul, Susan Vogel, Helen Bee, Inge Broverman, and Donald Broverman. "Sex-Role Stereotypes and Self-Concepts in College Students." *Journal of Consulting Psychology,* 32, 3 (1968), 287–95.

Siegal, Alberta E., ed. *Research Issues Related to the Effects of Maternal Employment on Children.* University Park, Pa.: Social Science Research Center, Pennsylvania State University, 1961.

Sobol, Marion G. "Commitment to Work." In *The Employed Mother in America, op. cit.,* pp. 40–64.

Steinmann, Anne, and David J. Fox. "Male-Female Perceptions of the Female Role in the United States." *Journal of Psychology,* 64 (1966), 265–76.

Stice, Glen, William G. Mallenkopf, and Warren S. Toegerson. *Background Factors and College-Going Plans Among High Aptitude Public School Seniors.* Princeton, N.J.: Educational Testing Service, 1956.

Terlin, Rose. *Job Horizons for College Women in the 1960's.* Washington, D.C.: U.S. Government Printing Office, 1964.

Useem, Ruth H. "The College Woman of the Sixties." *Women's Education,* 2 (September 1963), 1–7.

Wells, Jean A. *Economic Indicators Relating to Equal Pay.* Washington, D.C.: U.S. Government Printing Office, 1962.

———. *College Women Seven Years After Graduation.* Washington, D.C.: U.S. Government Printing Office, 1966.

———. *Continued Education Programs and Services for Women.* U.S. Government Printing Office, 1968.

Wilkening, Eugene, and Lakohnu Bharadwaj. "Dimensions of Aspirations, Work Roles and Decision-Making of Farm Husbands and Wives in Wisconsin." *Journal of Marriage and the Family,* 29 (November 1967), 703–11.

Women's Bureau. *Today's Woman in Tomorrow's World.* Washington, D.C.: U.S. Government Printing Office, 1960.

———. *Counseling Girls Toward New Perspectives.* Washington, D.C.: U.S. Government Printing Office, 1966.

———. *Fact Sheet* (April 1967).

Young, J. "The Federal Spotlight." *Honolulu Advertiser,* C–8 (February 26, 1968).

7 MARRIAGE ROLES, AMERICAN STYLE

Robert C. Williamson

The transformation in marriage and family roles is among the revolutionary changes of the twentieth century. Probably no one living in colonial America or even in the Victorian world would comprehend the complexity of forces that have invaded the home. Most present-day participants in these changes are not themselves fully aware of the implications.

Marriage has emerged from an institution based on certain biological and economic functions sanctified by religious authority, to a relationship oriented to companionship and affectional needs (Ogburn and Nimkoff, 1955; Burgess, Locke, and Thomas, 1963). The structural and functional aspects of this far-reaching change are controversial, even to the authorities of the family. It may well be that there is the ". . . beginning of the relative stabilization of a *new* type of family structure, one in which the family is more specialized than before, but not in any general sense less important, because the society is dependent *more* exclusively on it for the performance of *certain* functions" (Parsons and Bales, 1955, pp. 9–10).

We may examine the factors accounting for this redefinition of marriage and family roles. For one, the scientific revolution of the seventeenth and eighteenth centuries made possible the industrial urban society of the nineteenth and twentieth centuries. With this bureaucratized capitalist order emerged occupational specialization and role segmentalization along with geographic and vertical mobility. These processes, in addition to a heavy increase in population particularly in urban centers, led to the reshaping of our social institutions. With sweeping changes in the economy and government, the remaining social institutions have shifted their functions, both internally and externally. As a consequence, the traditional functions of the family have been transformed: economic production and services have shifted to the large-scale factory, corporation, and other managerial units; socialization of the young has been transferred to the school; care of the aged and handicapped has been assumed by governmental facilities. Finally, ideological movements and the rise of science have secularized traditional values. As a result, patriarchal, monogamous, and home-centered marriages, as decreed by religious orthodoxy, are confined to a minority of present-day homes. Although marriage has become a voluntaristic relationship and the commitment to it can be altered or suspended, it is still almost a universal institution.

The marriage relationship itself has undergone a number of basic changes. Young people now enter marriage after an extended period of relatively free courtship often including sex experimentation, having had ample opportunity to test themselves in various ways. The dating and courtship process is accompanied by an overtone of romanticism, which has a long tradition in Western culture. But at present, romanticism is more likely to be colored by the influence of peer groups and the effect of the mass media.

Despite the opportunities for more complete affectional, emotional, and sexual involvement (or possibly because of this opportunity), marriage has become more popular and universal. The age at marriage has dropped ever lower—22.8 years for the man and 20.6 years for the woman in 1965. Moreover, at least 92 percent of the United States' population is married at some point in their lives. This strong attachment to marriage is not surprising in view of neo-Freudianism and related ideologies along with the emphasis on affectional maturity that marriage signifies. The economic prosperity of the postwar world is another factor that encourages early marriage. Also, even more than in the past, society attaches high status to marriage. Most people feel that the maximum realization of the self can be achieved only in marriage.

The rise of women from the condition of chattel property to the status of an independent agent with social, political, and economic rights has had enormous impact on the nature of marriage roles. Not least, women have almost equal access to the employment world. In 1966, more than one-third of the United States labor force, or 25 million people, were women. More than one-third of wives are employed, especially in the early and middle years of marriage, and in some instances during the period of childrearing. As with other basic social changes, a complex of factors is related to the new economic role of woman. Higher education and the acquisition of occupational skills, expansion and diversification of the job market, increased demand for higher levels of consumption, and the introduction of contraception and family planning are among the major factors contributing to women's new role.

The twentieth century is also identified with a gradually rising divorce rate. Approximately one marriage out of five is terminated in the United States, and a few Western European nations (Britain and Scandinavia) are not far behind this ratio. A myriad of causes, including the centrifugal forces of urban life, the lifting of religious taboos, and the economic independence of women, have been suggested. However, most important is the high standard we place on marital happiness. A marriage that is not satisfying to the two partners can be dissolved, although for various social and individual reasons many unhappy marriages remain intact, at least for the outside observer.

The Nature of Roles

Roles in our society are regarded as the dynamic aspect of status (Linton, 1936). The position or status of husband, for example, presupposes the husband role, which in turn involves various role dimensions. These role dimensions constitute a "role-set" (Merton, 1957), that is, a number of behaviors reciprocal to the role-set of the wife. Some role behaviors are explicitly prescribed by culture, others are unique to the individual.

Role expectancies and behaviors are determined by the socialization of the individual and the immediate situational need. Roles may be ideal or actual, general or specific, internalized or externalized. More than occasionally, the role one anticipates in marriage does not prove to be realistic. For instance, the wife may pattern her role behavior on the image of a kindly, dependent aunt with whom she grew up, only to find that her young husband does not have the nurturant strength of her uncle. Or the composite of "wife images" on the movie or TV screen is hardly appropriate to the roles thrust upon her once the honeymoon is over.

In addition, roles are manifest or latent, direct or indirect. Roles may be contrived, as with the husband who assumes a devoted posture to his wife in order to cover up his extramarital liaisons. Roles may be conscious or unconscious, deliberate or spontaneous.

Marital and family roles perform traditional or perhaps universal functions. In examining the Western nuclear family, Parsons has described economic and power functions as *instrumental* roles. On the other hand, the wife or mother has an *expressive* role that is primarily concerned with affection and personality growth. These functions are diametrically opposed, even though they may be combined in the same person (Parsons and Bales, 1955, pp. 151 ff). Indeed, both the mother and children fall into the expressive function, the mother role being at the latent level more akin to the child role. Corroboration for this functional system may be found in family institutions of other societies (Zelditch, 1955).

This theoretical distinction between the instrumental and expressive role has only limited relevance when applied to marital interaction. Sex differences in personality are markedly less conspicuous now than they were at the beginning of the century. And it may be anticipated that sex differences will diminish even further (Udry, 1966, Chapter 3). Marital roles, along with sex roles in general, have become sufficiently blurred to discourage the observer from assigning role dimensions to husbands and wives on a neat instrumental-expressive axis. Individual factors influence both role expectancies and role performances.

Subcultural factors are related to instrumental and expressive roles. For instance, in the black community, instrumental values have been stressed by most observers. Yet this bias may be a matter of definition. Even the absent father may be a special means of realizing the instrumental role: only by the father abandoning the home can the family qualify for public assistance in a number of states. Indeed, the expressive function may be critical for both parents as they attempt to explain to their children what it means to grow up in a white society (Billingsley, 1968, pp. 23–33).

Conflicts in the Feminine Role

Among the role conflicts in our culture is the ambiguity of the role expectancies of women. College women are especially ambivalent in regard to their role in a male-centered culture (Komarovsky, 1946). Their background of family relationships and their own expressive role does not equip them to assume an instrumental role in society (Komarovsky, 1953). In dating and courtship, the girl is often forced to defer to the male by "playing dumb" and generally portraying a passive, dependent role. She may resort to "self-scapegoating," acceptance of negative stereotypes, as a member of the "inferior sex" (Seward, 1956, p. 176). Research data indicates that her choice between a traditional role and one of independence results from the pattern acquired in her own family structure as opposed to the values she derives from her peer group (Seward, 1945). According to recent evidence, conflicts about the feminine role are becoming less intense for the woman, especially as she becomes integrated into the college social system (Kammeyer, 1964). Presumably, she accepts a compromise between traditional and modern approaches to personality traits conventionally regarded as feminine and reconciles herself to a professional career and homemaking.

Six possible alternatives confront the modern woman (Kirkpatrick, 1963, pp. 444–66): (1) The "career path," with its total devotion to a profession or business activity. Marriage, if it occurs at all, is incidental to involvement in the outside world. (2) "Marriage-maternity-homemaking" stands at the other end of the continuum and remains the most frequently chosen "career" for women. As many have reflected, the monotony and obscurity of this role are balanced by emotional rewards and a feeling of normality. (3) "Low-fertility-companion" became a not infrequently chosen model during the low birth-rate period of the 1920s and 1930s and still remains as a compromise between maternity and the social and economic reality of the couple, notably the desire to provide nurturance to her husband. In view of the present threat of overpopulation, the companion role may become again a popular or even an officially sponsored alternative. (4) "Low-fertility-marriage-plus-career" attempts to combine the best of two possible universes, but may produce frustration for the husband. (5) "Fertile-marriage-plus-partial-career" is of particular appeal to the college graduate since it strikes her as a more realistic means of meeting the two primary goals, as studies of college women show (Empey, 1955). (6) "Fertile-marriage-plus-full-career" can be the most rewarding choice but also produces the most conflict.

Whatever the conflicts posed by work outside the home, practically all women plan a period of employment after marriage, usually until the arrival of the first child. A smaller number of wives plan to resume their career when the children are well advanced in school, or at the postadolescent "launching stage" into the outside world. Employment has become increasingly attractive to middle- and upper middle-class wives in contrast to a half-century ago when only the lower income household sent wives in large numbers to the job market (Foote, 1961).

However, according to one observer, role conflicts among women have become more acute in the postwar period (Friedan, 1963). The popularity of larger families, the stress on neo-Freudian psychology, and the increase in organizational activities have driven women away from the employment world. Even though women have increased numerically in the professions, they have declined since World War II in proportion to the population.

Marriage roles as interaction

Personality and the Selection Process

It is commonly said that "like marries like." Indeed, Americans are not unique in marrying endogamously by race, religion, class, and educational level. Also, to some extent we select mates similar to ourselves in physical appearance (Kirkpatrick and Cotton, 1951), in intellectual ability (Nimkoff, 1947; Snyder, 1966), and possibly in attitudes (Richardson, 1939; Snyder, 1964). Personality traits also suggest a homogamous relationship. In a large-scale sample of engaged couples, fourteen of forty-two selected traits were significantly similar beyond chance (Burgess and Wallin, 1953, p. 208). In a previous study, a median correlation of .24 was found in personality traits between husband and wife (Kelly, 1940). A recent Canadian investigation reports positive correlation of husband-wife traits as based on the Guilford-Zimmerman Temperament Survey (Pickford, *et al.,* 1966 a). Dissimilarity in personality was related to marital maladjustment, and the rating of the husband's traits was more predictive of marital adjustment than those of the wife.

It is difficult to determine the degree of validity and reliability in paper and pencil tests of personality. In any instance, the evidence for trait similarity has not been overwhelming. Moreover, investigation has focused on middle class, well-educated samples.

The debate concerning homogamy as a factor in mate selection revolves about the relevancy of the ideal mate concept to mate selection. It appears that we select our marital partner in harmony with certain images based on cultural norms, parental and peer attitudes, and idealization of the person we have already chosen. At best, the images become general guidelines, but are discarded when we are at the threshold of engagement (Strauss, 1946). Strauss found that more than half of his sample consciously compared the actual with the ideal mate, but were willing to compromise on a number of questions.

According to the findings of a college sample, young people have definite patterns of preference and rejection, yet this selectivity is highly flexible (Williamson, 1965). Subcultural factors are probably the most fixed, with a good deal of fluctuation on the question of personality traits. Judging from a study of ninety engaged persons, one concludes that the ideal mate exists at most as a generalized goal (Udry, 1965). As Udry says, "Ideal mate images can therefore be seen as resultants—reflecting need structures, changing in response to changing interpersonal relationships, responding to experiences with particular people—rather than determinants of heterosexual selections" (*Ibid.,* p. 482). The drift away from the sharply differentiated sex roles of the last century is a factor in the vagueness of the ideal mate concept.

Although homogamy may operate in social characteristics, the ideal mate image, if it exists at all, arises from the need to fulfill oneself through an individual who represents deep-seated characteristics very different from one's own (Winch, 1958). This theory of *complementary needs* proposes that a primary motive of mate selection is the gratification of personality deficiencies as based on Murray's classification—abasement, achievement, approach, autonomy, deference, dominance, hostility, nurturance, recognition, status aspiration, status striving, succorance (1938). In other words, one realizes his ego-ideal in a partner who completes, or compensates, for his own deficiencies. With the use of case histories, interviews, and various projective tests in a sample of twenty-five married couples, seventeen were classified into four possibilities depending on the pattern of dominance-submissiveness and nurturance-receptivity.

	Husband—Nurturant Wife—Receptive	Husband—Receptive Wife—Nurturant
Husband—Dominant Wife—Submissive	Ibsenian (from *A Doll's House*)	Master-and-Servant-Girl
Husband—Submissive Wife—Dominant	Thurberian	Mother-Son

Source: Winch, 1963, p. 590.

This theory that the narcissistic person leans on the mate in an anaclitic fashion has been only partially confirmed by research. A study of college couples in courtship offered little support of complementary needs

(Bowerman and Day, 1956). Likewise, the use of the Edwards Personal Preference Schedule for young married couples found that mate selection was more likely to occur because of similarity rather than dissimilarity (Blazer, 1963). The need for homogamy was particularly critical on the part of the wives, presumably because of their greater involvement in the marriage. However, mate selection may be both homogamous and heterogamous, varying with the stage of the courtship process. Couples studied over several months of courtship demonstrated that subcultural factors (ethnicity, social class, etc.) predominate in the early phase, followed in the middle phase by consensus of values, with need complementarity occurring in the later stages of emotional commitment (Kerckhoff and Davis, 1962). "Filtering factors," as a process of trial-and-error selectivity, shift from the usual sociocultural homogamy at the beginning of courtship to the deeper personality needs as one approaches engagement and marriage. One study comparing stable with unstable married couples suggests that the theory of homogamy hardly offers a satisfactory explanation for successful mating. Rather, a combination of needs and roles specific to the situation is the key motivating factor. Needs may call for complementary behavior at one point and homogamous behavior at another point (Murstein, 1967).

The significance of complementary needs in marital roles hinges on the effect of unconscious needs on role behavior. Role theory proceeds on the assumption of a ". . . process of interaction and the development of mutually reinforcing values and interaction patterns, all at a conscious level" (Burchinal, 1964, p. 660). Yet, it is questionable whether roles can be completely dissociated from conscious processes, or that the gratification of complementary needs is unconscious. Since marital roles are in an almost constant process of reassessment and reenactment by the individual, they can represent neurotic needs, as we shall later see.

A married couple enters marriage in a euphoric state. With the glow of the honeymoon only slightly diminished, the partners assume a number of implicit and explicit roles. These roles have been somewhat structured by the courtship process but now proceed in new directions, whether in sex behavior, household tasks, in-law relationships, or community life. The time required for adjustment varies perceptibly for specific areas of marital adjustment. Only 52 percent of a large married sample were satisfied with their sex relations from the beginning, while 12 percent never adjusted to them. In the choice of friends, however, the respective percents were 76 and 8 (Landis, 1946).

The two partners are confronted with a number of role problems in which processes of adjustment are worked out over a period of months or years. The techniques of compromise arise from a repertory of trial and error, insight, and improvization. We shall now examine two areas of adjustment in the initial phases of marriage—sexual adjustment and relations with in-laws.

Sex Adjustments

Perhaps three-fourths of the young people entering marriage today have had premarital sex experience, in some instances only with their spouse-to-be. There is no absolutely conclusive evidence as to whether premarital coitus has a positive or negative influence on marital happiness (Burgess and Wallin, 1953, pp. 362 ff), however, in at least one study orgasm adequacy of the wife has been correlated with premarital initiation, especially if it was with her future husband (Terman, 1938, p. 387). One could argue that the women who accept sex relations before marriage are those who are most likely to enjoy sex after marriage, and consequently there is no known causal connection in the premarital experience itself.

For the initiated, and even more for those experiencing coitus for the first time, the introduction into sex roles in marriage can be accompanied by feelings of guilt and anxiety. For the woman, conditioning against sex expression during most of her life means that a number of inhibitions must be unlearned. Frigidity is less frequent than formerly, but the fear of pregnancy and the woman's relatively weaker sex drive still remain as deterrents to her sex enjoyment. Too, some women may use coitus as a means of rewarding or punishing the husband. Unconscious "penis envy" is another factor. The wife may regard marital sex as an occasion to counteract her years of experience as a member of a suppressed minority.

Likewise, many husbands unconsciously fear castration caused by the wife. In addition, latent homosexuality may lead to impotence. Also, the wife can become a mother substitute and the husband unconsciously fears an incestuous relationship. His sex conflicts may become more acute in later years of marriage since the male sex drive declines as the female drive appears to become stronger (Kinsey, *et al.* 1948, 1953).

Sexual attraction and avoidance in marriage can be very complex. Periods of considerable sexual involvement with the partner alternate with periods of distance and disinterest. Cases of individuals who feel great emotional intimacy with the spouse and yet suffer from impotence and frigidity abound in psychiatric literature. For still others, the only area of intimacy in marital interaction is sex (Dince, 1968).

Fortunately, a number of factors have strikingly increased sex adjustment. A less repressive atmosphere is gaining ground in the socialization process. The civil rights accorded women in this century is gradually extending to the area of sex enjoyment. Men have begun to recognize women's sensitivity to the atmosphere in which sex activity is pursued and have learned to use a more skillful approach. Popular and professional literature abounds in techniques appropriate to intercourse and to other marital roles. Not least in importance, the fear of pregnancy has been drastically reduced as a result of better contraceptive methods.

In-law Problems

Newly marrieds must make many decisions concerning the roles they are to assume regarding their in-laws. Slightly more than half of one sample complained of difficulties with the mother-in-law (Landis and Landis, 1958, pp. 405–6). In another study, 36 percent were unhappy with the mother-in-law and 20 percent with the sister-in-law. Only 25 percent had no apparent difficulties with in-laws (Duvall, 1954).

The causes of in-law problems are partly an outgrowth of the transition from the traditional extended family to the nuclear family. Because of the emotional involvement of the parent who "loses a child" he, or more likely she, feels abandoned. Intergenerational tensions are also a cause of the problem since differential rates of aging and varying ideologies develop out of the phase of the life cycle in which one finds oneself. Cultural differences —ethnic, religious, and social class—can provide another gulf between the parental home and the new ménage.

Personality needs are central in this conflict. The parent projects on the newly married son or daughter a kind of wish fulfillment and is sensitive to any inadequacies of the partner. For instance, the mother wishes the daughter to receive the attention she was denied by her own husband. She may unconsciously perceive the son-in-law as a love-object with all the ambivalence this relationship implies (Simpson, 1960, p. 204). The Oedipal tendency makes the daughter-in-law especially vulnerable to the jealousy of her love rival. In view of the "Electra complex," the father occasionally has certain conflicts about his son-in-law but, being involved in his occupational role, he is less likely to intervene than is the mother. It is primarily the wife who is torn between divided loyalties and must reconcile her marital roles with those of her family. The obligations she has with in-laws can in some instances help her to define her role in the new marriage.

In the last decade or two, in-law difficulties appear to be less conspicuous, as the decline in mother-in-law jokes testifies. Among the reasons is the institutionalization of the nuclear family, with an overwhelming majority of couples establishing neolocal residence. On the whole, physical mobility has reduced contact with kin. Since, over the last twenty years, people have been marrying and having children at younger ages than previously, there is a smaller age difference between parents and their marrying children that is resulting in less intergenerational conflict. The higher educational level of today's parents and young people, abetted by improvement in mass media, has made for more understanding of tension areas between the couple and their relatives. Both wives and mothers are more frequently employed or in voluntary associations, which reduces the intensity of the emotional entanglement of the two households. In-law problems may be no less severe, but at least the proportion of persons affected has declined.

Empathy, Identification, and Role-Taking

It would be difficult to imagine a successful marriage in which the two partners failed to identify with each other. Although consensus is not complete between spouses in respect to their partner's roles, some minimal awareness is necessary. A study of married and divorced couples revealed a greater discrepancy in the attitudes about husband and wife roles among the latter. On the other hand, age, education, and occupation were of relatively less significance (Jacobson, 1952).

The precise degree of empathy and identification essential in marriage may be argued. For instance, in a sampling of "happily married" couples and couples in the process of getting a divorce, there was no significant difference in the awareness of the effects of one's own behavior on one's spouse (Clements, 1967). However, in the early years, several interrelated mechanisms appear to be established that utilize identification and role-taking (Mowrer, 1955).

Identification. In marriage, the process of identifying with the other partner emerges from role decisions and the specific situations of marital interaction. These decisions may concern sex relations, whom to invite to a dinner party, how to console "mother" after refusing her offer of living room furniture, or whether or not the wife should return to her old job. The identification process becomes more delicate as the deeper values of one or both partners is affected. To what degree the two partners retain their individuality largely depends on mutual respect for each other's attitudes and values.

Differentiation of Marital Roles. More often than not, young people enter marriage with somewhat prestructured role expectancies about how the husband and wife should perform. Questions as to whether the wife should keep her own name after marriage, whether she should work, the number of children desired, or whether the husband should assist with housework, find the partners with definite opinions (Burgess and Wallin, 1953). The single most important determinant, at least for women, is the influence of the mother, as the writer's questionnaire among a young married and unmarried sample indicated (Williamson, 1963). Equal to importance of the mother for the male was the experience of courtship in which attitudes about marriage were crystallized. Also highly critical was the influence of the father and the effect of the mass media.

At the same time, in most marriages the delineation of marital roles is a dynamic, constantly developing process, however stabilized it may appear. The change of the husband's employment, the birth of a child, the arrival of a new neighbor, all condition the interplay of roles for a couple. However, marriages differ in the degree to which the partners have dynamic or relatively static role relationships (Mowrer, 1955).

Emulation. A partner may imitate what he regards as the more desirable traits in the other. This mechanism, Mowrer asserts, is especially frequent in marriages where a cultural or age discrepancy occurs, as in Shaw's *Pygmalion.* Not infrequently, emulation has an exploitive element when it becomes a means of gaining concessions.

Idealization. This mechanism is particularly visible in courtship when it is fused with romantic impulses and the traits of the loved one are glamorized. To some extent, the mechanism is dysfunctional since it gives the marriage a certain degree of unreality. As idealization persists in marriage, it may be a factor in rationalizing a marriage and continues as a means of assuring marital unity. According to Mowrer, idealization is functional when the idealized trait becomes a reality.

Enhancement. There is sometimes an attempt to transform a questionable trait of the spouse. For the wife who marries downward, the lower class husband is marshalled into a complex resocialization process by which he is to become acceptable to her suburban social group. At a broader level, rationalization, sublimation, and displacement sometimes operate in this process (Simpson, 1960, p. 201). Identification with the spouse means an attempt to understand his needs and interests. With our intricate social world and its multiple role obligations, enhancement can assume various directions.

Interhabituation. A fundamental aspect of marriage is the interlocking of habit systems. These shared activities range from doing the dishes and giving the perfunctory kiss as one drives off to work, to the intimacy of the bedroom. It is uncertain at what point routine can emerge as a deep psychological bond, but even the ritualized marriage of the middle and late years derives meaning from these habit continuities. Occasionally, the highly stabilized marriage is most vulnerable to an extramarital liaison—except that the habit systems are frequently stronger than the desire for change.

Perception and Consensus

In any interpersonal relationship, role behavior depends on the ability of the individual to perceive the needs of his other partner. It relies on communication resources to transmit the empathic relationship into meaningful symbols. If we assume the validity of these propositions, several questions arise about which research findings are not altogether consistent: To what degree do the partners perceive accurately their traits and needs, and those of the mate? How does this ability relate to marital satisfaction? What sex differences exist in these capacities and needs? How does perception relate to the other dimensions of marriage role behavior such as communication, consensus, and decision-making?

We can hypothesize that perceptual sensitivity is a general factor on the part of each spouse and is positively related to marital adjustment. In one investigation, the satisfactorily married, as compared to individuals less satisfied with their marriage, show "significantly greater agreement of perception in regard to self and the perception of self by spouse; in regard to self and the parent of the same sex; in regard to spouse and parent of the opposite sex; and in regard to the perception of one's ideal self and the perception of one's spouse" (Luckey, 1960, p. 54). Most pertinent to the psychoanalytical viewpoint is the congruence of perception between the spouse and the personality of the parent of the opposite sex. At least, Luckey's data support the theory that images of the ideal mate are derived from parental models. Of equal relevance is the finding that the perceptual images of the wife are more critical than the husband's (Luckey, 1961). The less satisfied wives perceived their husbands as quite different from their fathers. Although this study does not necessarily support the importance of perceptual acuity, it does underline the implications of the quality of the perceptual product.

It is impossible to separate perception from the problem of identification. A preliminary study found insight and empathy important in the "self-other" relationship (Dymond, 1948). However, empirical investigations have not entirely confirmed this thesis. In a comparison of a small married sample and a random nonmarried sample, the implications were that, ". . . understanding of the mate had no relationship to marital happiness, nor was understanding a function of the similarity between the selves or the partners" (Corsini, 1956). In fact, husbands and wives were no more similar in their self-perceptions than the men and women of the control sample. Yet, those couples who had similar self-perceptions were significantly more happy.

Probably the most consistent evidence concerning aspects of marital interaction relates to the role of the wife. Research in marital adjustment finds that the wife must make the greater adjustment in marriage (Burgess and Cottrell, 1939; Locke, 1951), and the perceptions of the wife are more critical than the husband's in determining the mutual satisfaction of role behaviors.

The differences in the way that the two sexes perceive marital roles can be a function of the amount of time married and the specific area of behavior. For instance, perceptivity may increase during the first two years of marriage; men become increasingly more concerned with the instrumental aspects of role, whereas women stress the affective or romantic aspects.

Consensus on the role obligations of each partner is relatively flexible. There is some question as to how precise roles are and about the degree of implicitness and vagueness found in role behaviors, as a laboratory study of contrived marital roles demonstrated (Kenkel and Hoffman, 1956).

In all probability, intellectual as well as personality factors influence the ability to perceive roles. A study of "conceptual complexity," or the ability to conceptualize in diverse directions, suggests that the person free of rigidity and dogmatization is happier in marriage (Crouse, Karlins and Schroder, 1968).

Perception cannot be detached from the personality needs of the two spouses. One study focused on the ability of the spouses to evaluate each other according to the efficiency of their interaction. With the use of several personality, intelligence, and motor tests, cooperativeness between the spouses was measured, and the subjects with "high need satisfaction" gave significantly more favorable ratings of their spouse's personality and of the latter's ability to carry on cooperative activity (Katz, *et al.,* 1963). The findings corroborated our basic thesis that it is the wife who plays the critical role—that is, the wife who gratifies the husband's personality needs has the happier relationship.

One may ask whether the presence of marital difficulties makes for perceptual sensitivity. Or does the person with personality problems have a more realistic basis for perception? One study reports that the husband or wife who retains a romantic attitude in marriage tends to see the mate as having favorable personality tendencies, whereas conflict only sharpens the dissimilarities (Preston, *et al.,* 1952).

The Role of Communication

There is an arbitrary distinction between perception and communication. Husbands and wives depend on a number of cues to understand each other's feelings and motives. However, in the dialogue that constitutes much of marital interaction, various barriers exist that complicate the already existing tension between the mates. For one thing, there are differences in the media and style of communication as fashioned by sex-role socialization (Mead, 1949, Chap. 15). Also, differing environmental influences and subcultures have conditioned the two people to perceive and communicate about events in different ways. A husband may cling to the image of a taciturn and dependent female that he perceived in his mother. Educational, class, religious, and regional differences, although waning in American society, can shape the texture of communication. Even though most marriages are endogamous, the sociocultural matching is not perfect. Also marriages within certain subcultures have a "built-in" conflict. "Blue-collar marriages" are especially marked by communication blockages: inadequate insights, a limited range of verbal symbols, and the sharper differentiation of sex roles this subculture represents are examples of these blockages (Komarovsky, 1962).

The tendency of the partners to use open versus closed (depending on the degree to which the communication is available to the spouse), verbal versus nonverbal media, or public versus private discourse, is relevant. The communication pattern assumes a variety of styles and a repertory of anticipated and direct responses. The structure of interpersonal responses becomes a framework for both altruistic and antagonistic dialogue (Anderson and Badgley, Buerkle, 1961; Brownfield, 1953). A perceptive wife may gather her husband's restlessness at an evening party by an implicit signal and, therefore, provide the appropriate cue in order to arrange a gracious exit. Also, gestures, facial expression, and tone of voice may communicate to the husband that the wife could be effectively rewarded by a dinner out. A certain degree of "masking" usually operates in courtship, and a facade of communicative niceties may persist into the marriage and even endure through decades of family ritual.

Generally, it is the wife who must be the more responsive to the husband's communication and empathic needs. However, communication is critical for both spouses, according to the responses of a sample of California young marrieds (Hobart and Klausner, 1959). In fact, communication seemed to be more critical than empathy in the area of marital adjustment. "Psychological empathy" or "insight into how the mate rates himself as a person" could be more predictive than "marital role empathy," that is, insight into each other's role. For role disagreements, empathy proved to be more meaningful than communication. In other words, communication can only be considered in the entire context of marital processes, and its significance varies with each marriage.

As Udry indicates, selective communication is the answer. Destructive messages do not add to the marriage. Instances of these communicative gaps occur, for example, when the husband continuously reminds his wife that she must be attractive to the wives of his business associates even when this is not harmonious with her interests, or when the wife badgers her husband with the complaint that he is not spending sufficient time at home. Communications are only effective if the receiver is capable of making a change in his behavior. As Udry (1966) comments:

> The development of a problem will usually lead a couple to considerable conversation in the problem area. The abandonment of discussion in this area when the problem is discovered to be insoluble and diversion of communication into other, more satisfying channels is probably a step toward solidarity of the marriage. These comments are to be construed as speculative at this time and are only meant to emphasize that it is fruitful control and direction of the communication process which distinguishes satisfying marriages, not the volume of the material communicated or the amount of time spent communicating it [p. 280].

Marriage roles, decision-making, and the power structure

The appropriate climate for decision-making in marriage varies in time and cultures. We have already mentioned the shift from patriarchal control to a more equalitarian regime, but there are always individual variations. Basically, three types of relationships exist: husband-dominant, wife-dominant, and equalitarian. The structure can also be characterized in Lewinian fashion as democratic, laissez-faire, and authoritarian. Also, variations appear during the life cycle. Wife-dominance is prevalent during the campus years, but when the wife leaves employment and assumes family responsibilities a husband-dominant pattern tends to appear. An initially democratic marriage may be restructured in the event of a crisis, as with the unemployment of the husband, the discovery of an infidelity in the partner, or the onset of a severe handicap in the child. Indeed, parenthood itself alters the marriage relationship and the previous division of labor (Le Masters, 1957).

Power relationships vary with the areas of decision. The husband determines the choice and location of his work, and the wife decides on the socialization practices of the child, the social calendar, or her entry into the job market. The Detroit Area Study pointed to certain variables that demonstrate the influence patterns of husband and wife dominance. Generally, age has favored the wife; higher social status and income, the husband (Blood and Wolfe, 1960; Heer, 1958). Women with strong affectional needs more frequently deferred to their husbands. The relative dominance of one spouse influenced his or her particular area of decision-making; the dominant spouse is most likely to handle the financial transactions of the family.

Subcultural factors also condition the power relations within the family. It has already been mentioned that working-class husbands are less concerned with decision-making than white-collar and professional husbands. Negro marriages, especially in the middle class, seem increasingly to resemble the white culture, but patriarchalism and matriarchalism occasionally survive in urban areas as remnants of their rural and feudalistic past (Bernard, 1966; Frazier, 1939). More often, the urban Negro family is matriarchal because of the absence of the male household head. Catholicism may be only slightly related to a husband-oriented pattern; in fact, in the Detroit study the Catholics were practically indistinguishable from non-Catholics (Blood and Wolfe, 1960, pp. 25–26). Yet another investigation found Catholic women to be more tradition- (or "other"-) oriented, whereas Protestant and especially Jewish women were more career- (or "self"-) oriented (Steinmann, 1963). Subcultural differences often depend on the type of sample used. Farm families are predominantly equalitarian in structure, with a small minority either husband- or wife-oriented (Wilkening and Morrison, 1963).

The decision of the wife to enter the employment market has variable effects on the power structure. The working wife tends to have a greater decision-making role, yet this situation is conditioned by age, education, and income level (Blood and Wolfe, 1960, pp. 46 ff; Heer, 1958). The wife's employment is probably attributable to indirect effects, for example, the ideology of male and female relationships and the power needs of the two individuals. The wife who espouses male dominance and is unhappy at the prospect of having to go to work may insist on more dominance herself, or she becomes more subservient in order to bolster his feeling of dominance (Hoffman, 1960). At least one study showed working wives to be more patriarchal in orientation than nonworking wives (Middleton and Putney, 1960). Certain variables may affect the power structure regardless of the employment of the wife: for one, the positive association between the number of children and the authority of the husband.

The wife's employment affects marital adjustment as well as the decision-making role. Conversely, it is impossible to dissociate the power relations connected with dual employment from the adjustment of the two spouses. Studies are not altogether consistent in their findings regarding this relationship; however, a class relationship does exist. The net adverse effect of employment on marital satisfaction is less visible in the middle than in the lower class (Nye, 1963). The positive—or negative—effects of the wife's employment is a resultant of underlying variables; her assessment of the marriage may improve with this escape from household chores.

Altruism, Egocentricity, and Role Dimensions

In respect to the power relations within marriage, a fundamental question concerns the possible media for integrating the husband's and wife's needs for decision-making. How do empathy and identification function in the communicative devices and decision-making? What role dimensions are involved in this interplay?

Altruism appears to be a factor in marital role behavior and adjustment. An investigation of altruism in an adjusted and maladjusted sample revealed that the husband and wife enter into various role-taking behaviors, which are relatively specific to given situations (Buerkle, *et al.*, 1961). The subjects' altruistic responses to the Yale Marital Interaction Inventory were interspersed with individual needs: "conflict of interest" affected role reciprocity. Altruism was correlated with marital satisfaction, but was subordinate to particular sex role needs. Role changes within marriage or the total life situation as well as value orientations influence the altruistic interpretation. Indeed, a replication of the study with a revised inventory comparing an adjusted and maladjusted sample did not support the altruistic thesis

(Levinger, 1965). The failure to find empirical support for altruism would not rule out the possibility that the two develop a complex repertory of communicative and decision-making devices.

Decision-making in marriage encompasses a number of role dimensions, more often implicit than explicit, possibly unstructured as much as structured. Certain questions are pertinent to the relation to roles, decision-making, and the adjustment process. To what degree does the husband or wife consider his role more or less unitary or a set of more or less discrete behaviors? Casual observation as well as empirical evidence lean toward the viewpoint that specific factors control role relationships, including decision-making. In a factor analysis of the responses of 210 couples to the Locke Marital Adjustment Scale, several clusters appeared: companionship, consensus, affectional intimacy, wife accommodation, and euphoria (Locke and Williamson, 1958).

In an attempt to delineate role expectations and enactments, Tharp (1963) had groups: external relations, internal instrumentality, division of responsibility, sexuality, and solidarity. There were various sex differences such as the surprising finding that the husband's sexual interest was more associated with intimacy than was the wife's. Differences between role expectations and role enactments pointed to the intricacy of the decision-making process in various shared duties, household duties, parenthood, and community relationships.

Sex differences in role expectations and enactments imply that marital interaction is a profound learning experience and one in which flexibility of behavior is an indispensable factor. Decision-making undergoes an almost continuous alternation of egocentricity and altruism. Like roles, these interactional patterns are both cultural and unique, conscious and unconscious, with manifest and latent roles coming into play. This reciprocal role behavior is well described by Udry (1966):

> As two people become emotionally involved, each tends to respond to the other in terms of how he thinks the other sees him. This process usually goes on without conscious recognition by the persons involved. In this way, a husband may see that his wife expects him to be more forceful and dominant in the family decision making and respond to this expectation by first behaving in a more dominant manner, and finally by incorporating a conception of his husband role into a self-concept which is closer to his wife's conception of his role. A wife may see that her husband expects her to be more active and aggressive in their sexual relationship, and respond to this perception by behaving more in accordance with it. She then redefines her self-conception in terms of how her husband sees her. The couple may actually never have been aware of the discrepancy in their original conceptions, and the conflict in role expectations is not "resolved" by "give and take" or any rational adjustment consideration of the couple; rather it is done by a process of responding to one another's role expectations [p. 293].

One can hardly escape the conclusion that instrumental and expressive roles are deeply interwoven. Today's generation accepts an integrated approach to the role dimensions of marriage, not least because the present young people report parental models oriented toward interchangeability of function (Lovejoy, 1961). The choice of role behaviors depends on the resources the individual can tap—economic, physical attractiveness, household skills—as well as the quality of one's socialization and the intermittent demands of day-to-day situations. The degree to which the process of role dynamics can be harmonized with the subcultures on one side and decision-making on the other needs further investigation.

Power and Bargaining

Marriage can be conceptualized as a kind of exchange. As in all exchanges, rewards and costs are balanced from the vantage point of both participants. In the exchange setting of love, courtship, and marriage, the principle of least interest applies: the individual with less emotional commitment has the greater bargaining power (Waller and Hill, 1951).

Various kinds of power can be utilized. To mention only two examples, there is "coercive power," as in the ability to apply punishment to the mate, and "expert power," to be tapped when we apply knowledge to manipulate the other party (Hallenbeck, 1966). We have already noted that status of the husband, the employment of the wife, the presence of children, and the stage of the life cycle can be used as power resources. These resources are mainly external, reflecting the socioeconomic situation of the two mates (Blood and Wolfe, 1960; Blood, 1963). However, there are internal resources in the context of exchange theory, namely the weighing of alternatives as to the feasibility of divorce, or "terminating the exchange relationship embodied in the present marriage and entering into other exchange relationships providing a greater return for resources contributed" (Heer, 1963). Even if one partner does not contemplate a severance, he must reckon with the possibility that the other spouse does. Whatever the status of the exchange theory, these considerations enter into affectional and decision-making roles.

Marital interaction can be analyzed as a bargaining process. Bernard presents the models of this often conflict-ridden relationship: (1) *Assimilative models* include resocialization (or "brainwashing"), in which one spouse may choose to isolate the other spouse. Defense mechanisms such as "explaining away" or rationalization are also examples of assimilative models. (2) *Threat removal* occurs when one rejects communications from one's partner and refuses to enter into role-playing. The variations of the use of power, conscious or unconscious, become techniques by which bargaining takes place.

Models of marital interaction as drawn from game theory, are of two basic types. Zero-sum models occur when one spouse gains precisely what the other loses, and "mixed motive" models represent a situation in which both parties may win and/or lose with minimal likelihood of loss (Bernard, 1964). In both instances the parties have conflicting goals with alternative behaviors available, and each outcome has a certain payoff or value to the participants. In other words, the strategies are comparable to a game or conflict, whether in the sportsfield or at war. Whereas in the zero-sum model the gains and losses of the two players are balanced or cancel out, in the mixed motive model one party can be victorious. One problem with game theory is the assumption that the two parties are primarily concerned with a "mutually incompatible issue" (Kimmel and Havens, 1966). The model contradicts the basic premise of the marriage relationship as one of mutual identification.

Bargaining and conflict are interwoven in marriage, especially in the use of strategies. Escalation of a conflict can develop and one or both parties may move from one strategy to another until the marriage itself becomes threatened. Not infrequently, marriage proceeds by means of threats, commitments, and renewal of manipulative strategies based on the conflicting interests of the two spouses.

The public announcement of the forthcoming marriage, the promise (or refusal) of sex relations, or even the attractiveness of the menu possibly enhance the wife's power; the economic security offered by the husband constitutes his weapon. Returning to mother or to the office job would be the wife's verbal or actual counterattack. The advent of children could work both ways, but more favorably toward the husband. Yet the wife's threat of divorce can be powerful too, especially in view of the husband's fear of losing the children.

In the mixed model the two sexes may mobilize their respective strategies in the context of instrumental and expressive roles. The conflict generally proceeds more unconsciously and implicitly than the game theorists indicate.

The life cycle and marital role conflict

Thus far, marriage roles have been analyzed with reference more to the potential of conflict than to conflict itself. Also, we may ask whether changes in the life cycle have an affect on marital interaction. Do the husband and wife move closer together or further apart in the years following their marriage? How do changes in roles—the reproduction, socialization, and career launching of a new generation—shape the quality of marital adjustment? What are the patterns of role conflicts in modern marriage?

Disenchantment

A certain degree of disillusionment takes place in the years following marriage. A decline in romanticism occurs even in the first months of marriage, as compared to the courtship and engagement period. Young married couples in stages of courtship, engagement, and marriage showed an increase in disagreement scores and a decline of romantic responses, especially the males (Hobart, 1958).

Disenchantment is particularly observable in the later years of marriage (Pineo, 1961). In an analysis of Burgess-Wallin subjects twenty years after their marriage, the responses showed: (1) a decrease in marital happiness; (2) reduction of intimacy—less frequent kissing, less reconciliation of disagreements, and an increase in feeling of isolation; (3) decrease in shared activities, including coitus. These changes were more evident for the men than for the women. Moreover, the decline in marital satisfaction was not accompanied by a similar loss of personal adjustment.

Corroboration of the Pineo study is found in an investigation of the perception of personality traits in the spouse (Luckey, 1966). The sample included individuals married from two to twenty-one years and revealed a decline in both the favorable traits perceived in the mate and the marital adjustment score. The longer the respondents were married, the less they saw their spouses as cooperative and affectionate.

Variations in marital attachments for persons of middle age are documented in a study of over 400 upper middle-class marriages (Cuber and Harnoff, 1965). Five types of marriages were identified: (1) "Conflict-habituated" marriage in which tension becomes an accepted way of life with intermittent arguments and brawls; (2) "Devitalized" marriage in which the partners are reduced to a habit system as compared to early romantic and sexual affiliation; (3) "Passive-congenial" marriage which is devitalized from the beginning; (4) "Vital" marriage in which affectional fixation in each other is central and continuous for both mates; and (5) "Total" marriage which has much in common with vital marriage except that the marriage is more multifaceted. Although the analysis of these marriages was more impressionistic than statistical, the first two types, "conflict-habituated" and "devitalized," constituted a large percentage of the sample, indicating that disillusionment in marriage is not infrequent. Moreover, the authors conclude that ". . . there are very few qualitatively good man-woman relationships in this age in this class" (Cuber and Harnoff, 1963, p. 144).

The disenchantment process is attributable to a number of factors such as changes in sex interest, monotony in living routines, desire for change in the traits of the mate, growing detachment from the home with the exodus of children to school and eventually to their own careers, differential rates of aging, and role changes within the life cycle.

Stages in the life cycle are a particularly relevant variable. The first years of marriage allow the partners to develop their own interests, including outside employment of the wife. With the birth of the first child, the wife shifts to a maternity career with a succession of roles until the "launching stage." In a sense, the couple returns to the first phase of marriage and may retreat to their own world or to friends, community, and recreational outlets. Often this interest in friends or in extended kinship is designed to compensate for the loss of their children (Sussman, 1955). The woman especially makes a major adjustment at this period because of her loss of the maternal role. This psychological adjustment is further complicated by physical symptoms connected with the menopause.

A related aspect of the disenchantment process is "disengagement." In the Kansas City study of "adult life," couples aged fifty to seventy years showed a constriction of their activities and an increase in self-involvement (Cumming, *et al.,* 1960). This disengagement was more marked for nonworking wives than for the working. In some instances this disengagement from professional, recreational, and community activities brings the two mates closer together. However, interest often focuses on the self, and health problems only intensify this preoccupation.

Although a number of individuals in the middle and later years find their marriage more rewarding than in the early period, the romantic decline and reduction of sex interest begins to lessen the intensity of the marriage.

Nature of Conflict

Marriage has been described as "a tragic state of tension" (Keyserling, 1926). As implied throughout the chapter, marital roles have the potential for conflict, especially for the wife. Marital frustration is more significant today because we demand so much of marriage and because of the diverse commitments of the individual and the competing stimuli in our social universe. In urban and suburban living, the individual is caught between occupational duties, an array of voluntary associations, the problem of transportation and commuting, and most emphatically for "room at the top" in a highly mobile society.

Marriage can run the gamut of possible conflicts. At the lowest level are the "tremendous trifles" (Baber, 1953), whether a budgetary matter or who will clean the car. Below this conscious verbiage may lie deeper feelings. On the other hand, conflicts can become major dislocations of the marriage when they involve central but inconsistent values of the two partners. Conflict sometimes becomes ritualized in an interplay in which the facial expression or tone of voice, or even silence, may communicate hostility (Naegele, 1951). Aggression may be expressed directly to the spouse or displaced to children or other "neutral" objects.

Conflict has a variety of "causes" and seldom is it possible to isolate a single factor. Some major varieties are: (1) Cultural conflict. This can occur when the two partners are from diverse backgrounds or are moved from one social level to another with differing behaviors, attitudes, or values. In a situation of rapid mobility, the husband who is moving up the educational and managerial ladder may find the wife with only one year of college no longer responsive to his demands. (2) Situational demands. Role conflict and strain are included in this category. These conflicts may vary between economic pressures arising from different conceptions of the priorities in the budget to the general inadequacy of the financial base of the marriage or family. The demands of children, professional and community obligations, and in-law involvement are other areas of frustration for one or both spouses. There are conflicting role demands, such as the wife acting as wife, homemaker, and employee, not to mention den mother and chauffeur. A recent study suggests that conflict in marriage revolves about fairly specific issues like the working wife, money matters, sharing household tasks, and even whether or not to go to church (Scanzoni, 1968). (3) Personality needs and deep-seated value orientations. Spouses may be brought into covert or overt conflict due to differing values. For example, women with highly romantic attitudes toward marriage are found later to have lower adjustment scores (Terman, 1938, p. 149). Choice of friends, direction of recreational outlets, and hedonistic versus "ultimate" goals underscore the opposing needs of marital partners. One recalls the man who expects his wife to be the "clinging vine" type, whereas she has a role image of independence.

Most severe conflict probably emerges from unconscious needs based on the early socialization experiences of the individual. The first years of marriage often represent considerable narcissistic impulses in the struggle to find oneself in marriage (Simpson, 1960, pp. 207–08). Parental fixations and homosexual fixations may be latent or manifest. The complex history and neurotic structure of sex conflicts are well documented (Eisenstein, 1956). Destructive impulses toward self or mate operate in diverse and subtle ways. These unconscious systems are more likely the "cause" of marital discord than are the external or superficial grounds expressed in the divorce court (Goode, 1956, p. 88).

Role Conflict and Its Resolution

As implied above, role conflicts become a major basis for the disillusionment and deterioration of marital adjustment. Roles in disequilibrium assume various forms. Role discrepancies exist at various levels. There are differences in cognitive goals, communication levels, and instrumental problems (Spiegel, 1960). Fundamentally, marriage maladjustment appears to be largely interactional in character as a study of 1004 marriages indicated (Mathews and Mihanovich, 1963). It is difficult to determine ultimately how much marital conflict involves the definition and enactment of roles. However, an intriguing approach to the resolution of conflict has been conceptualized through manipulation of roles (Spiegel, 1960). Attempts to re-equilibrate role discrepancies constitute a continuum from coercing, coaxing, masking, and other techniques, to more positive media such as postponing and role reversal, joking, exploring, compromising, and consolidation. Some of these operate in the trial and error process of marriage illuminated by insight; others are more likely to be under therapeutic guidance.

Conclusions

This introduction into marital role behavior has primarily revolved about the question of sex differences. A fundamental point has been made that the wife makes the major adjustment in marriage because of the cultural definition of sex roles. Western society is currently in a state of flux in regard to sex roles and especially the woman's role is not precisely defined.

Marriage results in a number of strains for the husband and wife. It is not clear to what degree this ambivalence results from defects in the selection process or how much emerges in the interaction process of marriage. The extent to which homogamy or complementary needs, or some combination, determines the choice of mate or develops during marriage is a matter for future study. We also need further investigation into the role and effect of several processes in marriage: empathy, perception, and communication. One problem of empirical research in this area is the inadequacy of many testing instruments, especially in the marriage adjustment scale.

Research findings have been somewhat more explicit regarding the allocation of roles, the division of labor, and the media of decision-making in marriage. But personality needs, subcultural variables, and the specific situation produce discrepancies between role expectations and role behaviors.

As a final aspect of marital roles we have introduced the problem of the denouement of marriage and the dynamics of marital conflict. As in other aspects of role behavior, these questions must be seen from a number of viewpoints, for instance, differential socialization, unconscious processes, changes in the life cycle, and the pressures of an urbanized, upward mobile society that is constantly in change.

References

Baber, Ray E. *Marriage and the Family*. New York: McGraw-Hill, 1953.

Bernard, Jessie. "The Adjustments of Married Mates." In *Handbook of Marriage and the Family,* Harold T. Christensen, ed. Chicago: Rand McNally, 1964, pp. 675–739.

———. *Marriage and Family Among Negroes*. Englewood Cliffs, New Jersey: Prentice-Hall, 1966.

Billingsley, Andrew. *Black Families in White America*. Englewood Cliffs, N.J.: Prentice-Hall, 1968.

Blazer, John A. "Complementary Needs and Marital Happiness." *Marriage and Family Living,* 25 (1963), 89–95.

Blood, Robert O., Jr. "The Measurement and Bases of Family Power: A Rejoinder." *Marriage and Family Living,* 25 (1963), 475–77.

——— and Donald M. Wolfe. *Husbands and Wives: The Dynamics of Married Living*. New York: Free Press, 1960.

Bowerman, Charles E., and Barbara R. Day. "A Test of the Theory of Complementary Needs as Applied to Couples During Courtship." *American Sociological Review,* 21 (1956), 602–05.

Brownfield, E. Dorothy. "Communication—Key to Dynamics of Family Interaction." *Marriage and Family Living,* 15 (1953), 316–19.

Burchinal, Lee G. "The Premarital Dyad and Love Involvement." In *Handbook of Marriage and the Family,* Harold T. Christensen, ed. Chicago: Rand McNally, 1964 pp. 623–74.

Buerkle, Jack V., Theodore R. Anderson, and Robin F. Badgley. "Altruism, Role Conflict, and Marital Adjustment: A Factor Analysis of Marital Interaction." *Marriage and Family Living,* 23 (1961), 20–26.

Burgess, Ernest W., and Leonard S. Cottrell, Jr. *Predicting Success or Failure in Marriage*. Englewood Cliffs, N.J.: Prentice-Hall, 1939.

Burgess, Ernest W., Harvey J. Locke, and Mary M. Thomas. *The Family from Institution to Companionship,* 3rd ed. New York: American Book, 1963.

Burgess, Ernest W., and Paul Wallin. *Engagement and Marriage*. Philadelphia: Lippincott, 1953.

Clements, William H. "Marital Interaction and Marital Stability: A Point of View and a Descriptive Comparison of Stable and Unstable Marriages." *Journal of Marriage and the Family,* 29 (1967), 697–702.

Corsini, Raymond J. "Understanding and Similarity in Marriage." *Journal of Abnormal and Social Psychology,* 52 (1956), 327–32.

Crouse, Bryant, Marvin Karlins, and Harold Schroder. "Conceptual Complexity and Marital Happiness." *Journal of Marriage and the Family,* 30 (1968), 643–46.

Cuber, John F., and Peggy B. Harnoff. *The Significant Americans: A Study of Sexual Behavior Among the Affluent*. New York: Appleton-Century, 1965.

Cumming, Elaine, Lois R. Dean, D. S. Newell, and Isabel McCaffrey. "Disengagement: A Tentative Theory of Aging." *Sociometry,* 23 (1960), 23–35.

Dince, Paul R. "General Considerations of Major Sexual Disturbances in Marriage." In *The Marriage Relationship: Psychoanalytic Perspectives,* Solomon Rosenbaum and Ian Alger, eds. New York: Basic Books, 1968, pp. 145–56.

Duvall, Evelyn M. *In-Laws: Pro and Con*. New York: Association Press, 1954.

Dymond, Rosalind F. "A Preliminary Investigation of the Relation of Insight and Empathy." *Journal of Consulting Psychology,* 12 (1948), 228–33.

Eisenstein, Victor W. *Neurotic Interaction in Marriage.* New York: Basic Books, 1956.

Empey, LaMar T. "Role Expectations of Young Women Regarding Marriage and a Career," *Marriage and Family Living,* 20 (1958), 152–55.

Foote, Nelson N. "New Roles for Men and Women." *Marriage and Family Living,* 23 (1961), 325–29.

Frazier, E. Franklin. *The Negro Family in the United States.* Chicago: University of Chicago Press, 1939.

Friedan, Betty. *The Feminine Mystique.* New York: Norton, 1963.

Goode, William J. *After Divorce.* New York: Free Press, 1956.

Hallenbeck, Phyllis N. "An Analysis of Power Dynamics in Marriage." *Journal of Marriage and the Family,* 28 (1966), 200–03.

Heer, David M. "Dominance and the Working Wife." *Social Forces,* 30 (1958), 341–47.

———. "Reply." *Marriage and the Family,* 25 (1963), 478.

Hobart, Charles W. "Disillusionment in Marriage, and Romanticism." *Marriage and Family Living,* 20 (1958), 156–62.

——— and William J. Klausner. "Some Social Interactional Correlates of Marital Role Disagreement, and Marital Adjustment." *Marriage and Family Living,* 21 (1959), 256–63.

Hoffman, Lois W. "Parental Power Relations and the Division of Household Tasks." *Marriage and Family Living,* 22 (1960), 27–35.

Jacobson, Alver H. "Conflict of Attitudes Toward the Roles of the Husband and Wife in Marriage." *American Sociological Review,* 17 (1952), 146–50.

Katz, Irwin, Judith Goldston, Melvin Cohen, and Solomon Stucker. "Need Satisfaction, Perception, and Cooperative Interactions in Married Couples." *Marriage and Family Living,* 25 (1963), 209–13.

Kammeyer, Kenneth. "The Feminine Role: An Analysis of Attitude Consistency." *Journal of Marriage and the Family,* 26 (1964), 295–305.

Kelly, E. Lowell. "Psychological Factors in Assortative Mating." *Psychological Bulletin,* 37 (1940), 473 (A).

Kenkel, William F. and Dean K. Hoffman. "Real and Conceived Roles in Family Decision Making." *Marriage and Family Living,* 18 (1956), 311–16.

Kerckhoff, Alan and Keith E. Davis. "Value Consensus and Need Complementarity in Mate Selection." *American Sociological Review,* 27 (1962), 295–303.

Keyserling, Count Herman. *Marriage.* New York: Harcourt, Brace and World, 1926.

Kimmel, Paul R., and John W. Havens. "Game Theory versus Mutual Identification: Two Criteria for Assessing Marital Relationships." *Journal of Marriage and the Family,* 28 (1966), 460–65.

Kinsey, Alfred C., Wardell B. Pomeroy, and Clyde E. Martin. *Behavior in the Human Male.* Philadelphia: W. B. Saunders, 1948.

——— and Paul H. Gebhard. *Sexual Behavior in the Human Female.* Philadelphia: W. B. Saunders, 1953.

Kirkpatrick, Clifford. *The Family as Process and Institution.* 2nd ed. New York: Ronald Press, 1963.

——— and John Cotton. "Physical Attractiveness, Age, and Marital Adjustment." *American Sociological Review,* 16 (1951), 81–86.

Komarovsky, Mirra. "Cultural Contradictions and Sex Roles." *American Journal of Sociology,* 52 (1946), 184–89.

———. *Women in the Modern World: Their Dilemmas.* Boston: Little Brown, 1953.

———. *Blue-Collar Marriage.* New York: Random House, 1962.

Landis, Judson T. "Length of Time Required to Achieve Adjustment in Marriage." *American Sociological Review,* 11 (1946), 666–77.

——— and Mary G. Landis. *Building a Successful Marriage.* Englewood Cliffs, N.J.: Prentice-Hall, 1958.

LeMasters, E. E. "Parenthood as Crisis." *Marriage and Family Living,* 19 (1957), 352–55.

Levinger, George. "Altruism in Marriage: A Test of the Buerkle-Badgley Battery." *Journal of Marriage and the Family,* 27 (1965), 32–33.

Linton, Ralph. *The Study of Man.* New York: Appleton-Century-Crofts, 1936.

Locke, Harvey J. *Predicting Adjustment in Marriage: A Comparison of a Divorced and a Happily Married Group.* New York: Holt, Rinehart and Winston, 1951.

——— and Robert C. Williamson. "Marital Adjustment: A Factor Analysis Study." *American Sociological Review,* 23 (1958), 562–69.

Lovejoy, Debi D. "College Student Conceptions of the Roles of the Husband and Wife in Decision-Making." *Family Life Coordinator,* 9 (1961), 43–46.

Luckey, Eleanore B. "Marital Satisfaction and Its Association with Congruence of Perception." *Marriage and Family Living,* 22 (1960), 49–54.

———. "Marital Interaction and the Perceptional Congruence of Self and Family Concepts." *Sociometry,* 24 (1951), 234–50.

———. "Number of Years Married as Related to Personality Perception and Marital Satisfaction." *Journal of Marriage and the Family,* 28 (1966), 44–48.

Mathews, Vincent D. and Clement S. Mihanovich. "New Orientations on Marital Maladjustment." *Marriage and Family Living,* 25 (1963), 300–4.

Mead, Margaret. *Male and Female.* New York: William Morrow, 1949.

Merton, Robert K. *Social Theory and Social Structure.* Rev. ed. New York: Free Press, 1957.

Middleton, Russell, and Snell Putney. "Dominance in Decisions in the Family: Race and Class Differences." *American Journal of Sociology,* 65 (1960), 605–09.

Mowrer, Harriet R., "Getting Along in Marriage." In *Family, Marriage and Parenthood,* Howard Becker and Reuben Hill, eds. 2nd ed. Boston: Heath, 1955, pp. 341–65.

Murray, Henry A., *et al. Explorations in Personality.* New York: Oxford, 1938.

Murstein, Bernard I., "Empirical Tests of Role, Complementary Needs, and Homogamy Theories of Marital Choice." *Journal of Marriage and the Family,* 29 (1967), 689–96.

Naegele, Kaspar D. "Some Problems in the Study of Hostility and Aggression in Middle-Class American Families." *Canadian Journal of Economics and Political Science,* 17 (1951), 65–75.

Nimkoff, Meyer F. *Marriage and the Family.* Boston: Houghton Mifflin, 1947, p. 422.

Nye, F. Ivan. "Marital Interaction." In *The Employed Mother in America,* F. Ivan Nye, Lois W. Hoffman, eds. Chicago: Rand McNally, 1963, pp. 263–81.

Ogburn, William F., and Meyer F. Nimkoff. *Technology and the Changing Family.* Boston: Houghton Mifflin, 1955.

Parsons, Talcott, and Robert F. Bales. *Family Socialization and Interaction Process.* New York: Free Press, 1955.

Pickford, John H., Edro I. Signori, and Henry Rempel. "Similar or Related Personality Traits as a Factor in Marital Happiness." *Journal of Marriage and the Family,* 28 (1966a), 190–92.

———. "The Intensity of Personality Traits in Relation to Marital Happiness." *Journal of Marriage and the Family,* 28 (1966b), 458–59.

Pineo, Peter C. "Disenchantment in the Later Years of Marriage." *Marriage and Family Living,* 23 (1961), 3–11.

Preston, Malcolm G., William L. Peltz, Emily H. Mudd, and Hazel B. Froscher. "Impressions of Personality as a Function of Marital Conflict." *Journal of Abnormal and Social Psychology,* 47 (1952), 326–36.

Richardson, Helen M. "Studies of Mental Resemblance between Husbands and Wives and between Friends." *Psychological Bulletin,* 36 (1939), 104–20.

Scanzoni, John. "A Social System Analysis of Dissolved and Existing Marriages." *Journal of Marriage and the Family,* 30 (1968), 452–61.

Seward, Georgene H. "Cultural Conflict and the Feminine Role: An Experimental Study." *Journal of Social Psychology,* 22 (1945), 177–94.

———. *Psychotherapy and Cultural Conflict.* New York: Ronald Press, 1956.

Simpson, George. *People in Families.* New York: Crowell, 1960.

Snyder, Eloise C. "Attitudes: A Study of Homogamy and Marital Selectivity." *Journal of Marriage and Family,* 26 (1964), 332–36.

———. "Marital Selectivity in Self-Adjustment, Social Adjustment, and I. Q." *Journal of Marriage and the Family,* 28 (1966), 188–89.

Spiegel, John P. "The Resolution of Role Conflict within the Family." In *A Modern Introduction to the Family,* Norman W. Bell and Ezra F. Vogel, eds. New York: Free Press, 1960, pp. 361–81.

Steinmann, Anne. "A Study of the Concept of the Feminine Role of 51 Middle-Class American Families." *Genetic Psychology Monographs,* 67 (1963), 275–352.

Strauss, Anselm. "The Influence of Parent Images upon Marital Choice." *American Sociological Review,* 11 (1946), 554–59.

Sussman, Marvin B. "Activity Patterns of Post-parental Couples and Their Relationship to Family Continuity." *Marriage and Family Living,* 17 (1955), 338–41.

Terman, Lewis M. *Psychological Factors in Marital Happiness.* New York: McGraw-Hill, 1938.

Tharp, Roland G. "Dimensions of Marriage Roles." *Marriage and Family Living,* 25 (1963), 389–401.

Udry, J. Richard. "The Influence of the Ideal Mate Image on Mate Selection and Mate Perception." *Journal of Marriage and the Family,* 27 (1965), 477–82.

———. *The Social Context of Marriage.* Philadelphia: Lippincott, 1966.

Waller, Willard, and Reuben Hill. *The Family: A Dynamic Interpretation.* Rev. ed. New York: Holt, Rinehart and Winston, 1951.

Wilkening, E. S., and Denton E. Morrison. "A Comparison of Husband and Wife Responses Concerning Who Makes Farm and Home Decisions." *Marriage and Family Living,* 25 (1963), 349–51.

Williamson, Robert C. "Values and Subcultures in Mate Selection." A paper presented at the American Sociological Association meetings, Los Angeles, August 29, 1963.

———. "Dating, Courtship and the 'Ideal Mate': Some Relevant Subcultural Variables." *Family Life Coordinator,* 14 (1965), 137–43.

Winch, Robert F. *Mate Selection: A Study of Complementary Needs.* New York: Harper and Row, 1958.

———. *The Modern Family.* Rev. ed. New York: Holt, Rinehart and Winston, 1963.

Zelditch, Morris, Jr. "Role Differentiation in the Nuclear Family: A Comparative Study." In *The Family, Socialization and Interaction Process,* Talcott Parsons and Robert F. Bales, eds. New York: Free Press, 1955, pp. 307–51.

8 ROLE THEMES IN LATIN AMERICA

Robert C. Williamson

In Latin America, as elsewhere, relations between the two sexes must be viewed in a historical context with particular reference to the vast social and institutional transformation in this century. As with other developing regions of the world, the society has been emerging from a colonial past and is attempting to compensate for a long period of stagnation. Latin America is highly advanced compared to the Near East, Asia, and Africa, yet economic, social, and political barriers have prevented the area from realizing its full potential. Consequently, there is a frantic if uneven attempt to move forward along a number of fronts. These range from industrial production and the fulfillment of consumer demands to the implementation of civil rights. Latin America is attempting to accomplish in a few decades the degree of progress achieved by most Western countries in a century.

Fundamentally, the fabric of Latin American society results from the Spanish culture brought by the *conquistadores* as influenced by indigenous elements in the sixteenth and seventeenth centuries. It must be remembered that Spain and Portugal were outside the mainstream of European society during this period. Neither Spain nor her colonies were more than marginally affected by the intellectual renaissance, the scientific revolution, and the French enlightenment. The Iberian peninsula met the rise of conflicting faiths and ideologies by instituting the Inquisition.

When independence finally came to the New World, the national societies were in no way prepared for establishing democratic institutions or equalitarian societies. The basic ethnic pattern set down by the colonial system was retained, a society stratified by color and economic status, creating a four-fold society of whites, mestizos, Indians, and Negroes. Although the developments of the last century and a half have reduced considerably the effect of race, the rigid social class system has been only slightly broken by the growth of a middle class and remains one in which European ancestry is highly correlated with social status.

It is imperative to point out that any generalizations are bound to oversimplify the cultural disparities found in Latin America. For one thing, the twenty (twenty-one if Puerto Rico is included) republics composing Latin

America can be grouped, not without some strain, into five different categories: (1) The largest population belongs to the mestizo countries stretching from Mexico to most of Central America, Colombia, and Venezuela. (2) Countries in which roughly half of the population or more is Indian, including Guatemala, Ecuador, Peru, Bolivia, and perhaps Paraguay. (3) Countries largely European in character, such as Argentina, Uruguay, Chile, and Costa Rica. (4) The Caribbean area, varying between Spanish and Negro in Cuba, mestizo in the Dominican Republic, and negroid with some French influence in Haiti. (5) Brazil with its varied ethnic composition developing within the context of a Portuguese and African heritage. This framework is only one of several possible approaches to classification. In addition, one must consider the overwhelming differences these countries represent in respect to economic development and the overplay of social and political forces. Even within a given country, the range of characteristics is nearly infinite. The difference between a resident of Mexico City, São Paulo, or Buenos Aires and a villager in the remote hinterland is no less than the difference between a New Yorker and a Mississippi delta farmer. Beyond the usual rural-urban differences there are regional variations based on historical development, as well as the isolation of an area which even today still resembles a frontier. Limited transportation, communication, education, and access to the national economy are all relevant to the development of social institutions like marriage and the family. Also, the style of life is strongly determined by class lines, inevitable in an area that only in the middle of the twentieth century is gradually breaking with its feudal past.

In addition to the variations of national and regional lines, there is the uneven rate of social and economic development. At least half of Latin America is involved in an economic transformation characterized by industrialization and urbanization. In fact, Latin American cities are growing at a faster rate than the population itself, which is increasing more rapidly than anywhere in the world. The growth of the cities is in large part attributable to the *campesino's* desire to migrate to the city for its economic, educational, and social service benefits. This urbanization process is a major fulcrum of social change, however disappointed a migrant may be after he arrives. For example, unemployment is inevitable when we consider that urbanization is occurring faster than industrialization. The innumerable squatter towns, known variously as *rancho, barriada, callampa, villa miseria,* and *favela* offer a bleak outlook, yet most migrants hope for a better life than what they knew as rural tenants or subsistence farmers. The break in kinship ties and a traditional pattern of life may be bewildering and is possibly more abrupt than the changes in the family that accompanied industrialization and urbanization in nineteenth century Europe and North America. The transition to a nuclear and often broken family underlines the changes in sex roles in Latin America over the last two or three generations.

The family structure

The family in Latin America developed out of the patriarchal pattern inherited from Spain. Moorish influence was among the ingredients of Spanish culture since most of the peninsula was under Arabic control from the tenth to the fourteenth century (the fall of the Caliph in Granada occurred in 1492 marking the end of the occupation). Too, as no European women accompanied the *conquistadores* to the New World, liaisons with Indian women permanently affected not only the physical aspects of miscegenation but the quality of relations between men and women. The superior status of the male, inherent in Spanish and Moorish cultures, became accentuated with the newly acquired status of conqueror. Even when the Spanish overseers of the colonies arrived in the Americas with their wives, the mold was already set and liaisons continued premaritally and extramaritally with Indians and in successive generations with *mestizos*. As one Mexican psychoanalyst points out, "Woman is devalued to the extent to which she is identified with the native: man is elevated in virtue of his identification with the conqueror and the master" (Ramirez, 1961, as cited in Andreski, 1966, p. 53).

Another influence in the development of the family institution was Catholicism. The Roman Catholic Church has supported the inherent rights of the male over his property, including his wife, a dictum held generally throughout the Western world until humanitarian conceptions altered women's status during the last century. Catholicism as expressed in the insulated world of Latin America has maintained patriarchalism until the present age. Although the Church did not sanction the more libertine and aggressive impulses of the male, the message to the women was that her mission in life was to bear children. Humility, patience, and forbearance were among the highest virtues she could emulate. Moreover, belief in the divine purity of womanhood and premarital hostility were underscored by the Virgin Mary cult. Men could ignore whatever ethical doctrine the Church might offer, but women became the repository of the virtuous life. In a culture in which, until well into this century, the power structure was divided between feudal landowners, the state apparatus (including the military), and the clergy, the Church hierarchy was hardly likely to contradict the male-oriented needs of its secular ruling class. Also intrinsic in the Church doctrine was the Paulist undertone of antifeminism that equated woman with a temptress.

Courtship and Mate Selection. In order to understand either family norms or sex roles, it is necessary to look at the process by which young people choose their marital partner. The courtship system and the marital patterns have much in common with Latin Europe, but the cult of virginity receives special emphasis. Particularly in the middle class, the chief consideration is the sanctity of the daughter who is a candidate in marriage. Consequently, in all but the most cosmopolitan cities, the girl must be chaperoned during any social occasion involving members of the opposite sex. In a more traditional center like Panama City, the daughter of conservative middle-class parents can not even go to the grocery store alone and is constantly exhorted to beware of the dangers of male intentions (Biesanz, 1955). Throughout Latin America it is preferable for young ladies to move on village and city streets only in the protective custody of groups. Generally, chaperonage is of more concern to the middle class than to the lower class; however, the latter still pays it lip service. In a questionnaire study in two Central American capitals, the lower more than the middle class affirmed the necessity for an older person (*una persona de respeto*) to accompany a teenage daughter to a social affair (Williamson, 1962 a). But these practices have virtually disappeared in the more advanced and European cities of Santiago, Buenos Aires, and Montevideo. In the less formal social atmosphere of Brazil, the practice of chaperonage is confined to the more conservative segments of the population. In Ibero-America, the bestiality of the male appears to be a principal fear. Despite American influence, in San Juan, Puerto Rico a couple is supervised even after engagement (Scheele, 1956, pp. 442–43). This surveillance may persist into marriage if a suspicious young husband is worried about the possibility of an extramarital adventure on the part of his wife.

The selection of a candidate for marriage is left largely to informal relationships, such as casual meetings, although in the middle class it is more ritualistic. Also, indigenous-oriented communities insist on formal procedures, often initiated by the family of the male suitor (Beals, 1966, p. 49). In the colonial and early national period, particularly in Brazil, the male was likely to choose a bride ten or fifteen years his junior (Freyre, 1946, p. 353). However, the average age at marriage varies from twenty-seven for men and twenty-four for women in Argentina to twenty-three and nineteen respectively in Guatemala (Mattelart, 1964, p. 461). Of course, in village and rural life, marriage takes place in the teens, and in indigenous communities it often takes place shortly after puberty.

Marriage Patterns. In Latin America, marriage generally assumes three possible forms: (1) a civil ceremony followed by a religious one, (2) a civil marriage only, (3) free or consensual union (*union libre*), an arrangement similar to our common-law marriage. The free union is most discordant with Western culture. In most countries the religious ceremony cannot be held without the civil one, with the exception of remote rural areas.

Even in a highly European country like Argentina, more than a third of the births, at least until a generation ago, were illegitimate (Taylor,

1948). At the same time, the consensual union in rural areas is a stable arrangement. Explanations of this are the shortage of clergy, the arbitrariness of bureaucratic processes, and the lack of sanctions against consensual unions. In the mestizo countries or those with large Indian populations, the consensual union is practically universal, although Indians have their own institutionalized practices. No stigma is attached, at least in the lower class. For instance, in San Salvador only 7 percent of the middle-class marriages were consensual as compared to 52 percent in the lower class. Comparable figures for San José, Costa Rica were 1 and 21 percent (Williamson, 1962 a).

Generally, the consensual union has little stability; the "husband" is free to abandon his family. In Tobatí, a Paraguayan provincial town, the number of fatherless homes nearly equalled the complete ones, and in the latter, one-third were not legally married (Service and Service, 1954, p. 152). In most cities, absence of the father also characterizes many lower-class homes.

In those countries where the free union constitutes a third or more of the marriages, the arrangement tends to be stable and is a socially approved institution not entirely different from conditions in the North American frontier of a century or two ago. On the other hand, the *union libre* in urban society varies considerably from those households enduring the greater part of a lifetime to those of a relatively casual arrangement. In the shantytowns and slums, a mother may have children of various unions. A principal variable in the broken family is the undependability of the male and his indifference to the needs of his family—alcoholism and other antisocial habits being contributory factors. A woman may be reluctant to assume a marriage in which she can be permanently responsible for the welfare of the husband. Divorce is legal in several countries but is a very difficult process.

The extramarital behavior of the Latin American male is well known. As the wife is supposed to remain virtuous, it is expected that the husband will have his *querida* (mistress) and *casa chica* (literally, "little house"), the particular pattern being determined by region and class along with individual preference. With some exceptions, the rural environment offers considerably less opportunity than the urban milieu, and a town does not have to be very large in order to provide concubinage. Perhaps 60 percent of Panamanian men are absent from the home for prolonged periods, a testimony to the extent of the *casa chica* habit (Biesanz, 1955, p. 289). In Aritama, a lowland Colombian community of 2,400 people, extramarital behavior is normal for both sexes, as is sexual experimentation before marriage (Reichel-Dolmatoff, 1961). On the other hand, in the Colombian highland town of Saucío, monogamy is highly revered (Fals Borda, 1955, p. 206).

The tendency of men, at least in Mexico, to distinguish between "love" and the "sexual act" is relevant (McGinn, 1966). The husband may continue his notion of the purity of the woman into marriage and therefore he may find it more desirable to satisfy his physical needs elsewhere. "Because one proof of masculinity in Mexico is the number of children a man can produce, it may be that men use their wives to produce children; satisfy their sexual desires more fully outside marriage; and reserve their love for their mothers" (Fals Borda, 1955, p. 308).

At the same time, economic pressures in both the lower and middle class, as well as individual conscious and unconscious needs, prevent the perfect realization of the male's sexual norms. Impotence and homosexuality can become problems and are likely related to the need to prove masculinity. Two husbands of the *Five Families* had psychogenic problems and their dominance in the household was consequently reduced (Lewis, 1959). Even in the less complex semi-rural setting, conformity to the male or female norm of marriage showed variations (Reichel-Dolmatoff, 1961, p. 49). In Aritama, homosexuality, incest, and intercourse with animals were tolerated, if as less than wholesome outlets for the sex drive.

Kinship Roles. Latin American family life is conjugal or nuclear but the impact of extended kinship is greater there than in the United States. The *parentela* in Brazil, consisting of aunts and uncles and a series of cousins, provides a medium of security (Wagley, 1964). In this extended kinship system the boy has the possibility of finding an adult male model in an uncle who may substitute for the absent father. However, with migration to the city and geographic mobility within the city, these relationships do not function with the predictability they enjoy in the rural scene.

An important aspect of family life is the ritual kinship or *compadrazgo* (in Portuguese, *compadresco*). Standing for a child at baptism are his *padrino* and *madrina* who are more often relatives, but may be neighbors or friends. These *padrinos* are charged with both the spiritual and material welfare of the child, including the bestowal of gifts and adoption of the child in the event of the parents' death. According to questionnaire responses, the middle class adheres more rigidly to this "ritual coparenthood" than does the lower class, and *padrinos* are more frequently selected among relatives than friends (Williamson, 1968b).

The godparents or *padrinos* of the children also become the *compadre* and *comadre* of the parents. Consequently, within the family circle a three-way relationship may be established: parents-children, parents-godparents, and children-godparents. A taboo on sexual relationships between the parents and *compadres* exists, except in communities where sex relations are fairly relaxed, as in Aritama.

The elaboration of *compadrazgo* varies by nation, region, or community. In some societies, as in Amazon Town, a different set of godparents may be selected according to the occasion, whether baptism, confirmation, or marriage (Wagley, 1953, p. 152). Also, status relationships condition these kinship relationships. In Guatemala, Indians select *ladinos* (mestizos, or acculturated Indians) to be *padrinos* for their children, but the reverse is rarely true. The *ladino* can then expect the Indian to do certain chores for him (Whetten, 1961, p. 252). If the Indian parent should die, the *ladino* would adopt the orphan as an *hijo de casa,* although his role in the household might be largely that of servant.

With these forms of ceremonial kinship, sex identifications can proceed along multiple lines. The significance of the biological father is not the same as in our own culture. Often in the urban environment the system breaks down and no adequate substitute relationship exists, especially in the lower class.

Machismo, sex roles, and the value complex

It is of course impossible to separate sex roles from the total cultural complex. This relationship is all the more complicated because of the heterogeneity of cultures and subcultures that Latin America represents. We have already pointed to the ethnic diversity—white, Indian, Negro, and the various admixtures—and to historic, geographic, social, and economic development that has been discussed by nation and region. One has only to compare Mexico with Chile, for example. The former has undergone a social revolution that has become institutionalized. Also Mexico is often somewhat defensive because of the influence of United States culture. On the other hand, Chile tends to be isolated and highly European, particularly French in character. Or one might compare life on the Peruvian and Bolivian *altiplano* with its Inca heritage to the tropical lowlands and its negroid and mestizo culture.

Despite the diversity of Latin America, there are several prevailing value orientations. According to one much cited source (Gillin, 1960), these value clusters include: (1) Personalism—the belief in the intrinsic uniqueness of each individual, the *dignidad de la persona.* (2) A sense of subordination or hierarchy—the superiority of men over women, who in turn have their redeeming worth in the maternal and the sacred. (3) The tendency to accept the emotional and mystical over the rational and scientific. (4) The verbal facade—language being more a vehicle for expressing pleasant and esthetic sentiments than a medium for portraying reality. Feelings can be more important than thought, and a businessman or the president of a nation may write poetry with no need for apology. (5) Fatalism—life decided by forces beyond the self, whether in the bull ring, the political arena, or love and courtship.

Inevitably, sex roles are influenced by these and related value orientations, for instance, the differences between the two sexes are more deeply entrenched in Latin America than elsewhere in Western culture. Especially revered is the notion that every man and woman has his or her own individuality, as long as certain mores are not violated. Moreover, for both men and women there often exists a rapid fluctuation between passivity and violence, humor and tragedy, kindness and cruelty. These contrasts are found in other Western cultures—analyses of Russian culture have pointed to this problem—but inconsistency is salient in Hispanic America. It is in this context that we should examine a central cluster of values, *machismo* and the man-woman relationship.

The Male Prerogative. Machismo refers to (a) preeminence of the male, (b) his supposedly stronger sexual interest as compared to that of the female, (c) his consequent freedom from taboos in expressing this need, and (d) his need to demonstrate masculinity. The male cannot be content to rest purely on his reputation; he must prove to the world and to himself by a succession of conquests—whether overcoming the resistance of a neighbor's wife, a succession of interludes with a mistress, or, in the lower class, contacts with a prostitute—that he is a man.

The *machismo* cult is entrenched in Latin American culture. It appears in Spain and Portugal but its richest development has been in the New World. The heritage of *macho* in Mexico derives in part from the *conquistador* and in part from the warrior cult of the Aztec (Paz, 1961). It contains the idea of violence and boisterousness. "To the Mexican there are only two possibilities in life: either he inflicts the actions by *chingar* (doing violence to others), or else he suffers them himself at the hands of others" (*Ibid.*, p. 78). As the man is the active agent, the female must be passive, *la chingada.*

To some degree, *machismo* was fashioned by the frontier. For instance, the Portuguese colonizers and *fazendeiros* in Brazil were known to have their first sex experiences at the age of twelve or thirteen, more often with a Negress than with a white or Indian, and any male who did not terminate his virginity by early- or mid-teens was looked upon as somewhat suspect (Freyre, 1946, pp. 279 ff). This tradition of sexual experimentation has remained throughout most of Latin America. In a variety of cultures from Puerto Rico and Mexico to the pampa of Argentina, the male is expected to demonstrate his interest in the opposite sex at an early age and to continue this behavior through his entire adulthood.

Deference to the male is reported almost universally in Latin America; only in the most Europeanized cultures like Chile and Uruguay does the woman enjoy near equal rights. A male who does not have extramarital relationships is subject to ridicule whether in Aritama or on Margarita Island off Venezuela (McCorkle, 1965, p. 77). The presence of children in a succession of households provides substantial proof of potency. Birth control is of dubious appeal to men who will be on a poverty level whether they have ten or two children. In a rural community, children are useful as farm labor. And in the city, it is assumed that after the age of ten or twelve a boy will be self-supporting in some self-appointed enterprise like selling lottery tickets, watching cars, or shining shoes. However, with the dissemination of family planning services, the number of children as proof of potency has been undergoing revision in certain cultures (Stycos, 1968).

The *machismo* system is supported both culturally and psychologically. In reference to the cult of the Argentine *gaucho,* nomadic life and a solitary existence have existed for more than a century. Women have been few in number, and recreational as well as economic activities have operated in a male world. Romantic love or, indeed, love of any variety was unknown (Mafud, 1967). Sexual activity was entirely a physical act. The free and independent Martín Fierro served not only as the prototype for the well-known poem of José Hernández but reflected the nature of frontier life well beyond the borders of Argentina. One may ask, however, why the *machismo* tradition did not become accepted in the United States—or perhaps to some extent it did. The cowboy did have some resemblance to the *gaucho,* but the Anglo-Saxon heritage did not provide a comparable mystique for the male. A combination of forces—Methodism and other variants of Protestantism, the rapid spread of industry and urbanization, and the rise of feminism—added to the differences that separated Hispanic traditions from the values of the Anglo-American complex.

More than the cultural system, the nature of socialization accounts for *machismo* survival even in urban centers of Latin America today. There is some evidence that *machismo* results from inner anxieties of the male. For one thing, he suffers from the absence of adequate male figures. In 32 percent of a sample of Mexican homes, for instance, the father is missing (Ramírez and Parres, 1957). In many instances the father disappears before the child is born. Consequently, the child grows up with a hostility toward the father because of the latter's rejection of the family. The mother becomes the only love object. The aura surrounding the mother, infused as it is culturally by the ideology of the Church, can also become a problem for the male. *Machismo* then is a kind of reaction formation against guilt and anxiety arising from excessive feminine identification.

This ambivalent relationship toward woman and the inability to focus love on one mate explains the duality between the virgin and the fallen woman. Love and sex are separated, and for many males the former is absent or poorly developed. Only the mother remains sufficiently asexual to the male, and he continues to regard her as sanctified. Also, loyalty to the mother and Catholicism are mutually supportive. The maternal comforting and nontaxing aspects of the religion are attractive to the male. On the other hand, it is possible, although not yet supported by research data, that masculine aspects of Catholicism (sermons, fasting, communion, and confession—all administered by a male priest) have failed to appeal to most Latin

American men because they are a reminder of the forbidding and rejecting father (McGinn, 1966).

The woman of course must bear the brunt of this male cult. She can obtain status only by producing children, preferably more males than females. In a Mexican sample, 35 percent of the women preferred male children and the remainder were indifferent to the sex of the child.

Necessarily, there is a masochistic aspect of the woman's role as 77 percent of the sample accepted the notion of being *abnegada,* or the role of self-denial. Freedom of movement on her part is considered suspicious, and social activity must be confined to relatives or a few neighbors or friends. In Tepoztlán, even contacts with woman neighbors were regarded as dangerous since they might indirectly lead to contact with a paramour (Lewis, 1949). Similarly, any genuine attempt on the part of the husband to satisfy her sexually might elicit extramarital desires.

In the urban middle class, this sharp cleavage between the sexes appears to be waning. Demonstration of potency is a matter of personal preference, although there is a good deal of self-doubt when one departs from the norm, if current novels are a valid guide. In the upper middle class, appearance at certain cocktail parties with a mistress can be a mark of social status; however, the arrival of an illegitimate child receives more censure than it would in a provincial town.

Unquestionably, *machismo* places strain on the male. There is a considerable body of data indicating that alcoholism and violence are major indices of personal and social disorganization in Latin America. It is not clear to what degree they arise from psychosexual conflicts. Yet, alcoholic indulgence by the male is probably both a cause and effect of a psychologically unstable relationship with the opposite sex. In San Salvador, a large portion of lower class males spend one-third to one-fourth of their income on alcohol (Marroquín, 1962, p. 175).

The escape into violence and alcohol as an attempt to bolster male superiority may result from inadequate role models, poor communication, and absence of satisfactory channels for expressing feeling. The presence of a punitive father—or possibly worse, the absence of any father—means that one grows up with a sense of mistrust and deception since one is not punished for wrong behavior or the inability to conform to a given standard, but for being found out (McGinn, 1966).

As mentioned above, language does not always have much relation to reality. Talk flows freely, but its reliability and validity are open to question. On the other hand, this duality may be an aid to the development of romantic sentiment in the middle class (romanticism barely exists in the lower class), but the foundations of any deep and stable husband-wife relationship could hardly be developed since conversation focuses on the externals of the marriage relationship.

Any self-righteousness about the inherent moral superiority of the

Anglo-American pattern may, however, be deceptive. There appears to be more permissiveness in Latin American cultures toward deviancy, both intellectual and behavioral. Particularly in Brazil, sexual aberration is tolerated (Harris, 1956, pp. 158–59) and masturbation and homosexuality are permitted if not excessive or flaunted publicly. Spanish America may be less tolerant about unconventional sex norms. Homosexuality contradicts, after all, the *machismo* norm, although legal duress is rare. The language is possibly an index. An analysis of various epithets indicates that Mexicans are less accepting of both the homosexual and the fallen woman, if more tolerant of the political deviant, than the North American (Klapp, 1964). Yet it is the author's impression after residence in several Latin American countries that sexual deviancy is far more tolerated than in the United States. Professionals who would lose their license or tenure in United States communities are permitted to continue in their post, even though their upward mobility may be hampered.

Again we must remind ourselves that the sexual code varies markedly by country, region, social class, style of living, and degree of religious participation. The influence of mass media, including European and especially American films, has brought the emerging urban middle sectors even more into the mainstream of Western culture. In view of the need for upward social mobility, the *casa chica* can be too expensive, and for the new literate urban audience a politician is likely to be more effective if he can solve social and economic problems than if he appeals to the cult of the *caudillo* (the traditional type of political leader) and its facade of *machismo*. University students, as well as the middle class in general, increasingly resemble their North American counterparts. The converse is also true if we consider the recent episodes of student power in the United States. Today a girl in Bogotá or São Paulo must still be circumspect, but she no longer has to be accompanied by an aunt or older sister when she meets her *novio* (boyfriend).

Sex Roles: a Literary Note. Literature is a mirror of the folkways and values of a culture. Latin American novels reflect the change from a traditional patriarchal pattern to one of resistance toward the oppressed role of women. Women authors have especially focused on this theme. Increasingly over the last century there was a romanticized approach to family life. In the postwar period, however, realism and mysticism have appeared. Sex experimentation and a more equalized relationship between men and women are portrayed in recent novels. In some treatments, sex behavior has been detached symbolically from other areas of experience. At the same time, drama, novels, and short stories have turned to problems of impotence, frigidity, and homosexuality. There is a tendency to consider both men and women as suffering from basically the same types of motivation and conflicts, but with individual variations (Valenzuela, 1963). This new existential literature in Latin America indicates that sex roles are arbitrary phenomena and the inner existence remains apart from surface events including the whole range of sex responses.

This literature for the most part portrays a small portion of the urban middle and upper classes, and it is in this public that the authors find their readership. The writers are as much affected by what happens in London, Paris, or New York as by events in Mexico City, Rio de Janeiro, or Santiago. Although there is an equally important literature on the lower class with its economic and psychological struggles, the new literature of and for the middle sectors reflects the twilight of *machismo* in the urbanized world of Latin America.

Socialization and sex roles

Certain features stand out in the socialization patterns of Latin America. As has been implied, children grow up in a culture with strict father authority, but the woman dominates the home to a greater extent than in our culture. Generally, socialization assumes a more severe tone. For instance, in a comparison of five nations, only Italy surpassed Mexico in terms of autocratic authority within the home; the United States, Britain, and Germany were more democratic (Elder, 1965).

Nearly all accounts of the Latin American home mention the tight control of the father over the household, despite his frequent absence from the home. The mother, too, insists on her children's respect. Often this authority is supported by the law or a civil code. For example, the pre-Castro Cuban Civil Code stipulated: "The father, or in lieu thereof, the mother, has dominion over their legitimate children: and the children have the obligation to obey them while they remain in their control and to pay them respect and reverence always" (Nelson, 1950, p. 178).

One aspect of the restrictive atmosphere in the household is the concept of *respeto* a child is to have toward his parents. It is a type of response appropriate to the individual's age, sex, and social and economic status, and to the proper category of the other person (Manners, 1956, p. 144). The child grows up knowing not only his own relationship toward the parent, but perceives the deference of the wife in regard to the husband—she is to "wash his father's feet, to prepare the foods he likes if that is possible, to obey his sexual demands, and so on" (*Ibid.*). Often the child is required to address the parents with deference. For instance, in Tobatí, the formal address of "señora" must preface communications to the mother, grandmother, or aunt (Service and Service, 1954, p. 219). Children may be required to use "Usted" (the formal "you" form) to their parents.

At the same time, urbanization has engendered less formality and strictness in the socialization process than there was a generation or two ago. There is much more child orientation and permissiveness on the part of both parents, and the father is becoming more involved in household tasks. In recent times, he can even be seen carrying an infant on a village street in Mexico (Lewis, 1964, p. 505).

Still other differences exist in the patterns of socialization between Latin America and other Western cultures. Family size is larger despite the high infant and child mortality rate. For instance, in 1950 the Brazilian family had an average of 5.1 members as compared to 4.3 in the United States (Smith, 1963, p. 474). Any average of family size must be modified by class and urban-rural variations as well as the large number of broken homes. Despite the tradition of strong family unity in the Latin family, the larger size presumably makes for more diffuse interaction. Older siblings must assume a supportive role since the mother is occupied with a younger child or infant, especially when the father is missing. Also, with a high rate of mortality and separation, adoptions are relatively frequent, particularly in child-oriented cultures like Brazil. In Amazon Town, mortality and sterility worked together to encourage adoptions, for there was a need for children to help in the chores.

Other types of substitute parenthood complicate socialization. In the middle and upper class, servants have the predominant socialization role. Since servants have little commitment as socializing agents, some observers explain the corruption of Latin Americans as attributable to this practice (Andreski, 1966, p. 50).

Parental Identification and Age Norms. We recall that the male is caught in a psychological dilemma because of the absent father and the appearance of new siblings who are rivals for his mother's love. Unquestionably, this process has something to do with *machismo,* yet factors such as differential training of the male and high deference toward the fathers are worth looking at. It is significant that American children and Mexican children view their fathers somewhat differently. Mexican fathers are generally seen as more strict and irritable, but also more understanding and persuading. The American father is perceived as more relaxed and less certain of himself (McGinn, Harburg, and Ginzberg, 1965). Although more or less one-fourth of the fathers are missing from the household (the precise number varies by nation, region, and class), the father who is present may offer discipline and occasionally compassion in the child's development. However, in one of the few empirical studies of the subject, Mexican fathers were less consistent in their parental role than American fathers (McGinn, 1966). Also, when they were affectionate, it was decidedly not on a basis of equality. More often they were detached, and the boy unable to resolve this relation with his father often blamed himself when he was punished by the father. Consequently, the boy often manipulated both parents in order to keep on the good side of them. The feeling of love for the parents may have been in part simulated (*Ibid.*).

The father, if in the home, is expected to protect the chastity of the daughter and to insure the acquisition of *machismo* by his son. No less, the mother plays a role in this endeavor as her main object in life becomes the rearing of children. Probably most mothers indulge their children to the maximum possible within the psychological and material resources of the family and according to her own needs and obligations. Punishment is largely verbal—42 percent of a Guadalajara middle-class sample reported "scolding" as their most common form of punishment, 48 percent pointed to various kinds of deprivation, and only 10 percent chose physical punishment (Villaseñor, 1964).

Almost from infancy, sex differences are observable in the inculcation of sex roles. Girls are urged to be more modest in their toilet habits from the time training begins (Fals Borda, 1955). Boys, as compared to girls, are not restrained in their temper tantrums (Mintz, 1956, pp. 384 ff). Also, Puerto Rican parents become cautious about what they say in front of their children after they reach the age of five years.

Sex differences are marked in still other ways. In Bolivia, the boy until the age of seven is dressed only in a short shirt, whereas the girl must be fully clothed (Leonard, 1952, p. 152). In all cultures, tasks are assigned differentially. Girls are rigorously taught household skills even at an early age, boys are initiated into essential manual skills, whether fishing in an Amazon village or learning to ride a horse on the Argentine *estancia*. Both sexes, however, may be assigned agricultural chores. The boy often works harder than the girl, but he soon learns that he has the privilege of being his own boss.

Parents are continually anxious about the possibility of obscure sex drives being awakened by contact with the other sex. Consequently, the two sexes are firmly separated from each other even during childhood play. A study of the responses of lower- and middle-class children in Rio showed an overwhelming mutual rejection of the opposite sex (Pearse, 1958). The parents' responses underscored the necessity for strict segregation until after puberty, at which time chaperonage becomes desirable. Sex education on the part of the parents was firmly rejected, but about half of them did approve of schools assuming that function. These attitudes were shared by both *favela* (slum) and middle-class residents, but the lower class was less anxious for their children to grow up too fast.

Separation of boys and girls in the classroom explains much of the philosophy underlying socialization. It is difficult to determine to what degree the lack of coeducation has served to underline *machismo* and the subservience of the female. Only in rural areas are schools consistently mixed. Many urban elementary schools still remain segregated, and almost no high school, private or public, is coeducational. Even though education has come increasingly under civilian surveillance and administration, the educational tenets of the Roman Catholic Church and its rationalization of separate sex roles remain.

The process of adjustment to the opposite sex is initiated in the late teens. Chaperonage is the norm in the middle class except for some casual and often secretive flirtations, rarely accompanied by sexual activity. The male often indulges himself with a prostitute or, occasionally, with a servant. These customs vary according to region, and with greater numbers entering higher education the sex mores are changing. Yet even university students date far less frequently than American young people (Williamson, 1962 b). It is probable that the Latin American pattern will continue to gravitate toward the courtship norms of the rest of the Western world, different as they may be between Europe and North America.

Sex Roles and Achievement Motivation. How do family patterns affect achievement motivation, especially in reference to the male personality? According to a study comparing Brazilians with North Americans, the Brazilian son is permitted a great deal of freedom but is not encouraged to develop genuine autonomy (Rosen, 1962). Responses to the TAT and other tests revealed the Brazilian boys to be deficient in self-reliance and sense of achievement. The boys perceived that their parents had inflated ideas about their own scholastic achievement and other endeavors; the self-effacing mother did little to arouse independence and achievement motivation. Although the mother has the primary affective relationship with her son and consequently acts as chief disciplinarian, she cannot really encourage the boy's success-striving lest it compete with the husband's need for status. It is a predicament similar to that of Italian as compared to Jewish mothers in New Haven. Of course, these findings must be viewed in the context of Brazil's more relaxed social atmosphere, limited ceilings for upward mobility, and indulgence toward the male in contrast to the self-control imposed on the daughter.

Likewise, tests in Brazil, Mexico, and Colombia (except for Antioquia) indicate that the family milieu is not too favorable for the creativity and achievement of either sex, if one judges by the standards of Northwestern Europe, the United States, or Japan (Hagen, 1962; McClelland, 1961).

Women in Latin American society

The demographic structure of the sexes differs for the developing and advanced areas of the world. Latin America represents a young population; the average age of its citizens is twenty whereas it is twenty-seven in the United States. The small number of adults means a high dependency ratio that places a severe burden on the economic and educational systems. Also, the sex ratio favors males. Latin America has a sex ratio of 99.5 as a whole compared to 97.8 for the United States. Women more than men are drawn into domestic service and clerical employment in the cityward migration, whereas men are primarily agricultural migrants. Finally, no area of the Western world has as large a portion of unmarried people, even if we allow for the consensual union. Yet, fertility ratios are markedly higher for Latin America.

As pointed out above, woman's position in the society is an ambivalent one. Womanhood is revered as a reflection of the Virgin Mary cult, and the woman is also the acknowledged manager of the household. Also, she is protected by a number of laws—compensation equal to that of men for a number of occupations and welfare benefits for childbirth (among other social security benefits). Yet, many of the rights exist only on paper because of the bureaucracy in the courts and the lack of facilities in the urban environment. Most important, women have entered a number of careers from medicine to diplomacy to literature, in addition to the more traditional roles of nursing and social work. Politically, too, women have been franchised over the last generation. Ecuador was the first to give this right, in 1929, Paraguay the last, in 1961. Along with various national organizations, the Inter-American Commission of Women is making visible strides in extending social and economic equality to women.

Despite all this upward mobility, woman's status in most of the region, and not only in the working class, is possibly lower than anywhere outside the Arab world. One critic takes issue even with that comparison (Andreski, 1966 p. 49):

> The Moslems lock up their women and treat them badly, but at least they normally maintain them, do not disclaim the responsibility for the children, and do not persecute wives or concubines whom they have discarded. . . . The Moslems, moreover, refrain from interfering with other men's women, whereas a compulsive Don Juan not only treats women as mere objects for satisfying his lust or vanity, but also continuously commits, or at least attempts to commit, acts of trespass backed by force or fraud.

Whatever the bias of these remarks, certainly the lower-class males, and to a lesser extent the middle- and upper-class males, hardly encourage female self-esteem. Women have little sense of belonging in the society since the majority are barred from many occupations, still receive differential pay, and suffer from a less than adequate self-image.

The legal status of the wife in Latin America has a nineteenth century note. In a number of countries, the law still permits the male to have nearly complete authority over the wife. She is regarded as something akin to property rights. For instance, the Civil Code of Brazil is not unique in stipulating that a husband can file suit against his wife in order to have the marriage annulled if there is evidence that the wife was not a virgin at marriage (Cruz, 1967). However, in a number of countries, some degree of equality was accorded women during the 1920s. Argentina ratified its Woman's Civil Rights Law in 1926, for example. The Mexican Revolution brought women complete equality with men, on paper at least, in its Constitution of 1917. Most far-reaching in civil equality is Uruguay.

The problem of identity. Except for the upper middle class in a few capitals, the sex roles of men and women assume a separateness alien to Northwestern Europe and the United States. As we have seen, differentiation begins in childhood in expected roles, in assigned tasks and play activities, in dress. In adolescence, norms become even more accentuated. For instance, involvement of boys in gangs (Madsen, 1964, p. 55) assumes a variety of forms, but without this type of socialization the epithet of *niño bonito* (pretty boy) might be evoked in some communities. On the other hand, the girl is protected from contact with males or any other stimuli that might lead her into a loss of purity and femininity. As with our culture, the lower class may be more permissive, but even here freedom of activity for the female is more the exception than the rule, and in no class is she likely to feel equality to the male. It is no wonder that in Aritama all women, regardless of age, wish they had been born a male (Reichel-Dolmatoff, 1961). "Sexual promiscuity, laziness, and aggressiveness are, in the opinion of women, his 'birthright' [*su privilegio de nacimiento*]. Men 'have the authority to do whatever they please' " (*Ibid.*, p. 185). A woman who does not cater to this superiority is likely to be reprimanded verbally, and sometimes violently.

A questionnaire study of Argentine, Peruvian, and United States women (Steinmann, 1964) showed that the Latin American respondents are more concerned with the necessity of adequate fulfillment of the domestic and motherhood role. ("The woman who works can't be as good a mother," "Women are more responsible for marriage success than are men," etc.) In terms of self-assertiveness one often hears remarks similar to, "I feel I can accept nothing from others," or, "I prefer to listen instead of talk." On the other hand, there seemed to be more conflict among the North American sample as to how career and domestic roles of women are to be reconciled. It may be that the Latin American, although unhappy about her role, accepts it with less conflict. In any case, responses showed more homogenity for the Peruvian and Argentine samples than for the North American.

Institutionalized as these sex roles are, there is a discrepancy between the ideal and the actual. A questionnaire study of Mexico City secondary-school students showed that those personality traits that girls sought in future husbands were not entirely what they were to find in marriage: faithfulness, education, fondness for children, temperance in the use of liquor, good health, chastity, and piety were at the top of the list (Hayner, 1966).

The traits demanded by the boys were somewhat more realistic, since girls will have to conform to the male image. Indeed, it may be asked whether women, possibly for their own internal self-protection, tend to have a distorted perception of the men's conduct. This type of rationalization was found in a university sample in Bogotá, in which 18 percent of the women as opposed to 1 percent of the men stated that their fathers attended mass more than once a week!

Despite some tendency on the part of the female to gloss over reality, most adult women had no illusions about the realities of the opposite sex, at least if one may judge by the responses from samples in four countries (Williamson, 1962a, 1968a, 1968b). Concerning the projective item, "What percent of marriages you know are really happy?", over half of the respondents considered a majority of their peers to be unhappy in their marriage. While the men explained this difficulty in terms of economics and other forces, the women had rather more revealing explanations such as, "The husband has too much liberty," "The woman doesn't have a chance," etc. Complaints were more strongly voiced in the lower than in the middle class, but both samples considered marriage institutions to be better in Europe and the United States. Likewise, in San Salvador, El Salvador sample, only 69 percent of the middle class and 48 percent of the lower class would marry the same person if they had their life to live over, as compared to 79 percent and 54 percent respectively in San José, Costa Rica. According to many lower-class women, the greatest mistake was getting "married," which for most meant the *union libre* (Williamson, 1962a).

All in all, it appears that the female role, marital and nonmarital, is less distant from the European norm than is the male's. The woman's role seems to be more frustrating, but at least it is less conflict-ridden than for American women since there is less pressure to combine the career and wife roles. On the other hand, the Latin American male is far more independent, less loyal, and possibly suffering from internal anxiety in view of his rejection from the father. Certainly, alcoholic addiction and interpersonal violence, for instance, are more of a problem with the male than the female. In this connection, the feminine role is perceived by both Buenos Aires and Chicago youth as being more stable than the masculine role (Havighurst, *et al.*, 1965, p. 41).

The attitudinal component. The present author examined background items and attitudes toward social change and a variety of values toward modernism and traditionalism in a Bogotá and Santiago sample. A number of sex differences were revealed. It was no surprise to find women more religious than men, as measured by their attitudes and attendance at mass. Besides having a more restricted social life and less exposure to mass media in both Bogotá and Santiago, women also were more conservative in their political ideology. Both national and international leaders who were conventionally democratic were more accepted by women, whereas men were more favorable to candidates to the right and especially those to the left. On the modernism-traditionalism scale, women were less change-oriented within each country, although Chilean women were more liberal than Bogotá men, hardly unexpected in view of the differing social climates of the two countries. Sex differences were the most acute for the responses in a village outside Bogotá.

In the Bogotá sample, men appeared generally more secure than women. They tended to rate themselves in disproportionate numbers as members of the middle class, and indeed enjoyed the privileges of middle class—a wider social life, more movie attendance, and greater freedom of movement. They rated themselves higher in several personality traits (industriousness, sociability, self-confidence, *and* moodiness), but lower in introversion and nervousness. More than in the Santiago sample, there was little doubt that for *bogotanos* it was a man's world.

Occupational roles. The Latin American woman has been undergoing a gradual emancipation. It may be that her position in employment has made more impressive strides than her position within the home, especially in the more change-oriented areas. These changes are relatively recent. It was not until 1886 that women were permitted to work in the post office in progressive São Paulo, and a woman was finally matriculated in the law school in 1898 (Morse, 1958, p. 215).

Many women have entered the professions and even administrative positions. Politics itself has been increasingly open to them, in both legislative and executive positions. San Juan in Puerto Rico is only one of several major cities to have a woman mayor.

Despite these advances, most employed women are engaged in manual work since the absent or unemployed husband is more characteristic of the social class in which there has been little acquisition of skills by either sex. Although the employment of women has gained all over the Western world, it is the wife working in the early years of childrearing that is unique for Latin America. Thousands of women are employed in cities as servants and in other menial jobs. With industrialization, they are employed for routine tasks in textile mills and other types of factory labor. They form a large contingent of the lower rungs of civil service. The tendency to employ a disproportionately large number of personnel in most offices and factories means very low wages but also spreads employment among a growing and marginally employed population. Because of family responsibilities, women less often than men engage in "moonlighting" (holding a second position).

Some women choose prostitution as a second occupation or, for that matter, as the primary occupation. Authorities estimate as high as 4 percent of the urban female population may be prostitutes. In Bogotá in 1961, estimates ran from 10,000 to 25,000 prostitutes in a city with a female population of perhaps 300,000 between the ages of eighteen and forty-five years. These estimates would vary in terms of one's definition of amateur and professional in this "occupation."

The twenty republics vary markedly in their legislation restricting the use of women in unhealthier types of employment. Maternity leaves are universally given but the specific provisions differ by country and region. For both sexes there are elaborate social security benefits, especially in regard to medical and other types of insurance, but the system from its beginning has not kept up with a growing population and much of the public is unfamiliar with its program. At any rate, benefits are more a palliative than a solution to the problem. Even if the worker knows of the facilities, the cost of transportation across town and the possible loss of pay for hours away from the job are deterrents. But, like advances in education and housing, social security will undoubtedly improve with economic growth, slow as these goals may be in realization.

Career choice has come under study as another aspect of the occupational role of women. The author found that careers most preferred by women in the National University of Columbia were, in declining order, teaching, science (social or natural), social work, nursing, law, and medicine. Over 95 percent, however, considered marriage their primary goal. In a study of São Paulo high school girls, career choice was linked to life values. Girls who were traditionalist in life values were inclined to select a homemaking role, the transitionalists chose teaching, and occupations like commerce and law were preferred by the modernists (Gouveia, 1965, 1966).

In the total industrial labor force, women have moved away from their traditional employment status. In São Paulo, women have been leaving industrial types of employment for commercial and secretarial positions in recent years (Blay, 1967). Also, more women are found at present throughout São Paulo industries and there is now less separation between the sexes than formerly. Whereas in less advanced centers the movement by women into industry is a major event, for industrially advanced São Paulo it is a mark of upward mobility for women to move from secondary types of employment to the tertiary or higher service categories.

To what degree can Latin America resolve the inferior status of women? This problem is another symptom of social and economic underdevelopment. The advance of women can only proceed with the other basic changes: accumulation of capital for industrial formation and related aspects of economic growth; expansion of the educational system for the acquisition of social, academic, and technical skills; increased urbanization along with a solution of housing and other facilities within the urban community; and slowing down of population growth by birth control and family planning. It is not to say that patriarchalism and the *machismo* cult will give way easily even with these changes, but we have the history of the effects of industrialization, urbanization, and other cultural changes in the Western world. In its most classical form, the traditional prerogative of the Latin male is largely confined to areas that have had little impact from an urban, scientific, and technological culture. There is also the implication of family planning, a movement now underway in traditionalistic and strongly Catholic Colombia, not to mention progress on this front in Puerto Rico and Chile. These cultural changes must be accompanied by shifts in the value system because industrialization is not guaranteed to change the relationship between the two sexes.

Also, the improvement in woman's status may also depend on the growth of stable democratic processes in Latin America, a development that has if anything lost ground during the 1960s. Countries like Chile and Uruguay remain firmly in the democratic camp, if imperiled by economic problems, and at the other extreme are those like Haiti and Paraguay that seem never to emerge from dictatorships. Most countries do, however, shift back and forth between democratic regimes and dictatorial or junta rule. These processes depend on the style of the times, economic and social forces, the degree of and quality of involvement with the United States and the cold war—in the mid 1960s, the hopeful prospects of the Alliance for Progress gave way to the Johnson preoccupation with Vietnam.

Despite the forebodings of demographic pressures, economic stagnation, and political traditionalism, it would seem unlikely that the liberation of women from a castelike inferiority can be postponed forever. As this chapter has implied, progress at least is visible in the urban middle class.

References

Andreski, Stanislav, *Parasitism and Subversion: The Case of Latin America*. New York: Pantheon, 1966.

Beals, Ralph L. *Community in Transition: Nayón, Ecuador*. Los Angeles: Latin American Center, University of California, 1966.

Biesanz, John, and Mavis Biesanz. *The People of Panama*. New York: Columbia University Press, 1955.

Blay, Eva Alterman. "A Participação de Mulher na Industria Paulistana" ("Participation of Women in São Paulo Industry"). *America Latina,* 10 (January–March 1967), 81–95.

Cruz, Levy. "Brazil." In *Women in the Modern World,* Raphael Patai, ed. New York: Free Press, 1967, pp. 209–26.

Elder, Glen H., Jr. "Role Relations, Sociocultural Environments, and Autocratic Family Ideology." *Sociometry,* 28 (June 1965), 173–96.

Fals Borda, Orlando. *Peasant Society in the Colombian Andes: A Sociological Study of Saucio*. Gainesville: University of Florida Press, 1955.

Freyre, Gilberto. *The Master and the Slaves: A Study in the Development of Brazilian Civilization*. New York: Knopf, 1946.

Gillin, John P. "Some Signposts for Policy." In Foreign Policy Association, *Social Change in Latin America Today*. New York: Random House, 1960.

Gouveia, Aparecida J. "Preference for Different Types of Secondary Schools Among Various Ethnic Groups in São Paulo, Brazil." *Sociology of Education,* 39 (Spring 1966), 155–66.

———. *Professoras de Amanha: Um Estudo de Escolha Ocupacional* (*Professors of Tomorrow: A Study of Occupational Choice*). Rio de Janeiro: Instituto Nacional de Estudos Pedagogicos, 1965.

Hagen, Everett E. *On the Theory of Social Change.* Homewood, Ill.: Dorsey Press, 1962.

Harris, Marvin. *Town and Country in Brazil.* New York: Columbia University Press, 1956.

Havighurst, Robert J., Maria Dubois, M. Csikszentmihalyi, and R. Doll. *A Cross-National Study of Buenos Aires and Chicago Adolescents.* New York: Karger, 1965.

Hayner, Norman S. *New Patterns in Old Mexico.* New Haven, Conn.: College & University Press, 1966.

Klapp, Orrin E. "Mexican Social Types." *American Journal of Sociology,* 69 (January 1964), 404–14.

Leonard, Olen E. *Bolivia: Land, People and Institutions.* Washington, D.C.: Scarecrow Press, 1952.

Lewis, Oscar. *Five Families: Mexican Case Studies in the Culture of Poverty.* New York: Basic Books, 1959.

———. "Husbands and Wives in a Mexican Village." *American Anthropologist,* 51 (1949), 602–10.

———. *Pedro Martínez: A Mexican Peasant and His Family.* New York: Random House, 1964.

Madsen, William. *The Mexican-Àmericans of South Texas.* New York: Holt, Rinehart and Winston, 1964.

Mafud, Julio. "El Machismo en la Argentina." *Mundo Nuevo,* 16 (October 1967), 72–78.

Manners, Robert A. "Tabara: Subcultures of a Tobacco and Mixed Crops Municipality." In *The People of Puerto Rico: A Study in Anthropology,* Julian H. Steward, ed. Urbana: University of Illinois Press, 1956, pp. 93–170.

Marroquín, Alejandro. *San Pedro Nonualco: Investigación Sociológica.* San Salvador: Editorial Universitario, 1962.

Mattelart, Armand. *Manual de Análisis Demográfico.* Santiago: Centro de Investigaciones Sociológicos, 1964.

McClelland, David C. *The Achieving Society.* Princeton, N.J.: Van Nostrand, 1961.

McCorkle, Thomas. *Fajardo's People.* Los Angeles: Latin America Center, University of California, 1965.

McGinn, Noel F. "Marriage and Family in Middle-Class Mexico." *Journal of Marriage and the Family,* 28 (August 1966), 305–13.

———, Ernest Harburg, and Gerald P. Ginsburg. "Dependency Relations with Parents and Affiliative Responses in Michigan and Guadalajara." *Sociometry,* 28 (September 1965), 304–21.

Mintz, Sidney W. "Cañamelar: The Subculture of a Rural Sugar Plantation Proletariat." In *The People of Puerto Rico: A Study in Anthropology,* Julian H. Steward, ed. Urbana: University of Illinois Press, 1956, pp. 314–407.

Morse, Richard M. *From Community to Metropolis: A Biography of São Paulo.* Gainesville: University of Florida Press, 1958.

Nelson, Lowry. *Rural Cuba.* Minneapolis: University of Minnesota Press, 1950.

Paz, Octavio. *The Labyrinth of Solitude: Life and Thought in Mexico,* Lysander Kemp, trans. New York: Grove Press, 1961.

Pearse, Andrew. "Sexual 'Nature' and Sex Roles: A Brazilian Sample." Unpublished paper, 1958.

Ramirez, Santiago. *El Mexicano: Su Dinámica Psicosocial.* Mexico, D. F.: Pax-Mexico, 1961.

Ramirez, Santiago, and Ramon Parres. "Some Dynamic Patterns in the Organization of the Mexican Family." *International Journal of Social Psychiatry,* 3 (Summer 1957), 18–21.

Reichel-Dolmatoff, Gerardo, and Alicia Reichel-Dolmatoff. *The People of Aritama.* Chicago: University of Chicago Press, 1961.

Rosen, Bernard C. "Achievement Socialization and Motivation in Brazil." *American Sociological Review,* 27 (October 1962), 612–24.

Scheele, Raymond L. "The Prominent Families of Puerto Rico." In *The People of Puerto Rico: A Study in Anthropology.* Julian H. Steward, ed. Urbana: University of Illinois Press, 1956, pp. 418–62.

Service, Elman R., and Helen S. Service. *Tobatí: Paraguayan Town.* Chicago: University of Chicago Press, 1954.

Smith, T. Lynn. *Brazil: People and Institutions.* Rev. ed. Baton Rouge: Louisiana State University Press, 1963.

Steinmann, Anne. "Specific Areas of Agreement and Conflict in Women's Self-Perception of Men's Ideal Woman in Argentina, Peru and the United States." *Proceedings* of the 9th Congress of the Inter-American Society of Psychology, 1964.

Stycos, J. Mayone. *Human Fertility in Latin America.* Ithaca, N.Y.: Cornell University Press, 1968.

Taylor, Carl C. *Rural Life in Argentina.* Baton Rouge: Louisiana State University Press, 1948.

Valenzuela, Victor M. "El Tema Sexual en la Novela Chilena." *La Voz* (May 1963), 14–16.

———. "The Existential Novel in Contemporary Latin America." Unpublished paper, 1968.

Villaseñor Martínez, Irene. "El Mexicano: La Familia." Unpublished dissertation, University of Guadalajara, 1964.

Wagley, Charles. *Amazon Town: A Study of Man in the Tropics.* New York: Macmillan, 1953.

———. *The People of Brazil.* New York: Columbia University Press, 1964.

Whetten, Nathan L. *Guatemala: Its Land and People.* New Haven: Yale University Press, 1961.

Williamson, Robert C. "Some Variables of Middle and Lower Class in Two Central American Cities." *Social Forces,* 42 (December 1962a), 195–207.

———. "El Estudiante Colombiano y Sus Actitudes" ("The Colombian Student and his Attitudes"). *Monografías Sociológicas,* Universidad Nacional de Colombia, 13 (1962b).

———. "Social Class, The Status Quo, and Modernism: Some Attitudes in a Santiago Sample." Unpublished study, 1968a.

———. "Social Class and Orientation to Change: Some Relevant Variables in a Bogotá Sample." *Social Forces,* 46 (March 1968b), 317–28.

9 THE SWEDISH MODEL

Rita Liljeström

The official Swedish model of equality between men and women may be interesting to examine against the background of the current division of roles in Sweden within education, family, labor market, and political participation.

Official attitudes today

In a government report presented by Sweden in 1968 to the United Nations' Economic and Social Council concerning the status of women in Sweden, certain fundamental principles are suggested as a basis for a long-range international program for greater equality between the sexes. The Official Report states in part:

> The goal for a long-range program of "women's rights" must be that every individual, regardless of sex, shall have the same practical opportunities not only for education and employment but also fundamentally the same responsibility for his or her own financial support as well as shared responsibility for child upbringing and housework. If complete equality is ever to be reached in respect to these rights and responsibilities, there must be a radical change in deeply-rooted traditions and attitudes, as much among women as among men, and active measures must be taken by society which will stimulate a change in the roles of both men and women. The idea that women must be financially supported by marriage must effectively be opposed—even in law, as it is a direct obstacle to woman's economic independence and her chances to compete on equal footing with men in the labor market. By the same token, the traditional duty of the man to support his wife must be supplanted by responsibility, shared with her, for the support of the children. This support of the children should also find expression, from the man's side, in a greater share in the care and upbringing of the children [p. 3].

Certain points are worth emphasizing in this report to the United Nations. In the first place, a rapid advancement of women in the field of employment, in labor unions, and in political organizations is not possible as long as men do not accept their share of work in the home that is their duty as husbands and fathers. Thus, in Sweden, the expression "men's emancipation" has been used to mean the right of the man to stay at home while the children are small, when it seems appropriate for the mother to be earning the money. During recent years, demands have been made for changes in the laws whereby the father, like the mother when she interrupts her job, should have the right to a certain amount of free time with pay while the children are small.

In the second place, married women without small children should be regarded in the same way as unmarried women as far as the labor market is concerned. The old idea that women have a greater responsibility for the work in the home should be opposed and women's vocational ambitions stimulated. The active period of motherhood now takes only a small part of a woman's adult life because people marry at an increasingly younger age, have fewer children than formerly, and concentrate the births of their children in their younger years. It would, however, be unreasonable to expect married women to devote themselves to remunerative work as much as men do and at the same time do all the work in the home. Married women with jobs today have less free time than any other group in society. The current division of roles does not give women the same opportunities for advancement as men because employers find the risk of women leaving the job after marriage so great that they cannot invest in their education and advancement. The character of marriage as an institution for financial support, according to Western tradition, has thus become an indirect obstacle to women's emancipation in modern industrial society.

In the third place, the care and upbringing of children have increasingly come to be regarded as work necessary to society which, in principle, should be paid in a way comparable to remunerative work. The parent who stays at home to take care of the children should have the same economic status as the parent who earns the money. This attitude has characterized the directives for studies now being done in the field of family policy in Sweden. Apart from the fundamental principle that social measures and reforms must be made for all citizens regardless of sex, the Swedish government recognizes the necessity to make special provisions for women under *present* conditions.

The special reforms for women must, however, be set up in such a way that they stimulate *the integration of women in all areas of society.* This goal must be absolutely clear. Otherwise, there is danger that through special activities for women the traditional division of labor may become even further established, making it more difficult to bring about a practical equality between the sexes in the long run. Another complication in dividing the work of society according to sex is that people easily believe that a general reform policy is made to satisfy the needs of the male population, whereas problems concerning women must be solved by special arrangements or amendments. At the same time as special steps are taken to give women an equal position with men, women must be persuaded to enter areas traditionally regarded as masculine.

Women, as well as men, have an obligation to be active in labor unions and politics and to share the economic responsibility for the support of the children. They should not automatically be able to win social status and privileges through their husbands' contributions to society. On the contrary, women must be made aware of their personal responsibility as citizens. They must be activated to use their vote and their opportunities to be elected to posts of political responsibility. Moreover, women should feel responsible for putting to use the capital that society has invested in their education. It is, indeed, expected that capital investment will result in benefits to society.

The question of the roles of the sexes is, therefore, regarded as one of the main problems in connection with the reform work that is constantly being done in the fields of education, employment, and social, family, and tax policy. The Swedish government acknowledges the fact that the report to the United Nations (1968) may seem revolutionary and unrealistic to the leaders of many countries. In Sweden, however, there has been an increasingly favorable opinion toward these ideas. As in other Scandinavian countries, an intensive debate has been carried on during the last six or seven years in the mass media, in organizations, and in various sectors of society.

The climate of opinion in Sweden during the 1960s

Until the 1960s, a "moderate" opinion prevailed concerning the roles of the sexes, characterized by the concept of woman's two roles (Myrdal & Klein, 1956). The life career of a woman involved partly a period of child-rearing and active motherhood in the home and then, when the children had grown up, a return to remunerative work. The concept of woman's two roles involved problems of adjustment and transition with which society sought to help them. For one, it was suggested that housing and collective services be so arranged that housework could be minimized and rational labor-saving household devices introduced to a larger extent. Most important of all were the arrangements for the part-time care of children, including kindergartens, day-care homes, and afternoon homes. Moreover, conditions in both the labor market and in places of work would be so organized that woman's "double" life-career can be made easier by part-time jobs, extended time off with pay at time of childbirth, and increased opportunities for continued education and reeducation. Special attention can be given to opportunities for older women in the labor market, etc. It is worth noting that these measures were intended only for women, whereas the role of the man was taken for granted.

In an article, "The Conditional Emancipation of Women," Eva Moberg (1962) challenged the whole question of women's double roles. Among other things, she asserted the following:

> Actually, there is no biological connection whatsoever between the function of giving birth to and nursing a child and the function of washing its clothes, preparing its food and trying to bring it up to be a good and harmonious person. . . . The care and upbringing of a child is a purely human and moral matter and is in no way inherent in one's sexual function. . . . And all this in spite of the innumerable examples we have around us of unsuitable mothers of large families, men who have the makings of excellent, loving fathers, and childless women with a superior ability to bring up children. . . . The concept double roles can have an unhappy effect in the long run. It perpetuates the idea that woman has an inherent main task, the care and upbringing of children, homemaking and keeping the family together . . . we should stop hammering in the idea of woman's two roles. Both men and women have one main role, that of being human beings. . . .
>
> If we do not accept this, then we should clearly understand that we are helping to see that women's emancipation never becomes more than it is now: a conditional emancipation. Woman has been made free only under the unspoken condition that she still sees as her main task the care and upbringing of children and the creation of their environment. Just so long as she understands that this is her natural task, somehow built into her as a member of the female sex, then of course society recognizes her not as a fully free individual [pp. 108–109].

Radical participants in the debate have brought up the question of closed doors in the life situation of men: The demand for equality between the sexes should also mean that certain advantages that women enjoy are no longer kept for them alone. The burden of supporting the family should be shared, and both parents should have the joy of intimate contact with the children. Men have been forced into the harder, more impersonal every-man-for-himself life of the working force, while women have had a more sheltered position in the family. Equality should mean that men and women share more evenly the stresses and strains of competition outside the family and the intimacy of contact with the children. Expressing these ideas in terms of political action, Eva Moberg, among others, suggests that the current child allowance paid to every family with one or more children be increased with a child-*care* allowance paid, for example, for three years. This allowance should be large enough to permit one of the parents to remain home with the child during its early years or to pay for a substitute. In her words:

> The freedom of choice of the parents is thus increased. They can divide the housework and the remunerative work between themselves . . . in whatever way that suits each individual family. When the care of children is generally accepted as the concern of both parents, discrimination will decrease in the field of employment. If there are no financial or conventional obstacles for fathers to cut down on their jobs for the sake of their children, it is possible that many men will choose a field of work that was earlier reserved for women [pp. 29–30].

These thoughts and suggestions aroused a violent debate, a debate that spread far beyond the groups commonly concerned with "women's rights." With a bit of oversimplification it can be said that the front lines were manned on the one side by housewives and on the other side by working women and male supporters of each category. The controversy reached its climax when the Norwegian-Swedish study, *The Life and Work of Women* (Dahlström, 1962) was published. In it sociologists, social psychologists, and economists, in a series of essays, centered their attention upon the problem of sex roles. Once this contribution had been made to the debate, attention was definitely turned from "women's rights" to broader social questions, and the expression "sex roles" became common currency.

At first the new expression caused some confusion. Many took it up with relief. They could now relinquish the misleading terms "women's rights" or "the woman question." If a society shows sexual discrimination in the labor force, if its decision-making bodies, councils, and parliament contain an overwhelming majority of men, if sexual discrimination is practiced in connection with household tasks, it is as unreasonable to talk about "the problem of women" as to lay the blame for racial prejudice upon the Negro. Many found that the term "sex role" opened their eyes to the fact that it was, in the end, neither a question of man or woman, but rather of social pressure put upon individuals whose psychic dispositions and temperaments did not correspond to the social uniform for feminine and masculine. Others found the term "sex role" confusing, if not downright repellent. They associated it with sexual intercourse and venereal disease. Still another interpretation was that "sex role" concerned rules for courting or marriage proposal, or how one should go about initiating a sexual relationship. The misunderstandings themselves are strangely illuminating. I am inclined to agree that it is in situations such as the last one mentioned that a person's sex is of interest, but now instead our attention has been directed to child-rearing, division of labor, and recruiting according to sex. Moreover, the role and life situation of the male has been brought conspicuously into the picture.

Ever since the publication of *The Life and Work of Women,* new studies, debate books, articles, party programs, reviews, and adult education programs on the Swedish radio have kept the question of sex roles in the focus of interest. It is interesting that laughter and ridicule, which so often characterize the attitude toward feminine-masculine, have been directed in Sweden toward traditional behavior and have become a weapon for radicals. The article about "woman's conditional emancipation" was thought to represent, at the time it came out, a rather extreme and unrealistic expression of an "angry young woman." It is therefore remarkable that the government's long-range program corresponds on important points with the ideas that jolted public opinion not so long ago.

The reader should, however, keep in mind the rational themes that so strongly saturate discussion on social issues in Sweden. The rationalists, who in Sweden are sometimes called "cultural radicals," have reached a kind of dominance in the climate of opinion. Professor Hans Zetterberg (1965) describes them in the following way:

> Rationalists have a great deal to say concerning the content of radio and television programs and control the editorial and cultural pages of the large newspapers. The rationalists have transformed political debates into seminars in economics, political science, and sociology, [that is] debates between rational experts. The solutions which are suggested are, in effect, practical social science [p. 14].

In other words, the attitude expressed by the Swedish government does indeed dominate the articulate Swedish climate of opinion, but how broadly it is accepted and how deeply it has penetrated and at what rate the population will take advantage of the new opportunities still remain to be seen.

The problem of the traditional lines of education

The nine-year basic school was legally established in Sweden in 1962. In the outline of studies that states specifically the principles governing the work of the basic school, the ideal of equality is clearly expressed. The school shall promote the democratic principle of "equality between the sexes." The school shall also help the students ". . . as objectively as possible to assess their qualifications for different lines of study and work." It also states that girls who have interests in technology and science ". . . should be encouraged to develop them" and that ". . . the conventional attitude toward these matters should be opposed." During the eighth grade all students are given *vocational orientation,* a subject that is accorded great weight. In this orientation is also included practical occupational experience for a total of three weeks, during which time the pupils can work in at least two places of their own choice.

Studies of jobs chosen by boys and girls during their practical vocational orientation show that the choice of vocations still is strongly bound to sex—in other words, girls choose typically "feminine," and boys choose typically "masculine," vocations. The most popular areas of work for girls during both of the academic years 1965 and 1966 were public health and nursing. All signs indicate that this field will be expanding greatly in Sweden, and considering to what extent young peoples' choice of occupation is associated with their sex, care of the sick should be occupying an increasingly large proportion of working women. The need to change the distorted recruitment to the nursing professions is illustrated in a striking way by a mathematical figure that shows that every third Swedish girl would need to work in the field of nursing and medicine if a larger proportion of men could not be recruited.

The strongly traditional tendency in pupils' practical vocational orientation is also illustrated clearly in a study made in a middle-sized Swedish town, Västerås (Thorsell, 1967). The most popular occupations among boys and girls during the school year 1965–66 are shown in Table 1.

TABLE 1 THE TOP OCCUPATIONS IN THE PRACTICAL VOCATIONAL ORIENTATION AMONG PUPILS IN VÄSTERÅS, SCHOOL YEAR 1965–66

Boys, total	*Girls, total*
1. Auto mechanics (34)	1. Primary school teacher (53)
2. Air Force jobs (24)	2. Kindergarten teacher (43)
3. Electricians (23)	3. Child nurse (43)
4. Bakers (23)	4. Sales girl (39)
5. Laboratory assistants (21)	5. Hairdresser (35)
6. Military jobs in the local regiment (19)	6. Office girl (35)
7. Photographer (16)	7. Nursing assistant (25)
8. IBM data machine operator (15)	8. Animal care (19)
9. Draftsman (14)	9. Store decorator (16)
10. Salesman (14)	10. Travel bureau assistant (16)
11. Jobs with railroad (14)	
Total placements = 469	Total placements = 473

The above results of young peoples' sex-bound vocational choices have been the object of a great deal of attention. The following trends characterize the educational choices being made today: Young people seek areas of activity "typical" for their sex. The boys who are studying in the "gymnasium" show a greater interest in technical, mercantile, legal, and administrative professions. Girls are most interested in language, artistic, psychological, teaching, and service professions. The same tendency continues to dominate in the university.

Moreover, boys are better prepared than girls to enter professional training that will take many years; their level of ambition in regard to careers is higher. Girls are satisfied with short-term training; they have lower ambitions concerning level of work, and they are distributed among a few different vocations. Even in school, boys' general fields of study are more vocationally oriented, their choices of subjects more precise, made with a thought to vocational aims and expediency. In a study of motivation for courses taken at the gymnasium it was found that ". . . the boys say that they cannot manage without a higher education, and the girls say that in gymnasium they receive a general education and learn things for which they will always have use later on." We seemed to find in these answers an uncertainty as to what use this education really would be to them. This uncertainty has now a masculine and a feminine variation: "You have to have it" and "You can always use it" (Härnqvist & Grahm, 1963).

"Inner" obstacles

Traditional Attitudes

The social changes in the Scandinavian countries up to the present time have meant, in effect, that a legal and formal equality has not been met by a corresponding equalization of roles. In spite of the fact that many *outward* obstacles have been removed, there remain obstacles that are partly of another type having to do with deeply-rooted ideas, role expectations, role ideals, values, and habits among, for example, employers, work supervisors, fellow workers, husbands, and, not least, among women themselves. These are obstacles based on conventions in the pattern of social relations itself (Dahlström, 1962). They have to do with inhibited and extinguished motives and with aspirations and interests that were not encouraged or aroused. These "inner obstacles" are now the center of interest for sociologists. By getting at them it is hoped that the educational situation itself can be changed.

In adolescence, the decisive asymmetry in the position of both sexes takes place, an asymmetry particularly apparent in relation to the opposite sex and in attitudes toward choice of and preparation for vocation. As boys and girls of this age are confronted by the world of sex and the world of vocation, the breach between boys and girls, in terms of the psychological and social conditions under which they must live, is widened. In relation to the opposite sex, new rules begin to function concerning initiative and responsibility. A girl must learn to "keep to herself" in love and to be passive and to refrain from all direct initiative in seeking a partner. She is given the role of an object. On the other hand, she is responsible for the boy's initiative. She is the one who puts on the brakes, restrains and sees to it that her partner does not go too far, all in spite of the fact that the biological and psychological changes of adolescence dispose her to activity, self-expression, and emotional intensity. One has at this point a glimpse of a separation of initiative and responsibility that probably leaves its traces in the continued development of sex roles. Responsibility rests, to a great extent, with the one who does not have the right to initiative.

In education and vocational training we see striking differences in recruitment. The girls begin with better grades and come, to a large extent, from higher social classes. They make a poorer showing at the end of every stage of education than the boys. The girls show a progressively deteriorating curve of performance (Holter, 1962 b). Whether the lowering of quality is due to sexual differences in the maturing process or differences in the support of the environment, the pattern does not disclose. It seems likely, however, that there is, at all stages of education, an environmental pressure working to the advantage of boys by stimulating their motivation.

The rules of sex roles themselves can be assumed to have an inhibiting effect upon intellectual accomplishment. Girls are subjected to stricter demands concerning mores, obedience, and the ritual following of rules, whereas boys are encouraged to have a freer and more experimental way of life. Moreover, parents' ambitions are greater for the careers of their sons—with greater pressure and even greater encouragement as a result. The vocational interest of girls is considered something more secondary—something to fill out the time of waiting, or "something to fall back on." Any vocational interest shown by girls easily becomes unrealistic, with less attention to security and economic independence and more simply to trying out their talents and interests.

During the exploratory phase, the different futures of boys and girls become particularly real to them. Boys aim toward both starting a family and earning money. They do not run the same risk as girls that these two future prospects will conflict with one another, and therefore they can have more purposefulness, rational planning, and realistic self-appraisal. For girls, marriage and the creation of a family become all-encompassing. The fact that in our culture marriage is surrounded by mystique, romance, and vague hopes must give rise to a fatalistic and unplanned attitude which, in turn, must affect a girl's education and choice of vocation.

The choice of a vocation that is traditionally associated with one or the other sex has been interpreted as an expression of fear and inability to cope with the dissonance between the traditional sex roles and the stereotype of the vocational role. Especially for young people, the fear of going too far in behavior not typical for one's own sex is very great. Since the sex-role pattern is better integrated with the personality than the vocational behavior pattern, for which the young person still lacks knowledge and experience, the sex-role stereotype tends to take over. Adjustment to the norms of society for feminine and masculine behavior are of deep importance for the young person since self-image and feeling of identity are particularly connected with sex. Therefore, the feeling of deviance from the expected sex role can lead to anxiety and fear. Not until this type of conflict can be openly discussed and made the object of conscious thought and evaluation by young people themselves can it be possible to change the traditional sex role stereotypes.

Young peoples' contact and knowledge of different vocations and lines of education is greatly limited and consists of a few vocational stereotypes. School authorities are now making an intensified effort toward vocational guidance. In the report to the United Nations (1968) the following instructions were given concerning the goals of vocational guidance:

In practical vocational orientation it must be made clear that girls' vocational interests should be stimulated and that students must choose in a less conventional way. Thorough information must be given about the income of different vocations so that girls can become aware that the income of many traditional women's occupations often is worse than for traditional men's occupations. The lack of such information means a departure from the goal of objectivity in vocational orientation. In instructions for future vocational guidance it should be explicitly stated that objectivity in vocational orientation should not only give the students a description of the current occupational structure but also of new occupations which will be needed in the future. The students should also be given concrete examples of girls and boys who dared to break away from traditions in their choice of vocation. In teaching one should go out to places of work and study such examples.

It must also be pointed out for girls that if they choose shorter vocational training, they can have difficulty asserting themselves in regard to jobs in the future. Neither should girls' education be regarded as a type of insurance which could be good to have in case they married and their husbands should die, become sick or be divorced. Such reasoning leads girls to have lower vocational ambitions than boys.

In one important aspect basic school is helping directly to change the traditional sex roles. Boys, as well as girls, are given obligatory training in homemaking, cooking and child care. With this training it can be hoped that housework and child care can be regarded as a job for both husband and wife in families of the future. In general, a knowledge of homemaking must be seen as a form of every citizen's education, in which everybody should have a certain amount of knowledge, whether one has a family or not. Even in textbooks and educational material, traditional ideas about women's and men's work must be weeded out. Instead, both text and illustrations should stimulate a less stereotyped attitude concerning that which is masculine or feminine, for example, by showing men engaged in housework and service occupations and women in, for example, technical jobs. At the present time a survey of textbooks in the social sciences is underway in the Women's Commission of the National Bureau of Employment. The national textbook commission is now constantly watching to see that textbooks do not give students a traditional picture of women's or men's work (p. 24).

Cultural Lag in Communication Media

This special control of the way in which masculine-feminine is presented in textbooks can be seen as a result of the more or less strict analysis of the contents of textbooks that were published during the 1960s, in which attention was drawn, for example, to the cultural lag in regard to social relations. The textbooks of the primary schools showed an agrarian picture of the world, with three-generation families, textbooks in community studies showed parts of industry with nothing but men, while interests and hobbies were consistently stereotyped according to sex. An inclusive and radical reorientation of textbooks and a new awareness on the part of the authors of textbooks has gone into effect during the past years. Observations have even been made of the methods of the press in reporting and commenting upon the sex-role debate, and weekly magazines have been attacked in a book, *The Shrunken Feminine Ideal* (Backberger, 1966), which analyzes the picture of the world and the definition of reality that women's magazines give their readers.

An analysis of the contents of children's books (Liljeström, 1966) can serve as an illustration of the way in which the mass media help to perpetuate traditional sex roles. We asked 456 children from twelve to fourteen years of age to name two or three books that they had read. The results showed that Enid Blyton's gang and mystery books were the uncontested favorites of both sexes for this age range. But, with the exception of the Blyton books, it happened only rarely that boys and girls named the same books. It was more uncommon for boys to mention girls' books than the reverse. The samples chosen for content analysis included the ten books mentioned most often by girls—all with female main characters—and the ten most mentioned by boys—all with male heroes.

Typical of the girls' choices were four books set in a job environment, three nurse stories and one airline hostess story. No so-called girls' classics were included. On the other hand, six classics were included in the boys' top ten: *Twenty Thousand Leagues Under the Sea, Treasure Island, The Last of the Mohicans, Robinson Crusoe,* and *Robin Hood.* Nine of the girls' books and four of the boys' books were part of a series in which the reader, in book after book, followed the fate and adventures of the same main character. The person's name in the title of the book told the potential reader *whom* the book was about, thus contributing to continued and relatively permanent acquaintance with the same person. For many readers it was not just a question of another book but of a well-known fictitious person. This continuity of the main character that is typical of so many children's books is noteworthy and demonstrates young people's need to identify and recognize.

The categories used in the analysis of contents were intended to measure to what extent the descriptions of male and female differ in their orientation with respect to four of Parsons' pattern variables (1952). The individual's behavior in social relations showed a fourfold variation, as follows:

1. The extent to which an open display of feelings is permissible or relationships require a control of feelings (affectivity vs. affective neutrality).
2. The extent to which one's attention is drawn to outward attributes or to accomplishments (ascription vs. achievement).
3. The degree of intimacy—anonymity in relationships (specificity vs. diffuseness).
4. The extent to which relationships are subjective, unique, and individualized or bound by standardized rules and principles to

which the parties involved must submit (particularism vs. universalism).

One pole of each of the above-mentioned dimensions is found in primary groups: The emotional, intimate, individual, and less performance-oriented relationships are typical of the family and relations between good friends. The opposite pole is characteristic in the civil service, bureaucracies, organizations, and work where emotional discipline, merits, impersonality, and standardized rules in relationships between people are expected.

Harriet Holter (1962a) has presented the hypothesis that girls are brought up for primary group, and boys for secondary group, relationships. In other words, the sex roles differ in respect to the different social techniques they must learn in relation to other people. Although both boys and girls learn, to a great extent, the same general manners and types of behavior, differentiation according to sex makes them give different priorities to different types of behavior. An analysis of sex roles can therefore concentrate upon variations in the order of priorities given to different norms. Both women and men are expected to have feelings and also to be objective, but women are expected to have more feelings and to be less objective than men. Femininity and masculinity in our culture are the result of differences in gradations and priorities.

The sex-role differences revealed in content analysis (Liljeström, 1966) of children's books in general bears out these assumptions. Without presenting the results in detail, they may be summarized as follows:

1. The main characters in girls' books expressed themselves much more emotionally than do the boys' main characters.
2. Verbal interaction in the boys' books occurred almost exclusively within a sex-and-age-homogeneous group. In the case of girls' books, while communication with peers of the same sex also tended to dominate, all categories of recipients of spoken lines, including elders as well as peers, were represented. Moreover, the analysis of the recipients of spoken lines revealed differences between girls' and boys' books in interaction structure. The main characters communicated in different types of situations. It seemed as though authors more often placed girls in situations where norms for affective orientation had the priority, and boys in situations that called for affective neutrality. In other words, perhaps boys' and girls' behavior is not so different in itself, but they are placed in situations that call for different kinds of behavior.
3. A frequent indicator of affective orientation was the use of physiological signs such as blushing, hot cheeks, cold shivers, choked throat, nausea, broken and trembling voice, etc. Of a total of ninety-eight items of this type, seventy-two occurred in girls' books as contrasted with the small minority of twenty-six found in the boys' books.
4. A fourth sex-role difference concerned relative emphasis on outward at-

tributes versus accomplishment. Although the girls' books devoted much more time and interest to personal characteristics than did the boys', in terms of the relative amount of attention to ascribed versus achieved qualities, the character descriptions in the boys' books put more emphasis on the person's ability to achieve and produce.

As for outward attributes, the main characters in the boys' books were males whose appearance and clothes gave little rise to comment. They were fairly anonymous agents carrying on action and intrigue. Girls' books, on the contrary, underlined the importance of clothing and appearance.

The sex role differences are brought out in Table 2. The qualities of the main characters for boys' and for girls' books are arranged according to the number of items recorded for each category, weighted on the basis of the amount of text devoted to them:

TABLE 2 WEIGHTED NUMBER OF ITEMS FOR QUALITIES OF MAIN CHARACTER

Girls' books		*Boys' books*	
1. Clothing	69	1. Knowledge	27
2. Appearance	59	2. General impression and facial expression	19
3. General impression and facial expression	50	3. Appearance	18
4. Character	34	4. Character	14
5. Knowledge	24	5. Clothing	13

One notices immediately that the first and last places in rank order change places. *Clothing* is the characteristic most written about in girls' books and least mentioned in boys'. *Knowledge* is exactly the reverse.

Children's books reflect a social reality, but they also help to conserve this reality. If there is to be an equalization of roles and a change in the traditional division of labor, as we see it in young peoples' choice of occupations, it is necessary that influence and examples that hold boys and girls to limited concepts of their own sex roles be seen for what they are, and that alternative role models also be offered. An attempt has been made to do this in Sweden with the analysis of contents used as a weapon to reveal such one-sided influence. In a less scientific way, content analyses have also been made of newspapers and their way of commenting and reporting the current sex-role debate, and the values of the weekly magazines have been examined in a debate book. Besides content analysis of various kinds of sex-role prototypes, considerable interest has been devoted to the type of inner obstacles associated with woman's low self-confidence that results from her marginal situation between a traditional and a modern style of life, in a situation where rank and status are out of balance (Liljeström, 1968).

Changed life careers

Family Roles

Of the 7.8 million inhabitants of Sweden, about 22 percent were children under sixteen years of age in 1967. Sweden is probably one of the few countries in the world with such a low proportion of children, with a birth rate in 1966 of 15.8 living children per 1000 average population. Half of the families with children under sixteen years of age at home had only one child. Only 16 percent of the families with children had three or more children. However, the children in the last-mentioned group are one-third of all Swedish children. This means that 7 percent of the population between eighteen and sixty-six were bringing up one-third of the new generation. One-parent families are naturally also included and make up one-tenth of all families with children.

In the life career of women, the period of childbirth is now coming at a younger age. Whereas the average age of marriage as recently as 1930 was 30.1 years for men and 27.8 for women, it had gone down to 25.9 for men and 22.9 for women in 1960. One-fourth of the women are now marrying before their twenty-first birthday. The vast majority of children are born during the early years of marriage. The active years of parenthood are earlier and many vital decades without preschool children still remain for the mothers. Much is being said about the right of both parents to be with their children during the relatively short time they are small, and about the unreasonableness of wives being economically dependent.

In connection with the life careers of both sexes, attention has been drawn to the age difference that has accompanied the traditional sex roles. According to Holmberg (1966):

> In Sweden there are at present about 300,000 widows and 125,000 widowers; in the population over 66 years of age about every other woman is a widow but only every fourth man is a widower. This is a reflection of the age difference between the partners in a marriage. The men are an average of 3 years older than their wives but, on the other hand, live 3 years less. The result has not only been a disproportionate number of widows in our society—the average married woman must look forward to 6 years as a widow. Moreover, this age difference has brought about or encouraged an authoritarian relationship between husband and wife which is not so desirable for the attempt to equalize the sex roles. This system means that women have less experience of life than their partners when they marry, that women do not have time to educate themselves as well as men before they marry, that women risk ending up in a subordinate situation. Sex roles are naturally part of the cause of these age differences between husbands and wives, but the age differences, in their turn, also strengthen the traditional sex roles at the same time as they create a widow problem [p. 3].

Reeducation

The Parliament voted in 1967 for a thorough expansion of adult education—one can call it a possibility for reeducation—which is comparable to young peoples' education in terms of the competence it fosters. Adult education is relatively more important for women than for men. The early age of marriage, combined with the long time that an education takes, means that many women do not have time to finish their education before they start a family. Childbirth makes study time longer for women, but it seems to have an accelerating effect on the student father. Studies are also interrupted more frequently for university women students. When the children have become older and the duties in the home have decreased, women want to continue their interrupted studies or begin studies they had no opportunity to carry on before. It is then of primary importance that society provide the same opportunities for adult education as it provides for youth.

The proportion of women in training for the labor market was 17 percent in 1959–60 and 46 percent in 1965–66. Not less than 41 percent of the students who were forty-five years of age and older were women. During 1966, measures were intensified in a special campaign aimed at the women's labor force, according to the following report of the labor board (Official Report to the UN, 1968) :

> During the period the campaign to inform the public of employment opportunities for women was intensified. One of the measures taken to interest women in a wider choice of occupations and to make them realize the need for longer and more qualified training was to repeat the radio series "Hemmafru byter yrke" ("The Housewife Changes Her Occupation") . In connection with these broadcasts comprehensive information on labor market and social matters was given at conferences arranged by the county labor boards in which women's organizations, public authorities, etc., participated. Study circles based on the radio series were organized in most counties under the auspices of various educational associations [pp. 69–70].

Economic Participation

Women's participation in the economic and social development of Sweden has increased markedly in the sixties. The rapid rise in the employment of married women that was noticeable in the fifties has continued at an even faster rate. The increase is especially remarkable if one includes *part-time* working wives.

A tendency toward lowered remunerative activity has appeared among unmarried women as well as men because more and more young people continue their education much longer than in the past.

Of the total number of people with jobs in 1966, 40 percent were women. Of the female population between fourteen and seventy-four years of age, 70 percent had belonged to the labor force during a longer or shorter time. In regard to working time, there were important differences in comparison with men. Of the total number of working women, 36 percent had part-time jobs involving less than thirty-five work hours a week, as contrasted with the analagous figure for men of only 3.8 percent.

Within the same age range of fourteen to seventy-four years, more than three-fourths (77 percent) of those who could not carry on remunerative work in 1966 were women. As indicated in Table 3, the reasons why those women did not have jobs were mainly connected with housework and childcare (Official Report to the United Nations, 1968, p. 74).

TABLE 3 REASONS FOR LACK OF REMUNERATIVE WORK, 1966

	MEN		WOMEN	
Reason	*(000)*	*Percent*	*(000)*	*Percent*
Studies	109.4	30.6	123.1	10.3
Illness	124.0	34.6	186.7	15.6
Childcare	–	–	201.6	16.8
Household	6.8	1.9	487.6	40.7
Could not find work	–	–	29.6	2.5
Part-time work	–	–	24.7	2.1
Other reason	117.3	32.9	166.1	14.1
Total	357.5	100.0	1197.3	100.0

The tendency toward increased employment is, however, strong in Sweden, especially among those between thirty-five and fifty years. In this group in 1965, more than four out of ten women had more than half-time, usually full-time, work. The division of the sexes among various types of jobs in the Swedish labor force is, however, greatly slanted. About 80 percent of all working women are engaged in occupations where less than 10 percent of the men on the labor force are working (Holmberg, 1966). The predominant women's jobs are those of office workers and saleswomen. The division of work into typical women's jobs and typical men's jobs makes it hard to apply formally the principle of equal wage.

Roles of men and women in Swedish organizations

The first big step toward general suffrage was taken in 1907. Women in Sweden were given the right to vote in 1919. One year later they also were given the same legal status as men. If participation in elections is the first step toward political participation, both sexes have taken that step completely. There is no difference between the voting participation of men and women—or rather—the negligible difference that exists is to the women's advantage. The younger women, even up to forty to forty-four years of age, exercised their voting rights to a greater extent than the men in the 1960 elections (Rudebeck, 1965). In international perspective, this phenomenon is remarkable. Even the difference in the parties backed by Swedish men and women voters was negligible.

For the sake of honesty, it should be added that the virtually obliterated differences between men and women in voting participation are not matched by a corresponding equality of political knowledge. In connection with the 1960 election, a number of voters were asked to answer nine questions about politics in general as well as about the various parties' views on particular questions. Women's knowledge was considerably less. Whereas the proportion of correct answers among men was between 31–95 percent, for women it was between 11–80 percent. If increasing the level of political knowledge can be called the second step in political participation, the cross-section of women has not yet caught up with the cross-section of men.

Greatest is the distance to the third step: participation in political representation and posts of responsibility. In Parliament women have consistently been underrepresented. Although they make up more than half of the population, women have never occupied more than 14 percent of the seats in the second chamber.

The results and reflections made in a newly published book from Finland in which the sociologist, Elina Haavio-Mannila (1968), reports the findings of her study of women's participation and influence in organizational life, will doubtless find an echo in the rest of Scandinavia. The author collected information concerning 402 organizations randomly selected from the organization register. She arranged these organizations into four categories with respect to their chief aims and purposes:

1. *Economic organizations* that aim to take care of resources for material adaptation. For example, labor unions, farmers' cooperatives, etc.
2. *Political organizations,* the aim of which is to decide how the collective resources shall be used and distributed.
3. *Leisure-time organizations* with the main purpose of providing an outlet for peoples' tensions and giving them recurrent excitement and relaxation, for example, organizations for youth, sport, culture, hobbies and pleasure.
4. *Organizations for unity,* which gather people around a particular new value system of religious or idealistic nature. Under this category is also placed charity.

In order to comprehend the relative influence of men and women in the different types of organizational activity, their participation on the boards of the organizations was determined. It was found that 47 percent of board memberships were all-male, although women were not excluded from general membership. The level of their participation in these groups, however, was obviously below that of the 44 percent of organizations whose boards included both sexes. In 9 percent of the groups, the boards were exclusively made up of women. Women were more often members of the boards of political organizations than of labor unions, economic groups, or sports clubs. Organizations that work for unity were found to contain on the average more women on their boards than any of the other types. This was true in spite of the fact that veterans' associations and several other purely male groups were included in this category. In 51 percent of these organizations, at least one woman served on the board.

The activity of the organizations can be outwardly or inwardly directed. Taking care of material resources and deciding their use are outgoing purposes, which are concerned with the outer environment. Relieving tensions and caring for group unity, on the other hand, are important for the inner social adjustment and aim to make social interaction easier and more pleasant.

Organizations strongly dominated by men are directed toward material resources (economy) and toward relieving tensions through leisure-time activities (sports, etc.). Organizations where both sexes participate (at least one woman on the board) are, surprisingly enough, political. Their purpose is to support certain values and to influence the use of society's material resources. This may mean that when an organization wants to carry out its program successfully among the public and to influence public opinion, it cannot afford to choose its members or board members from one sex only but must collect all its able people.

The specialization of organizational life reflects the kind of traditional division of the sexes that one finds, for example, in the family. The men dominate in the instrumental activities but both sexes cooperate in the expressive activities. In the case of inwardly directed activity, men dominate in organizations that give an outlet for tensions, and women are well represented in religious and idealistic groups. The old roles are even manifested in the fact that the duties of chairman and treasurer are usually given to men, whereas women usually have the job of secretary.

The difference between the sexes in the more inwardly directed, leisure-time activities is due to the many norms limiting social relations between men and women during leisure time. In the interests of protecting the family, these norms favor attendance at meetings limited to the same sex. In view of the increased opportunity open to working women for contact with men, it is noteworthy that the housewives are the ones who show special enthusiasm for joining women's organizations.

Traditional sex roles in organizations create problems in regard to future action. If that sector of organizational life where women have some influence has specialized forms of activities and goals related to the traditional female sex role, how can it then point the way to women who want to try new fields of activity? Even the political women's organizations adjust often to the social handicaps of their members by compensating monotonous work and isolation in the family with a many-sided recreational program. Along with political programs and studies, courses in being a hostess, fashion shows, table-setting contests, excursions, theater visits; and social evenings are arranged. Although such tactics meet vital needs of the members, they fail to steer these needs into paths that lead to political influence. How can they then change their own situations? Of course it is nice when the party women's organization sings at the old peoples' home, but it does not promote equality in the unions and councils.

In this chapter we have shown the Swedish model in a double exposure. On the one side, the radical climate of opinion and political unity behind supportive measures and reforms. On the other, the persistent traditional choice of occupation among young people and cleavage in the labor market. The modest political representation in the midst of this contradictory pattern and the research and debate are centered upon "inner obstacles" that are holding back the equalization of men's and women's roles and keeping them both from becoming well-rounded human beings. Out of such a dialectical struggle there is hope for the emergence of new and more dynamic patterns of sex-role interaction in the future.

References

Backberger, Barbro. *Det Förkrympta Kvinnoidealet* (*The Shrunken Feminine Ideal*). Stockholm: Bonniers, 1966.

Dahlström, Edmund, ed. *Kvinnors Liv och Arbete* (*The Life and Work of Women*). Stockholm: Studieförbundet Näringsliv & Samhälle, 1962.

Haavio-Mannila, Elina. *Suomalainen Nainen ja Mies* (*Finnish Women and Men*). Helsinki: Werner Söderström Osakeyhtiö, 1968.

Härnqvist, K., and Å. Grahm. "Vägen genom gymnasiet" ("The Way through Gymnasium"). *Sou,* 15 (1963).

Holmberg, Per. *Kynne eller Kön?* (*Temperament or Sex?*). Stockholm: Raben & Sjörgren, 1966. Conference paper.

Holter, Harriet. "Fra Barn til Voksen" ("From Childhood to Adulthood"). In *Kvinnors Liv och Arbete* (*The Life and Work of Women*) Edmund Dahlström, ed. Stockholm: Studieförbundet Näringsliv & Samhälle (1962a), pp. 159–88.

———. "Kjønsforskjeller i Yrkesatferd" ("Sex Differences in Vocational Behavior"). In *Kvinnors Liv och Arbete* (*The Life and Work of Women*), Edmund Dahlström, ed. Stockholm: Studieförbundet Näringsliv & Samhälle (1962b), pp. 327–75.

Liljeström, Rita. *Jämställdhetens Villkor* (*The Conditions of Equality*). Stockholm: Sveriges Radios Förlag, 1968.

———. *Kynne eller Kön?* (*Temperament or Sex?*). Stockholm: Raben & Sjörgren, 1966. Conference paper.

Moberg, Eva. "Kvinnans villkorliga frigivning" ("The Conditional Emancipation of Women"). Pamphlet, 1961. Reprinted in Eva Moberg, *Kvinnor och Människor*. Stockholm: Bonniers, 1962.

Myrdal, Alva, and Viola Klein. *Women's Two Roles*. London: Routledge, Kegan, Paul, 1956.

Official Report to the United Nations on the Status of Women in Sweden, 1968.

Parsons, Talcott. *The Social System*. London: Routledge, Kegan, Paul, 1956.

Rudebeck, Lars. "Det politiska systemet i Sverige." In *Svensk Samhällsstruktur i Sociologisk Belysning*, Edmund Dahlström, ed. Stockholm: Svenska bokförlaget, 1965, pp. 453–54.

Thorsell, Siv. "Pryo—den praktiska yrkesorienteringen i teori och verklighet" ("Vocational Guidance in Theory and Practice"). Studier och Debatt. In *Arbetsmarknadens kvinnonämnd*. Stockholm: Svenska Kommunalarbetarförbundet, 1967, p. 6.

Zetterberg, Hans. "Traditioner och Möjligheter i Nordisk Sociologi" ("Traditions and Possibilities in Nordic Sociology"). Uppsala: *Sociologisk Froskning*, 1 (1966).

10 MALE AND FEMALE IN THE GERMAN FEDERAL REPUBLIC

Ursula Lehr and Hellgard Rauh

Sex-role stereotypes in contemporary German social sciences

The German philosopher, Immanuel Kant, gave a description of the roles of man and woman in his "Anthropology" that reflects very well an extant stereotype. According to Kant (1798), in the original state many centuries ago, man acted as a "warrior-hero," marching boldly into the unknown world followed by his submissive (*demütig*) wife who carried the man's household equipment. This stereotype of the man who faces the problems of the world and deals with them, and of the wife who as his humble servant takes care of the house and of the hero's comfort, can be recognized in the contemporary ideologies on family life written by German sociologists like Schelsky (1955 a, b), Wurzbacher (1951), König (1946, 1957), Baumert (1965), and others. Although these authors pointed to the decline of the dominating "father figure" in Germany, they nevertheless consider as typical and natural a sex-role differentiation in our society in which the man represents the outer-directed, active, competent leader, whereas the woman can only live a meaningful life in the nuclear-family organization.

If we follow Schelsky's ideas on the change from the three-generation family to the nuclear family, we may conclude that emotionality, "womanhood," and activity in the intimate small-group atmosphere of the family are what the wife has necessarily to contribute for the preservation of the family. The wife—at least in our society—is made to preserve the precious blessings of the cozy German home. This picture arises from Schelsky's (1957) analysis of the new German Woman Movement after World War II. He doubts whether the world of the man, i.e., the world of politics, of business, and of industrial production, can be at all positively influenced by women. Thus, he criticizes women's ideology from the viewpoint of a traditional male ideology. When discussing the problem of admitting women to leading positions in society, he says:

> The question whether woman, especially one who wants to preserve her genuine personality (*ihr ursprüngliches wesen*), is capable of doing well in these positions of leadership has not been mentioned in these publications at all [p. 415].

The same author who criticizes Lersch (1947) for not considering social influences on sex-role concepts accepts within another context his social stereotypes of "womanhood" as being identical with the "genuine nature" of women. Therefore, we can say that Schelsky and others who helped to correct the common notion of the father-centered German family structure were not able to rectify their own stereotypes of sex roles and to free themselves from the traditional biases regarding sex differences.

The influence of these stereotypes certainly is greater in those books written or planned before or during World War II, even if published after the war. An example in this case is Lersch's *The Nature of the Sexes* (1947), which still adheres to the dichotomous view of man as genuinely rational, active, socially adjusted, and competent in dealing with the outside world and, in contrast, woman as genuinely ("by nature") sensitive, emotional, passive ("pathic"), though an indispensable maker of the intimate, warm climate of the typical German family.

The old "patriarch" has gone; the "good housemother," however, is still regarded by some psychologists and sociologists as the ideal realization of the female role created solely to take care of the needs of her family. Like many other authors, Lersch sharply criticizes Otto Weininger's (1919) pessimistic opinion of women's abilities. Neither Lersch nor most of the other authors consider women as inferior human beings, though they believe women to be different in a way that cannot be explained by social factors, and that only in the realization of the innate qualities of "manhood" and "womanhood" does human life have value, dignity, and beauty. Martha Moers (1948), herself one of the first women university professors, criticized these male views in part. Evaluating many empirical findings on sex differences, she stated that there were no traits exclusively characteristic of each of the sexes. However, behaviors and modes of feeling connected with motherhood would distinguish any woman from a man. Such characterization of motherhood and feminine development, no matter how carefully analyzed, reflects a certain ideology.

Fifteen to twenty years after the war, certain stereotypes of genuinely female tasks still determine many sociopolitical decisions and actions. According to Stahl (1964), the traditional image of the woman, centered around serving (*Hingabe*), sacrificing, and silent caring for others, still influences today's educational objectives and methods in many schools and colleges. The increasing number of married women working and the entrance of women into various leading positions in the industrial society are regarded as a "betrayal" of the genuine feminine role and as an assimilation of the woman's role with the man's.

Pichottka (1964) concluded from her experience in child guidance that young mothers today are practically unprepared for the tasks of motherhood because of concentration on job and career training. Even this very progressive author apparently is influenced by a stereotype that regards the world of industrial work, science, and politics as characteristics of the male role, whereas taking care of people, especially those of one's own family, serving, and helping, are regarded as the dominant traits of the female role. The same view is expressed by Rosner (1963), who feels that there are no means of adjusting the nature of woman to the requirements of a modern industrial world that remains an unfriendly world, alien to any woman. In line with this thinking, Weegmann (1966) and Scharmann (1962) hold that women should be employed only in those jobs that satisfy their intrinsic needs for helping and caring within an intimate, close, and friendly atmosphere.

However, even authors who regard industrial work as a new "natural" field for the realization of women's abilities are usually convinced of the necessity of differentiating the type of work according to sex-typical differences in the mental abilities and tendencies of men and women. According to Bramesfeld and Graf (1949), women are better at work requiring manual dexterity and tolerance of monotony. Automatic work and work at the conveyor belt are regarded by them as better suited to women than to men because of women's acceptance of drudgery and their greater emotionality and fantasy.

If we take the opinions of these "experts" who rarely refer to research findings as representative of German thinking on the problem, we might better call the West German contribution to this volume "Static Sex-Role Concepts in Changing Society." However, we doubt whether these opinions are really representative of the actual thinking and behavior with regard to sex roles.

Our doubts are based on and fostered by:

(1) Statistics on education and on the development of women's work during the last sixty years; (2) Biographical studies on the life histories and work-life histories of men and women from different age groups; (3) Studies on similarities and differences in the behavior of boys and girls, and of men and women, in present-day West Germany; and (4) Studies comparing attitudes of boys and girls toward various problems (moral standards, work, ideals, etc.).

Unfortunately, we cannot offer findings equivalent to those presented by Blood and Wolfe (1960), Shanas and Streib (1965), or Hill (1965), as no work of this type has yet been undertaken. However, some studies show a clearer change in actual sex roles than in the sex-role concepts studied by most scientific and nonscientific authors.

Changing society and changing sex roles—evidence from empirical research

The Equality of Educational Opportunities

The change in society's attitude toward sex roles can best be demonstrated by a short summary of the history of equalization of rights for men and women in Germany (Bundesminister, 1966). The women's emancipation movement at first concentrated its efforts on getting girls admitted to institutions for higher education. In 1865, in Berlin, the LETTE-Verein was founded to provide better educational opportunities for girls. The first "Lyzeum" was opened in 1868 in Berlin as a private institution, and in 1898 the first six women finished their high school training with the "Abitur," the German high school degree. In the same year, the first women were admitted to medical examinations, but they had to go to Switzerland in order to get their training. The turn of the century, however, saw the entrance of women into German universities. Since then, the percentage has risen steadily, as shown in Table 1 (Bundesminister, 1966):

TABLE 1 PERCENTAGE OF FEMALE STUDENTS TO TOTAL NUMBER OF STUDENTS

Year of Census	*Percentage*	
1908	0.5	
1911	4.1	
1914	4.9	
1924	9.8	
1934	14.0	
1937	11.6	
1955	17.8	(West Germany only)
1961	26.6	(West Germany only)

It should be noted that in 1961, 84 percent of the men and 70.4 percent of the women who had received a university degree were established in their vocations.

In the lower schools, a study of unmarried youth (EMNID, 1965) indicated an interaction between social class of parents, educational ceiling, and sex of children, with workers' children in general, and girls in particular, overrepresented in the lower forms. A tendency toward upward mobility appeared in the parents' sending their children to a school one level higher than that of their own.

Analysis of the reasons for the sex-differential education suggests that vocational education is less often important for girls in their parents' and their own eyes; either their own interests are more family-oriented or their parents' interests keep them from higher education. Boys, on the other hand, more often refer to poor school achievement or special vocational interests. In the lower social classes, girls more often than boys are expected to earn money for the family and to help with younger siblings. Boys are allowed more freedom socially, educationally, and financially (Baumert, 1965). In the higher classes, although the tendency is more equalitarian, parents often show greater interest in the education of their future sons-in-law than in that of their daughters, since social prestige depends solely on the male's professional status.

These findings can serve only as examples for the variety of attitudes toward the education of boys and girls existing in this country. They certainly should be supplemented by careful interview studies in order to uncover the underlying motivational structure. Such intensive investigation might be expected to reveal a complex of dynamics that characterize the ways in which a changing society influences its people's attitudes toward sex roles, and vice versa.

Sex Role and Worker Role

Many writers feel that the increase in working women can be regarded as the most impressive social change in this century. Actually, this rise is not as revolutionary as current discussions of the problem would suggest. The official records of the former *Deutsches Reich* and of the German Federal Republic demonstrate a very stable percentage of working women, as seen in Table 2 (Bundesminister, 1966):

TABLE 2 PERCENTAGE OF WORKING WOMEN RELATED TO TOTAL NUMBER OF WOMEN

Year of Census	*Percentage of Working Women*
1882	24.2
1895	25.1
1907	30.3
1925	35.4
1933	34.1
1939	36.1
1950	31.4
1956	34.8
1961	33.1
1964	33.4
1966	31.4

This table shows that there was almost the same proportion of working women in 1907 as in 1966, and that before the war as well as in the early sixties there was even a greater percentage of working women than today. The change in the composition of the working population was apparently a consequence of the war, since the postwar generations show a more "natural" distribution of the sexes.

Although the general quantitative change in the occupational field with respect to sex roles is not at all dramatic, an impressive qualitative change in the correlations between sex role and worker role can be demonstrated by comparing the proportion of women in the so-called "male" occupations in 1965 and 1950, as shown in Table 3 (Bundesminister, 1966):

TABLE 3 PERCENTAGES OF FEMALE EMPLOYEES IN "MALE" OCCUPATIONS *

	1950–1951	*1964–1965*
Window dresser	7	89
Technical designer	15	71
Optician	19	73
Goldsmith, silversmith	28	91
Shipping agent, shipowner	28	39
Dental mechanic	31	83
Banker, bank employee	37	77
Men's tailor	43	486
Wholesale dealer, retail businessman	60	94
Insurance agent	64	118
Industrial agent	68	117
Tourist traffic agent	85	351
Pharmacist	95	705
Book-seller	154	282
Hair dresser	296	1202
Furrier	330	503
Merchant, salesman, shop assistant	450	493
Cook	122	24

* 100 male employees correspond to . . . female employees in each occupation listed.

From this table it can be noted that a variety of different occupations representing different degrees of "prestige" show an increase of women workers. The general trend is clearly toward admitting women to skilled work and to higher vocations requiring training in special colleges (e.g., pharmacists or tourist specialists). In the highest professions, however, women are still the exception. Female managers, for example, as well as female professors, are still quite rare: in 1964 there were only four female full professors at West German universities.

Analyses of differences in the work area as experienced by men and women, based on the life histories of 500 women and 160 men aged twenty to seventy years, again points to qualitative differences in the working situation of women compared to that of men (Lehr, 1969). In general, women find the first two years of their occupational career to be more stressful than do men; this picture changes, however, during the third year (see also Argelander, 1923; Wurzbacher and Jaide, 1958). Positive social contacts and recognition by superiors and colleagues are more decisive factors for the adjustment of women to the worker role than they are for men, for whom type of work appears to be more important. As far as social background variables are concerned, girls from integrated homes adjust more easily to the training conditions than do girls from broken homes. These variables are not significant for men (Thomae, 1958).

Reasons for leaving the occupational career differ for men and women; women are more likely to stop working because of family and social situations, while men more often are forced to do so because of extrafamilial circumstances like war, unemployment, company bankruptcy, etc. More specifically, women may quit work in order to take care of their parents, whereas sons, even in such urgent cases, are supposed to go on working. Furthermore, marriage and childbirth frequently lead to an interruption or termination of a woman's working life.

These findings hold especially true for the life histories of women born at the turn of the century. Their working lives were characterized by repeated interruptions of this kind. They were expected to come to their parents' home when somebody was in need. A woman's role was primarily that of a "good daughter"—or in later years that of a "good sister"—who was not supposed to have any occupational ambitions of her own but, rather, was expected to help her brother in attaining his goals. Women born between 1920 and 1930 reported an attitude of their parents quite different from that of the older group. Here the parents frequently advised them to continue their occupational training or to get some years of professional skill, and frequently it was the mothers of these women who helped care for the grandchildren or the whole household. The experiences of World War I and of the periods of inflation and depression apparently led to a reevaluation of occupational training and occupational careers for women.

Those women who continued working remained in the same position or occupation for a longer period of time than did men. Job changes were usually due to social aspects of the working situation. Women more often than men tended to stay in the same job just because of a positive social atmosphere there, even though a change might have meant a promotion in terms of more responsibility, higher occupational status, or simply greater income (Lehr, 1969; Wilms, 1966).

The reasons for a change in working location are different in the different generations of women, although no such generational differences were found among men. Whereas the older women reported motives such as "regard for family" or "social contacts," the motives of the younger women approximated those of men, including "promotion," "salary," "working conditions," etc. This generational difference among women may be interpreted to mean greater "openness" of the life space of younger women that may be expected eventually to result in an assimilation of woman's attitude toward work with that of the man. This interpretation can be further substantiated by comparing the experiential aspects of the present working situation of the different age groups of women during the period from 1960 to 1965 (Lehr, 1969). The youngest women experience their work primarily as something that is fun and gives satisfaction because they feel "competent" and "efficient." Satisfaction about achieved independence from parents as well as from the husband seems to be another major motivational aspect of their work situation. Only in the oldest group, aged sixty to seventy, does the experience of a job as a "life task" rank highest, and satisfaction over achieved independence appears much less important. This may be a socialization effect insofar as independence would seem a much less appropriate goal for them than task fulfillment or maintaining a certain security in life.

Generally speaking, there are differences in the worker role between men and women of the older age groups that disappear in the younger generation. The question, however, cannot be solved as to whether these differences between younger and older women's attitudes are a generational effect or whether the social situation in which the younger women live is simply more amenable to letting them adjust better to the conditions of work. In any case, there is much evidence that the worker role that a generation ago was an "additional role" to that of wife, housewife, and mother, is now becoming more self-fulfilling and satisfying in itself.

Changing Sex Roles in the Family

The constitution of West Germany, the *Grundgesetz* of 1949, for the first time in the history of this country declared men and women to have equal rights. This principle became effective as a law in 1953, and necessitated many changes in the Code of Civil Law, especially those laws regulating family life. Up to that time, these laws had been determined by a patriarchal model of family life, the husband having the right of decision over everything within the family: he decided where to live and where to work; he could cancel any occupational contracts of his wife if in his eyes she did not take care of their household well enough. He was responsible even for his wife's property unless a special contract had been made before the marriage. Among other things, he determined the school to which their children would go, the disposition of their property, etc.

Since 1953, husband and wife have been considered partners with equal rights and responsibilities. This change in constitution and law had been in part prepared for by a long process of democratizing the personal aspects of life. In view of the changes between 1933 and 1945, this process might have been stopped completely. In any case, many of the case histories analyzed by Lehr (1969) show a high proportion of equalitarian regulations in the husband-wife relationship even for that time. Baumert (1965), Wurzbacher (1951), and Schelsky (1955b) demonstrated how the postwar period with its high economic stress was met in many families by the wife's becoming the leading contributor or at least sharing with the husband the tasks of finding food, fuel, and jobs. As Schelsky and Wurzbacher implied, this change was paralleled by an increase in the number of two-generation families. These small cells of social life were used as a shelter from the storms and stresses of the fight for survival and from the coldness and unfriendliness of modern industrial society with its increasing bureaucracy and impersonal regulation of many affairs.

Several authors, including Schelsky (1955a), go so far as to speak of the wife's dominating position, especially with respect to her educational function. Mitscherlich (1963) even referred to the contemporary society as "fatherless," a characterization that could mean that Schaffner's (1948) theory of the German authoritarian father, as expounded in his book *Father Land,* had been rejected completely. Empirical findings on this issue are not unequivocal. Some still substantiate the traditional image of wives and mothers. For instance, in the EMNID study in 1955, 59 percent of the West German men and 53 percent of the women accepted the statement: "The wife cannot learn to obey soon enough" (Fröhner, Stackenberg, & Eser, 1956). Similarly, though less markedly, West German adolescents differentiated their parents' roles on selected semantic differential scales (Seward & Larson, 1968). "Mother" was usually seen as more passive and sensitive, though stronger; "father" as more active, wiser, braver, and friendlier. There was little difference in the ways boys and girls perceived their fathers and mothers. In comparison with American high school students, West German girls and boys conceptualized women as having more courage and leadership.

Certainly, these observations do not justify a changed view of West Germany from a "father-land" to a "mother-land," since there is no real proof that these perceptions of father and mother are the result of recent developments. Studies on the earliest memories of adults born before 1910 showed that, even during the years of their childhood, the mother was apparently more often experienced to be the dominating figure in the family than was the father (Holzapfel, 1964; Lehr, 1965, 1969; Schott, 1964). Only lower-class boys were more father-oriented than mother-oriented. According to Rainwater (1962), this differentiation of power structure in the German family in relation to social-class membership still seems to hold true: the dominant father seems to be characteristic only in the lower social classes. Even these fathers feel that they are much more understanding and tolerant toward their wives and children than their own fathers were. To what extent there has really been a change toward greater tolerance, even in the lower social classes in the last sixty years, is difficult to say since, according to Kaufmann (1963), fathers and mothers generally tend to believe that the childrearing methods under which they grew up were more restrictive and authoritarian in comparison with their more tolerant and democratic attitudes toward their own children.

Perhaps equalitarianism is the most characteristic feature of today's

West German families, not patriarchalism or matriarchalism. This view is largely substantiated by Rainwater's (1962) study that can be regarded as a most valid representation of the intrafamilial sex-role differentiation in Western Germany. It is further supported by the fact that 84 percent of the EMNID (1955) sample agreed with the statement, "Men and women have equal rights."

Changes in legal rights as well as in the way husbands and wives see themselves and their parents, and the way they are characterized in turn by their own children today, point to role changes within the family. Husbands have, for the most part, given up their traditional dominant attitudes, and wives, their submissive and passive behavior. In spite of many traditional holdovers in our progressive time, the evidence indicates a "leveling" of the sex roles within the family of postwar West Germany.

Unfortunately, there are not many studies on parental value systems and attitudes to direct their childrearing practices, and there are even fewer hints from psychological data that differentiate parental attitudes toward boys and girls. Actually, we have to refer mainly to American authors in order to find some relevant information. Devereux, Bronfenbrenner, and Sucie (1962, 1965) compared American and German pupils who answered questionnaires on their parents' behavior toward them. They found that German parents showed more "parenting" behavior and emotional involvement than did the Americans. Moreover, U.S. parents preferred to spend their time with the child of their own sex, while German parents preferred the child of the opposite sex. Except that boys were more often spanked than girls, and girls more often than boys had to assume responsibility, the subjects in the above-mentioned study did not feel that they were reared very differently with respect to their sex. These results are consistent with those of the EMNID 1955 survey insofar as 68 percent of the subjects reported that they would apply spanking or scolding to boys and 54 percent to girls in case of needed punishment.

Again, we have to differentiate with regard to historical and social-class effects. Analyzing early childhood memories of men and women, Lehr and Thomae (1965) found that women's childhood memories tended to have a more negative, men's a more positive, shade. Women more often than men remembered frustrations and punishments. This was especially true for older women of lower social class and for younger women (born between 1920 and 1939) of higher social class. Upper-class older women and lower-class younger women, on the other hand, reported much liberty as children. During adolescence, restraint and stress characterized men more than women. Again, historical differences were found only in women insofar as younger women of lower classes reported more restraint than older ones, and younger women of higher classes more liberty than older ones during adolescence. If we compare only the younger generation of women and men interviewed by Lehr, we may say that socializing parental control strongly intervened in the lives of upper-class girls in the first ten years of life, while girls as well as boys from lower social classes, after having enjoyed a liberal childhood, felt parental controls tightening during adolescence.

With respect to the value systems according to which parents tried to socialize their children, little information from empirical studies could be found. Asked to name the foremost virtues they would like to see in girls and boys, men and women did not differentiate clearly between the sexes, according to the EMNID (1955) findings. From boys they expected primarily achievement, efficiency, alertness; secondarily, good manners, modesty, readiness to help others; and finally, obedience. From girls below sixteen years of age, men as well as women expected good manners, modesty, and readiness to help others in the first place, as well as achievement, industry, and efficiency. Typically "female" traits like "motherliness" and housewife virtues were mentioned by only 11 percent.

There are two cross-national studies comparing parental values in Germany and the United States. Unfortunately, they questioned *mothers* only with respect to what they expect their *boys* to do and become (Karr & Wesley, 1966; Wesley & Karr, 1968). According to research findings, in most areas U.S. mothers expect independent behavior of their sons earlier than do German mothers, except for bladder control and all activities involving traffic dangers (e.g., bicycling, touring, going shopping). The greatest differences between expectancies of U.S. and German mothers concern social independence, which American mothers encourage in their sons about three or more years earlier than do German mothers. The behavioral areas German mothers most strictly control could be classified as "home activities" such as obedience, cleanliness, orderliness, and good manners. Of greatest concern to American mothers are "away from home activities" including peer associations, leisure-time activities, expressing opinion, and church attendance. Whereas German mothers are more controlling with respect to toilet-training, U.S. mothers are so with regard to personal hygiene and sex behavior. The following lists represent a rank ordering of those "virtues" that mothers of six-year-old sons most frequently mentioned in the U.S. (Portland, Oregon) and West Germany (Münster):

Münster, West Germany	Portland, Oregon, U.S.A.
obedience	sociability
honesty	respect for others' and their rights
academic achievement	affectionate behavior
orderliness	self-reliance
readiness to help	obedience
cleanliness	religiosity

sociability	responsibility
good manners	individuality and independence
politeness	curiosity, thirst for knowledge
lack of obstinacy	academic achievement

In discussing their study, Wesley and Karr raise the question of whether the free naming of the value areas they used really reflects the cultural value system or, rather, those areas mothers have most trouble with, or a mixture of both.

Comparative studies based on more national and local samples are needed since cultural and social differences seem to be more prominent and effective in the realm of values and beliefs than in that of actual behavior.

Socialization Effects on Contemporary German Youth

The change in behavior, attitudes, and expectations of the older generation should enable us to predict a far-reaching leveling of sex-role differences in the generation born after the war. Schelsky (1957) expressed this view a decade ago, and there are more arguments for it than he could take into consideration such as findings from recent studies on achievement, interests, social attitudes, ideals, and goals of boys and girls.

With respect to school achievement, girls generally tend to do better than boys. Girls are more often consistently high achievers, whereas boys may show negative or fluctuating development (Kemmler, 1967; Knöpfler, 1964; Mierke, 1963; Rank, 1962; Schmidt, 1965). According to Kemmler (1967), there are more overachievers among girls and more underachievers among boys. She relates this to the differential working behavior of the sexes and the greater "vulnerability" of the boys. But if we examine the results more closely, the explanation is apparently more complex, involving an interaction among social class, teachers' judgment, sex, and behavior.

According to their school achievements and their teachers' vote, girls should have a better chance than boys to go to secondary schools. The reverse is true: more boys enter these schools, in the first place because they tend to make a better showing on tests than expected and, secondly, because parents more often register their sons for secondary schools than their daughters. This differential parental behavior has an even greater effect when one realizes that it counteracts the teachers' tendencies, so that the weights on the scales change in favor of the boys.

The area of interests in contrast to school achievement reveals many differences that clearly reflect traditional sex-role differentiation. When offered a choice among eleven areas of leisure time activities including athletics, art, languages, youth club, craftswork, etc., girls mainly chose social welfare activities, craftswork, and music as their favorite fields, while boys more often named sports and working on technical problems as their hobbies. Generally, the interests of the high school girls appeared more education-centered, whereas those of the boys were focused on physical activities and technical achievement (Lemberg & Klaus-Roeder, 1965).

Studies dealing with the relationship between adolescence and cinema or television preferences also stress sex differences to a certain degree. Westerns and detective stories are most preferred by boys under ten and by girls over ten years of age. Although boys show a major interest in sports news, Stückrath and Schottmayer (1967) report that girls, too, show an increasing interest in such topics. In 1955, the same authors found a much more "female" interest pattern in girls than they did ten years later.

Social class and education very often interact with sex-role influences. While boys and girls from high schools are to the same degree highly interested in television and broadcasts on politics, boys and girls from vocational schools prefer hit parades (Lückert, 1965). Generally, girls prefer television, boys prefer movies—which corresponds to certain differences with respect to allowed freedom between both sexes (Maletcke, 1959).

In summary, our information regarding sex differences in interests appears somewhat inconsistent due to a variety of methodological problems. In some studies, the instruments used definitely facilitated responses in agreement with the traditional sex stereotypes. In other cases, the discrepancies may be attributed to social-class influences or to regional factors. Studies conducted in Hamburg certainly must lead to findings differing from those sampled around Munich, although both are metropolitan areas. Finally, these divergencies indicate the different ways children and adolescents react to the increasing differentiation of the social sex roles in certain areas, especially in politics, sports, and even technical problems that were almost entirely a "privilege" of the men up to very recent years.

Moral Attitude and Moral Judgment

Adolescents' attitudes and thinking on guilt, rights, laws, and punishment may also reflect consistency and change over the past decades relevant to understanding social sex roles. Fortunately, a study first undertaken by Kelchner (1932) has been replicated four times since World War II by Thomae (1965) and students, Engels & Thomae, 1950; Kleiss, 1959, and Michaelsen, 1967. In essays on "guilt and punishment," the subjects mentioned capital crimes most often as reasons for guilt, but whereas the same percentage of boys did so in 1929 as in 1966 (34.3 percent versus 33.5 percent), there was a marked increase in the percentage of girls mentioning it in 1966 (1929, 31.6 percent versus 1966, 55.2 percent). Sexual offenses as reasons for feeling guilty were found three times more often in the boys' essays and over five times more often in the girls' essays in 1966 than in 1929. Generally, girls in 1966 wrote down more examples of feeling guilty by violating laws than in 1929, probably reflecting a shift toward more external orientation.

There was also a shift in perceived motivation for transgression of laws and rights from 1929 to 1966 on the part of both boys and girls. Economic deprivation was seldom seen as explanatory while insanity and avidity were often mentioned as motives in 1966. Most interesting, however, is a comparison of the ways guilt was defined in the two studies by the two sexes. An increased skeptical and critical attitude toward the generality of legal and social norms showed up in 1949 only to disappear again thereafter. Boys' definitions of guilt did not change very much, but girls in 1966 in comparison with their counterparts had moved away from irrational-ethical definitions toward rational-social ones. "Private" small-group oriented definitions of guilt decreased in boys as well as in girls, though more definitely in girls, in favor of more expanded public-oriented definitions.

Again, we may conclude that in the area of moral judgment as well as in other areas, changes in girls' opinions and attitudes are more impressive than those in boys, indicating a shift from a "my home is my realm attitude" to a more expanded, outer-world oriented attitude similar to that of the boys.

Ideals and goals of life can reflect socialization effects most impressively. In light of a number of studies on children's ideals since the turn of the century, we may compare different generations of adolescents empirically (Bergler, 1962; Bertlein, 1960; Elias, 1917; Engelmann, 1954; Friedrich, 1901; Glöckel, 1960; Goddard, 1904; Kesserlring, 1919; Lobsien, 1903; Richter, 1912; Schmeing, 1935).

According to Glöckel (1960), preadolescents and adolescents of 1960 as well as those of 1934–35 (Schmeing, 1935) generally prefer persons of their immediate social environment—parents, teachers, friends—as "ideals." This trend has been consistently stronger in girls than in boys. In various studies from the beginning of the century up to 1960, boys relatively more often than girls of the same age described as their "ideals" persons of public life such as political figures, sportsmen, writers, scientists. Interestingly, in all these studies, girls more frequently chose their ideals among persons of the opposite sex. Physical characteristics like beauty, body features, clothes, etc., were prevalent in the girls' characterizations of their "ideal person," whereas boys more frequently were impressed by their hero's achievements, success, and prestige. Müller (1967) found similar sex differences in children's essays on "If I could transmute then. . . . ." Generally, the sort of people chosen as ideals were the same in 1934 and in 1960. However, in 1960 people of the primary group, especially parents, were chosen, at least by boys, as anti-ideals more frequently than any time before, indicating an intensification of an authority conflict.

In both generations, 1934 and 1960, the ideal was found to change with the age of the subjects. The younger children preferred as ideals accessible persons in their environment, but for the older boys and girls inaccessible persons prevailed as ideals. This distinct crossover from closer to more remote ideals was taken as a sign of the psychological beginning of adolescence. In 1960, boys as well as girls reached that turning point about one year earlier than their age-mates in 1934. Glöckel (1960) interpreted this result in terms of psychological acceleration. With regard to the "ideal persons" young people chose, the agreement of reactions across generations may be interpreted in terms of a relative sex-role stability within a changing society.

Another area in which sex-role stereotypes were investigated with regard to sex, social class, and age difference was the future-time perspective of children, adolescents, and young adults. On the model of Allport's (1960) and Gillespie's (1955) cross-national studies, several investigators have asked groups of German youth to write essays on such fictive topics as "My life up to the year 2000" (Czisch, 1961; Goerdt, 1965; Höhn, 1967; Oblinger, 1958). In these fantasy life courses, boys more often than girls described aspects of their future work lives, and girls more often than boys wrote about their future husbands and families. These sex differences to some extent seem to be dependent on the residential areas in which the subjects live. Czisch, for example, failed to find any sex differences since both boys and girls in the Stuttgart area where he conducted his study were strongly family-oriented.

The largest sex differences were found among students from vocational schools (i.e., working girls and boys below the age of eighteen who have to attend school once a week). In high school students, on the other hand, these differences were rather small. Höhn (1967) found similar differences between working girls and high school girls, as can be seen in Table 4:

TABLE 4 PERCENTAGES OF GIRLS AND EXPRESSED GOALS

Goals	WORKING GIRLS		HIGH SCHOOL GIRLS	
	No.	*Percent*	*No.*	*Percent*
Marriage only	129	49	3	3
Marriage and career	102	39	88	73
Career only	24	9	29	24
Neither	8	3		
Totals	263	100	120	100

Age of subjects proved to be another important factor. The largest sex differences in future-time perspective were found in the youngest age groups. Though still apparent, sex differences diminished with age of subjects: girls over eighteen became relatively more work-oriented and boys more family-oriented (Goerdt, 1965). A more recent study by Pfeil (1968) confirms these results. However, less than half of her twenty-three-year-old women mentioned family-centered goals and about one-fifth mentioned work-oriented goals. Even at that stage of life, when founding one's family becomes the main "task" (Havighurst, 1963), women do not restrict their expectations to the world of the "home" although they clearly recognize that success and promotion in the work world is still easier for men than for women. Sex-role stereotypes seem to change at different speeds in the different areas of society.

Conclusions

As we have shown, social sex-role stereotypes in West Germany still prevail in many "experts' " opinions and still determine social and political decisions. At the opposite extreme, stereotyped opinions advocating complete interchangeability of sex roles have disturbed responsible people. They learned that at the turn of our century the man was the active, decision-making, and authoritarian leader, and the woman, the passive, obedient, submissive complement, silently managing the home. Now they are told that since the middle of our century women have become more and more dominating, actively entering into the external world, and men, who have lost their dominant position, eventually will become superfluous.

Neither of these black/white pictures of social sex roles seems to hold against empirical findings. With regard to the "old" role division, we can object that even around 1900, the woman had a prominent social position though admittedly mainly within the home and family. Secondly, some of the "proofs for a dramatic change" proved to be misinterpretations of statistics. With regard to the "new" stereotypes, one may wonder if they are not partly the result of methodological shortcomings. Discussions on the female role in industry, politics, and science became such an attractive topic for many writers that they seriously neglected the male role. Of all that has been written on the woman's role in society, little is based on empirical findings and even less is suitable for generalizations. Sex-role changes that actually can be traced throughout the past seventy years may be largely attributed to the woman's access to higher education, political life, and equal rights with regard to major familial decisions. However, those "objective" legal changes usually tend to lag behind the actual social readiness for such changes.

The social sex-role differences we have reported in West Germany today were usually those of degree only and tended to refer to the sexes' expectations, attitudes, opinions, and judgments rather than to actual behavior patterns. Whereas no essential changes in the male role during the past seventy years could be inferred from our data, there was a leveling of sex-role differences, especially in the younger generation from the higher social class living in industrial cities.

There has always been a great temptation to speculate on social sex-role differences. However, before prematurely generalizing from findings, one should keep in mind that sex is only one among many other covarying and contravarying variables that determine human behavior.

References

Allport, G. W. "Values and Our Youth." *Teachers College Record,* 63 (1961), 211–19.

Argelander, A. "Über die Motive der Berufswahl und des Berufswechsels." *Zeitschrift pädagogische Psychologie,* 24, (1923), 46–51; 98–105.

Baumert, G. "Einige Beobachtungen zur Wandlung der familialen Stellung des Kindes in Deutschland." In *Jugend in der modernen Gesellschaft, Neue wissenschaftliche Bibliothek,* L. v. Friedeburg, ed. 5: Soziologie, pp. 310–20. Köln-Berlin: Kiepenheuer and Witsch, 1965.

Bergler, R. "Die psychologische Struktur der Leitbilder Jugendlicher." *Vita Humana,* 5 (1962), 34–60.

Bertlein, H. *Das Selbstverständnis der Jugend heute.* Berlin-Hannover-Darmstadt: Verlag Schroedel, 1960.

Blood, R. O., Jr., and D. M. Wolfe. *Husbands and Wives.* New York: The Free Press of Glencoe, 1960.

Bramesfeld, E., and O. Graf. *Praktisch-psychologischer und arbeitsphysiologischer Leitfaden für das Arbeitsstudium.* München: Carl Hauser Verlag, 1949.

Bundesminister für Arbeit und Sozialordnung, ed. *Frauen-Enquête: Bericht der Bundesregierung über die Situation der Frauen in Beruf, Familie und Gesellschaft.* Bonn: Bonner Universitätsdruckerei, 1966.

Czisch, G. "Untersuchungen über die Zukunftserwartungen Jugendlicher." Bonn, 1961. Unpublished paper.

Devereux, E. C., Jr., U. Bronfenbrenner, and G. J. Sucie. "Patterns of Parent Behavior in the United States of America and the Federal Republic of Germany: A Cross-National Comparison." *International Sociology Science Journal,* 14 (1962), 488–506. German translation in *Jugend in der modernen Gesellschaft, Neue wissenshaftliche Bibliothek,* L. v. Friedeburg, ed. Köln-Berlin: Kiepenheuer und Witsch, 1965, 335–57.

Elias, M. "Ideale judischer Kinder," *Zeitschrift pädagogische Psychologie,* 18 (1917), 464–74.

EMNID—Institut für Meinungsforschung. "Jugend zwischen 15 und 24: Untersuchung zur Situation der deutschen Jugend im Bundesgebiet." Bielefeld: M. v. Stackenberg Verlag, 1952.

———. "Jugend—Bildung und Freizeit, 3. Untersuchung zur Situation der deutschen Jugend im Bundesgebiet." Stiftung Jugendwerk der Deutschen Shell, 1965. Unpublished paper.

Engelmann, W. "Untersuchungen über die geistig-seelische Entwicklungsbeschleunigung im Wertungsbereich." Heidelberg, 1954. Unpublished dissertation.

Engels, H., and H. Thomae. "Schuld und Sühne im Urteil jugendlicher Arbeiter der Gegenwart." *Unsere Jugend,* 2 (1950), 361–66.

Friedrich, J. "Ideale der Kinder." *Zeitschrift für pädagogische Psychologie,* 3 (1901), 38–64.

Fröhner, R., M. v. Stackenberg, and W. Eser. *Familie und Ehe: Probleme in den deutschen Familien der Gegenwart.* Bielefeld: M. v. Stackenberg Verlag, 1956.

Gillespie, J. M., and G. W. Allport. *Youth's Outlook to the Future—A Cross-National Study.* New York: Doubleday, 1955.

Glöckel, H. "Eine Vergleichsuntersuchung zur Frage des jugendlichen Idealerlebens—Ideal und Gegenideal." *Psychologie Rundschau,* 11 (1960), 1–20.

Goddard, H. H. "Die Ideale der Kinder," *Zeitschrift für experimentalische Pädagogik,* 5 (1904), 156–73.

Goerdt, P. "Zukunftserwartungen der Berufsschuler der Gegenwart." *Die Deutsche Berufsschule,* 61 (1965), 10–16.

Havighurst, R. J. "Dominant Concerns in the Life Cycle." In *Gegenwartsprobleme der Entwicklungspsychologie—Festschrift für Charlotte Bühler,* L. Schenk-Danziger and H. Thomae, eds. Göttingen: Verlag für Psychologie, Hogrefe, 1963, pp. 27–37.

Hill, R. "Decision Making and Family Life Cycle." In *Social Structure and the Family—Generational Relations,* E. Shanas and G. F. Streib, eds. Englewood Cliffs, N.J.: Prentice-Hall, 1965, pp. 113–39.

Höhn, E. "Partnervorstellungen junger Mädchen." In *Psychologie und Pädagogik,* H. Horn, ed. Weinheim-Berlin: Verlag Julius Beltz, 1967, pp. 317–66.

Holzapfel, R. "Untersuchungen zur Präsenz der frühen Kindheit." Bonn, 1964. Unpublished paper.

Jaide, W. "Selbstzeugnisse jugenlicher Industriearbeiterinnen." In *Die jungen Arbeiterinnen,* 2nd ed. G. Wurzbacher, W. Jaide, *et al.* München: Juventa Verlag, 1958, 39–132.

Kant, I. "Anthropologie." In *Pragmatischer Hinsicht,* K. Vorlander, ed. 6th ed. Leipzig: Meiner Verlag, 1922. 1st. ed. Königsberg, 1798.

Karr, C., and F. Wesley. "Comparison of German and U.S. Childrearing Practices." *Child Development,* 37 (1966), 715–23.

Kaufmann, I. "Untersuchungen zur Elternrolle an Hand von 200 Biographien." Bonn, 1963. Unpublished dissertation.

Kelchner, M. "Schuld und Sühne im Urteil jugendlicher Arbeiter und Arbeiterinnen." *Zeitschrift für angewandte Psychologie,* 63 (1932), 1–147.

Kemmler, L. *Erfolg und Versagen in der Grundschule.* Göttingen: Verlag für Psychologie, Hogrefe, 1967.

Kesserlring, M. "Untersuchungen über Ideale im höheren Jugendalter." *Zeitschrift für pädagogische Psychologie,* 20 (1919), 12–37; 89–103.

Kleiss, G. "Schuld und Sühne im Urteil jugendlicher Arbeiter—Nachuntersuchung 1956." Erlangen, 1959. Unpublished paper.

Knöpfler, H. "Schulische Entwicklung und Berufsbewährung in psychischer, somatischer und sozialer Sicht." Bonn, 1964. Unpublished dissertation.

König, R. *Materialien zur Soziologie der Familie. Beiträge zur Soziologie und Sozialphilosophie.* Bd. 1. Bern: A. Francke Verlag, 1946.

———. "Family and Authority: The German Father in 1955." *Sociological Review,* n.s., 5 (1957), 107–127.

Lehr, U. *Die ersten sechs Lebensjahre in der Erinnerung Erwachsener und Jugendlicher.* Göttingen: Verlag für Psychologie, Hogrefe, 1965, pp. 159–67.

———. *Beruf und Lebensschicksal—Untersuchungen zur weiblichen Berufsrolle.* Frankfurt am Main: Athenäum Verlag, 1969.

———and H. Thomae. "Konflikt, seelische Belastung und Lebensalter." Forschungsberichte des Landes Nordrhein—Westfalen, Nr. 1455. Köln und Opladen: Westdeutscher Verlag, 1965.

Lemberg, E. "Auberschulische Bildungsinteressen der Gymnasialjugend." In *Studien zur Soziologie der Gymnasialjugend,* O. Schafer, E. Lemberg, and R. Klaus-Roeder, eds. Heidelberg: Quelle und Meyer, 1965, pp. 153–212.

Lersch, P. *Vom Wesen der Geschlechter.* München: Erasmus Verlag, 1947.

Lobsien, M. "Kinderideale." *Zeitschrift Pädagogische Psychologie,* 5 (1903), 323–44; 457–94.

Lückert, H. R. *Beiträge zur Psychologie der Gegenwartsjugend.* München-Basel: Ernest Reinhardt Verlag, 1965.

Maletzke, G. *Fernsehen im Leben der Jugend.* Hamburg: H. Bredow Institut, 1959.

Michaelsen, U. "Schuld und Sühne im Urteil jugendlicher Arbeiter und Arbeiterinnen, Machuntersuchung, 1966." Bonn, 1967. Unpublished paper.

Mierke, K. *Begabung, Bildung, Bildsamkeit,—Betrachtungen über das Bildungsschicksal des mittelmässig begabten Schulkindes.* Bern: Gemeinschaftsverlag Hans Huber, 1963; Stuttgart: Ernest Klett, 1963.

Mitscherlich, A. *Auf dem Wege zur vaterlosen Gesellschaft,—Ideen zur Sozialpsychologie.* München: Piper Verlag, 1963.

Moers, M. *Frauenerwerbsarbeit und ihre Wirkungen auf die Frau.* Recklinghausen: Verlag Bitter, 1948.

Müller, R. G. E. "Psychologische Analyse projektiver Aufsätze von Schülern im späten Kindesalter." *Schule und Psychologie,* 14 (1967), 379–87.

Oblinger, H. "Zukunftsvorstellungen des Volksschulkindes." *Schule und Psychologie,* 5 (1958), 107–19.

Pfeil, E. *Die 23jährigen—eine Generationenuntersuchung am Geburtsjahrgang 1941.* Tübingen: Verlag J. C. B. Mohr, 1968.

Pichottka, I. "Wollen und Können der Mutter in der heutigen Erziehung." In *Die Mutter in der heutigen Gesellschaft; Gesamtbericht über den 63, Dtscher Fürsorgetag in München,* H. Muthesius, ed. Köln-Berlin: Grote Verlag, 1964, pp. 186–97.

Rainwater, L. "Social Status Differences in the Family Relationships of German Men." *Marriage and Family Living,* 24 (1962), 12–17.

Rank, T. *Schulleistung und Persönlichkeit, Wissenschaftliche Jugendkunde.* Heft 4. München: Barth Verlag, 1962.

Richter, A. "Statistische Erhebung über die Ideale von Volksschulkindern." *Zeitschrift pädagogische Psychologie,* 13 (1912), 254–64.

Rosner, L. "Frauenarbeit—Provisorium auf Dauer." *Der Volkswirt,* 18 (1963), 831–32.

Schaffner, B. *Father Land: A Study of Authoritarianism in the German Family.* New York: Columbia University Press, 1948.

Scharmann, D. L. "Die Situation der berufstätigen Frau in der industriellen Gesellschaft." *Zentralblatt Arbeitswissenschaft,* 16 (1962), 113–16.

Schelsky, H., ed. *Arbeiterjugend gestern und heute.* Heidelberg: Quelle und Meyer, 1955a.

———. *Wandlungen der deutschen Familie in der Gegenwart.* 3rd ed. Stuttgart: Enke Verlag, 1955b.

———. *Die skeptische Generation—Eine Soziologie der deutschen Jugend.* Düsseldorf-Köln: Verlag Diederichs, 1957.

Schmeing, K. "Ideal und Gegenideal—Eine Untersuchung zur Polarität der jugendlichen Entwicklung." *Zeitschrift für angewandte Psychologie,* 70 (1935), 1–136.

Schmidt, M. *Somatische und psychische Faktoren der Reifeentwicklung, Wissenschaftliche Jugendkunde.* Heft 9. München: Verlag Barth, 1965.

Schott, O. "Untersuchung zur Präsenz der frühen Kindheit." Bonn, 1964. Unpublished paper.

Seward, G. H., and W. R. Larson. "Adolescent Concepts of Social Sex Roles in the United States and the Two Germanies." *Human Development,* 11 (1968), 217–48.

Shanas, E., and G. F. Streib. *Social Structure and the Family: Generational Relations.* Englewood Cliffs, N.J.: Prentice-Hall, 1965.

Stahl, M. "Ehe und Familie im Lebenshorizont des jungen Mädchens von heute." In *Die Mutter in der heutigen Gesellschaft: Gesamtbericht über den 63. Dtscher Fürsorgetag in München,* H. Muthesius, ed. Köln-Berlin: Verlag Grote, 1964.

Stückrath, F., and G. Schottmayer. *Fernsehen und Grobstadtjugend.* Braunschweig: Westermann Verlag, 1967.

Thomae, H. *Vorbilder und Leitbilder der Jugend. Deutsches Jugendinstitut,* Bd. 6. München: Juventa Verlag, 1965.

———. "Familienzusammenhalt und Berufsbewährung." In *Jugendliche in der Berufsbewährung,* W. Hagen, H. Thomae, E. Mansfeld, and F. J. Mathey, eds. Stuttgart: Verlag Thieme, 1958, pp. 115–37.

Weegmann, I. "Frauen sind anders." *Arbeitgeber,* 18 (1966), 462–63.

Weininger, O. *Geschlecht und Charakter,* 8th ed. Wien-Leipzig: Verlag Braumuller, 1919.

Wesley, F., and C. Karr. "Vergleiche von Ansichten und Erziehungshaltungen deutscher und amerikanischer Mütter." *Psychologische Rundschau,* 19 (1968), 35–46.

Wilms, D. "Ausbildungsprobleme bei veränderter Struktur der Frauenerwerbsarbeit." *R.K.W.—Rationalisierung,* 17 (1966), 267–69.

Wurzbacher, G. *Leitbilder gegenwärtigen deutschen Familienlebens.* Dortmund: Ardey Verlag, 1951.

———W. Jaide, *et al.,* eds. *Die junge Arbeiterinnen—Beiträge zur Sozialkunde und Jugendarbeit,* 2nd ed. München: Juventa Verlag, 1958.

11 MALE AND FEMALE IN THE GERMAN DEMOCRATIC REPUBLIC

Alfred Katzenstein

While numerous researchers are investigating remote facets of our rapidly changing society, less attention has been directed toward the more personal aspects of living whose development has lagged behind material progress. Changes in private spheres have become visible only after conspicuous evolution in such public domains as technology, education, physical science, economics, and even the law. The greatly accelerated pace of postwar readjustment, however, has brought out new developments in intimate behavior, including that of sex roles, which previous generations believed to be eternal verities of "human nature."

In the case of Germany, where recent history has split a single people into two parts with as diametrically contrasting living conditions as those of the Federal Republic and the Democratic Republic, there is fertile ground indeed for research into all levels of social response. Since adequate understanding and appraisal of the present scene can be achieved only in the perspective of its antecedents, a brief overview of the past is needed (Müller-Mertens, Paterna & Steinmetz, 1965).

The past

From Caesar to Kaiser

Following the downfall of the Roman Empire, it became apparent that in Germany the prevailing hedonistic attitude with its delight in sensual enjoyment transmitted from the ancient pagan cultures and congruent with early Germanic tribal patterns contrasted sharply with the rising asceticism of Christianity's rejection of pleasures as "low fleshly lust." The increasing dominance of ascetic submissiveness as a publicly professed way of life proceeded by no means in a straight line. On the contrary, history shows victories and defeats for this way of life—the defeats resulting from the inherent opposition of the people, who rebelled against the restrictions and used every available opportunity to break away from them.

Particularly in periods of warfare, which frequently assumed the character of religious conflicts, many subterfuges and emotional outlets were found. Thus, during the Crusades the fashionable "Minne" adoration—at first a purely lyrical and platonic current—reverted to more earthy extramarital liaisons. Moreover, the sixteenth and seventeenth centuries were characterized by the openly sensuous climate of the Renaissance, later toned down by the moral intolerance and the brutal terror of the Inquisition as well as by the spreading fear of syphilis. The impending ruin of feudal power, responsible for the stilted, oversophisticated Rococo with its impotent ritualism, was in turn followed by the vital and forceful middle-class rebellion of the *Sturm und Drang* period. With consolidation of the economic and political power of the rising middle class, suppression of sexuality reached its climax in the hypocritical dual morality of the nineteenth century.

Until World War II, public life of Western culture in general, and of Germany in particular, was characterized by a strictly hierarchical structure of society with clearly defined levels of absolute power and authority and complete submission to authority. This hierarchy extended into the family and later also into public education. As feudal lords, army officers, factory owners, bankers, and finally Storm Troop commanders were absolute bosses whose orders were unthinkingly obeyed by their subordinates who in turn exerted an equally unquestioned authority over their underlings, so husbands at home and teachers in school demanded the utmost submission and obedience.

The dual morality that allows one behavior pattern to be professed publicly while another is practiced in private induces a dichotomy of sex roles to the disadvantage of women. In Germany up to 1945, this situation was an inherent aspect of the hierarchical social system together with the persistent need to contrast the superiority of the "true German" ingroup with the evil outsider. The implied threat that outside influences were undermining and pervading the ingroup gave rise to the fear of being considered an agent of foreign influences and thus open to political punishment and social ostracism. Such fear acted as a formidable pressure for conformity and submission. Once these patterns had become the accepted and expected norms of behavior, they brought great benefits to those in power. Asceticism, obedience, and conformity directly increased economic productivity, an important asset to the rising power élite who were at a geographic disadvantage in a "world" centered around the Mediterranean.

Similar trends were found far beyond the borders of Germany as Walker and Fletcher (1965) indicate:

> It is not surprising that by accepting the sexual code of the church, the "Christian" nations rapidly outdistanced their competitors in the race for worldly prosperity. An incalculable number of man-hours were saved for them for such non-sexual and progressive activities as money making, getting on in the world, soldiering and the conquest of dissolute nations [p. 107].

Aside from this direct consequence of submissiveness and asceticism, there appears to be a more indirect but equally important psychological effect. Thus, Mannstein (1967), pointing out that rigid moral inhibitions in private life facilitate the commitment of crimes against supposed enemies, states:

> Strangely enough the dangers of sexual deviations are denounced publicly and from the pulpits much more strongly than all cruelties and outrages of regular armies of so-called civilized and christian states . . . as if every smallest deviation from the numerous norms (in sexual relations) should create the feeling of sin and prepare the subject for absolute obedience in military matters [p. 145].

The absolute power of the leaders, be they called Herzog, Kaiser, or Führer, together with the ever present threat of disgrace, failure, social degradation, and isolation, created a pervasive atmosphere of insecurity and anxiety. This emotional climate not only prevented the healthy maturing of the individual but also favored an exaggerated assertion of authority and self-righteous domination of the weak by the strong. In this society, weak was identified with female; strong with male. Masculinity was regarded as a badge of natural superiority and the display of attributes presumed to represent it was applauded. In a climate in which a child was kept in continuous fear of corporal punishment, ridicule, loss of love, and social ostracism, the individual was restricted by moral and legal prohibitions to the point of stultification. One bitter proverb goes: *Verboten ist alles was nicht erlaubt ist!* (Everything is forbidden that is not allowed!) Under such conditions, even the tamest and most law-abiding conformist was bound to fail, and, provided that he was able to keep his transgressions well hidden, to be beset by guilt feelings. The most horrible threats, of course, loomed in the sexual sphere. Autoerotic and homoerotic play were said to result in most dreadful diseases and, if discovered, immediately led to public degradation and expulsion from the group. Even thoughts and desires were supposedly fraught with fearful consequences: premarital sex relations were reputed to cause infections of the most indescribable kind.

A young man, restricted on all sides and expected to direct all his energy to developing hardiness and occupational skill, did not take long to find out that others were more successful because they belonged to one or another of the various "patriotic" male societies. Examples were the Army, certain semimilitary organizations such as the notorious Storm Troops, dueling student fraternities, sporting clubs, and numerous others. The camaraderie in these groups and their usually high ranking and well-to-do "old men" (sponsors) not only offered occupational and financial advantages, they also provided, under cover of drinking bouts, outlets for expressing sexual and aggressive impulses. Here the strict social sanctions were removed. Each organization had its own code of conduct well separated from the openly proclaimed morality that it professed to defend. Any disagreeable consequences of such behavior were quickly "adjusted" by the group leadership that, in return for protection, demanded "only" absolute faithfulness and obedience. These "patriotic" societies were a powerful tool in the hands of those who pulled the strings. But the deep rift between the public laws of conduct and those practiced privately or under the anonymity of the group corrupted the character of the young people and dangerously undermined the social fabric. Apart from this, the excesses of these groups left numerous victims—not adversaries felled in noble duels as so frequently claimed in their beer-songs, but weak and helpless women and children. The unmarried mothers who had been unable to undo the consequences of acts to which they had frequently been coerced, and the children to whom they gave birth with their human dignity destroyed, had to face a life of misery and degradation.

"The People" on Trial

The question may well be asked why only man's role has been dealt with so far. During all of its written history until 1945, Germany has essentially been a man's world. The young girl learned that man was superior, that he was to be obeyed, and that even her thoughts and her logic were better kept to herself if in conflict with his superior judgment. During the first decades of the twentieth century, progressive political parties and groups in Germany undertook to change the worst features of this rigid, dehumanizing pattern. In politics, this led eventually to the fall of the empire (*Kaiserreich*) and to the founding of the Weimar Republic, events that soon were paralleled by similar changes in other spheres.

Advocates of women's rights, who became more influential with the increasing strength of socialist and communist parties, were successful in achieving votes for women, political equality, admission to academic institutions, and teaching positions. On the other hand, they were unable to effect such needed changes as legal equality. The law discriminated between men and women as it still does in West Germany, with respect to inheritance and property rights as well as in many other areas. Moreover, there was no equal-pay-for-equal-work provision.[1] Nevertheless, more and more women began to use their new freedom, and some were even elected to the *Reichstag*.

A cautious development of new family relations also became discernible. Although the majority of people, still firmly grounded in an almost feudal way of life, adhered closely to the tightly organized, politically and socially conservative churches, families increasingly became a sort of economic enterprise with a legally defined mutual obligation to provide for their members' welfare. The great economic changes of the twenties with their increased competition, their deep economic crises, their millions of unemployed and homeless, strained the family bonds to the breaking point. Numerous parents, no longer able to provide their growing children with the necessities of life, had to depend instead on the small earnings that their children, exploited as cheap labor, were able to bring home. Under these circumstances, it was inevitable that the educational development of the children suffered. On the other hand, many young couples were unable to marry and settle down since they could nowhere find jobs to support them. In general, a more liberalized pattern of family life and interpersonal relations developed in the larger cities of the Rhein and Ruhr area, currently the Federal Republic, while with the exclusion of a few larger cities, living conditions in what is now the territory of the German Democratic Republic remained extremely backward.

During this period, another development assumed increasing importance with regard to sex roles. It had never been easy to tolerate the frustration of erotic and sexual needs imposed by the conventional pattern of behavior, but at least the sources of temptation had been more or less well hidden. Now, however, a whole industry arose to confront young people with temptation all day long, a temptation made irresistible by skillful psychological tricks. Advertisements, commercials, artificial stimulation of sexual desires, deceptive promises of sexual extravagances and secrets—all these were omnipresent. If at least the schools had taken a clear position against this audio-visual flood, young people might have been better prepared for it. But most educational authorities in Germany pretended not to see. Entertainment and the publicity industries did not exist as far as they were concerned, except when they disseminated legends and ideals that corresponded to the feudalist prewar value system. Then whole schools with principals and school bands marched in formation to cinemas, or listened to radio plays. As a result, most young people were deeply torn between the hard line of conduct propounded in public pronouncements by their school and other authorities, and the glittering, enticing sweetness of life that literature and screen, radio and theater depicted with such beguiling vividness.

Unfortunately, this was not the only failure of the school system. Instead of preparing the younger generation for its tasks in a rapidly transforming society, schools in Germany in the twenties tended to perpetuate old beliefs and customs and to foster regard for aristocratic superiority. They also continued to rely upon fear and anxiety as primary motivators. Fear of corporal punishment, fear of ridicule, fear of God's omnipotence and omniscience, combined with fear of illness and infection, social failure and ostracism, were to imbue the growing child with submissiveness and docility and, of course, were apt to cripple character development.

By its mode of selecting applicants for higher institutions of learning on the basis of their parents' ability to pay substantial tuition fees, the educational system of the German *Reich* contributed to the maintenance of the existing hierarchical stratification, while the separation of boys and girls in school and college, with few exceptions, tended to maintain the inequality of sexes. Even in their less conspicuous aspects such as teaching aids, textbooks, pictures on school walls, etc., the "media" propagated the "noble" traditional values of German military greatness and the dangers of equalitarian new-fangled ideas. It goes without saying that men were always presented as successful executives and superior breadwinners, while modest and busy women cared for kitchen and children.

The Weimar Republic was thus characterized to a greater extent than any previous period by a coexistence of contradictory social influences and contrasting styles of living. The impact of the new ideas was felt differently in different social classes. While the ruling circles proved almost completely impervious, the working class and some strata of the peasantry as well as groups of intellectuals were receptive to these influences. In these groups, we also find the formation of a vanguard that increased rapidly and made itself felt in the communities. Even to those who did not want to see, it soon became obvious that within the confusing array of forward and backward movements the seeds of spiritual independence and rational humanism were rapidly spreading. Apart from organized labor, more and more young people were drawn into socialist and communist as well as middle-class student movements, the so-called *bündische Bewegung,* and began to take a hard critical look at what we would call today The Establishment. Marx and Engels, Lenin, Freud, and Gandhi were read and eagerly discussed by millions of young Germans. Fearless people like doctors Hodann (1932), Hirschfeld (1926–1930), and many others exerted all their influence in favor of an honest and sane morality and a healthier position on sexual matters.

Nazis and Führer

Then the Nazis came into power, brutally crushing everything that seemed to have even the slightest progressive threat. They began systematically to revive and strengthen all those influences that had ever been repressive and apt to produce submissiveness, conformity, and easily manageable aggression. This was the situation when, in 1945, the murderous Third Reich finally collapsed under the powerful assault of the Allied armies. The majority of young Germans who had survived, as well as their elders, had been subjected to a thorough conditioning and indoctrination with regard to the specific sex and racial role they were expected to play. They had come out of the Nazi educational process technically expert but emotionally primitive and immature to the point of being incapable of independent thinking. Trained from early childhood to hide insecurity and cowardice under exhibitions of masculine prowess and group aggression against the weak, in total defeat they still proudly proclaimed their behavior to be true comradeship and faithful obedience to the Führer, but meekly renamed it *Befehlsnotstand* (extenuating circumstances due to enforced execution of orders).

The present

Economic Changes

In 1945, many thoughtful people asked whether it would ever be possible to redress the faults of centuries of Prussian educational repression. Today, after almost twenty-five years, there is little doubt about the answer to this question. The mental attitude of the average citizen of the German Democratic Republic shows a completely different outlook. The change that has taken place has not remained a surface phenomenon but has begun to penetrate such private planes as the conception of sex roles and the character of family living. Before describing this aspect in some detail, a sketch of some background facts is required.

The German Democratic Republic, which had always been the economically most backward part of Germany, was completely prostrate by the end of the war in 1945—its cities in ruins and its population uprooted. Within the last twenty years, it has developed into one of the advanced industrial states of Europe. Of the 18 million people living today within its boundaries, approximately one-third had actively taken part in the Nazi war effort and had been thoroughly indoctrinated in the ideology of "master race" and "masculine superiority"; one-third of the German Democratic Republic's population was below fifteen years of age at the time of the unconditional surrender, whereas the last third was born after the war. In spite of an inordinately high percentage of invalids, children, and people of retirement age in 1966 (Schneider 1967, p. 12), economic growth has been made possible by the increasingly active participation of women, who at present constitute 47 percent of the working population.

A special chapter would be needed to describe how, with an overwhelming majority of former Nazis, not only was the economy developed, but the formation of a democratic state began to take shape simultaneously. Job security—a pious wish even under the Weimar Republic when fear of economic failure and unemployment were ever present—has been established and is in fact so much taken for granted that hardly anybody here speaks about it. Men and women from all walks of life feel economically secure. They know that there will always be a decent job for them. This guarantee is not only laid down in the Constitution, but a network of labor laws makes it almost impossible for anyone to lose his job. In addition, the great manpower shortage that currently exists in the German Democratic Republic and probably will continue for some years tends to increase the importance of each individual worker and to enhance his job security. Although the sting of economic insecurity and the resulting pervasive anxiety has thus been widely removed, there has been no lack of effective incentives. Apart from the heightened social prestige that goes with executive position and intellectual eminence, there are very real financial and other material advantages scaled according to responsibility and social significance of work. As a result, there is considerable striving for more and higher education and training. Evening and correspondence schools attract a steadily increasing group of people, while the regular system of higher education is also being continuously enlarged.

School Reform

In a series of interconnected laws and directives, the right of all young people to education up to the most advanced level has been realized. Neither the financial capacity nor the social status of parents, but the student's own knowledge and ability, determine how far he will progress beyond the ten-year school level compulsory for all. Attendance at all institutions of learning is completely free, and more than 90 percent of all full-time students receive a substantial monthly state allowance similar to that given to veterans in the U.S. under the G.I. Bill of Rights. All students with average grades of B or better, regardless of their parents' income, receive an additional allowance for learning efficiency. Evening-and correspondence-school students obtain one to two days' paid additional leave per month (study days) from their places of employment.

These measures have greatly enlarged the student population and have transformed the educational privilege of a small minority into a right for all. The number of university students in the German Democratic Republic more than tripled from 1951 (31,512) to 1966 (106,422), with women constituting approximately one-third of the student population (Staatliche Zentralverwaltung für Statistik, 1967, p. 476). The present aim is to send one out of four children to trade schools and universities. Of equal significance is the change in the content and spirit of education. Sympathy and understanding is fostered for others, especially those who are weak and exploited. Women's role in the fight for freedom and peace as well as in cultural development is emphasized. The use of physical superiority as threat or pressure is condemned, and prohibition of corporal punishment in school is implemented by disciplinary action and discharge in cases of infraction by teachers who have failed to comply. Even observers from West Germany (Commandeur & Sterzel, 1965) who profess to dislike the socialist system "for personal and political reasons" consider the "unified educational system of the GDR an impressive advance," and conclude: "Pedagogues in the Federal Republic are perfectly right when they point out ever more frequently that the German Democratic Republic is superior to us in some respects with regard to school education" (p. 59).

Incidentally, sex education constitutes an inherent part of the school curriculum. Influential educators demand an earlier start with information on sexual matters, which at present takes place in the ninth to eleventh class (ages fifteen to seventeen), in order to anticipate "hidden coteachers." As a result of the frank treatment of these questions in schools, public lectures, PTA meetings, and numerous books widely read by older children and students, a change in attitude is taking place. Fears, inhibitions, and anxieties based upon irrational acceptance of asceticism and guilt feelings due to traditional secretiveness are lessening. The whole sphere of sexuality is fast losing its flavor of something shameful, forbidden, and unclean. Of course, much remains to be done. One of the primary tasks at present is the better preparation of the teachers themselves for the treatment of these problems. Grassel (1967) has recently conducted several attitude polls of pupils and teachers in this sensitive area. In Table 1 pupils' attitudes toward sex education are shown (p. 180):

TABLE 1 PUPILS' ATTITUDES TOWARD SEX EDUCATION

Attitude	*Percent of Pupils*
Interesting and information-extending	23.5
Normal subject matter	19.4
Involving nothing new	20.8
Negative	13.9
No answer	22.4

The general trend of these results is obviously positive.

In another survey, the same investigator explored teachers' attitudes toward premarital intercourse, with the results shown in Table 2 (p. 195):

TABLE 2 TEACHERS' ATTITUDES TOWARD PREMARITAL INTERCOURSE

	Percent of Females	*Percent of Males*
In favor	72.0	63.0
Opposed	16.2	20.6
Undecided	11.7	16.2

On this issue also, the results are again in the positive direction.

School and sex information doubtlessly contribute greatly to the final formation of sex roles. Heightened self-reliance in women as well as men develops from the knowledge that everyone is needed and that everyone has the right to avail himself of all educational advantages. Self-confidence is further enhanced by the fact that literally every citizen is asked to participate actively in decision-making of one kind or another. Asked why students in the German Democratic Republic seemed to be rather unperturbed, whereas those in other countries were clamoring for a voice in the management of schools and universities, my younger daughter, aged nineteen, a first year medical student, replied:

> We are always asked to become members of decision-making bodies on the campus. It is sometimes difficult to find enough candidates to volunteer for election to those functions. Even those who do, sometimes wish they would be spared some of these steering board meetings, which also require preparation, in order to have more time available for study. Who of us would go to ask for more participation in management?

Work, Women, and the Law

Everyone has ample occasion to prove his capacity in his occupation as well as in public affairs. There remains also the fact that, due to the tremendous losses of men during the war, the older age groups have been depleted, with the result that men are outnumbered three to one. Women are consequently more eager to admire and even spoil men instead of pushing them into defensive positions. On the other hand, the continuous appeals of all political parties for understanding and application of rational solutions in difficulties of an interpersonal nature are getting results, and one sees frequent examples in clinical interviews and PTA steering boards of physically hard-working, powerfully built fathers trying to carry on a reasonable and constructive dialogue with their family members. Of course, the behavior of millions of men will be so varied that any single denominator can only be an approximation. Yet, one may well say that men in general have moved in the direction of greater self-confidence, less stress on physical prowess, and a more rational acceptance of and respect for the dignity and value of women and children.

With regard to women, concerted and persistent efforts have been made to facilitate their constructive and creative participation in the work process beyond their own homes. Nurseries and day-care centers have been established in most enterprises and districts. But, although there has been a rapid and steady increase (Winter & Hesselbarth, 1965, p. 234) during the last fifteen years, available facilities remain far behind the growing demand. The twofold responsibility of modern women has been recognized by numerous special provisions. In the 1961 Code of Labor Laws of the German Democratic Republic, paragraphs 123 to 133 deal with the advancement of working women. Thus, section 2 of paragraph 123 reads (Borrmann, 1966):

> The organs of the state and the managers of enterprises bear direct responsibility to create the preconditions to enable women to participate in the work-process, to develop their creative abilities and to fulfill simultaneously their high social mandate as mothers [p. 27].

Married women, as well as unmarried women with dependents, are entitled to receive an additional day's leave per month, the "household day," fully paid. Single women, including widows and divorcees with one or more children, receive paid sick leave when one of their children falls ill. All women receive fourteen weeks of fully paid maternity leave and, in addition, may stay home for a whole year without losing their right to whatever jobs they held before. Pregnancy, once the scourge of working families, has lost much of its threat. Knowledge about and availability of a variety of contraceptive devices contribute to increased freedom from the consequences of "blind nature." Painless childbirth methods are propagated, and all medical services are completely free. Beyond this, in addition to a number of minor benefits, the state pays mothers 500 Marks at the birth of the first child, and 600 and 700 Marks respectively for the second and third child.

The new Family Law (*Ministerium der Justiz,* 1966) provides for better protection of women and children in case of divorce, or pregnancy of an unmarried mother, and requires all district councils to establish marriage and family guidance clinics. It also continues the policy previously established of absolute equality for children born out of wedlock with those born in complete families, and it outlaws any discrimination against the unmarried mother.

One of the best-known marriage counselors of the German Democratic Republic, L. Aresin, speaking to West German reporters about the fact that, in the German Democratic Republic as in other countries, childless couples are eager to adopt children, commented, as quoted by Commandeur & Sterzel (1965):

> But this is not quite simple, for there are not enough children for adoption because the unmarried mothers which in your state primarily put children up for adoption, here want to keep their children. This is quite simply related to the position of the unmarried mother. It happens only very rarely that in our state a girl gives her child away. She simply does not have to fight against so many prejudices. She is equal in all respects to the married mother [p. 96].

Laws and provisions that give special consideration to women make it possible for married women, in addition to caring for their children, to assume places in the economy, thus becoming independent of men for social and intellectual stimulation and in a position to contribute their own experiences to family discussion. Rarely does one find a man in this new kind of family relationship who would have wished to revert to the earlier situation. The number of working women has increased steadily from 40 percent of the total working population in 1950 to 47 percent in 1966 (*Staatliche Zentralverwaltung für Statistik,* 1967, p. 23).

No wonder that the West German reporters (Commandeur & Sterzel, 1965), speaking of women of the German Democratic Republic, expressed amazement that:

Their men don't even feel discomfort that women have placed themselves next to them as equals on the job and in society and that in some cases they have to tolerate women as bosses. Emancipation over there is much further advanced than in West Germany [p. 87].

Boys' and Girls' Ideals

Children educated in the new family and influenced in a similar direction by the school take the social equality of men and women for granted. As a result of these changing educational influences, the ego-ideals of young men have radically changed from that of the Nazi youth. They are striving for a harmoniously integrated personality. Although they want to be physically fit, intellectually alert, and aspire to positions of social importance such as engineer, physician, scientist, and explorer, they show more concern and active interest than any previous generation in matters of homemaking and family life. They consider it perfectly natural to prepare a meal and to play with and take care of their small children. Twenty-five years ago a man would not appear in public pushing a baby carriage, while today it has become a commonplace.

The development of the ego-ideals of girls has come closer in some respects to that of their masculine counterparts. They too are eager to play an active role in the economic and political life of the nation, but marriage and motherhood remain the center of their attention. Although girls generally are striving to establish home and family and to become understanding, capable, and loving mothers, only a very small percentage of them would like to stay home and become full-time housewives, even if they could afford to do it.

In daily life, very high demands are made on boys and girls. Much knowledge must be acquired even during the first ten years of school, and since there are positions available in the higher income brackets for all qualified applicants, most pupils exert considerable effort to "make the grade," with girls frequently coming out at the top of the class. Starting with the fifth grade, school lasts six to seven hours daily including Saturday, and an average of three hours' homework per day is required. Thus, adolescents are left with relatively little time on their hands. What leisure time there is is frequently spent in sports, dances, youth group activities, and hobby groups, all of which are quite generously supported by public funds. Recent research has shown the strong drive of GDR youth (Seward and Williamson, 1969).

New Trends in Marriage and Divorce

In spite of the acceleration of physical growth and earlier onset of puberty, initial sexual relationships continue to occur at approximately the same age level. From a number of investigations concerning sexual experiences of young people (Borrmann, 1966; Friedrich & Kossakowski, 1962;

Grassel, 1967), it is possible to conclude that first coitus usually takes place a little later than the Kinsey (Kinsey *et al.*, 1948, 1953) reports indicate for corresponding groups in the United States. About 10 percent of first contacts occur before the age of sixteen. By the age of eighteen, 60 percent of young workers have had their sexual initiation, while for academic youths the proportion is only 30 percent.

During the decade between 1955 and 1965, there has been a trend toward earlier marriages, according to a report by Eberhard and Weise (1968) as indicated in Table 3 below (p. 82):

TABLE 3 AVERAGE AGE AT MARRIAGE

Date	*Men*	*Women*
1955	29.5	26.4
1965	28.1	25.5

During the same period, within the age range of eighteen to twenty-five, the number of marriages increased while at the same time the age differences between the marital partners decreased.

The consistent realization of equal rights for women in the German Democratic Republic finds indirect expression in divorce statistics. In this connection, the interesting point is that while in absolute numbers both marriage and divorce rates have declined, the number of women initiating divorce proceedings has increased progressively from year to year. In 1958, 53 percent of all divorces were requested by women; in 1965 the figure stood at 59.6 percent. This change is even more pronounced when only those divorces are analyzed that were based on marriages of less than sixteen years' duration. For marriages that had lasted over twenty years, the majority of divorce proceedings were started by the husbands. In general, where men have taken the initiative in the divorce, the percentage of women pleading against the proceedings has steadily declined—from 8.3 percent in 1958 to 5.0 percent in 1965. According to Eberhard and Weise (1968), this tendency may reflect the strengthening of women's economic independence that makes holding on to the marriage at least for economic reasons less necessary.

Social Change and Conflict

In this paper I have made an attempt to acquaint the American reader with some of the changes taking place in the German Democratic Republic with regard to sex roles and their cultural background. In my endeavor to picture the major trends, I have had to neglect minor details that are interesting and sometimes contrasting. I felt that it was necessary first to provide an understanding of the changes that have taken place before attempting to describe on the basis of a few examples the process of change itself, which has by no means terminated. The rapid changes in every area of society—economy, law, public health, and child welfare, as well as in the roles of men and women—present a complex adjustment problem to the individuals concerned. The difficulties are compounded by pressures and propaganda from the West disseminated over the television and radio networks. As a result, people are not only finding it difficult to adapt to new developments, but some even approach them with a strong inner opposition fostered by arguments and emotionally toned appeals from across the border.

As a clinical psychologist, one is able to observe many of those adjustment problems that affect the private lives and indirectly the health of people. Thus, a woman with great intellectual capacity and excellent job advancement opportunities may seem to have solved the problem of the amount of time to spend with her children who are relatively well provided for in nurseries. Yet, traditional values are still so deeply ingrained that with every difficulty, whether illness or the emotional disturbance of a child that could occur as easily if the mother were a housewife, a feeling of maternal inadequacy is apt to develop.

Within the home, the division of labor between husband and wife is in transition and often a source of emotional conflict. While many men have been willing to take over a large share of domestic chores, others are resistant to this trend. Thus, women are in some cases still at a disadvantage in vocational development.

It is not only the negative attitudes of others that hold women back, but often their own anxiety over the strict requirements for school and job causes them to seek an escape in marriage and motherhood. More and more women are able to overcome these difficulties by means of various protective measures and special promotion benefits on their behalf. Those who are still in a less fortunate position see the development of others and experience a stronger impetus to follow their lead. On the other hand, those who strive so intensely that they achieve their educational and professional goals at the cost of minimum relaxation and recuperation, labor under severe strain. Overtaxing their compensatory capacities frequently results in psychogenic illnesses, psychoneuroses, or other forms of emotional disturbance. To meet this new crisis, educational and health authorities have become increasingly sensitized to prophylactic intervention.

Special problems are presented by the changes in attitudes sometimes required of women in executive positions. On their jobs they exert executive leadership and organizational talents, yet at home they stand for sensitive, understanding, femininity, and motherliness. This may become quite difficult in the occasional event where a woman may be more successful, or in a higher income bracket, than her husband. In reading the previous sentences, the question arises, "What is meant by femininity?" No doubt the social status and the public roles of women have undergone considerable change, but what about her behavior in the most private realms? To what extent are decisiveness, strength, coolheadedness, which are important assets on the job, irradiating into the sexual relationship at home? An answer to this question at this time, unfortunately, must rely on "anecdotal" evidence such as an analysis of the German Democratic Republic woman's behavior in novels and short stories of recent date, clinical impressions, etc., and is obviously tentative and inconclusive. We may cautiously conclude, however, that considerations of financial improvement, prestige, and power have lost some of their importance in the area of intimate behavior and are outweighed by personal and emotional factors. Increasing public emphasis on the affirmation of healthy sensuous pleasure and acceptance of mutually enjoyable sex relations appear to have had a liberating effect on women's behavior. The clinician as well as the marriage counselor still sees cases of frigidity, but one has the impression that these are fewer. The greater freedom in the intimate sphere has led to occasional experimenting without lasting effects. For example, from a purely logical point of view, there is no reason why a young woman should not take the initiative in asking a stranger to dance with her. Yet, in practice, few attempts in this direction are made. Women generally recognize quite clearly that equal rights and social status do not necessarily imply equal role-playing. Accordingly, they have generally perfected age-old methods of indirectly stimulating the initiative of potential or actual male partners rather than taking the initiative themselves.

The smooth integration of occupational and private duties constitutes a challenge for the modern woman that may tax her capacities. Thus, the female student, having obtained the same right to education as her male counterpart, faces a difficult dilemma: Is it preferable for her to finish her studies before getting married and having children? Some educational and medical (male) authorities are distinctly in favor of this line of action. Doubtless, the studies would be less interrupted and the demands made upon students, which frequently approach the limit of their capacities, would be met more adequately. By the time a girl student has her doctorate, however, she may be twenty-seven or twenty-eight years old, an age at which most compatible men are married. Thus, she might have to pay for her professional advancement with a lifelong private loneliness.

Another problem that arises in connection with changed conditions stems from the fact that young people in their early twenties with a B.S. or a similar educational qualification sometimes earn considerably higher salaries than their parents. This favors early independence but also causes frictions, particularly in those cases where the parents still adhere to older traditional value systems.

New solutions

As new problems arise, various ways of coping with them also develop. Conflicts, although full of stresses in each individual case, are also frequently the cradle of more general solutions. An example may be given: The additional rights and the special protection accorded working women not only have beneficial effects but they also have drawbacks. Thus, a manager, thinking along purely business economic lines, may prefer to employ young men rather than women, since the latter not only are to be granted additional days off (household days) and pregnancy furloughs but also, as experience shows, have a higher rate of sickness leave due to their children's illnesses, are exempted from night shift for one year after the birth of a child, etc. Thus, the organization of a smooth line of production is made much more difficult. To some extent, such discrimination may pass unnoticed. In a number of industries, the shortage of labor actually forces managers to take all comers, and no discrimination in employment preference is possible. However, in certain enterprises it may well happen that the enterprise-centered "economic" thinking, behind which old prejudices are usually lurking, slows down the rate of change in the sex composition of the plant. In other places, it may become obvious that men have better chances for advancement than women. If these processes surpass a certain limit, a compensatory mechanism is set in motion. The women who have been put in a disadvantageous position will appeal. There is an effective chain of appeal and control of the rights of working women. Each plant has an especially elected commission for the protection of women's rights, and the shop-steward committee is obliged to expose and repair all wrongs done consciously or unconsciously to women. When it sometimes happens that these bodies for one reason or another do not act on the appeals, women may then take their cases either to the courts, which quite frequently decide in their favor, or to the press. At the staffs of certain women's weeklies and some trade-union journals, they usually find great willingness to investigate the complaint and, if necessary, to exert public pressure by addressing specific open questions to the manager.

Thus, we see that the emergence of a new level of greater freedom and equality for women by no means occurs in an atmosphere of complacency and lack of internal contradictions. On the contrary, the changes give rise to various new inner and interpersonal conflicts. Through the pattern of personal difficulties and contradictions created by the new conditions, the social scientist may well observe the slow development of new behavioral standards and more humane ways of living together.

Note

[1] At the present writing, according to Sokolowski and Wrochno (1965, p. 174), Convention No. 100, "Equal salary for equal work," of the UNO, has been ratified by only forty-six (including all socialist countries) of its members. Even some of these signers, however, still pay women a lower wage for the same work as men.

References

Borrmann, Rolf. *Jugend und Liebe.* Leipzig: Urania-Verlag, 1966.

Commandeur, Werner, and Alfred Sterzel. *Das Wunder Drüben sind die Frauen.* Bergisch Gladbach: Gustav Lübbe-Verlag, 1965.

Eberhard, K.-H., and W. Weise. "Entwicklungstendenzen und Faktoren der Ehelösungen." *Neue Justiz,* 22 (February 1968), 76.

Friedrich, W., and A. Kossakowski. *Zur Psychologie des Jugendalters.* Berlin: Volk und Wissen, 1962.

Grassel, H. *Jugend, Sexualität, Erziehung.* Berlin: Staatsverlag der Deutschen Demokratischen Republik, 1967.

Hirschfeld, M. *Geschlechtskunde.* Stuttgart: J. Püttmann, 1926.

———. *Sexualerziehung.* Berlin: Universitas-Verlag, 1930.

Hodann, M. *Geschlecht und Liebe.* Berlin: Büchergilde Gutenberg, 1932.

Kinsey, Alfred C., W. B. Pomeroy, and C. E. Martin. *Sexual Behavior in the Human Male.* Philadelphia: Saunders, 1948.

———. *Sexual Behavior in the Human Female.* Philadelphia: Saunders, 1953.

Mannstein, B. *Liebe und Hunger.* München; Wien; Basel: K. Desch Verlag, 1967.

Ministerium der Justiz. *Familiengesetzbuch der Deutschen Demokratischen Republik.* Berlin: Staatsverlag der Deutschen Demokratischen Republik, 1966.

Müller-Mertens, E., E. Paterna, and M. Steinmetz. *Deutsche Geschichte von den Anfängen bis 1945.* Leipzig: VEB Bibliographisches Institut, 1965.

Seward, G. H., and R. C. Williamson. "A Cross-National Study of Adolescent Professional Goals." *Human Development,* 12 (1969), 248–254.

Sokolowska, M., and K. Wrochno. *Die gesellschaftliche Stellung der Frau im Lichte der Statistik Medizin und Soziologie.* Berlin: Volk und Gesundheit Verlag, 1965.

Schneider, W. "Das Gesundheitswesen der Deutschen Demokratischen Republik." *Institut für Planung und Organisation des Gesundheitsschutzes,* 2 (August 1967).

Staatliche Zentralverwaltung für Statistik. *Statistisches Jahrbuch der Deutschen Demokratischen Republik,* 12 (1967). Berlin: Staatsverlag der Deutschen Demokratischen Republik, 1967.

Walker, K., and P. Fletcher. *Sex and Society.* Harmondsworth: Penguin, 1965.

Winter, K., and W. Hesselbarth. "Einige Angaben über die gesellschaftliche Stellung der Frau in der DDR." *Medizin und Soziologie, Berliner Symposium,* 3–5, 12 (1964). Berlin: Volk und Gesundheit Verlag, 1965.

12 WORKER, MOTHER, HOUSEWIFE: SOVIET WOMAN TODAY[1]

Mark G. Field and Karin I. Flynn

The dictum attributed to Engels that the culture of a society reflects its attitudes toward women (Shim, 1967) has become firmly rooted in Soviet ideology, and each one of the great Soviet leaders of the past has found it necessary from time to time to reaffirm the complete equality of the sexes in Soviet Russia. In a strictly Marxist sense, woman is a member of the traditionally oppressed and exploited class, and her liberation and flowering can come only through a proletarian revolution, the abolition of the private ownership of the means of production, and the advent of socialism, the first stage on the road to full communism. To paraphrase countless Soviet broadsides, only under a Soviet type of social structure can a woman really be free, can she really be "human," can she fully realize her own potentials unfettered by the restrictions common under feudalism and capitalism where she is nothing but slave and chattel, the property first of her father and then of her husband.

Some ideological considerations

To start with the obvious, and in spite of all the brave talk of feminists, there is a "difference" between men and women, though not necessarily one that automatically implies "inferiority" of one sex to the other. Oscar Wilde, when asked by a lady to explain the nature of that difference, is supposed to have paused and replied: "Madam, I can't conceive." (Money, 1963, p. 63). Marxists, and particularly Engels, regarded the division of labor between man and woman for the procreation of children as the first division of labor. Later on he added that the first class antagonism in history was the development of tensions between man and woman in monogamy, and that the first oppression was that of the female by the male (Fréville, 1950). Seen through the prism of the Marxist optic, the battle of the sexes was the prototype of the class struggle—man appropriated and enslaved woman (or several women) as his private means for the production of children to whom his private property could be transmitted. To ensure that this property was passed on to his "real" children, man enforced strict monogamy on his wife (or wives), hence the strictures against the adulteress, while he himself enjoyed the double standard, philandered, and encouraged prostitution.

The introduction of industrialization, according to Marx and Engels, was accompanied in its early phases by the employment of women (and often children) in factories and plants, usually at the expense of their health and domestic functions as wives and particularly as mothers. It is enough to read certain passages from *Capital* (Marx, 1906) or from Engels' *The Condition of the Working Class in England* to realize that part of the reason for the seriousness of the Marxist indictment of industrial capitalism stemmed from the working conditions of factory women. Engels (1958), for example, wrote:

> When women work in factories the most important result is the dissolution of family ties. If she works for 12 or 13 hours a day and her husband is employed . . . what is the fate of the children? . . . this can be seen by the increase in the number of accidents to little children which occur in the factory districts. . . . Many midwives and others who assist at childbirth state that female factory operatives experience more difficult labor in childbirth than other women, and that miscarriages are more frequent among them than is normal. . . . It is quite common for women to be working in the evening and for the child to be delivered the following morning, and it is by no means uncommon for babies to be born in the factory itself among the machinery [pp. 160–61].

The approach of Marx to this question, however, is a more dispassionate one. While he excoriates the ruling classes for their exploitation of women and children, he finds in a truly dialectic fashion that industrialization also has its positive aspects since, by providing employment opportunities to women *outside* of the home, it liberates them from the tutelage of their fathers and husbands. The disintegration of the traditional family thus leads to a higher stage of the history of mankind where women will truly achieve freedom and equality through their participation in the productive processes. In his words (1906):

> However terrible and disgusting the dissolution, under the capitalist system, of the old family ties may appear, nevertheless, modern industry, by assigning as it does an important part in the process of production, outside the domestic sphere, to women, to young persons, and to children of both sexes, creates a new economical foundation for a higher form of the family and of the relations between the sexes. . . . Moreover, it is obvious that the fact of the collective working group being composed of individuals of both sexes and all ages must necessarily, under suitable conditions, become a source of humane development; although, in its spontaneously developed, brutal, capitalistic form, where the labourer exists for the process of production, and not the process of production for the labourer, that fact is a pestiferous source of corruption and slavery [p. 536].

The Bolshevik revolution was thus looked upon by its theoreticians as the opportunity to liberate woman from her servitude and to provide her with the same rights and opportunities granted men, particularly in the economy. Fannina Halle (1933), for example, pointed out that since the Soviets seized power, hardly anything had been written or said about the economic development of the new Russia without reference to the significance of the expanding growth of women's labor. Thus, the employment of women in the Soviet Union was not only congruent with the economic needs of that society, but also with the basic tenets of its official ideology and practical policies. It is quite clear, for instance, that at least in its first years the regime looked upon the Soviet woman as one of its "natural" allies, for had it not liberated her and did she not owe her freedom and opportunities to the Soviet regime? It was furthermore assumed by the regime that even the obstacles to educational, occupational, and political opportunities caused by her biological role as mother could and would, insofar as possible, be removed (Massell, 1968). Maternity was to be recognized as a social function and society was to assume the care, education, and training of children and adolescents. The abolition of private property in the means of production was to have repercussions in the marriage relationship, which was to be based on truly monogamous love and founded on mutual attraction, equality, and dignity. When love ceased to exist, the marriage bonds would be automatically dissolved. Common-law marriages were to have the same validity as registered ones: no social stigma was going to be attached to unmarried mothers, nor would there be made any distinction between the child born in wedlock and the natural or illegitimate child.

The history and the vicissitudes of Soviety family law show the unrealistic nature of many of these ideas, given the realities and demands of Soviet society. Abortions, legalized in 1920, were made illegal in 1936, except for very specific and restricted medical cases. Divorces were made more difficult and costly and measures were taken to force fathers to support their children. In 1944, divorces were returned to the courts with no statutory ground being given for the dissolution of the marriage, this being left to the discretion of the superior court. Unregistered marriages lost their validity and equality with registered marriages; illegitimate children were from then on to carry their mother's name (the name of the father remaining a stigmatizing blank on the birth certificate); the mother could not sue for paternity nor could the child inherit any of his father's property (Inkeles, 1959).

Some measure of relaxation and liberalization was introduced in the wake of reforms following Stalin's death in 1953. For example, abortion on "social" grounds was relegalized in 1955 (Field, 1956) and a more liberal divorce law was introduced on January 1, 1966, making divorces simpler and cheaper but still avoiding the issue of illegitimacy (Juvilier, 1967). It is likely that in the near future, illegitimate children will be able to use their father's name and that paternity suits will be allowed, therefore putting an end to their unfair stigmatization. However, this is only one more step toward, rather than the final realization of, the complete emancipation of the woman. Indeed, as long as it is not possible for society to undertake the complete care of the child for every woman who wishes to have it so, and as long as she is saddled with domestic duties, her equal participation in political, social, and economic activities will be hampered.

Demography and the economic role of Soviet women

In the area of demography and economics, some of the basic explanations of the role of Soviet women may be found. In the Soviet Union perhaps more than in most other industrial countries, women do not merely constitute a reserve labor force, nor do they constitute, as is often the case, an important but still a minority of the labor force; they are, in the Soviet Union, an integral and indispensable part of that force. Indeed, it may be fair to say that the Soviet economy and Soviet society, at least until now, could not operate, barring drastic structural changes, without the labor provided by women.

Throughout Soviet history, women have constituted a majority of the population, reflecting not only their greater life expectancy but also the selective male losses incurred by such events as World War I, the two revolutions of 1917, the civil war, foreign intervention, the epidemics and famine of the twenties, the industrialization drive, the forced collectivization of agriculture, the purges of the thirties, and finally, in the forties, the traumatizing effects of World War II. In 1926, according to the first census taken by the Soviet regime, women constituted 51.7 percent of the population; in 1939, that percentage rose to 52.1; in 1946, it was estimated at 57.4 percent, representing an excess of 25 million women in a total population of about 176 million.

In 1959, according to the first postwar census taken fourteen years after the end of hostilities, women still constituted 55 percent of the population. Population losses and deficits of births due to World War II and its immediate aftermath have been very roughly estimated at about 45 million (20 million as birth deficits and 20 million men and 5 million women as excess mortality). There are, however, wide variations in the percentage of women to the total population in the several republics that constitute the Soviet Union, with those areas that were most exposed to the brunt of the German invasion showing the highest percentage, and those areas that were spared (Central Asia, for example) showing the lowest. Furthermore, the 20 million surplus of women noted in the 1959 census is not distributed evenly among all age groups of the population, but is concentrated primarily among those cohorts old enough at the beginning of the war to be selectively affected by hostilities. For example, in the age groups over thirty-five in 1959, the number of women per 1000 of the population does not fall below the 600 mark. Statistically speaking, this indicates that one-third or more of these women had either no chance of finding a marriage partner or were widowed. Of the population aged sixteen to fifty-nine in 1946, it can be estimated that 60.3 percent were women and approximately *one-half* of all men alive in 1939 did not survive the war (Dodge, 1966).

These losses are also reflected in the 1959 statistics about marriages: more than 90 percent of the males between the ages of thirty and sixty-nine were married in 1959, but among women, only 72 percent in the thirty-five to thirty-nine group, 62 percent in the forty to forty-four group, 54 percent in the forty-five to fifty group, and less than half in all age groups older than fifty. The poignant loneliness of the Soviet woman has been expressed, better than statistics can ever do, by Vladimir Semenov (1959) in a poem addressed to a Soviet girl:

You tried to find him everywhere
He must exist
He is someplace.
You asked:
Where is he? Where?
There was no answer.
Your youth is gone.
You paled and withered.
You, whose beauty shone once,
You do not know the verity
That a wife to no one
You long since are
A widow . . .
You do not know that he was killed
in War
Before you met him.

At the same time, only an increasing birth rate could even begin to partly compensate for the losses and deficits caused by the war. As a result, women have been encouraged to increase the number of children they have while, at the same time, not withdrawing from the labor force. Thus, the decree of July 8, 1944 encouraged large families by establishing honorific titles for women who brought more than five children into the world. In addition, the 1944 decree seems to have had two other purposes: (1) it was an attempt, in line with other conservative measures adopted in family law since the mid-thirties, to imbue men with a more responsible attitude toward their family obligations; and (2) it was also a recognition that, as a result of the war, many women would find it impossible (statistically speaking) to bear children in wedlock. It thus afforded unmarried women some financial provisions for the support of their children who were desperately needed by the regime to compensate for the war losses. As we have already seen, unmarried mothers were prohibited from suing for paternity or for alimony, a measure that was designed, as Juviler (1967) has suggested, ". . . to spare a man and his legal family the financial and emotional shocks that might arise from paternity and support suits, from his official acknowledgment of paternity, or from an extramarital child's bearing his name" (p. 52). In effect, the decree actually licensed men to increased irresponsibility toward their illegitimate children since it was aimed precisely at an increase of the fertility rate of both married *and* unmarried women.

While we may expect, in the not too distant future, a change in family law that would tighten the responsibilities of parents for their children, and while the drastic sex unbalance that characterized the Soviet population in the postwar period is gradually disappearing, some consequences of that war are still affecting Soviet society and provide additional background to an understanding of the role of women. For example, the excess mortality and the birth deficits of World War II have led to a very sharp reduction in the number of entrants into the labor force fifteen to twenty years after the end of the war (Feshbach, 1966). In 1959, when the number of new entrants into the labor force was at about its lowest ebb, M. Ya. Sonin (1959) wrote that ". . . it is more important than ever to free this small generation (or cohort) from being tied to household work—to ensure an even, 'natural' growth of the work force" (p. 88). At the same time, the smaller number of people who have, in recent years, entered adulthood and the child-begetting ages will also mean another potential drop in the labor force a generation from now.

The significance of women in the Soviet economy and particularly in industry was illustrated by the 1959 census and is summarized in Table 1 (*Zhenshchiny i deti v SSSR,* 1963, p. 79).

The table reveals that more than four-fifths of all employed women were occupied in production—industry, construction, transportation, agriculture, and so on—and less than one-fifth in the occupations that might be called services, such as education, public health, science, and medicine. By 1965, the picture had not substantially changed. Figures on the number of women occupied in agriculture, that is, as farm hands on collective farms, are not available for the more recent years (collective farmers are not "employed" or salaried by the state), but in 1959 almost 30 million women as against 18,600,000 men comprised the labor force on the land (Karcz, 1967).

While women are engaged in practically all types of work, they are underrepresented in the occupations that embody directive, managerial, decision-making, and executive functions, and they tend to be overrepresented in the subordinate and junior positions and in the menial jobs. On the other hand, if one were to compare the Soviet figures for professions such as engineering and medicine with those of Western countries, one would see a far greater proportional participation of women in the Soviet Union. There are some indications, however, that the regime may not be completely satisfied with those professions having heavy female representation such as medicine and teaching. Indeed, in the last few years, the proportion of women in medicine has slightly decreased and will probably continue to do so as more and more of the entering classes are more evenly balanced as to sex, an indication that the highly skewed figures of the past were due primarily to a shortage of men and to their going into the more technical occupations (Parry, 1967).

TABLE 1 EMPLOYED WOMEN IN THE SOVIET UNION BY TYPE OF EMPLOYMENT, 1959

	Women (000)	*Percentages of Total*
Women employed in sector of material production, including:	38,342	80.5
Industry, construction, transportation, and communications	14,152	29.7
Agriculture	20,764	43.6
Trade, public catering, procurement, material-technical supply and retail	3,178	6.8
Women employed in nonproductive sectors, including:	9,204	19.4
Housing, communal housing services, organs of administration and banking	2,276	4.9
Education, science public health and medicine	6,928	14.5
Not assigned to any sector, not giving or inaccurately giving place of work	59	0.1
Total, Women Employed *	47,605,000	100.0

* Excludes members of families of collective farmers, and of workers and employees engaged in subsidiary (private plot) agriculture.

As to teaching, the Minister of Education of the Russian Republic declared in 1966 that the overwhelming majority of school teachers and students in pedagogic institutes and academics were women, who do their job "with great tact and skill," and yet, the Minister continued, "There should be more men entering our . . . institutes and . . . academies" (Prokofev, 1966).

Women have thus become an integral part of the Soviet labor force, not so much because of ideology as because of manpower shortages and economic needs. There is still little likelihood that, for the present time at least, the regime wants or can afford to release them from their occupational obligations, although it will continue, within its limitations and needs, to attempt to improve their working and living conditions. With time, it is also quite likely that a greater proportion of women will eventually be employed in white-collar, semiprofessional and professional occupations rather than manual and unskilled jobs, particularly as more mechanical power and automation become available to the economy and industry becomes less labor-intensive and more capital-intensive.

Recent literature indicates that part-time employment will be available for housewives within a year or two. This would both ease the workload of some women who are now working full time, and it would make it possible to employ others whose family commitments prevent them from taking a full-time job. An article by Sonin and Savranskaia (1966) points out that this is done in Czechoslovakia for those (primarily women) who wish either a shortened workday or partial workweek with corresponding remuneration. The authors go on to say:

> One cannot forget that, besides production work, a woman as a rule still manages the household and brings up the children; many of them like to change to shorter working hours. If such an order is introduced, then housewives who want to work but who cannot be away from home all day will go into social production (especially in the service sphere). Investigations carried out in several districts and cities say that by this it is quite possible to draw approximately a quarter of the housewives to work. [p. 1].

This statement, interestingly enough, implies that women will be freed from their household drudgery only to be primarily employed in the servicing industry which, with its centralized facilities for washing, dry-cleaning, shoe repairing, and home delivery of products or mail order purchases, does not in essence distinguish itself from housework, nor is it held in any higher esteem. As a matter of fact, the authors point out that students graduating from secondary schools scrupulously avoid employment in this area and, if they accept such a job, frequently hold on to it for no longer than a year (Sonin and Savranskaia, 1966). And yet, it is likely that this kind of employment, given the gradual shift in the production of most household items of consumption to commercial enterprises, will become more available to women than the less suitable and more arduous occupations in agriculture, construction, and heavy industry. It is quite possible that the occupational distribution of women will, in time, tend to resemble that of other industrialized and urbanized societies.

Educational status of Soviet women

The indispensable underpinning for full participation of women in the life of a country is undoubtedly that of education. While in predominantly agricultural countries women can and do contribute significantly to the work force through farm work even though they may have little or no education, as soon as a society begins to industrialize, urbanize, and mechanize, the importance of literacy and education becomes overwhelming. While in the period between 1926 and 1959 the proportion of women in the agricultural labor force increased from 50 percent to 62 percent, the proportion of the total female labor force engaged in agricultural pursuits diminished from 91 percent to 53 percent. This decrease was due to industrialization and the increased educational levels of women that enabled them either to specialize in some area of agriculture or to shift to more gratifying and less backbreaking jobs in other sectors of the economy (Karcz, 1967).

Before the Revolution, not more than 15 percent of the students in higher and secondary educational institutions were women (Beilin, 1935); by the school year 1927–28 the percentage had already climbed to 28 percent, and by 1940–41, to 58 percent. Since then, the percentage of women students in higher and secondary specialized schools has fluctuated, dropping to 53 percent in 1950–51, and to 42 percent in 1961–62, and then increasing again to 44 percent in 1965–66 (*Zhenshchiny i deti v SSSR,* 1963; *Vestnik Statistiki,* 1967). While there have been fluctuations in the percentage of women in educational institutions, the absolute number of such women keeps climbing.

An examination of levels of education by sex shows that in 1959 the men, though fewer in number, had somewhat higher rates of education than the women, and the rural population trailed behind the urban population, as the figures in Table 2 (Itogi Vsesoiuznoi, etc., 1962) will show. It can be surmised in the absence of precise statistics that the situation as of 1968 could not be radically different.

An examination of these figures reveals that residence (urban or rural) is probably one of the most important factors in determining access to education, particularly higher or university education. There are, of course, differences in the rates between the sexes, but these differences are not as marked as those due to residence. As might be expected, the largest discrepancy exists between urban men and rural women (7.5 times) in the realm of completed higher education. But in the urban population there were less than one-third more men than women with this level of education. In the rural areas, the rate was 50 percent higher for the males than for the females. The greatest equality (given the basic differences between urban and rural settings) was among those who had either an incomplete higher education or an incomplete intermediate education. There was more uniformity in the educational levels of the rural and urban populations among those who had only either an elementary or an incomplete seven-year school education. As a matter of fact, the rates of those with only this level of education for both sexes were higher in the rural than in the urban setting.

While the general level of education has risen considerably in the last two decades, the women's educational rate has risen faster than that of the men, if only because the women started from a more disadvantaged position. It seems, however, that women are channeled more frequently into the lower reaches of the educational system and that men still dominate the upper reaches. For example, women constituted exactly half of the students in semiprofessional schools in 1965–66, but only 44 percent in professional schools (*Vestnik Statistiki,* 1967). It is quite conceivable that cultural, economic, geographic, psychological, and social factors inhibit the full participation of women in education and this accounts for the rather large variations in the educational level of women in the different Soviet republics. Although women of the Central Asian Republics have progressed faster between 1939 and 1959 than those in most of the other republics, they are still trailing considerably behind the more industrialized sections of the Soviet Union. As is the case in most societies, the very fact that education is available for all at low or no cost does not necessarily secure equal participation of all groups. It might be added that although the educational status of Soviet women is not quite at par with that of men, it is surpassed by very few other countries, the United States included.

TABLE 2 EDUCATION OF POPULATION 10 YEARS AND OLDER, 1959, BY SEX AND RESIDENCE

	Higher Education Completed *	*Incomplete Higher and Incomplete Secondary Education* *		*Elementary and Incomplete 7-Year Education*
Urban and Rural Population				
Men and Women	23	338	310	162,464,288
Men	27	365	377	70,442,003
Women	20	318	258	92,022,285
Urban Population				
Men and Women	40	429	298	80,282,263
Men	45	442	358	35,172,835
Women	35	420	252	45,109,428
Rural Population				
Men and Women	7	249	321	82,182,025
Men	9	289	396	35,269,168
Women	6	219	264	46,912,857

* Expressed in rates per 1000 population.

The Political Role of the Soviet Woman

A brief review of the political role played by women in the Soviet Union seems to indicate that it falls somewhat short of the complete equality proclaimed by the Constitution and the ideologists. The most important political organization, the maker of policy and the wielder of power, is the Communist Party of the Soviet Union. In 1924, the Party was composed of 8.2 percent women; it doubled by 1932 to 15.9 percent, but declined by one point in 1941. The magnitude of the role played by women during World War II was reflected in the sizeable increase in their proportion in the Party —17 percent by 1945, and about 20 percent by 1950. Since then, this proportion has remained more or less stationary. Three percent of the adult female population belongs to the Party as against five times as many among the corresponding males. The participation of women in leading Party organs has been rather trivial. In conclusion, the role of women in the Party is more than a token one, but it does not approach any degree of equality. In the *Komsomols* (Communist Youth League), the proportion of women members has always been higher than in the Party, a situation consistent with the observation that women are found in larger numbers in lower ranks and junior positions than in higher levels. At the present, between two-fifths and one-half of the *Komsomol* members are women. In the higher *Komsomol* organs, while women are better represented than in the Party, they are still in the minority. In the soviets, which are the formal governmental structure but not the real holders of political power, the percentage of women is below their proportion in the adult population. Among Soviet leading organs such as the Supreme Soviet of the USSR, the proportion of women varies from less than one-third to about 43 percent in local soviets. This representation should not, however, be lightly dismissed: symbolically and visibly, the role of women in the soviets is an important one, and does represent a major advance over prerevolutionary days.

In the labor unions, state-controlled organs to ensure maximum productivity, women are fairly well represented, varying from 30.8 percent in top union organs to a high of 66.8 percent among labor organizers (*Zhenshchiny i deti v SSSR,* 1963).

In the period 1918–67, women have been awarded one-third of all awards, medals, decorations, and other signs of distinction, a most respectable performance.

In conclusion, women participate in the political life of the Soviet Union at a rather restrained and subdued level, particularly in the light of professed ideology. Time and again, the press has deplored the lack of greater participation of the distaff side in Party and other activities and has called for remedial action, but little has been accomplished. The regime, particularly the Party, is caught in a dilemma between the "inherited symbolism" of the working-class struggle and the formerly disinherited and dispossessed (including women), and the "logic of elitism" that requires it to lead and manage the society and thus take into its ranks those who can best further that leadership (Fainsod, 1963, p. 247). Somehow the woman, just like any worker or peasant, does not quite easily fit into that group.

The social roles of the Soviet woman

The Soviet Housewife—A "Dependent"?

One of the characteristics of the traditional, agrarian society was its "undifferentiated" nature: the family as a social unit was a kinship structure (a group of people related to each other by particularistic ties of descent and marriage) as well as an economic structure (a group of people working together in a common enterprise). In addition, it often was a religious group united by common symbols and an educational enterprise, since parents taught their children the skills necessary for adult life and work. The survival of the family over time depended on its ability to produce enough food and other implements, to bear children, and to socialize its young. The position of women as daughters, then wives, mothers, and grandmothers, was fairly clear and unambiguous and, given their limitations due to child-bearing and physical strength, they participated in the economic life of the group, often assuming a very important role in it.

One of the basic features of an industrialized society results from the shift of its locus of economic activities from the kinship group and the land to the factory, the plant, the mine, or the office. These require large concentrations of specialized manpower. People are brought together for the specific purpose of economic production and not related to each other by particularistic ties. The family, as such, has lost its major productive focus, and the members of the family who work must be able to leave their homes and "go to work." When both husband and wife work today, in most instances they do not work side by side. Indeed, the hiring of a spouse *qua* spouse would contravene the "achievement" or "universalistic" orientation of industrialized society. At the same time, as the family ceases to be a productive unit but continues as a consuming group, it must increasingly purchase commercially produced items, sometimes at a lower cost than an equivalent produced at home. This then requires additional cash income, and the commercial production of consumer goods and services opens employment opportunities for women who thus transfer their economically productive hours from the home to the plant, factory, or the office.

While the process of industrialization has had roughly similar effects on the role of women and the family wherever it has occurred, we suggest that there may be certain elements peculiar to the Soviet situation. The first, and perhaps the most significant, is the extraordinary loss of manpower suffered by the Soviet Union between 1917 and 1945. The second is the tempo of the industrialization and collectivization drive launched by Stalin in the late twenties, which required the fullest economic participation of the population. The third factor is the existence of an explicit ideology that encourages women to take part in the economic and social life of the country. Finally, equality of rights means, of course, equality of obligations in all activities.

The involvement of woman in economically productive processes outside the home has not, in any way, meant that she could leave the domestic sphere with impunity and concentrate exclusively on her job or her profession. Indeed, today's modern woman, including the Soviet woman, has one foot at home and one foot in industry, and maintains a precarious equilibrium between the two. Unable because of her domestic obligations to devote herself fully to a job or a career, she is often held down and stigmatized because of the "menial" nature of the functions she is called upon to perform as a housewife and mother. She resents her continued status as a "dependent," with the implications that in a family situation the man has the higher status and prestige. In the light of the critical role that Soviet women played during the war and in the postwar reconstruction, the calls on the part of the regime for her active participation in the "building of communism," and the official statements of her equality, it is humiliating for many a Soviet woman and housewife to have the word *izhdivenka* (dependent) entered in the blank calling for her occupation in her passport. Thus, the wife of a demobilized officer and the mother of two wrote:

> Well, what kind of "dependents" are we? Even when we watch television we are knitting sweaters for the children. Our work is not easy; every woman, every real housekeeper knows this. We wash, scrub floors, clean, cook, sew, knit and mend; we alone raise our children—as a rule successfully—and help raise the children of others. We get neither vacation nor holidays. Then why aren't we respected; why are we treated so contemptuously? [Tatu, 1965, pp. 96–97].

This contempt seems to result, again, from the fact that the functions of the housewife, while "necessary," do not compare favorably with those required in the larger economic system. Furthermore, these functions contradict the claims of the equality of women, since men are not "stuck" with the same work.

One answer to the dilemma would be for the Soviet woman to establish and maintain her claim to equality through her employment in the society's economy, leaving behind once and for all the stigma of domestic functions. The theme that only through "hard" work on equality with man can the Soviet woman "earn" her respect and independence is sometimes sounded in the Soviet press by the more fundamentalist believers in female equality. Witness the following letter, printed in *Literaturnaia Gazeta* in 1967, entitled "Freedom for the kitchen?" (Lebedinskaia, 1967) :

> One often hears women who have devoted themselves entirely to housework in families where the fathers can afford everything needed complain bitterly that their husbands reproach them for their inability to save money. Any woman who has any self-respect at all would not only dig

ditches but do the dirtiest work, if only to avoid hearing humiliating reproaches and to have the right to spend the money she has earned as she sees fit [p. 12].

In a later discussion in the same paper, Larisa Kuznetsova (1967) again formulated the dilemma faced by the Soviet woman. "It would be criminal," she writes, "even to look askance at those women who voluntarily choose the home and the family as their life's work and who are great in their world of selflessness and love." And yet, these women suffer from a lack of esteem in their society. The author continues:

Cooking, washing floors, and doing the laundry are the same sort of difficult and unskilled labor that we object to when done in industry by women. The entire difference, however, is that industrial labor is of social importance and is paid for by the state, while housework is restricted to the private sphere and earns neither moral nor material rewards [p. 12].

There is little doubt, from a perusal of the Soviet sources, that the woman who deliberately chooses to become a housewife and mother and to restrict her activities to husband, children, and hearth is not considered a "complete" Soviet woman because she is not participating fully in the building of the new society and because her position and "dependence" are too strongly reminiscent of the bourgeois housewife of a former stigmatized past.

That some attention should be paid in the Soviet Union to the theme of the woman who retreats voluntarily or under compulsion into domesticity and dependency is not, of course, accidental. It does reflect certain aspects of social reality and certain demands made upon the Soviet woman. The solution to this "problem" offered in fiction, the theater, and propaganda is her recognition, or the recognition on the part of those around her who would keep her in a dependent position, that not only does she have duties toward her state and fellow-man that transcend the narrow circle of her family, but that she could not be happy living as a "parasite" or "kept woman" because she would not be a "complete" or "real" person. The reality and the wholeness of her person can come only through her full participation in "life" and in the building of communism. That solution is, of course, well-suited to a society with a leadership that claims a feminist ideological heritage through Marx, Engels, Lenin, and the Russian revolutionary movement (Fréville, 1950). It is also convenient because of the Soviet Union's need to utilize female labor due to the manpower situation that makes the nonparticipation of women in the economy a problem probably more serious in the Soviet Union than in almost any other contemporary society.

The woman who chooses to participate and earn her independence on the basis of her occupational and other achievements is likely to be defined as exemplary, *provided* she does not totally neglect her other functions. We can thus delineate four general types of social roles of the woman in the Soviet Union based on her participation in the life of the country outside her home. Needless to say, these types are artificial constructs for the purpose of analysis. The first two types, the "strong" women, are positive heroines; the third and fourth types, the "weak" women, are considered socially regressed and thus negative representatives of their sex.

Four Types of Soviet Women

Comrade Positive is the prototype of the *femme engagée,* the heroine of production who, in spite of tremendous obstacles, finds it possible to combine useful, productive work or study, with her family life and obligations. Like a tower of strength, she provides continuity and support to those around her and is able to transcend the narrow circle of her family. This positive, if somewhat manic and hyperactive, type of woman is endowed with endless energy and boundless devotion to the cause of building a communist society. She is the woman who is eager and ready to "prove herself" (*Slovo o nashikh zhenshchinakh* 1958). We find her, for example, described in *Pravda,* typified in six girls working at the foundry of the Likhachev Automobile Works in Moscow: "Their job is to pour hot mixtures into molds. Their work is strenuous, requiring no small exertion of muscles, eyes, and nerves." But mornings the girls walk to the foundry ". . . as though carried by the wind. One would imagine that they are hurrying to a ball, a date, a skiing party," so eager are they to pour "hot mixtures" into the molds (Hindus, 1961, pp. 279–80). But that is not all; they also decide to contribute a Sunday to work on the construction of a new stadium. One of them, however, a "frail, delicate, white-faced girl," failed to show up. "Neither her fragility, nor her pallor saved her from the sharp rebukes of her teammates."

These girls presumably find their ideal in someone like junior lieutenant Tereshenkova, the first woman cosmonaut, who proved the value of women in "building the glory of the state" (Topping, 1965):

> To millions of Soviet women, junior lieutenant Tereshenkova is a promise of the future . . . [she] represents Soviet women as the Kremlin pictures them when an ideal Communist society, still a dream of the future, becomes a reality. She wears her hair in the latest, most popular, short, fluffy "kitten cut," but to Soviet propagandists, her space feat is proof that Soviet women are on "equal footing in work that calls for great courage, physical endurance, and much knowledge."

Comrade Positive is the one who will repay her debt to the society that gave her a free education and training, regardless of any obstacles that might confront her. If she cannot find employment in the foundry or the field, she at least will devote herself to social and community activities, for example, taking care of children whose mothers do work, setting up kindergartens in her building, or watching after the local authorities to see to it that they build the necessary facilities to take care of the children. At all times she wants to be prepared to have a good answer should her children or grandchildren ask her: "Mama (or Babushka), what did you do to help build communism?" (Chelovek i kollektiv, 1962)—a question aimed at mobilizing anticipatory anxiety, like the World War I poster depicting a deeply furrowed father being queried by his small son: "Daddy, what did *you* do during the war?"

Comrade Willing, But . . . is not less positive than the previous type, but some objective barriers keep her from fully participating in the building of communism. Her family situation, for example, prevents her from seeking employment; she is the "household prisoner" who is constantly trying to extricate herself from the "secondary" tasks of housework and childraising in order to go to work. She is ashamed of performing daily menial and unrewarding tasks and feels that, in the meanwhile, life outside is slipping by with real and important work waiting for her. It is, of course, primarily for her that the regime makes some special efforts by investing in creches and kindergartens for the care of her young children, and since the building of a sufficient number of such institutions takes time and money, the waiting period for her liberation is sweetened by official attempts to raise her public image. *Pravda,* for example, has pointed out that housewives constitute a huge (labor reserve) army and they undoubtedly perform useful and needed work, but *Pravda* continues: "Ask these women, 'Are you satisfied with your position?' and the majority of them will answer this question in the negative. Only necessity has forced them to give up their occupations, and at the first opportunity, they will return to their beloved jobs" (January 6, 1962). Although the regime, understandably, does not blame her for her condition, there is an undertone in the comments about her type that implies that she is sometimes apt to give up too early and too easily in her efforts to find a solution to her dilemma.

In order for her to remain in this category and not to slide into the next, more opprobrious one, it must be shown that she is trying in every possible way to extricate herself from the secondary tasks of childrearing and housekeeping in order to go to work. Here again, one must not discount the influence of her environment, her friends, "the collective," the *Komsomols,* and the sympathetic husband who understands how much his wife suffers from having to stay home when excitement and joy await her outside of the confines of her home. Witness, for example, the anguished cry of the husband who writes: "I am very ashamed that I must maintain at home a young woman whose desire is to work" (Chelovek i kollektiv, 1962).

Comrade Reluctant is the negative type, as she is too easily inclined to slide into nonparticipation and lacks sufficient motivation or drive to involve fully herself in the life of the country. The dutiful and often spoiled and lazy daughter who awaits marriage in her parents' comfortable home, or the submissive wife who accepts the more traditional, i.e., "bourgeois" female roles centered around home, husband, and children, thus emerges as the standard "negative" person so dear to Soviet didactic literature (Dunham, 1960).

The temptation on the part of Soviet girls and women to remain in or backslide into dependency and domesticity might be called, to borrow from another context to be sure, "social regression" (Slater, 1963, pp. 339–64). Social regression may be defined as a tendency, either of individuals or of a group, to withdraw into largely self-sufficient roles leading to isolation from a larger network of social relationships and participation and the consequent failure to perform socially needed roles. The problem of social regression is particularly acute in a politically monolithic society such as the Soviet Union, which demands the full participation of *all* its members and their undivided loyalty to the regime. A case in point is Vera, the object of some attention on the part of *Pravda* (Mikhailova, 1962).

Vera completed a high school technical course on the assumption that she would later enter a higher institute or a university. In the meantime, she went to work in a plant as a lathe operator. There she met a nice fellow whom she soon married, although he had only seven years of education and certain old-fashioned ideas about the place of women. When he told her to stop working at the plant and to stay home and take care of their infant daughter, she passively acquiesced. Vera's mother, a good Soviet citizen, then wrote an anguished letter to *Pravda* and asked: "How did this happen? And am I the only one guilty of the fact that instead of a young specialist I raised an ordinary housewife?" *Pravda* did not quite think so and sent a correspondent to interview Vera and make a report. The fault, it asserted, lay in Vera's "collective," her school, her *Komsomol* comrades, and her coworkers at the plant who had forgotten her. Her husband must, of course, bear the large share of the responsibility: the selfish oaf has a wife who takes good care of him, a nice little daughter, work he loves, and a good group at the plant. He has, meanwhile, imprisoned his wife within the four walls of dependent domesticity, and even Vera herself has forgotten that these four walls are her prison. The solution *Pravda* suggests is that the *Komsomols,* the collective, everyone is obligated to help Vera find her true happiness, which is in collectivism. Family life is nice but, *Pravda* tells us, it always must be organically tied to creative work and education—to the life of the country. If one multiplies Vera by several million (about eleven million able-bodied women are neither working nor studying), and if one then juxtaposes this figure against the decreased number of new entrants into the labor force of the sixties, one realizes how critical Vera's attitude may be to the regime.

Comrade Parasitic is a more socially regressed type than Vera, who revealed to the correspondent from *Pravda* some degree of shame and discomfort at no longer working. Comrade Parasitic, on the other hand, does not work, does not want to work, and apparently does not feel that she ought to work if she has either parents or a husband to support her. Letters to *Pravda,* for example, all express the righteous indignation of women who have taken it upon themselves to blame their unemployed sisters and to support public morality. We are informed, for example, by the Moscow Comrade Z. Nemchinova that Ala, a young woman in her apartment, married a neighbor and the day after the marriage registration she did not return to work. Nemchinova and other neighbors,

> . . . assured her [Ala] that one must work and study. But the young woman did not listen to . . . [their] advice. Soon Ala became pregnant and somehow she got a job only in order to receive compensation for the statutory leave. . . . After the birth of the child she did not return to work. At home her mother does everything for her . . . one simply marvels at how a young, healthy woman can satisfy herself with such a life.

The tone of other letters to *Pravda* is more ominous: some of them even raise the question of *forcing* such women to work. Indeed, according to the 1961 Decree of the Presidium of the Supreme Soviet of the RSFSR, "On the strengthening of the struggle with persons who shirk socially useful labor and lead an anti-social, parasitic life," (*Sovetskaia Iustitsia,* 1961) Ala could technically be classified as a parasite and be subject to prosecution by a Comrades' Court, although there is not much evidence that women, by contrast to many men, have been convicted of "parasitism." But under present conditions, the official attitude seems to be that these women are considered as little more than deserters, kept women, and social prostitutes. If, in addition, they have received a specialized or technical education, they are considered to have accepted the training under false pretenses and to be swindling the state and *the people* in their refusal to work.

Working Conditions

Granting that most women in the Soviet Union should and must work, the question that has been raised in the pages of *Literaturnaia Gazeta* is, "What kind of work should women do?" In the past few years, two viewpoints have been expressed on the subject. One is that equality of the sexes means that women must undertake exactly the same kinds of jobs as men to justify that equality: any kind of differential or preferential treatment would smack of inequality and discrimination. The other viewpoint is that a woman, simply because she is a woman, is entitled to some respect and should be spared certain types of work—the heavy and dirty jobs, for example—which should be left to the men. In a review of the controversy prepared by Vera Bil'shaia for the *Literaturnaia Gazeta* (1959), the author quotes a woman reader named Nilova, who had written that ". . . only with sweat on her face can a woman compel respect for herself, not only as a mother but also as a human being." This is perhaps an extreme viewpoint. We have seen that there is specific labor legislation regulating the work of women and forbidding their employment in certain kinds of occupations—including underground mining. Yet there is plenty of evidence, some of it gathered by Nemtsov (1957; 1958) and published earlier in *Literaturnaia Gazeta,* that women are employed in the roughest, most difficult, and physically most strenuous occupations, including coal mining, asphalt paving, stevedoring, and foundry work. Nemtsov asks why women should perform such jobs, particularly when men are available to do them, and why, in general, such jobs are not performed by machines now that the Soviet Union has a technology so advanced that it can put a manned satellite into space. He then suggests several explanations, the most important being a culturally ingrained lack of respect for the woman that leads to her being considered a natural candidate for the heaviest and dirtiest jobs. In other words, it does not shock Soviet people to see women used as beasts of burden. As a result, men will be appointed as foremen over women because of their sex and not on the basis of their qualifications.

The second factor is the usual one of bureaucratic inertia and costs: managers will not install labor-saving devices if they are not forced to do so. Nemtsov had complained to an engineer that in a certain plant men in one shop worked in almost surgical cleanliness making radio tubes, while the casting shop next door where most of the heavy work was performed by women was dirty and poorly ventilated. The engineer saw nothing anomalous in this situation, explaining that "technology determines everything." When Nemtsov asked, "What about the people?" the engineer muttered something about an extra milk allocation to women doing arduous work.

Two more factors also help to determine the jobs available to women: one is that girls finishing the intermediate schools often do not have a specialized education and can work only in relatively unskilled jobs. The other is that in certain districts there are no alternate employment possibilities for women who are presently engaged in totally unskilled or rough occupations.

Domestic Work: "The Squirrel in the Cage"

The fate of the Soviet housewife is not, from what one can read and observe, a particularly happy one. Since the family today has become primarily a consuming unit, the purchase of the necessary items for the family's daily needs is a woman's job. With the poor development of shopping and retail facilities typical of the Soviet Union, it is likely to be the equivalent of a full-time occupation. Domestic duties are further complicated by the difficult housing conditions under which most urban families must live, in particular, the frequent necessity of sharing kitchen and bathing facilities with several other families in the same apartment.

In addition to her housework, the woman has to care for the children. The average housewife may spend as much as three hours a day shopping and as much time preparing food, cleaning, making beds, washing dishes, and doing the myriad other tasks that women, particularly when they have no labor-saving devices, must perform. Consequently, men, according to time-budget studies, have twice as much if not more free time at their disposal than women, as shown in Table 3 (Prudenski and Kolpakov, 1962):

TABLE 3 TIME BUDGETS, NONWORKING TIME, MEN AND WOMEN *

	MEN			WOMEN		
	Hours	*Minutes*	*Percent of Total*	*Hours*	*Minutes*	*Percent of Total*
Free time	3	09	20.0	1	43	10.8
Housework and self-care	2	43	17.3	5	10	32.6
Time for sleep and meals	8	58	57.1	8	11	51.7
Expenditure of time connected with production work	0	53	5.6	0	47	4.9
Total Nonworking time	15	43	100.0	15	51	100.0

* Based on a sample of 1,477 families, Moscow and Novosibirsk, 1959.

But women were running in their apartments like "squirrels in a cage" (Nemtsov, 1957). It is, of course, at that point that the vaunted equality guaranteed in the Constitution completely breaks down.

Women, like men, are expected to put in a full day's work at the office, in the plant, or in the field, but Soviet men, jealous of their masculinity and spoiled by their indulgent mothers and submissive sisters, refuse to help their wives in their household duties. What would the neighbors say if they saw him washing the dishes or making the beds? No wonder, then, that some Soviet women have taken to complaining in the newspapers that they are asked to work just as hard as their husbands on the job, but that at home their husbands will not lift a finger to help.

At this point, it may be of some interest briefly to summarize what remedial steps have been proposed in the Soviet press (Nemtsov, 1957):

1. Strict or stricter adherence to labor regulations on the work of women, and possibly reserving some of the "lighter" types of work for women.
2. Greater flexibility in the employment of married women with children: part-time work, elimination of night shifts, shortening

of the work day, and work that can be done at home. These suggestions are being considered by the regime, but no major move has yet been made toward their implementation except, as noted earlier, part-time work.

3. Reducing the women's domestic load: more institutions for the care of children, better and more household appliances, and relief from some food preparation through more restaurants and better commercial processing and preparation of food, such as precooked meals by catering organizations.
4. General cultural reshaping of national attitudes by artists, writers, and film makers who should stop romanticising hard work by women, or even its routine acceptance. Youth should be inculcated with an attitude of greater respect for women so they will not find it "natural" to see girls employed as stevedores or coalminers.

Childbearing, Work, and the Birth Rate

We must raise another consideration: If woman plays a crucial role in the economic life of a society, she plays an even more indispensable role in the bearing and raising of children. To some irreducible degree these functions and regular employment in industry conflict, and too great an emphasis on woman as a worker might depress the birth rate below a desirable level. With better medical care and environmental conditions, a lower infant mortality rate and consequent longer life expectancies, a society can maintain itself with a proportionately much lower birth rate than it could in earlier times.

From the viewpoint of society, furthermore, the removal of an unskilled and easily replaceable woman from the work force so that she may bear a child or several children will be less costly than the removal of a woman who has had many years of costly professional training and education. Moreover, a professional woman who took five or ten years to complete her childbearing cycle would find that some of her skills had become obsolete by the time she returned to work, a situation not facing the unskilled person. There might, therefore, be more of a tendency for a professional woman to restrict her childbearing than for a nonprofessional, leading to a division of labor not only between the sexes, but also within the female sex according to sociooccupational levels. Soviet data, summarized in Table 4 (*Zhenshchiny i deti v SSSR,* 1963, p. 68), indicate that farm women have more children than women workers, and the latter have more children than women employees, a category that includes professionals. This may, of course, be partially the result of geographical factors and the supply of housing as well as of Soviet policy, which encourages large families among the lower-income population. We might further surmise that it is possible for a professional woman to find a career, a kind of interest and commitment similar to that found by a man, and that she might not be inclined to have a large family, if she chooses to have any children at all.

Research on displaced Soviet women indicated that professional women and specialists tended to be consistently more satisfied with their jobs than men, but that women responded to their work experience predominantly according to the occupational level and only incidentally according to sex; the higher their type of job, the greater their satisfaction with it. With mechanization and automation, unskilled women workers may well be gradually withdrawn from the labor force, not necessarily to go back to their homes, but perhaps to engage in social, welfare, and cultural work. Professional women will continue their full-time commitment to their work equally with men. From a functional viewpoint, the elimination of women from the pool of skilled and professional talent would be disastrous in terms of their contribution to society. By the same token, the elimination of the childraising role, or its toning down and replacement by other institutional arrangements, might present other problems we will briefly mention below.

TABLE 4 FAMILIES ACCORDING TO NUMBER OF CHILDREN UNDER 16 YEARS BY OCCUPATIONAL GROUPS (Percentage of all families) 1962

	Employees	*Industrial Workers*	*Collective Farmers*
With one child	50	46	40
With two children	41	39	32
With three children	8	12	19
With four or more children	1	3	9
Total	100	100	100

Motherhood

What about the children? This question must be raised because the mere physical production of children is *never* enough to ensure the continuity of a society. They must be "socialized," i.e., transformed into reasonably well-behaving members of the adult world. Traditionally, socialization has been a family function, with the mother playing the most important role as an extension of her childbearing functions.

The logical application of Engels' scheme of the societal and public upbringing of children by agencies other than the family, toward which Soviet society on ideological grounds seems to be heading, raises the very critical question of maternal deprivation—the psychological correlates of institutional upbringing upon the personality of children brought up without a close relationship with the mother. It has been found that this does produce a deleterious effect on personality, on the intellectual level, and on social adjustment, that is for all practical purposes irreversible (Bowlby, 1952; World Health Organization, 1962). It is in this light that the Soviet scheme for the institutional upbringing of children, which is consonant with Marxist ideology, the belief in the plasticity of the individual, and the importance of the milieu and economic needs, should be examined with critical interest. If the hypothesis of the effects of maternal deprivation is a valid one not only for Western cultures, then the Soviet scheme should be a source of important information for the planners of institutionalized societies. Some evidence has come to light that Soviet children raised in orphanages or children's homes, i.e., raised in a nonfamilial atmosphere, invariably perform more poorly in their school work than those who come from families, even though these families might be economically deprived. One of the main reasons for this is that the children in institutions do not have a single adult person with whom they can identify and establish a continuous relationship. In one Soviet school, for example, children could not recognize themselves in group pictures because someone had forgotten to hang mirrors. In another such institution, the personnel were so busy in routine tasks that they had hardly any time to converse with their charges (Field and Anderson, 1968).

There is also some indication that a great deal of the juvenile delinquency that increasingly seems to plague Soviet society may be due, among other things, to broken families and to families in which the mother, because she either has to work or wants to work, neglects her children. If she is lucky she has her own mother or a relative to cook and mind the children when she is at work (Fischer, 1961). However, most women have to cope alone with every aspect of their occupational and domestic life. Needless to say, not too much individual attention can be devoted to the upbringing of children if the mother works between forty and forty-five hours a week. Furthermore, the lack of day-nurseries, kindergartens, and boarding schools forces working mothers to leave their children alone as soon as they are old enough to care for themselves. And even a loving and doting grandmother is not always an ideal substitute for a mother: she is particularly prone to overindulge her grandchildren and thus is frequently blamed if the youngsters get into trouble (Parygina, 1968).

The mother's lot, at least from the evidence we have in the Soviet sources, seems to be a particularly difficult one. She is expected to work outside the home and often is blamed if, as a result, her children bear the familiar characteristics of parental, particularly maternal, neglect. If she stays at home to care for her children and household, she receives little recognition and is criticized for her withdrawal from the "real" life of building the new society. And if her children grow up into responsible adults, she will earn no particular credit.

It is possible that as Soviet society becomes more prosperous and the critical need for women in the economy recedes, the traditional role of motherhood will receive more unequivocal support. Indeed, the recognition of the critical role played by mothers was well-stated in an article by N. I. Pirogov (Garina, 1967), published in *Izvestiia* in 1967:

> *The upbringing of society* must go hand in hand *with the upbringing of children.* . . . All who are preparing to be useful citizens must first learn to be people. . . . Let women realize that by tending the cradle of a human being, by establishing the games of his childhood and teaching his lips to say his first words . . . they become the chief architects of the society [p. 6].

The article further asks that the importance of the task of childraising be recognized on a par with that of giving birth and it argues that only a mother, and not a kindergarten or other similar institution, can give the child the individual attention he requires. The author then faults a society that esteems a woman who works in a factory more highly than one who stays at home supervising the growth and upbringing of her children. It is therefore quite possible that as the industrialization drive reaches a plateau in the Soviet Union and the demand for womanpower begins to decrease, greater official recognition will be accorded to the importance of motherhood for the emotional and intellectual balance of society and that this mechanism of socialization will be judged, after all, as more effective than the institutional arrangements of the type suggested by the more utopian Marxists.

"Womanhood"—or the Rediscovery of Femininity

The emphasis on equality and the large-scale employment of women in the economy, the ideological rejection of the bourgeois-like qualities of the wife and daughter with their implication of parasitism, have all tended to play down, if not to eliminate from the Soviet scene, any of the accepted concerns with femininity that seem so commonplace in the West. And yet, this concern has not disappeared—indeed it seems to be reappearing with great vigor. What is it, then, that Soviet men expect from Soviet women and from which they find it so difficult to part? A survey conducted in different areas of the Soviet Union revealed that Soviet men want ". . . wives who are sincere, cultivated, loyal, who like family life, domestic comfort and children" (Kasiukov and Mendeleev, 1967, p. 18). These results seem to indicate that after fifty years of propaganda to emancipate Soviet women from the domestic and bourgeois virtues and to turn them into equal participants in the building of a new society, there is still a longing among Soviet men for "feminine" women and feminine qualities. The obvious lack of femininity so often observed by visitors to the Soviet Union and apparently a source of pride for those who believe in absolute equality, was publicly lamented in 1967 by an elder poet, Ilia Sel'vinskii in the *Literaturnaia Gazeta,* who called, among other things, for the idealization of "feminine charms":

> Feminine beauty is not a bourgeois prejudice. Woman is the most perfect being that nature ever created. The esthetic of feminine beauty is vital to the whole country, to men, as well as women. Some of the greatest masterpieces of poetry, painting, and sculpture have been dedicated to feminine charm [p. 12].

Sel'vinskii further complained about the apparent indifference of women and young girls to their appearance. According to him, even leading women in the professions do not concern themselves sufficiently with this.

There are, on the other hand, increased indications that Soviet women are just as interested in how they look as their counterpart in the West (Curtis, 1967), and that this concern with their appearance is not, as it formerly was under Stalin, interpreted by the moral censors as kowtowing to an ideologically alien and subversive culture. The young women of the Soviet Union, conscious of the fact that their mothers have aged and even died prematurely as a result of the heavy burden they carried, seem determined not to share their fate. Perhaps the remark of a Moscow girl to an American friend expresses this feeling (Frost, 1965):

> Russian women work. A full week—that's tiring. They also run the house. Shop. Stand in line. Take care of the children. Do the wash. Stand in another line. After they are married, they haven't got five minutes to look in the mirror, let alone take care of what needs to be done. They get their work done somehow but simply have no energy left to look after themselves. So they deteriorate. But our generation will be different, I assure you. . . . Our generation is different! We know what the trouble is, and we *care* about our appearance [p. 17].

The Russian woman who "cares" spends her money on cosmetics and attractive clothes as far as they are available. She dyes her hair, demands more household appliances as well as more creches and kindergartens, and seems on the whole as anxious as any woman in any industrialized society to be recognized both as a person *and* as a woman.

Conclusions

An examination of the status and the role of woman in Soviet society may shed some light not only on the specifics of the Soviet situation but, in more general terms, on the fate of woman in the contemporary, large-scale industrialized or industrializing society. The Soviet case, though it has its unique cultural and structural features, may represent in an acute and concentrated form, the relatively new dilemmas and uncertainties of modern woman, torn between her blurred feminine identity and her role as a wife and mother with the economic trivialities of her domestic pursuits on the one hand, and the uncertainties, temptations, pitfalls, and opportunities of an occupational world that often needs her services and yet has looked with ambivalence on her equal participation and status in that world.

Note

[1] Reprinted with the permission of the publisher from Donald R. Brown, ed. *The Role and Status of Women in the Soviet Union* (New York: Teachers College Press) © 1968. This chapter represents a revised and updated abridgement of the original paper. The first version of this paper was presented at the Mary Winsor Symposium, Bryn Mawr College, April 23–25, 1964. The assistance of the Russian Research Center at Harvard University in making this study possible is gratefully acknowledged.

References

Beilin, E. A. *Kadry spetsialistov SSSR* [*Specialized Personnel of the USSR*]. Moscow, 1935, p. 348. Cited in Alex Inkeles and Raymond A. Bauer, *The Soviet Citizen*. Cambridge: Harvard University Press, 1959.

Bil'shaia-Pilopenko, Vera L'vovna. "Kto prav: Vl. Nemtsov ili E. Nilova?" ("Who is Right: Vl. Nemtsov or E. Nilova?"). *Literaturnaia Gazeta,* January 10, 1959.

Bowlby, John. *Maternal Care and Mental Health,* 2nd ed. Geneva: World Health Organization, 1952.

"Chelovek i kollektiv" ("The Individual and the Group") *Pravda,* March 23, 1962.

Curtis, Charlotte. "Soviet Women Cherish Their Femininity." *New York Times,* October 9, 1967.

Dodge, Norton T. *Women in the Soviet Economy: Their Role in Economic, Scientific, and Technical Development*. Baltimore: Johns Hopkins Press, 1966.

Dunham, Vera Sandomirsky. "The Strong Woman Motif." *The Transformation of Russian Society*. Cyril E. Black, ed. Cambridge: Harvard University Press, 1960, pp. 459–83.

Engels, Friedrich. *The Condition of the Working Class in England in 1844*. W. O. Henderson and W. H. Chaloner, trans. and eds. New York: Macmillan, 1958.

Fainsod, Merle. *How Russia is Ruled*. Cambridge: Harvard University Press, 1965.

Feshbach, Murray. "Manpower in the U.S.S.R.: A Survey of Recent Trends and Prospects." *New Directions in the Soviet Economy, Part III, The Human Resources*. Washington, D.C.: U. S. Government Printing Office, 1966.

Field, Mark G. "Re-legalization of Abortion in Soviet Russia." *New England Journal of Medicine,* 255 (August 30, 1956), 421–27.

——— and David E. Anderson. "Family and Social Problems." *Prospects for Soviet Society*. Allen Kassof, ed. New York: Praeger, 1968 pp. 386–417.

Fischer, Markoosha. "The Grandmothers." *Harper,* Special Supplement, May 1961.

Fréville, Jean, ed. *La Femme et le Communisme: Anthologie des Grands Textes du Marxisme*. Paris, 1950.

Frost, G. "What Russian Girls Are Like." *New York Times Magazine,* January 24, 1965.

Garina, Ye. "Izvestiia v krugu sem'i: Y kolybeli chelovek" ("Izvestia with the Family

Circle: At the Cradle of a Human Being"). *Izvestiia,* August 17, 1967. Also available in English, *Current Digest of the Soviet Press, CDSP,* 33.

Halle, Fannina. *Woman in Soviet Russia.* New York: Viking Press, 1933.

Hindus, Maurice. *House without a Roof.* Garden City, N.Y.: Doubleday, 1961.

Inkeles, Alex. "Family and Church in the Postwar USSR." *The Annals of the American Academy of Political and Social Sciences,* 263 (May 1949), 33–44.

Itogi Vsesoiuznoi Perepisi Naseleniia 1959 Joda 1962, Table 20, 74–79.

Juviler, Peter. "Family Reform on the Road to Communism." *Soviet Policy Making: Studies of Communism in Transition.* New York: Praeger, 1967.

Karcz, Jersy F., ed. *Soviet and East European Agriculture.* Los Angeles: University of California Press, 1967.

Kasiukov, I., and A. Mendeleev. "Mnenie sotsiologa: Nuzhni li talent sem'ia-ninu?" ("Sociologists Opinion: Must a Family Man Have Talent?"). *Nedelia,* 12 (March 12–18, 1967). Also available in English in *CDSP,* 19, 13.

Kuznetsova, Larisa. "Kak chei zhe udel' kukhnia?" ("Whose Job Is in the Kitchen?"). *Literaturnaia Gazeta, CDSP,* 19, 33, (July 12, 1967).

Lebedinskaia, L. "Svoboda dlia kukhni?" ("Freedom for the Kitchen?"). *Literaturnaia Gazeta,* February 22, 1967.

Marx, Karl. *Capital: A Critique of Political Economy.* Edited by Friedrich Engels, translated from Third German Edition by Samuel Moore and Edward Aveling, and revised and amplified according to the Fourth German Edition by Ernest Unterman. New York: Modern Library, 1906. First ed., Hamburg: Meissner, 1890–1894.

Massell, Gregory J. "Law as an Instrument of Revolutionary Change in a Traditional Milieu: The Case of Soviet Central Asia." *Law and Society Review,* 2, 2 (1968), 179–228.

Mikhailova, O. "Spravedlivaia obida" ("A Justified Vexation"). *Pravda,* January 6, 1962.

Money, John. "Development Differentiation of Femininity and Masculinity Compared." In *The Potential of Women,* Seymour M. Farber and Roger H. L. Wilson, eds. New York: McGraw-Hill, 1963.

Nemtsov, V. "Ob uvazhenii k zhenshchine" ("On Respect toward Women"). *Literaturnaia Gazeta,* June 11, 1957.

———. "Eshche raz ob uvazhenii k zhenshchine" ("Once More on Respect toward Woman"). *Literaturnaia Gazeta,* April 12, 1958.

Parry, Albert. "Soviet Women Physicians: A New Numerical Balance?" *Review of Soviet Medical Sciences,* 4, 1 (1967), 13–21.

Parygina, Natalia. "Zhiteiskie besedy: Dobrota vo vred" ("Everyday Conversation: Kindness to a Fault"). *Pravda,* January 26, 1968; *CDSP,* 20, 4.

Prokofev, M. K. *Komsomolskaya Pravda,* May 20, 1966; *CDSP,* 18, 23 (1966).

Prudenski, G., and Kolpakov, B. "Questions concerning the Calculations of Non-working Time in Budget Statistics." *Problems of Economics,* 12 (1962), 31.

Sel'vinskii, Ilia. "Proza o prekrasnoi dame" ("Prose about the Beautiful Lady"). *Literaturnaia Gazeta,* April 12, 1967.

Semenov, Vladimir. "Dva stikhotvorenia: ("Two Poems"), *Novii Mir* (*New World*), Vera S. Dunham, trans. 7 (1958), 137–38.

Shim, Eduard. "A nu-ka, vziali!" ("Ready, Heave!"). *Literaturnaia Gazeta,* (February 1, 1967), 12.

Slater, Philip E. "On Social Regression." *American Sociological Review,* 28 (June 1963), 339–64.

"Slovo o nashikh zhenshchinakh" ("A Word about Our Women"). *Literaturnaia Gazeta,* October 7, 1958.

Sonin, M. Ya. *Vosproizvodstvo . . . rabochei sily v SSSR i balans truda* (*Productivity of the Work Force in the USSR and the Balance of Labor*). Moscow: Gosplanizdat, 1959, p. 88.

Sonin, M. Ya., and Savranskaia. "Sotsiologicheskie zametkicheloveki rabota" (Sociological Notes—Man and Work). *Literaturnaia Gazeta,* September 22, 1966.

Tatu, Michel. "Are Soviet Housewives Citizens?" *Atlas* (February 1965), 96–97 (trans. from *Le Monde,* 1963).

Topping, Audrey R. "First in Space—But Not in Femininity." *New York Times Magazine,* June 30, 1965.

Vestnik Statistiki (*Statistics Bulletin*), 1, 1967.

World Health Organization. *Deprivation of Maternal Care: A Reassessment of Its Effects.* Geneva: Public Health Papers, 1962.

Zhenshchiny i deti v SSSR: statisticheskii sbornik (*Women and Children in the USSR*). Moscow: Gostatizdat, 1963.

13 THE SEXES: IDEOLOGY AND REALITY IN THE ISRAELI KIBBUTZ

A. I. Rabin[1]

That there is often a discrepancy between plans and actual achievements, between the "ideal" and the "real," is hardly a novel observation. In fact, many of us could point to accomplishments that fell short of the blueprint. However, the gap between the desired and the accomplished does present us with a challenge. We frequently ignore successes, the fulfilled expectations, for they do not leave us with any problems; they do not raise any questions.

Although the Kibbutz society has many accomplishments to its credit, "complete equality" between men and women is not one of them. Progress in this particular area has been slow and uncertain; there remains a discrepancy between ideology and reality. The background, history, and current status of this discrepancy are the major concern in the pages that follow.

Israeli "Culture"

It is rather difficult, if not impossible, to speak of an "Israeli Culture." The country of modern Israel is of such recent origin, and its population is composed of so many groups of diverse backgrounds, that a common culture and modal sex roles related to such a culture cannot be found. Nevertheless, the broader cultural setting, with some attention to its major components, will be described in order to serve as a backdrop for the Kibbutz social system and the sex roles within that system.

Israeli society consists of four major subgroups that reflect some important cultural differences. European immigrants, immigrants from Eastern and, especially, Arabic-speaking countries, the native Arab minority, and the native-born Jewish citizens (*sabras*) make up the bulk of the population of Israel. Although heroic and even frantic efforts at integration and assimilation are being made, some of the cultural differences between these segments of the population remain. These differences may persist for some time to come because of continuing immigration and due to the fact that even a "pressure cooker" as compared with a "melting pot" does not work instantaneous miracles.

Even the European or Western immigrants do not constitute a homogeneous cultural group. Some arrived before World War I and soon after—primarily from Eastern European countries such as Russia and Poland. The bulk of immigrants, however, arrived shortly before and after World War II. A large percentage of these arrivals was from Western European countries such as Germany and Austria. Immigrants from Eastern European countries continued to trickle into Palestine, as the country was then called, between the two world wars, with occasional waves of immigration propelled by the political upheavals in those countries. The early Eastern European immigrants came from the typical *shtetl* (Zborowski & Herzog, 1952) culture that was characterized by a patriarchal family pattern and organization. Later, immigrants from Eastern Europe, as well as those who came from the West, represented different kinds of familial settings.

The years after World War I brought about important social and cultural changes. Among them was the "emancipation" of the woman and her increased participation and authority outside the confines of the family circle. Many women fought side by side with men in the various post-World War I revolutionary movements in Russia and elsewhere. Similarly, increasing participation of women in the professions and greater equality with men with respect to education and authority in the family circle particularly characterized the German and other Western European immigrations during the 1930s and later. Thus, the European immigrants over a period of some fifty years have represented different cultural trends—the earlier patriarchal types of families with clear-cut distinctions and differentiation of sex roles and the later transitional patterns representing greater liberation of the woman and a rapprochement between the sex roles of the two sexes.

Most of the immigrants of the second group, those from the Arabic-speaking countries (Egypt, Syria, Iraq, etc.), arrived after the end of World War II and upon the establishment of the state of Israel in 1948. These Eastern immigrants and their children constitute, at this writing, more than fifty percent of the country's Jewish population. The vast majority of this group may be characterized as "Levantine" in culture. Most relevant in the present context is their patriarchal type of family and the supreme authority of the father. Sex roles are clearly defined in this sort of setting. Besides taking care of the household, bearing children, and caring for them, the woman's functions also extended into economic activities outside the home as part-time farmer, artisan, trader, etc. The setting was not unlike that existing today in many of the rural and some of the urban areas of the Arab countries—including the practice of polygamy.

The third segment of Israel's population is composed of native Arabs, Moslems, and Christians. The vast majority of this group represent traditional values similar to those found in the Eastern Jewish immigrant group, discussed in the preceding paragraph. A very small minority of women can be called emancipated. By and large, the Arab community is still patriarchal with the male head of the family the undisputed ruler and the woman in a rather subservient position to him. Although the woman is very heavily involved in the family's economic enterprises (farming, gardening, trading) in addition to giving birth to children and taking care of the home, the male has the high status and supreme authority. This is especially true in Moslem families because the Koran allegedly dictates the differential in sex roles and in the power and status structure.

Sabras, or native-born, non-Arab Israelis, make up the fourth and last group. The majority of the young adults in this group are descendants of the Western and European immigrants. The emancipation of the woman that started in Europe continued in Israel and is reflected in her status in *sabra* society. The Kibbutz society, which is the focus of our present concern, is composed primarily of European immigrants—the founders—and their descendants who are, of course, *sabras.* Immigrants from the Eastern, Arabic-speaking countries have contributed a negligible number to Kibbutz society. We must, therefore, consider that segment of European immigrants that initiated the Kibbutz movement and its ideology and then follow the evolution, changes, and revisions of that ideology as embodied in the modern Kibbutz society consisting of veterans and *sabras* alike (Rabin, 1961).

Kibbutz: History

As indicated above, the veterans—founders of the Kibbutz movement that dates its beginning to the year 1910—were young pioneers, men and women, who arrived in Palestine from Eastern Europe. Many of them were disenchanted with the radical socialistic movements and revolutions in Russia, not only because of their lack of success in the ascension to power prior to the Bolshevik revolution, but because the internationalist ideology did not in fact eliminate narrow nationalism and anti-Semitism. Many of these young men and women who migrated to Israel imported socialistic ideologies of various hues along with a Jewish nationalism—an aspiration to rebuild a Jewish homeland devoid of anti-Semitism and persecution. Part of this nationalistic aspiration was to develop a new country on a sound economic basis. These pioneers stressed the need for abolishing the traditional "Jewish" occupations—trade and commerce—and advocated a "return to the soil" as an avenue for personal salvation and sound economic planning. Embracing agriculture was not merely due to economics but due to the influences of Tolstoy and his disciples, who found the greatest happiness in a return to "mother earth."

Barren or swampy land and unfriendly neighbors were not the most ideal conditions for the new settlers in Palestine. They had to band together and help each other to work the land; for security reasons and for the sake of self-protection against marauders, neighbors, and nomadic bands, they joined together into well-knit and well-disciplined fortress-villages. For these reasons and for the sake of social justice and equality, "to achieve socialism in our day," they established the communal settlements known as Kibbutzim (plural of Kibbutz).

During the second decade of the twentieth century, a few small Kibbutzim were established. However, the 1920s and 1930s brought large waves of immigrants into the country. The Kibbutz movement grew by leaps and bounds during this particular period. Some further growth took place during and immediately after World War II. Since then, relatively few new Kibbutzim have been established. The new immigrants of the 1950s and 1960s had little interest in communal living, in its socialism, and in the romanticism of the "return to the soil." Most of the immigrants of this period came from the Near Eastern countries and from the Soviet satellites, with little interest in the earlier Kibbutz ideologies. Thus, it is possible to state with some degree of certainty that as far as growth via immigration is concerned, the Kibbutz movement has been relatively static for about fifteen years. Some growth occurred and will take place from within: if Kibbutz members increase their rate of reproduction. This trend might be reasonably predicted.

In the latter part of the 1960s, one finds some 220 Kibbutzim in the country. The total population in these villages is somewhat under 100,000 persons, less than 5 percent of the country's inhabitants. The vast majority of these Kibbutzim are organized into three major federations that differ politically from each other and represent the socialist political spectrum from left of center (mild social democratic ideology) to the extreme left, short of international communism. The federation that has most consistently maintained many of its ideological principles through the years, including the equality of sexes, is the most leftist politically and is the main concern of the subsequent pages (Leon, 1964; Rabin, 1965).

Kibbutz Ideology

The Kibbutz movement represented drastic changes, even revolutionary perhaps, from the old form of life that the young immigrants had experienced in the countries of their origin. Life in the new country moved in new directions in several areas. The innovations were consciously planned and inaugurated as a result of fairly well-enunciated ideologies that carried an amalgam of social justice and nationalism.

Politically, Jewish Palestine under the British mandate formed a "government within a government." Although the overall governmental apparatus, especially the higher echelons, was in the hands of the British, the Jewish community governed itself to a considerable extent. A good deal of political freedom and activity was possible within this framework. All shades of political opinion and parties were represented in the community, which constantly vied for the "souls" of the incoming immigrants. Political activity and activism flourished, and the developing Kibbutz movement was fairly well divided among some of the major political parties. Hence, the division into federations, mentioned above.

Most salient, of course, was the economic revolution undertaken by the Kibbutz. In addition to the abandonment of the various trades (semi-professional and professional occupations of the diaspora) for the "return to the soil," the Kibbutz embraced the principle of economic collectivism. The principle essentially eliminates private property and the opportunity to accumulate wealth. All means of production are owned by the Kibbutz community collectively. Economic collectivism continues even under the conditions of high industrialization that have developed in the Kibbutzim during the past two decades. The community supplies the needs of the individuals who comprise it. No distinctions with respect to economic rewards are made between different occupations. All members of the community, regardless of occupational status, education, or expertness, have equal rights economically as well as politically. With the exception of such personal belongings as apartment furnishings, books, and radios, private property is eliminated. Each person receives according to his needs and, generally, resources are allocated to various economic, social, and educational enterprises upon the decision of the entire collectivity.

Complete equality in the economic sphere is intimately bound with political and social equalitarianism. Democracy of a radical nature evolved as the major principle in the government of the Kibbutz. Supreme authority was lodged in the "town meeting" type of weekly discussion in which all adult members participate. All the power and authority of individual coordinators and directors of various activities, and of the committees that serve as advisory and/or executive bodies, are delegated via the town meeting, which represents the total membership. Power is delegated for a limited period of time, one, two, or three years, depending on the job. This conferred power and authority can be removed at any time if the membership of the Kibbutz deems it advisable. Thus, the entrenchment of power of an "encrusted nobility" is definitely avoided.

Consonant with the economic collectivism and with the basic democracy of the social organization and control of power is the social equality in this essentially classless society. Since there are no differentiated formal rewards connected with different occupations, and since there is no accretion of power via accumulation of wealth and consequent control over resources, there is not expected to be any marked difference in social status among the members of the Kibbutz. However, according to some observers, reality does not quite conform to this ideal state of affairs. In actuality, members differ in levels of ability, productivity, and contribution to the economy. Although leadership is formally transmitted democratically, individuals do differ in the amount of power and influence they have. Political, cultural, and economic leadership emerges. This fact accounts for the emergence of social status and a certain degree of inequality. It can be said, however, that the opportunity for perpetuation of status independent of merit, ability, and achievement for the benefit of the collectivity, is absent when compared with any modern Western society.

The Family in the Kibbutz

Economic collectivism, as a major characteristic of the Kibbutz, also wrought some important changes in the structure of the Kibbutz family. The common economic enterprise that has been an important binding force in the maintenance of the family unit for centuries has been eliminated. As one author puts it (Leon, 1964), "The economic factor plays no role in the formation of the Kibbutz family, in its maintenance or—in the event of failure—in its dissolution" (p. 129). As we shall see presently, there are important bases for the existence of the family in its altered form in the Kibbutz, but the economic factor is not one of them. In addition to the elimination of the woman's traditional economic dependence upon a male breadwinner, the children, too, are not dependent upon their parents economically. The Kibbutz as a whole is responsible for their well-being in every respect. However, another important exclusive prerogative of parents in relation to their children has been partially relinquished in the Kibbutz—the raising, upbringing and socialization of the young. Thus, another cardinal aspect that characterizes the traditional family has been removed. Some writers went so far as to question the existence of the family in the Kibbutz (Spiro, 1954). However, the "family" definitely exists—primarily as a psychological, rather than an economic or legal, entity. The following statement puts it in a nutshell: "The Kibbutz family rests upon positive personal, rather than impersonal economic foundations" (Leon, 1964, p. 129). This is further corroborated by the findings concerning the positive intrafamilial relations in the Kibbutz (Rabin, 1965).

Freeing the Woman

"Emancipation of the woman" was part and parcel of the ideal of the new family structure in the Kibbutz. With the elimination of the traditional economic dependency of the woman upon her husband, and with the establishment of communal nurseries that liberated the woman from the four walls of her domicile, she was expected to be well on her way to complete equality with the man. Moreover, the central kitchens and dining rooms in the Kibbutz were designed to remove the woman from her traditional position "by the kitchen stove" in the ordinary family setting. She no longer had to cook and prepare meals as well as serve them three times a day. She became free to do "other things." Whether she did, in fact, become engaged in doing other things beyond the usual and conventional realm of feminine occupations is another story with which we shall concern ourselves in greater detail in a later section of this chapter.

At first, equality between the sexes was embraced literally and with a vengeance by the Kibbutz woman. An attempt was made to eradicate, as far as possible, all differences except, of course, the physical and physiological ones that had to be fatalistically accepted and tolerated. In a way, femininity was defended against, and the defense employed was a sort of reaction formation. There was not only a denial of femininity, but an attempt to achieve some sort of masculinity in order to justify equality. Equality of rights was also extended in interpretation to equality in obligations and in the specific kind of obligations.

With respect to the latter point, women have often tried to justify equality between the sexes by assuming obligations and by undertaking certain physically taxing jobs that tested the endurance of their masculine counterparts as well. Along with such efforts involving physical prowess, beyond what was customarily demanded of women, were other behavioral alterations that pointed to certain transformations in self-concept directed by the ideal of complete equality.

Grooming and personal attractiveness had become the sacrifices upon the altar of equality between the sexes. If woman is equal to man, there is no reason for her to play up to him, to make herself feminine and attractive to the male. Apparel and grooming became relatively insignificant for the Kibbutz woman. This neglect was in part connected with the existing economic conditions and a consequence of the kinds of heavy labor women had frequently undertaken; it was also, however, due to the ideology of equality and to the reaction against being the "fair and weak" sex that had to employ feminine guile and cunning to ensnare the man. Old Eve relinquished her persuasion of Adam for a new garden of Eden!

Additional victims of the campaign for equality were the etiquette and manners that characterized European, especially urban, society. These changes were not so much a part of the new and equal woman, but were reflected in her treatment by the man. The assumption was that woman, since she is equal to man, should not be treated by him with any special consideration. Opening the door for the woman, offering her help in negotiating steep climbs, etc., became quaint and antiquated customs that not only betray inequality but are also remnants of the culture of the "chivalrous" bourgeois society against which the Kibbutz revolted so thoroughly and assiduously. Manners and etiquette were viewed as superficial and insincere external manifestations of interpersonal relations that lacked in the genuineness and truthfulness upon which Kibbutz society was to be based.

The foregoing paragraphs describe a strife for equality in status via an attempt to equalize the roles. Since role and status are intimately intertwined (Parsons, 1951), the consequent accompanying role changes were inevitable. Status and prestige had been traditionally connected with "masculinity." Thus, in order to achieve equality, the attendant change of roles was in the direction of masculinity. A possible change of roles on the part of the men in the Kibbutz will be touched upon later.

Another related pattern of behavior characterized the early Kibbutzim, especially those formed by former members of such youth movements as *Hashomer Hatzair*. Puritanical standards with respect to sexuality and the undemonstrativeness in the public interaction between husband and wife were among such patterns. This extreme reserve and apparent affective control almost represented a denial of sex and sexuality, of tenderness and attraction, between man and woman. This extreme modesty was apparently not altogether unrelated to the attempt to deny the existence of real differences between the sexes, except for the most obvious ones—physical and physiological—which were minimized and whose public salience was drastically reduced. In a sense, the implication has been that it is in poor taste to stress the differences between man and woman, especially in public, and to display emotions in relation to each other.

Childrearing

Of immense importance in the attempted process of changing sex roles in the Kibbutz movement was the development of its unique childrearing and educational system. The importance stems from two sources. First, the new educational system, termed "collective education," was designed to contribute to the emancipation of the woman by removing the child from the family setting that had traditionally required the constant vigilance of the mother and her consequent confinement to the home. Second, the tenets of collective education involved practically no differentiation between the sexes in the educational process and a delay of any recognition of differences to the latest possible date—that of late adolescence and early adulthood. Let us, then, review briefly the childrearing practices in the Kibbutz and their effects upon the status of the woman or, rather, upon her potential status.

When the Kibbutz mother returns from the hospital following delivery, her baby (usually about one week old) is placed in the Kibbutz creche or "baby house." Here, the infant shares a room with about three or four other babies who are within a few weeks of its own age. The closeness in age depends, of course, upon the birth rate in the Kibbutz. The group of four or five infants is in the charge of a *metapelet* (caretaker) who has full responsibility for the physical care and well-being of the group of babies. The *metapelet* is usually a mature person, a mother herself, who has had some experience in caring for children, as well as some formal training in practical and theoretical aspects of childcare.

The mother of the infant returns to reside with her husband in their apartment. However, during the first six weeks following the birth of the child, she remains free and is not obligated to return to work. During this period, she ordinarily maintains the closest relationship with her offspring; she feeds him (breast-feeding is encouraged), diapers him, plays with him and, generally, spends most of his waking hours with him. At night, however, the baby remains in the infant house and the mother returns to her apartment or to attend some community social or cultural evening activities. Occasionally, if the need arises, she may be called by the night watch to attend to her baby.

Following the first six weeks, after a feeding rhythm has been established, the mother returns to work on a half-time basis. Naturally, she is less constantly available to the child, but is present for the feeding periods and spends considerable time with the infant after working hours. During this period, the role of the *metapelet* in caring for the child increases markedly. She attends to matters of cleanliness, extra feeding when necessary, and the relieving of the child's discomforts. When the baby is about four months old, the mother resumes full-time work. Contacts are further reduced to more irregular visits during the day and to regular attendance at bedtime.[2] After nine months, a regular regimen commences. Contacts between mother and child and between the child and other members of the biological family become confined to two or three hours daily, after work, in the parents' apartment, and extend to longer periods of time on the Sabbath and during holidays. However, the parents may visit at any time.

Subsequent to this period, the role of the *metapelet* further increases in importance. She assumes almost exclusive responsibility for the habit training, teaching, and socialization of the young infant and child. These functions are subsequently taken over by a series of *metaplot* (plural of *metapelet*), teachers, and educators as the child progresses through the primary and secondary grades until he reaches the age of eighteen.

At no point following her return to work does the mother regain the close and continuous contacts she had with the child during the first few months of his life. The father's interaction with the child, during the visits to the parents' apartment, equals that of mother's following the period of early infancy and exceeds that of fathers in conventional society. However, there is little differentiation in the extent of authority or discipline that either of them may exercise in relation to the child. Actually, they do not exercise many controls, for these are lodged in the *metapelet,* peers, and teachers (Rabin, 1965).

Consonant with the general ideological orientation of the Kibbutz, complete equality of the sexes is a cherished ideal in the educational process. This is reflected in the equal and nondifferential treatment of boys and girls in the educational system, reaching the ultimate in coeducation. Boys and girls learn and live together from infancy to maturity, without any distinction in their functions or roles. Until recently, the same curriculum applied to boys and girls through the primary and secondary grades. In the later years of the *Mosad* (high school), some differentiation in roles takes place in connection with the small auxiliary farms that are worked by the students. The boys assume responsibility for the heavier chores while the girls gravitate to the physically less taxing activities connected with the economy. In sports, too, there is fairly early recognition, around the latter part of the latency period, of sex differences in capacities for exertion and in the several competitive activities. Toward the latter part of adolescence, the girls tend to drop out of most sport activities while the boys' nightly practice in the open-air basketball court, in preparation for various league competitions, is a common sight in many Kibbutzim. However, during the first ten or twelve years of life, there is little emphasis upon different or separate games, sport activities, or other kinds of recreation for boys and girls.

This lack of differentiation has been further stressed in clothing. During most of the week the same type of shorts or jeans, and shirts or blouses, are worn by boys and girls. Only on holidays, and especially in recent years, do the girls wear dresses and begin to emphasize different aspects of their femininity such as occasional frills, girlish hairdos, ribbons, and so on. There has been an increasing sensitivity to clothes, grooming, and femininity on the part of the adolescent and adult female population of the Kibbutz. In part, it has been attributed to "outside" influences—effects of the broader Israeli culture that will be discussed presently in greater detail. However, much of it was stimulated by the Kibbutz membership itself.

Sex Differences and Identification

The Kibbutz experiment in the equalization of sex roles depends upon the educational process that is responsible for the production of the new generation. As mentioned above, the differences in the childrearing practices and attitudes toward boys and girls in the Kibbutz educational setting are minimal. There is a conscious effort, in keeping with the ideology, to minimize sex differences. As we indicated, this program is relatively successful.

There are several lines of evidence concerning the education process (Rabin, 1965). A group of Kibbutz ten-year-olds were asked to "draw a person," and then to draw a person of the opposite sex. Using an index of sexual differentiation, the Kibbutz children were compared with non-Kibbutz Israeli children reared in the traditional family setting and with a group of American children of the same age. The conclusions were that ". . . non-Kibbutz and American fourth graders achieve higher levels of sexual differentiation than Kibbutz children . . . girls are superior to boys on the measurement of sexual differentiation in the non-Kibbutz and American samples; Kibbutz girls do not differ in this respect from Kibbutz boys" (p. 117).

It appears, therefore, that awareness of sex differences is reflected less in the drawings of Kibbutz children. Also, the earlier maturity and awareness of such differences of non-Kibbutz girls does not appear in the Kibbutz girls.

Due to the very structure and nature of the Kibbutz intrafamilial constellation, the identification of the Kibbutz child, as compared with that of the non-Kibbutz child, is less centered on the same sex parent; it is more diffuse. Thus, Kibbutz boys have as their models not only father figures, but mothers, *metaplot,* and peers; the girls apparently use as their identification figures not only their mothers and/or *metaplot,* but the fathers and peers (male and female) as well. There is, therefore, little evidence of direct sex-role instruction in Kibbutz childhood, although there is some opportunity for incidental learning (Sarbin, 1955) of such roles. Also, a corollary of the diffuse identification is, of course, a certain vagueness about the traditional line of demarcation and distinction between masculinity and femininity or the differences in sex roles.

The third and final point that should be made deals with the sexuality of Kibbutz adolescents. Quite consonant and continuous with the emphasis upon equality of roles and functions, the sexual drives and their manifestations that are prompted by maturation during puberty are quite consistently avoided or evaded. I concluded elsewhere (Rabin, 1965):

> Kibbutz adolescents seem to be highly tempted by, and concerned with, sex, but they suppress it mainly for ideological reasons and because of the external pressure in the Kibbutz setting. However, it appears that the controls of heterosexuality become more relaxed when the Kibbutz youngster enters the Army where his ideology is not so salient and where external social controls of the Kibbutz recede [p. 206].

It may be readily noted, therefore, that, developmentally, little differentiation between the sexes and a deemphasis of any juxtaposition of masculinity and femininity are part of the education process in the Kibbutz. This state of affairs is maintained until, due to biological (sexual) maturation and social relaxation of rules, the young people can no longer "hold out." There begins the inevitable recognition of the biological "facts of life" and sex differentiation that extends to a much broader arena. The relationship between the biological differences and the sociocultural aspects and sex roles were amply discussed and documented by Seward [1946 (1954)] and others (e.g. D'Andrade, 1966).

Contacts and Conflicts

Upon joining the armed forces—a compulsory obligation—Kibbutz young men and women are exposed to a greater extent to "outside" influences and the larger cultural context. Although there is universal compulsory military service for women as well as for men, there are important differences in the length of service and in the types of functions and demands made upon the members of the two sexes. Women's obligatory service is much shorter than men's, there are more classifications of exemptions for women, and they are assigned to various clerical, instructional, or similar noncombatant duties. The latter are, generally, in marked contrast to the demands made of the larger proportions of men inducted into the armed forces. Thus, in the army and even more so in their now more frequent contact with civilians outside the Kibbutz, the Kibbutz-reared young men and women are exposed to marked differentiation of the roles and functions between the sexes. This is combined with the inevitable observations of the distinctions between the roles of males and females in the adult Kibbutz society itself, which we shall discuss at some length in the later sections of this chapter. All of these serve as an antidote to the blithe path of absence of any sex differences in the educational process. Some conflict, especially in the girls, arises as a result of this paradoxical situation—the discrepancy between the years from birth to eighteen on the one hand, with the facts of the adult reality on the other. The ideology that the Kibbutz youth has lived during the first eighteen years of his life is no longer a useful guide. A reorientation has to take place.

In his discussion of sex differences and cultural institutions, D'Andrade (1966) states:

> Maleness and femaleness are institutionalized as statuses in all cultures. Such statuses become psychological entities for most individuals. Usually individuals learn to want to occupy the sex status they are assigned; however, special cultural conditions can affect the degree to which one sex envies the status of the other [p. 201].

In our particular instance, it appears that perhaps the boys "learn to want" to occupy the male status, but with respect to the girls there may be a serious question. For one thing, even growing up in a children's society does not make them entirely oblivious to the ambivalence, nay dissatisfaction, of their own mothers and their female friends with their status in the Kibbutz. Thus, it is possible that some of the girls "learn" *not* to "want" the social status and roles women occupy in their community. Moreover, the Kibbutz economy (productive) and, therefore, authority, is predominantly in the hands of males, as we suggested above. The educational system, although it stresses equality, is permeated with traditionally masculine values. This, too, is a further source of frustration to the girl.

Plans and Suggestions

Attempts to deal with these issues, especially the inequality and dissatisfaction, are of two kinds. First come the suggestions that involve the changes in reality in order to adapt to the ideology. One series of suggestions (Golan, 1962) spells out steps for the placement of men in "service" branches (tractor driver, machinist), although it may remove them from their jobs for six months or a year. This will give women greater opportunity to enter the agricultural and manufacturing enterprises of the Kibbutz. Additional suggestions include advanced professional preparation in the service branches and improvement of working conditions in these branches for mothers of young children.

Another series of suggestions involves a certain change in position—a recognition of the "fundamental character differences" between the sexes and a certain accommodation or adjustment to them. From this general position flow suggestions for the change of the school curriculum, especially at the secondary level, to permit greater variability and parallel tracks to prepare female students for their differential tasks in the community. Another more far-reaching trend, which has been dominant in one particular Kibbutz federation, is an almost complete return to the traditional division of labor and to a concomitant strengthening of the family unit (Shafer, 1967).

In other Kibbutz federations, there is also an increasing tendency, due to popular demand, to give women more time with their offspring (Levine, 1968). This trend brings about a considerable strengthening of family ties. A major question is, "At what point does this revival of the importance of the family unit spell out a threat to the collectivism of the Kibbutz community?" Only time will give us an answer to this question that is crucial to the perpetuation of Kibbutz life. More details about these issues follow.

Centralization and Regression

The presence of central educational and childcare institutions in the Kibbutz are paralleled further by some additional centralization and specializations of activities that have been traditionally within the purview of the housewife. Thus, not only is the woman "liberated" in her daily routine from childcare and control activities, but from many other chores as well. Since there is a central dining room in the Kibbutz that supplies the food, the woman is spared the traditional tasks of marketing, preparation of food, and serving of food to members of her family. Also, since the typical Kibbutz has a central sewing and mending shop, these chores are also excluded from the woman's daily routine. The question arises, however, as to what kinds of activities and functions replace the chores of yore in the life of the Kibbutz woman.

Actually, it was the women who became the *metaplot* in the children's houses, and the kindergarten teachers. The women, too, became the cooks and functionaries in the central kitchens and dining rooms of the Kibbutzim. Similarly, they also took primary responsibility for sewing, mending, and such sundry tasks required by the entire Kibbutz. "The objective needs force on most of the women just those jobs from which the Kibbutz promised to liberate them" (Golan, 1961, p. 97). Instead of doing a little bit of each chore in her own home, the Kibbutz woman undertook one task at a time as a specialized occupation. Spiro (1956) summed up the situation rather succinctly by stating that, ". . . instead of cooking and sewing and baking and cleaning and laundering and caring for children," the Kibbutz woman ". . . cooks *or* launders *or* takes care of children for eight hours a day. She has become a specialist in one aspect of housekeeping. But this new housekeeping is more boring and less rewarding than the traditional type" (p. 229). Spiro's analysis with respect to the greater specialization of the traditional household activities appears quite reasonable, but his evaluation and conclusion may be questioned. It is not less rewarding in all instances. In many situations, Kibbutz women are given the opportunity to achieve a high level of competence in their branches of activity via advanced specialized training, be it in education, dietetics, clothes designing, etc. Thus, many of the specialized jobs need not be so devoid of the "initiative and creativity" that, according to Spiro, were characteristic of the "traditional type of housekeeping." This is not to deny that monotony and dissatisfaction may not be felt in many instances of the type of specialization alluded to above.

The general picture with respect to feminine occupations in the Kibbutz that emerges gives little support for the ideological equality and nondifferentiation between the sexes. The actual state of affairs is such as to indicate that the vast majority of Kibbutz women are engaged in education and "nonproductive" service activities, whereas the men are mostly involved in agriculture, management, and income-producing services. One survey (Golan, 1962) reports 35 percent of women in education, 38 percent in services (nonincome producing), 8 percent in agriculture, and the remainder in a miscellany of other occupations. On the other hand, 32 percent of the men were engaged in agricultural pursuits, 27 percent in "productive" services, and 11 percent in management; only 5 percent were in educational occupations and 6 percent in service jobs.

A more recent survey (Shafer, 1967), based on 818 interviews in eighteen Kibbutzim, throws some further light on the division of labor. The percentage of men in each Kibbutz engaged in occupations defined by them as strictly masculine, such as agricultural jobs, jobs involving animals, work in the service of the economy, and central social-political activities (full-time), was determined. Similarly, the percentages of women in strictly feminine occupations (defined by the women themselves) were also determined. The definite feminine occupations were kitchen work, care of children, clothes supply store saleswoman, and nursing. The results obtained from the 818 individuals by means of this survey lead to the following summarization:

A. (1) The percentage of men working in masculine occupations varies between 53 percent and 84 percent. (2) The percentage of women in feminine occupations ranges between 50 percent and 84 percent.

B. (1) The percentage of men working in feminine jobs is very low and reaches in no Kibbutz more than 10 percent; out of the eighteen Kibbutzim studied, in ten there are no males doing feminine jobs. (2) The percentage of women in masculine occupations ranges between 5 percent to 20 percent; in six out of the eighteen Kibbutzim there are no women in masculine occupations.

The remaining percentages of males and females were in occupations that were not strictly defined as either masculine or feminine. The overlap is obviously not very great, and the polarization of occupations along sex lines is widely accepted. Most Kibbutz members who responded to this survey seem to agree that certain jobs are unsuitable for men and others are not suitable for women. Only 13 percent of the sample claimed that there are no such sex-linked jobs. It was also interesting to note that about two-thirds of the Kibbutz members interviewed stress the difference in physical strength between the sexes as the main reason for the unsuitability of certain jobs for women. The range of reasons for the unsuitability of certain other positions for men is wider, such as the absence of the proper approach, problems of efficiency, social norms, and the fact that these jobs are "contrary to nature."

From the foregoing opinions and facts of employment, it is quite apparent that the *de facto* situation is a clearcut division of labor in the Kibbutz, corresponding to sex, which parallels fairly closely the state of affairs in the "outside" society.

The imperceptibly slow drift or regression in the position of the woman in the Kibbutz from occupational equality to lower status occupations, possibly less interesting ones and less gratifying ones, has brought about considerable resentment and dissatisfaction. Whenever a family leaves the Kibbutz it is usually the woman who is the main instigator of the move. According to Shafer (1967), it is the growth of the family and its strengthening in the Kibbutz that brought about a change from the earlier days when the aim of equality was achieved, at least in part. Women participated in most of the agricultural, construction, and physically strenuous work done by the Kibbutz. There was less participation on the part of men in work that was defined by the surrounding society as feminine. To be sure, there were men who worked in the kitchen, but there is no evidence that they participated in infant care or in the care of clothes. It may be argued, however, that it was not the family that reduced the greater equality present in the earlier periods of the Kibbutz existence.

Perhaps the inability, of the membership to maintain that equality, due to physical and psychological causes, contributed to a strengthening of the family to the extent of bringing the children to sleep in their parents' apartment, in several Kibbutzim of one of the federations. Between the years 1948 and 1955, the regular occupation of women in productive agriculture dropped from 11.1 percent to 6.3 percent. During those years, the percentage of men engaged in these occupations rose from 27.6 percent to 33.4 percent. By 1955, more than 66 percent of the women worked in various service jobs as compared to 11 percent of the men.

Female Discontent

The discontent of the Kibbutz woman and the erosion of her occupational equality have given rise to what became known as the "problem of the woman." The Kibbutz movement has been concerned with the problem of the woman, or the girl, for quite some time. One example of such interest and concern is illustrated by the attitude survey the present author was asked to undertake by one of the three large Kibbutz federations (Kibbutz Artzi) in 1962. What follows is a report of some of the relevant results published earlier (Rabin, 1963 b, 1968).

A forty-item questionnaire, designed to tap the attitudes of Kibbutz seventeen to eighteen-year-olds (graduating high school seniors) to their form of life, education, and sex roles, was administered to over 300 subjects. Generally, despite the discontent mentioned above, there are no marked differences between boys and girls in response to the final item of the questionnaire—"My future is in the Kibbutz." The vast majority of both sexes (about 90 percent) circled the "yes" in response to this item. The others circled the question mark (?), and only one respondent, a girl, circled the "no." Thus, only one out of more than 300 respondents was sure that her future was *not* in the Kibbutz.

A number of the items were especially designed to tap opinions and attitudes involving the woman's status in Kibbutz society. Some interesting sex differences in the responses appeared. Significantly, more girls felt that "There are not a sufficient number of interesting jobs for women in the Kibbutz." A good deal more dissatisfaction on the part of the girls is reflected in a number of additional items on which the girls responded differently from the boys. The girls feel that they wished to be more with their parents when they were younger and that, "I would want to take care of my own children more than my parents cared for me." They are also more ambivalent about the peer-group continuous living unit that is almost a family surrogate in the Kibbutz. They are more attracted by nice clothes and anticipate making new friends in the army and in the "outside," which appears more attractive to them than to the boys. The girls also feel that city boys are more polite to girls than Kibbutz boys. However, despite some of the responses mentioned above, a significantly larger percentage of the girls admit that they miss the Kibbutz when they are away from it for a few days.

The most significant difference between the sexes was obtained on one item that concerns an opinion regarding feminine interests, "The girl enjoys taking care of a household more than most other jobs in the Kibbutz." The vast majority of boys agree with this item, whereas the girls disagree in large numbers. This item seems to highlight the difference between the sexes in their conception of femininity. There is no denying that the girls want prettier clothes, want to mother their children more than their mothers did, and would like a more gentlemanly attitude on the part of the boys. Along with all this, however, they do not wish to become conventional housewives or work on household duties. They do not enjoy this type of work, although the boys think they do. This, too, is at the basis of the difference in the opinions between the boys and girls as to the sufficiency of interesting jobs for women in the Kibbutz. This difference in viewing feminine interests and opportunities is rather remarkable considering the fact that the boys and girls have spent all of their lives in close proximity to each other—in the peer group—from infancy through adolescence.

Of special interest in the foregoing discussion is the apparent paradox that underlies the dissatisfaction of Kibbutz girls with their roles in the Kibbutz. On the one hand, they wish to be more feminine (clothes, children, etc.) in the traditional or conventional sense of the word. But, on the other, they show dissatisfaction with housekeeping duties and other service occupations that are often their lot in the Kibbutz. However, this is not any different from the situation that prevails in Western society. Women wish to have the opportunity to enter all kinds of occupations that have been traditionally the domain of the male, but, at the same time, love to care for their children and maintain their "femininity" and feminine attractiveness. The Kibbutz, perhaps not unlike the external society, is dominated by males and traditional male attitudes that serve as obstacles to women's entering a variety of occupations that are not forbidding because of the physical demands that they make. Also, the young women's own emphasis on clothes and on increasing their involvement with the care of their children serve as a complementary force in the direction of greater differentiation between the sexes and their roles in Kibbutz society, along more traditional lines.

Despite the concern with the "problem of the woman" in the Kibbutz, with her alleged dissatisfactions and disaffections, there is also evidence to the contrary. One study of 400 adult female members in seventeen Kibbutzim (Katz, 1964) yields some interesting conclusions, some of which are relevant to our discussion. These are quoted below:

(1) There is great stability in the female membership of the Kibbutz, and the particularly serious defections are concentrated in a very small number of Kibbutzim.

(2) The reasons for leaving the Kibbutz are not all due to the mother's attitude toward collective education. We found a nega-

tive attitude towards the children's house only in a few instances. This was an expression of a fundamentally negative attitude toward the Kibbutz in general and towards this form of life. . . .

(3) About 87 percent of these women see in the Kibbutz their way of life; 13 percent are in conflict. The attitude towards collective education is positive in 80 percent, critical but not negative in 17 percent, and definitely negative in 3 percent of the cases [p. 4].

Thus, it would appear that these young Kibbutz-born mothers are generally satisfied with their mothering function in the Kibbutz setting. These results are quite consonant with those of earlier reports (Rabin, 1963a, 1964) that conclude that most of the mothers (83 percent) were fully accepting of collective education. Some minor criticisms were raised; the 17 percent of mothers who indicated an ambivalent and/or critical attitude to Kibbutz childrearing were primarily concerned with the insufficiency of contacts with their children, with separation from them at night, and with inadequacies of the *metapeleth*. A further conclusion (Rabin, 1964) is that, ". . . it appears that the 'maternal drive' or the need for mothering is, by and large, gratified under the conditions of collective education" (p. 142).

Some additional findings of interest in the present context have come to light in one of the reports cited above (Katz, 1964). Contrary to various reports, including some mentioned earlier in this chapter, women participate quite actively in agriculture. In the seventeen Kibbutzim surveyed, 27 percent are engaged in agriculture, 35 percent in education, and 38 percent in other occupations and services (nursing, manufacturing, professional clothing production). Thus, the occupational picture is not identical in all Kibbutzim. The high involvement in education and service occupations still remains the common denominator, nevertheless. The same report also indicates that the vast majority of female Kibbutz members participate in the Kibbutz meetings—weekly "town hall" equivalents. However, participation is rather passive. Although they may often serve as members of important committees, they rarely chair those committees or become coordinators in the several branches of the economy. Their representation in the leadership is, therefore, very limited. These findings are essentially corroborated by Shafer's study (1967), referred to earlier in this chapter.

Similar results are reported by Shapiro (1963), who finds that one-third less women participate in the Kibbutz general meetings, 22 percent of women as compared to 43 percent of men serve as coordinators of work branches or as committee members in the Kibbutz hierarchy, and the ratio of women to men in central Kibbutz posts (e.g. treasurer, secretary) is one to eight.

The overall picture, therefore, is one in which several clear trends become discernible. In the first place, there seems to be a fairly clear-cut division between masculine and feminine occupations in the Kibbutz. The former are mainly the economically productive occupations—the ones that create capital. The latter are the occupations involving service and consumption—childrearing, education, food processing and service, etc. The managerial functions are almost entirely in the hands of men as well. Thus, it is not only physical strength that determines the occupational role; the dominant male segment has acquired the positions of control and power in Kibbutz society.

Secondly, there seems to be a misperception on the part of many males of the extent to which the Kibbutz woman is satisfied with her lot. Many men seem to feel that there are all kinds of interesting opportunities for women in the Kibbutz setting. This view is apparently quite discrepant with the way women themselves appraise the situation.

The third point worthy of emphasis is that Kibbutz women are not as active politically as the menfolk. They do not participate in as large numbers, with as great frequency, or with as much activity as the men in the deliberations of the legislative body of the Kibbutz democracy—the general Kibbutz "town hall meeting." Whether this passivity is the cause or the effect of less representation in the management functions of the Kibbutz is difficult to say. Suffice it to state, however, that such a relationship exists.

The fourth and final point to be made at this juncture is that the attitudes and behavior of many of the women themselves are retrogressive with respect to equality of the sexes. Kibbutz mothers want to be more with their babies; Kibbutz adolescent girls hope to take care of their own children more than their parents took care of them. In some of the Kibbutzim of one of the federations, children reside, at least overnight, in their parents' apartment—primarily at the instigation of their mothers. Thus, we note that the growing tendency among the women themselves is to attempt to strengthen their motherly and wifely functions—the traditional feminine roles that have set women apart from men during millennia of recorded history. Whether these trends in the direction of traditional femininity and of strengthening the family, and thus the allocation of different roles within it, are due to external influences or to something intrinsic within the persons involved, is a question not easily answered. On the one hand, the greater affluence and industrialization of Israeli society in recent years have allowed for greater leisure and a lessening of the tension and activism characteristic of a pioneering country. As a consequence, women began to drop out of the front lines and started to assume a more passive and "feminine" role in the affairs of the community. This greater passivity along with the "expressive" feminine qualities rather than the "instrumental" masculine ones became more enchanting to the Kibbutz women as well, especially since their achievements and status under the philosophy of alleged equality did not gain them much. On the other hand, it is quite possible that after the frontier-like conditions of Kibbutz existence have nearly disappeared and after some of the "non-feminine" demands upon women have been relaxed, their "maternal" or "instinctive" needs for nurturance of children and for passivity, vis-à-vis the male, reassert themselves and demand opportunity for expression.

The facts are that, as we mentioned earlier, in order to achieve equality between the sexes there was a period of denial of *any* differences between them. This expressed itself in the woman's imitation of the roles and functions that have been traditionally designated as masculine. There was no attempt in the opposite direction—for males to assume the roles and functions that have been traditionally labeled as feminine. Despite these efforts, women have drifted back to their traditional roles and occupations, in part because the males had not been ready or willing to be replaced by women, nor did they wish to replace women in their areas of endeavor. Perhaps Jessie Bernard (1968) is right in stating that, "In a sense, any attempt to equalize unequal statuses can raise only one by lowering the other. In a sense, sexual equality is paid for by men" (p. 14). Even Kibbutz men, despite the ideology, the full implications of which they probably did not realize, were not able fully to implement the program of equality for women. Perhaps the women themselves, as indicated above, did not really wish for or insist upon the implementation.

Epilogue

Out of a highly variegated combination of groups originating in various parts of Europe and the Middle East evolved a unique social group or subsociety in Israel called the Kibbutz. This new society or subculture was consciously constructed according to a carefully formulated doctrine or ideology that places high value on collectivism—economic, social, and psychological—and upon complete equality among its members. "Emancipation of the woman" was part of the rebellion against a patriarchal type of family and society and an important aspect of the strife for equality.

At first, equality was interpreted as not only equality of rights and opportunity, but equality of role and status as well. There was a maximum denial of any existence of possible genetic and characterological differences between the sexes (with the exception of the physiological ones). This was expressed in a denial of "femininity" in dress and behavior and an assumption of behavior and appearance that reduced feminine attractiveness and increased women's similarity to males. The demanding conditions of a pioneering existence and literal interpretation of ideology facilitated such a trend.

This equality was further expressed in the extreme stance of coeducation with little emphasis on sex differences, and was further facilitated by changing the family structure and by removing the woman from its traditional housewifely functions. As time progressed it became apparent, however, that equality of roles was impractical. Women have assumed almost exclusive responsibility for the Kibbutz services—childcare, education, health, food services, clothing, etc. At the same time, men were found primarily in the productive and managerial positions of the economy. There developed a great gap between ideology and reality. At the same time also, women's discontent with their lot in the Kibbutz became a central problem.

The discontent apparently is traceable to two sources. In the first place, the promised equality of opportunity and freedom of occupational choice never fully materialized. Secondly, many women began to have second thoughts about their "liberation" from the household, especially from the care of their children. The need to be more with their children has been asserting itself very strongly among the mothers who were themselves born outside the Kibbutz as well as among those *sabras* born and reared in the Kibbutzim (Rabin, 1963 a, 1964). Counteracting the feminine discontent is the increased amount of time women in Kibbutzim are spending with their offspring. Concomitant with this trend is a consolidation of the nuclear family unit. According to many, such a course is endangering the very existence of the Kibbutz, for it may tend to weaken its collectivist foundations.

Thus, we may note a gradual accommodation between ideology and factual reality. Ideology tends to be modified in the face of experience, although experience may be directed by ideological principles. Changes in the school curriculum that will prepare woman for the kinds of functions she is undertaking anyway, and the increase in family centeredness without relinquishment of the fundamental formal and legal rights of equality in the Kibbutz democracy, are some of the major indications of this accommodation.

Postscript [3]

As to the future of the Kibbutz—prediction is a mighty hazardous business. With the risks (of prophecy) in mind, it should be recalled that, thus far, the Kibbutz has been the most viable utopian experiment in history; it has lasted for nearly three generations. Its strength, where others have faltered, lies in the careful attention to education and ideology and to a sort of "participatory isolation" vis-à-vis the larger society. This attention to education and participation in the larger society, despite a certain kind of exclusiveness, helps the perpetuation of the Kibbutz by the younger generations. I see the greatest danger to Kibbutz existence in the strengthening of the family unit within it—a process opposite to that occurring in society at large. At any rate, I see the Kibbutz as viable for another fifty years and, perhaps, longer. There is also the possibility that developing ideologies, economic and familial, in the larger society, may broaden the population base of the Kibbutz society. Also, there is some evidence that the Kibbutz is trying to be flexible and is now sending a number of people to medical school and other professional institutes, thus eliminating important sources of dissatisfaction in the system.

The Kibbutz has been constantly changing; it is not static. It will continue existence in a modified form but will maintain the cardinal principle of economic collectivism for a long time to come.

Notes

[1] The author is grateful to Gideon Levine and to Dr. Menahem Gerson of the faculty of "Seminar Hakibbutzim" (Oranim, Israel) for their helpful comments on an earlier version of the manuscript.

[2] In many Kibbutzim, mothers are currently also given an hour in the morning to be with their children.

[3] Personal communication to editor (GHS) in reply to a request for a prophecy concerning the future of the Kibbutz.

References

Bernard, Jessie. "The Status of Women in Modern Patterns of Culture." *The Annals of the American Academy of Political and Social Science,* 375 (1968), 3–14.

D'Andrade, Robert G. "Sex Differences and Cultural Institutions." In *The Development of Sex Differences,* Eleanor E. Maccoby, ed. Stanford, Calif.: Stanford University Press, 1966.

Golan, Shmuel. *Sugyot Hakibbutz (Studies of the Kibbutz)*. Merhavya, Israel: Sifriyat Poalim, 1961.

Golan, Yona. "The Woman in the Kibbutz." *Hachinuch Hameshutaf,* 13 (1962), 37–42.

Katz, Frieda. "Kibbutz Children as Parents." *Hachinuch Hameshutaf,* 14 (1964), 3–7.

Leon, Dan. *The Kibbutz.* Tel Aviv: Horizons, 1964.

Levine, Gideon. Personal Communication, 1968.

Parsons, Talcott. *The Social System.* Glencoe, Ill.: Free Press, 1951.

Rabin, Albert I. "Personality Study in Israeli Kibbutzim." In *Studying Personality Cross-Culturally,* B. Kaplan, ed. Evanston, Ill.: Row, Peterson, 1961.

———. "Maternal Attitudes to Kibbutz Child Rearing." Paper delivered at the 40th Annual Meeting of the American Orthopsychiatric Association, Washington, D.C., March 1963 a.

———. "Some Differences in Attitudes Between Boys and Girls Graduating from the Kibbutz High Schools." *Hedim,* 72 (1963 b), 157–63.

———. "Kibbutz Mothers View 'Collective Education.'" *American Journal of Orthopsychiatry,* 34–1 (1964), 140–42.

———. *Growing Up in the Kibbutz.* New York: Springer, 1965.

———. "Some Sex Differences in the Attitudes of Kibbutz Adolescents." *Israel Annals of Psychiatry and Related Disciplines,* 6, 1 (1968), 62–69.

Sarbin, Theodore R. "Role Theory." In *Handbook of Social Psychology,* G. Lindzey, ed. Vol. I. Reading, Mass.: Addison-Wesley, 1954.

Seward, Georgene H. *Sex and the Social Order.* New York: McGraw-Hill, 1946 o.p. Harmondsworth, Eng.: Pelican, 1954.

Shafer, Joseph. *The Reflection of Children's Sleeping Arrangements in the Social Structure of the Kibbutz.* Tel Aviv: Ichud, 1967.

Shapiro, Renven. "There is a Chance for the Woman in Active Femininity." *Hedim,* 75 (1963), 31–41.

Spiro, Melford E. *Kibbutz—Venture in Utopia.* Cambridge, Mass.: Harvard University Press, 1956.

———. "Is the Family Universal?" *American Anthropologist,* 56 (1954), 839–46.

Zborowski, Mark, and Elizabeth Herzog. *Life is with People.* New York: International Universities Press, 1952 (Schocken, 1962. Paperback).

14 MILIEU DEVELOPMENT AND MALE-FEMALE ROLES IN CONTEMPORARY GREECE

C. D. Spinellis, Vasso Vassiliou, and George Vassiliou

Milieu development

Persistent Patterns

Greece, a country with a documented history of more than twenty-five centuries, is a land in which people have been exposed to changes, at times explosive, in the many variables influencing their development and behavior. The reviewer of Greek patterns of life, including social sex roles as they have developed through the centuries, will therefore be surprised to discover that they have undergone little change until recently. Many Helens of Sparta (or Troy) trigger trouble, whether of a sexual or other nature. Iphigenias are still sacrificed in various ways so that men can go on accomplishing and "conquering." One could find in many places a Penelope waiting for an Odysseus, and there are many Odysseus' venturing around in endless endeavor. Achilles, in modern dress and many disguises, is still trying to prove himself. Menelaos struggles on to save face in various situations, and here and there a desperate Agamemnon attempts to unite individualized efforts around a common goal.

The modern Greeks, who always appear "unpredictable" to the untutored observer who must judge from appearances ("Who can understand a Greek?"), have retained traditional patterns. According to these patterns, what are the roles assigned to man and woman? It is this question that will be examined in the pages to follow.

In order to secure a multifocal, multidimensional description, information will be derived from statistics as well as from current legislation, and it will be supplemented by conclusions from qualitative observations and quantitative research data collected through a variety of studies conducted at the Athenian Institute of Anthropos. Finally, we shall attempt to trace the functional use of the prevailing patterns and point out the areas of conflict created by the rapidly changing variables involved.

Changing Picture

It might be helpful to have in mind the tremendous changes that modern Greece has undergone from Homer's time (ninth century B.C.), the building of the Parthenon (fifth century B.C.), the Roman conquest (second century A.D.), the Byzantine Empire (fourth to fifteenth century), the Ottoman occupation (1453–1821), and the War of Independence (1821), down to the emergence of the Greek state (1830). From 1828 to 1961 (National Statistical Service of Greece, 1967), the population increased from less than 800,000 to over 8 million people while the area more than doubled in size during the same period.

The changes that have occurred during the twentieth century, however, are mainly due to the processes of urbanization, industrialization, and modernization—with the effects on the cultural norms and social structure that are visible in all developing countries. Forty years ago the urban population was approximately 31 percent and the rural population 54 percent of the total population. The accelerating process of urbanization equalized the distribution of urban and rural areas (43.3 percent urban and 43.8 percent rural). It is interesting to note, however, that while the rural population decreased and the urban increased, the semiurban population remained on the same level including approximately one-eighth of the whole population (National Statistical Service of Greece, 1967).

Meanwhile, the sex ratio of the Greek population has been shifting during the past century. According to the 1961 census, for every 100 males there are 105 females, which gives a ratio of 49 percent males to 51 percent females. Women are currently playing a visible role in the country's economic life: out of every ten Greeks economically active, three are women. In rural areas they constitute an even larger labor force: out of every ten people economically active, six are women. Moreover, for every five women seeking employment for the first time, there are 4.5 men. The general unemployment rate follows the same trend: 5.91 percent for both sexes, of which 4.90 percent represents males and 7.98 percent, females.

Some additionally useful information appears in the educational achievements of the two sexes. Statistics show that Greek women are less educated than men, and also that they occupy less important positions than men in the area of education. Nevertheless, illiteracy, defined as inability to read and write, dropped for women from 80 percent in 1907 to 27 percent in 1961, with corresponding figures for men of 40 percent and 8 percent respectively. Recent data (National Statistical Service of Greece, Higher Education, 1968) covering the academic year 1965–66 reveal that out of every ten graduates, 3.3 are women. During the same year, of the 293 doctorate degrees awarded, 45 went to females.

At the undergraduate level, a marked sex difference appears. In professional schools, including nursing, social work, decorative arts, home economics, business, and farming, the enrolled females outnumber males 58.6 percent to 41.4 percent. The technical schools, by contrast, have a 93.8 percent male student body (National Statistical Service of Greece, Technical and Professional Education, 1968). The same sex-ratio trend characterizes the figures concerning instructors. In the professional schools, out of every ten people engaged in teaching, four are women, while in the technical schools only 0.6 percent are female.

Unfortunately, at the present time there is no information available on the volume of female workers and employees in public or private enterprises.

Legal Reflections

In Greece, the legislation enacted to protect women or to raise their status by conferring on them various privileges or rights gives only a crude image of the ascribed roles. For one thing, legal provisions do not always result from existing conditions but are often imported from France, Germany, Switzerland or other countries, and are more likely to represent an outside ideal rather than a local reality. For another, since laws are seldom amended as soon as patterns of behavior and attitudes change, they are subject to cultural lag. With these precautions in mind, we may examine some of the legal enactments relevant to the roles of Greek men and women.

Since 1952, women have had the legal right to play an active role in the political life of the country as they have had the right to vote and to be elected members of the Parliament. Thus, *de jure* at least, the old distinction between the "man's world" of the public sphere in contrast with the "woman's world" of informal relationships in restricted circles no longer exists. Moreover, women, after their thirtieth birthday, may become jury members or members of the mixed courts. In the mid-1950s another interesting law was passed that allowed women to hold any public office, with the exception of arbitrator and priest, and to be hired on equal terms with men. For protective reasons, based on various treaties originated by the International Labor Office and signed by Greece, women may not be employed in unwholesome occupations or on night shifts. Moreover, working women benefit from social security. In addition, working mothers receive a bonus at the birth of each child and a leave of absence of six weeks before and six weeks after delivery. Working women also retire five years earlier than men, on their sixtieth birthday.

While Greece officially subscribes to the principle of equal pay for equal work, substantial differences in salary exist in private enterprises. Data collected from companies employing ten people or more during the month of February 1968, reveal that the *average* monthly salary for males is

5,112 drachmas (approximately $170), while it is 2,912 drachmas (approximately $97) for females (National Statistical Service of Greece, 1968). The *average* hourly pay is 14.68 drachmas (48 cents) for males and 10.35 drachmas (34 cents) for females. These differences are most probably due to the fact that women occupy lower levels in the industrial hierarchy.

The reality of women's inferior status is reflected in the Greek Civil Code, which underlines their need for protection as well as their subordinate role in the family. The law, for instance, gives the daughter the right to sue her father or her mother and claim her dowry, while at the same time stating that "the man is the head of the family and makes all decisions concerning conjugal life provided that his decision does not constitute an abuse of right." It would be fair to mention parenthetically that this provision was copied from the German Civil Code and that it also existed in the French, Austrian, Prussian, and other European codes. According to Greek law, the man is the breadwinner of the family because he is the person mainly responsible for bearing the economic burden of marriage, and only if he is unable would the wife be expected to share the economic burden. Moreover, the woman does not lose her financial independence after marriage. Finally, according to the law, the father has the exclusive right of *patria potestas,* i.e., the right to represent the child in case of legal or financial transactions and to rear, train, educate, and punish it. Only if the father is unable to do so is this power exercised by the mother. This stipulation, however, is so broadly construed that it is less restrictive than it appears.

This review of legal provisions emphasizes the existing discrepancies between life and law that are presumably symptomatic of the inevitable dislocations of a country in the throes of rapid cultural change.

Research findings

From research studies using both projective and objective methods and conducted by the Athenian Institute of Anthropos on representative national samples, as well as those specifically based on the Athenian population, certain clear trends concerning social sex roles have emerged (Vassiliou, 1969; Vassiliou, Georgas, & Vassiliou, 1967; Vassiliou & Vassiliou, 1968).

Masculine Roles

The first striking fact is the absence of any concept of *equalitarian* role: All roles seem to be superordinate or subordinate (Triandis, Vassiliou, & Nassiakos, 1968), with the male role dominant and superordinate. The man is supposed to have more freedom of movement and to be less restricted than the woman. He has implicit permission to "trespass" certain social barriers. Moreover, he is expected to be highly competitive and upwardly mobile, asserting himself in any situation. Typically, he has been persuaded to pursue the goals that he shares with his family and mostly with his mother. In this effort he counts on his ingroup—those people who show concern for him, who are for the most part members of his family, who are his friends. He characterizes them as "for me" people. Within this group he is supposed to be loyal, trustworthy, and sincere, responding to the generosity of his friends with even greater generosity. In short, his behavior toward the ingroup is expected to accord with the highest value of the milieu, the *philotimo*. He must fully respect, obey, and folow authority. Outside his ingroup, however, he is expected to be competitive, to outmaneuver his rivals, cheating them if necessary, and to defy any "stranger" authority. In this way, he cannot be characterized as authoritarian or antiauthoritarian. Authority will be followed or defied by him according to its position inside or outside of his ingroup. The one basic rule of his social performance is that he must excel. Under a number of influences stemming from his parents, mainly his mother, he is induced to believe that there are two places in society: the first and the nonfirst. Anything other than the first position is not significant.

Feminine Role

From antiquity to the present, the woman has played a rather secluded social role. Early in her life her behavior is restricted and she is required to follow the prevailing moral code much more closely than is the case of the average boy of her age. In fact, Greek women, according to the traditional patterns, are not expected to become involved in socioeconomic activities. While these patterns have been slowly evolving into new forms, other social changes have been so rapid that they have accelerated the movement in this area. Woman's increased participation in industry has, nevertheless, failed to elevate her position sufficiently to shape for her a social role similar to that of the male. Consequently, she is not counted as a primary member of the ingroup. Her affiliation is indirect, "through" a male—father, brother, son, husband.

A negative stereotype concerning woman seems to prevail. It is almost equally shared by both men and women since the women themselves have accepted and internalized it. Responses of the female subjects were often clearly influenced by such an autostereotype (Vassiliou, 1966).

Marital and Family Patterns

Characteristics attributed to the "Proper Man" and the "Proper Woman" are mainly related to family obligations. To be a good household provider is considerably more important than other characteristics. The characteristics attributed to the "Proper Woman" are related to good housekeeping and mothering and secondarily to characteristics referring to the woman as an individual—beautiful, well-kept, educated. "Proper Man-Proper Woman" roles are fulfilled within marriage and not through pursuing goals of individual actualization. Happiness in life is seen as depending on marriage.

Under the impact of many variables, marriage tends to be durable. A number of conventions have become embedded in society precisely for the purpose of maintaining the family and preventing disruption and divorce. They are mainly concerned with mutual concessions, forgiveness, and obedience of the wife to the point of accepting unquestionably the views of the husband in order to avoid open conflict.

Among a large number of family roles that we have studied in Greece (Triandis, Vassiliou & Nassiakos, 1968), the least intimacy is attributed to the husband-wife relationship. The central relationship seems to be the parent-child, and mainly the mother-son role, which is viewed as more reciprocal than other family roles. The Greek family in general emerges through a variety of studies as child-oriented. It is in this sense future-oriented also, since a great part of its activity and planning aims to secure the means for the child's advancement on which the family's advancement is based. Of course, advancement is defined differently as one moves up the social ladder.

In Greece, social mobility has increased to a great extent during the last century. As elsewhere, one of the main contributing factors is education. Education is the variable that correlates highly with income. Providing the best possible education for the son is all-important for the family's future advancement. When there is no son, the daughter is used as a substitute for the fulfillment of the family's ambitions. For a number of reasons, however, social advancement is much more feasible for a boy than a girl. Parents' preferences concerning the sex of their child are influenced accordingly. In most rural areas, the word "child" is synonymous with "boy." When asked how many children they have, parents answer, "I have two children and two girls," meaning that they have two boys and two girls.

Male-Female Ambivalence

The arrival of the child triggers a number of intricate changes concerning family roles. The woman whose role has changed little by becoming a wife, changes dramatically by becoming a mother. From that moment she assumes a role that is idealized and considered "holy." Despised and suspected as a woman, she is revered, trusted, respected, and obeyed as a mother. Strange as it may sound, she will eventually warn her son that there are three evils in life—"the fire, the woman, and the sea." Her son will grow up despising other girls and considering them untrustworthy and treacherous, while remaining highly loyal to "the only trustworthy person in this life," his mother.

The father-daughter role is associated with behaviors connoting a helpful orientation involving both nurturance and superordination. It is also associated with attitudes like "greatly admire," "be interested in," "feel sympathetic toward," "love," "enjoy," etc., most of these behaviors connoting affectionate admiration.

When the man-woman relationship is presented stripped of family ties, the male ambivalence that has been built in from earliest training emerges. Greek subjects perceive this as a hostile relationship involving such behavior as annoyance, reprimanding, scolding, and quarreling. This relationship is also associated with "outgroup" behavior such as competition, exploitation, rivalry, and jealousy.

Not only is the male ambivalent toward the female, but the female is ambivalent toward the male. This was supported by our studies of family relationships that revealed a pattern of factors consistent with the interpretation of female ambivalence toward the male. Relationships of daughter-father, wife-husband, sister-brother, bride-groom were high in a factor we have named "ingratiation with contempt." This factor reflects the ambivalence of the female who "fears, lies to, and cheats" on the one hand, and "cries with and caresses" on the other. The same study also pointed out that the perceived lower status of the woman is reflected in such attitudes as "not competing with" the male, "not being an enemy of" the male, "not supposed to grow impatient with" him, and "not indignant of" him.

Personality Differentiation

It is interesting to note that other studies have provided indications that women are more creative, inventive, and resourceful than men (Georgas & Vassliou, 1967). On the other hand, another picture of the woman emerges in the light of the survey results. Females predominate in subgroups giving "don't know" answers, are less informed, are least aware of current events, are less involved in decision-making, and are the most unsophisticated concerning patterns of desirable social action. In addition, there are data indicating that when people move from simpler to more complex milieux, the woman's personality differentiates less than the man's.

Discussion

Sex Roles and Family Transaction

The roles of men and women seem to be circumscribed and well-delineated, with little overlapping. Up to a few decades ago, the primary group was mainly, sometimes even exclusively, the meeting ground of the two sexes. Men and women would live, work, and act together within this social context as relatives or as husband and wife. The roles shaped according to fixed patterns, prevented conflicts, confusion, and, in the case of the growing child, difficulties in developing an appropriate identification. Given their subordinate position, however, women, under various circumstances, often antagonized each other bitterly. It is understandable then that in woman-to-woman relations, mutual suspicion, negative feelings, and antagonistic tendencies could be detected. It is also understandable that the woman, having accepted the assigned subordinate role, will be "tricky" and "deceitful" concerning the male (father, husband, son, friend, etc.), "cheating him with contempt."

As has already been mentioned, a radical reversal for the woman occurs when she finally becomes a mother. The highly idealized role that is assigned to her from then on is blended in such a way with her subordinate role as to produce an intricate interplay of social dominance and subordination, the main focus being the child.

We have previously described the Greek family as child-oriented. There is a shared interest in the child's future. The child is the agent for the actualization of goals and plans that are expected to benefit the whole family. As may be expected in such a case, a son is preferred to a daughter. One need not look for psychoanalytical interpretations of such sex preference when there are strong socioeconomic reasons to account for it.

Within such a family transaction, mothers carrying over early ambivalence toward males develop contradictory attitudes toward their sons. On the one hand, they tend to load their sons with ambitions, build up their prestige, and generate in them a relentless drive for achievement. On the other hand, their overprotection, overabundant care to the point of pampering, and praise of small achievements often results in low self-confidence and easily threatened self-esteem. On assuming the assigned superordinate role, such a male is constantly in need of a source of dependence. Yet, he finds himself depending psychologically on a woman who ranks as his social dependent. In the case of marriage, this means that on frequent occasions, while the husband is the weaker he is obliged to play "the strong" and, at the same time, while his wife is the stronger she is obliged to play "the weak." Thus they contribute mutually to the preservation of marriage.

The question is often raised whether the role of the woman in the Greek milieu is "favorable" or "unfavorable." We feel that such questions are traps to be avoided. Roles, attitudes, and subjective culture in general are shaped by the very needs for adaptation that are imposed on the individuals by the transaction of all other interrelated variables that are shaping the milieu. Consequently, it does not make sense to hypothesize that this transaction will lead to favorable roles for the one and unfavorable for the other. All roles are necessarily "favorable" in the sense that all roles are functional. Nevertheless, under the contemporary rapid changes that alter the milieu more rapidly than the traditional patterns can change, a number of conflicts arise that render certain role demands increasingly difficult to meet under the given circumstances. The prevailing, well-circumscribed, complementary male-female roles are conducive to syntonic transaction within the family.

Role Strain outside the Home

Within the secondary groups, however, recent developments are creating a difficult situation (Vasiliou, Georgas, & Vassiliou, 1968). As the woman becomes increasingly involved as a worker, employer, or professional, she does not have available role descriptions suited to the new kind of relations in her occupational life. Due to the emerging conflicts, the woman today is facing more stressful situations. Knowing only the traditional patterns that have shaped her role, she is in need of new patterns, more syntonic with the requirements of her present milieu.

The man is also exposed to a series of conflicts. Although they are not as devastating as the role strains in the case of the female, they are nevertheless stressful enough to have visible consequences on the performance and the overall adaptation of the male. For one thing, the Greeks, who have been accustomed to work rather independently, cooperating only with people with whom they had "ingroup" ties, are now obliged to become "organization men." Having been previously in a group in which their position, their role, and their value orientation were clearly described and taken for granted, they now find themselves in the middle of a group that is not based on ingroup ties, where one is supposed to cooperate with "strangers," and where one is supposed to develop novel concepts concerning equalitarian roles. The difficulties that naturally arise under the circumstances are obvious. Instead of cooperating within the organizational framework, the Greek tends to compete with his colleagues. According to his traditional patterns, it is he as an individual who has to excel. Inasmuch as the organization is not his ingroup, he cannot perceive shared interests and cannot develop shared plans and ambitions for future achievement. In order to understand his organization as his ingroup, he requires personalized concern by the authority. With an outgroup authority in the role of the "boss," he will adopt defiant and elusive tactics against him. This behavior in turn sets up a vicious cycle, making it difficult for the boss to show concern for him. The result is self-defeating.

Peer relations, on the other hand, are hindered by the tendency that each one has to form his own ingroup within the organization in order to rival the others. Role demands increase due to the changing conditions that impose increasingly heavier requirements for social achievement, coupled with the high need-achievement of the male from birth. Under the circumstances, to be a "Proper Man" becomes increasingly stressful.

Unquestionably, the trend is toward an increased overlapping of social sex roles. But history, tradition, culture, and the prevailing value orientation are such decisive variables in the Greek milieu that one could reasonably speculate that the rate of this increase is bound to be slower than in other cultures.

References

Georgas, J., and Vasso Vassiliou. "A Normative Rorschach Study of Athenians." *Journal of Projective Techniques and Personality Assessment,* 31 (August 1967), 31–38.

National Statistical Service of Greece. *Statistical Yearbook of Greece.* Athens, 1967, 1968.

National Statistical Service of Greece. *Statistics of Education during the Academic Year 1965–1966—Higher Education.* Athens, 1968.

National Statistical Service of Greece. *Statistics of Education during the School Year 1965–1966—Technical and Professional Education.* Athens, 1968.

Triandis, Harry C., Vasso Vassiliou, and Maria Nassiakos. "Three Cross-Cultural Studies of Subjective Culture." *Journal of Personality and Social Psychology,* 8, 4 (1968), 1–42. Monograph Supplement.

Vassiliou, George. *A Preliminary Exploration of Variables Related to Family Transaction in Greece.* Athens: The Athenian Institute of Anthropos, 1966.

———. "Aspects of Parent-Adolescent Transaction in the Greek Family." In *Adolescence: A Psychosocial Perspective,* Gerald Caplan and Serge Lebovich, eds. New York: Basic Books. 1969, pp. 122–132.

———, J. Georgas, and Vasso Vassiliou. "Measurements of Variations of Manifest Anxiety in Relation to Socioeconomic and Cultural Determinants." In *Evaluation of the Results of the Psychotherapies,* Stanley Lesse, ed. Springfield, Ill.: Charles C. Thomas, 1968, pp. 329–36.

Vassiliou, George and Vasso Vassiliou. "A Transactional Approach to Mental Health: An Experiment in Greece." In *New Directions in Mental Health,* Bernard F, Riess, ed. New York: Grune & Stratton, 1968, 280–301.

Vassiliou, Vasso, J. Georgas, and G. Vassiliou. "Variations in the Manifest Anxiety Due to Sex, Age, and Education." *Journal of Personality and Social Psychology,* 6, 2 (1967), 194–97.

PART THREE

THE SEXES in THE EAST

15 MEN AND WOMEN OF INDIA TODAY

S. N. Sinha

A role represents the dynamic aspect of a status. Every individual has a series of roles derived from the various social patterns of interaction. Roles seem to reduce the ideal pattern of social life to individual terms.

Social roles provide convenient links between the individual and society inasmuch as the relation of an individual's perception of his own role to its perception by others largely determines the nature of his social functioning. A person's social role cumulatively combines many separate roles in a complex pattern of social interaction. An individual at any one time occupies age, sex, family, occupational, and many other roles. The content of the roles may be either nebulous or clearly defined, continuous or discontinuous. Benedict (1938) says that discontinuity in roles arises from contradictory expectancies and the individual's lack of preparedness for future roles.

In East Asian countries such as India, continuity in roles is perhaps more evident than in other cultures since, from childhood, individuals are continuously conditioned to responsible social participation. This is unlike the sharp discontinuity evidenced in cultures of the West, with marked transitions in role expectations from childhood to adulthood to old age.

Parsons (1936) has analyzed the tensions arising out of role discontinuity or role strain in occupational and family systems. He suggested that, within the occupational roles themselves, strains arise from conflict over the father's determination to choose his son's occupation and social status. Similarly, role tension, strain, and discontinuity, characteristics of old age in Western cultures, are beginning to be experienced in Indian culture due to the disintegration of the joint family system. The discontinuity in tradition from middle age to old age may be more striking than from childhood to adolescence.

Contrary to the well-delineated roles in the world of work, those in family and friendship circles are likely to be less differentiated and more varied. In East Asian countries like India, the formalized role relationships to be played in the outside world are tested within the family. The remnants of the joint family system have reduced role strains and discontinuities to some extent. However, there are large areas of ambiguity in role relations not because the roles change, but because social perception and expectation of roles are not always uniform or specified.

Social context in change

Sex Role Differentiation

In India, girls are apt to be relatively docile and are considered "good" by conforming to adult expectations. This tendency may be partially explained by the fact that it is possible to initiate girls directly into many important aspects of adult feminine behavior, such as housekeeping and looking after younger children, at an early age. In semi-industrialized cities of India, since the father ordinarily does not work at home his son, left without a tangible male model, obviously cannot emulate his father's professional "expertise" and skills. In rural areas and nonindustrialized cities, however, there is the possibility of a gradual initiation of the son into his father's occupation and the activities (pottery, dyeing, and printing of textiles) associated with the adult male role. Hence, in the rural situation, the father's semi-professional skills provide a meaningful model for boys to emulate if they so wish.

In the cities of contemporary India, there is no sex differentiation in the process of formal education up to high school and even as far as the college level. Sex differentiation seems to be primarily related to social status and area of residence. It is important to note that education embraces equality of status for both sexes—the girls requiring education primarily to compete in the marriage market, and the boys, to face the employment market. Postgraduate professional education, which is restricted to males, is no longer limited to the children of higher and middle socioeconomic groups. In the sphere of liberal education, equality of opportunity exists because of the tendency throughout the social structure to segregate the occupational sphere from the social sphere.

For male adolescents, athletics and other masculine activities have become an important avenue of achievement and competition. The outstanding feature among urban female adolescents today is the wearing of tight dresses to accentuate sexual attractiveness. These different patterns of behavior define roles that tend to polarize the sexes while at the same time emphasizing certain common psychological features of total personality such as the need to compete.

In India, most females have yet to earn the title of "breadwinner" despite a sizable proportion of career or working women. The earnings of working women by and large tend to be of a supplementary nature, contributing to the pool of family income. Of utmost importance to the sex-role structure of the adult male is a job or a vocation, and this approved occupational role is a fundamental and integral part of his social status.

Two important alternative tendencies in the feminine role of adult women have appeared; simple domesticity, on the one hand, and a full-fledged career, on the other. Until the 1930s, there was a rigid distinction between respectable married women and those who followed the masculine pattern by seeking a career. At present, these rigid distinctions have faded out for urban middle-class women. In the rural lower class, farming and other unskilled occupations tend to be equally shared by both sexes. According to Dixit (1968), there is no clear-cut sex demarcation of occupational roles. Since a large majority of working women in the urban upper middle-class remain unmarried, perhaps the primary status-carrying role for them would be that of a housewife. It may be noted here that, in spite of the very great progress of the movement to free women from the traditional domestic pattern, only a small minority of women have taken advantage of the emancipation open to them from the traditional domestic pattern.

As an alternative to that of simple domesticity on the one hand and a full-fledged career on the other, a glamour pattern has emerged among certain modern young women of India. To the girls growing up in the metropolitan cities, such a role holds certain attractions. It appeals especially to those girls who are excluded from the struggle for power and prestige in the occupational sphere as a direct path to a sense of superiority and importance. This "solution," however, has obvious limitations inasmuch as it runs counter to the usual patterns of moral conduct and fosters conflict with community and personal standards.

The more emotionally mature women in their thirties tend to choose the affectionate companion pattern. This type of role, with its strong emphasis on the virtues of fidelity and devotion to husband and children, offers them the highest level of a certain kind of security. Today in India, the effect of the specialization of occupational roles is to narrow the range within which common human interests can be shared. This narrowness would tend to encourage the domestic role for nonprofessional women, or the glamorous role for professional women. Outside of marriage, however, except for professionals like doctors, lawyers, and teachers, there seems to be a notable inhibition against easy social intercourse, especially in mixed company. A man's contact with other women is checked by the danger of the situation's being defined in terms of rivalry with the wife. Friendship without sexual-emotional involvement, however, is permitted within the occupational sphere on the basis of specialization of interest.

Youth and Age

The stark realism of adults has prevented their acceptance of youthful idealism. Youth in almost all societies of today's world is a period of considerable strain and insecurity; if this were accepted by adults, they would have to turn their backs on security, their predominant value. Youth culture may have important positive functions in easing the transition from the security of childhood to the hazards of full adult status in the various occupational fields.

In comparison with other societies, India assumes an extreme position in permitting participation of the aged in the most important social structures and interests. In rural and semi-rural parts of the country, formal retirement from farming or the maintenance of small independent enterprises is unknown. There seems to be merely a gradual relinquishment of the main responsibilities and functions with advancing age. In urban industrialized areas and the large cities of India, an individual's occupational status centers in his specific job, which carries the liability of abrupt termination rather than "retirement."

Retirement leaves the older man in a peculiarly functionless position in specific social situations. Status in the community, which had accrued in a large measure from holding a specific job, is decreased, though not to a critical degree. While retirement loosens ties to the job, it does not lead to isolation from the family or the community. Old age is not a problem from the point of view of maintaining adequate role relationships, although it is correlated with increased insecurity and dependence.

Caste System

A number of social mobility studies have focused on departures from traditional caste-based occupations. The traditional relationship between caste and occupational roles has changed considerably in modern India. Today, Brahmins, who possess the highest rank among the Hindu castes, are found in all grades of occupations (Ghurye, 1961).

Mukherjee (1965) has shown that although one may find various occupations within a single caste, a considerable number of people engaged in various handicrafts tend to follow their traditional vocation. However, according to data of Bopegamage and Veeraraghavan (1967), deviations from the traditional caste occupations are most frequent among the highest castes and the tendency gets weaker as one moves down the scale. It would be erroneous to conclude that departures from the traditional caste occupations are indicative of progressive trends in a changing society unless some evidence is obtained as to whether present occupations are judged as higher, equal, or lower in relation to traditional vocations. Mukherjee (1965) pointed out that rural people tended to rate their occupations as equal to their caste occupations to a larger degree than was the case with the urban population, which believed their current occupations to be superior, or falsely superior, to their traditional occupations, due to the effect of white-collar jobs. Hence, the village-based caste system along with the joint family setting has considerably lessened social and geographic mobility.

In the Poona research project of UNESCO formulated by Veeraraghavan (1965), preference scores for religious groups on a scale, ranked social distance in the following order, from highest to lowest: high caste Hindu, Christian, lower caste Hindu, and Muslim. These findings suggest that among the various religious groups, high caste Hindus (Brahmins) were accepted easily in one's social groups, Christians and Harijans were next, and Muslims were not at all easily accepted. In Southeast India, a majority of high caste groups, with high status, were mostly professionals, prosperous industrialists, and landlords. People coming from the intermediate castes were mostly clerical workers, teachers, and small business people. People from the bottom of the caste hierarchy were by and large untouchables, the servant castes, or had served either as laborers in agricultural areas or as industrial laborers in urban areas. The controversy between blue-collar and white-collar workers can also be explained in terms of caste origin. The majority of white-collar workers come from the high caste groups, whereas the blue-collar workers are of lower origin. A comparison of the views of urbanites with those of rural people reveals that Brahmins who had stayed in the city had become valueless and felt that they enjoyed less status than previously, or no status at all.

Our evaluation of the caste roles in the city and rural areas explains the differences in status. In Veeraraghavan's (1965) study, empirical evidence was obtained to show that caste was a more important factor in the village than in the city. The low rank assigned to the caste factor in urban areas may not, however, be taken as indicating that the role of caste dynamics is irrelevant in the city. Caste plays a significant role in both town and country. In terms of self-identification, however, rural people tend to appraise their own status and roles primarily on the basis of caste. Caste appears to be the predominant frame of reference for the villager. From his earliest years, the villager is well-acquainted with caste categories and has to be more aware of caste gradations than the urban child, whose caste consciousness develops much later and perhaps very slowly (Dixit, 1968).

A gradual change in the importance of caste is explicit in the urban dweller's attitude toward marriage and intercaste relations. Caste roles tend to be less emphasized by industrial workers in the large cities of India than they are by rural people. The behavior of urban people toward lower caste shows less rigidity and social distance—they were perhaps willing to have lower caste neighbors and fellow workers. This pattern of acceptance of lower caste may not be due so much to crumbling social distinctions as to expediency (Veeraraghavan, 1965).

The urban population perceives the caste hierarchy in more fluid terms than their rural compatriots. They see it as offering greater hope of moving up the social ladder. Social mobility is positively valued by urban people since it fosters greater individual achievement and enterprise.

To sum up, it may be observed that there is sufficient evidence to suggest that in India, rural and urban people have different images of the status structure, as status evaluations of urban population tend to be more elaborate and more achievement-oriented.

Another dimension in the caste system is sex. Caste roles tend to operate differentially for males and females. Caste dynamics seem to have influenced men as far as the world of work and politics goes, but affect women only in relation to matrimonial affairs. Sex-role ascriptions on the basis of caste have almost disappeared among the higher, while persisting among the lower, castes.

Subcultures

A critical subculture in India is, of course, religion, and it affects relations between the sexes. Women have the greatest responsibility in ceremonial matters. The women invariably pray for the men of the family on behalf of husbands, sons, and brothers. The assumption of ritual responsibilities by the women for the welfare of the social unit is an exceptionally effective way for them to identify themselves with the most pressing interests and crises of the group. The prominent place that women occupy in conducting religious ceremonies accounts for the status they have in preserving the family as a social unit.

Also, various subcultures such as Sikhs, Jains, or Parsees, exemplify typical roles that members of subreligious groups can assume. Many of these subcultures have taken on various occupational, vocational, and avocational roles. As a subculture, the Sikhs have striven to obtain jobs in the defense services as representatives of a warrior community. However, those who have not successfully achieved this goal, due to the rigorous selection of armed forces personnel, have assumed other occupational roles in independent businesses. There are various sects within Sikh society but, by and large, the Sikh subculture tends to maintain a rigid, closed system, the norms of which emphasize dominance and the soldierly ideal. Failure to actualize these norms induces cutthroat competition in various forms of business or independent enterprises.

Among the Sikhs, some of the major religious practices and social customs tend to diverge from the rest of the Hindu culture. There is no standardized worship for Sikh religion, which has been markedly democratized. Offerings and prayers to their *guru* (spiritual teacher) constitute the main form of worship. Certain social customs such as marriage are conducted in a very simplified manner, without the performance of elaborate ritual ceremonies or the social obligations of the "dowry" (goods and cash given to the bridegroom's party by the bride's father or relations as a prerequisite for the settlement of marriage).

A special feature of the Sikh female sex role is her partial masculinization. Sikh women seem to accept masculine roles, and their behavior patterns manifest marked trends toward dominance, a simulation of the Sikh male behavior pattern.

This brief survey shows that there are all kinds of subcultural variations within a culturally heterogenous country like India. Segregation, isolation, discrimination, or withdrawal of social support for any subculture from the rest of the community is ruled out, as these subcultural groups mutually interact with the entire cultural fabric.

Roles outside the home

Political Roles

The Indian Constitution, which came into effect in 1950, grants women the same right of property ownership as men. An adequate sample of the national population would show a clear majority against the notion of equal inheritance, since at the present time the family must pay all the expenses for a girl's marriage. In a survey conducted by the Indian Institute of Public Opinion, 45 percent of the urban and 60 percent of the rural West Bengal people conceded that women should have the same property rights as men.

Hindu women have been in the political arena since the days of British domination over India. They have shared the political burden since 1857, when the crusade for Indian Independence was started and wars of independence were waged against the British. During the preindependence period of the 1930s, women began to hold high offices in provincial government. Indian women exercised adult franchise by 1935, as seats were reserved for them in each provincial legislature. Since that time there have been women governors, ambassadors, and even a Prime Minister.

In the *Panchayats* or Councils, small, self-regulated, autonomous administrative units of the governmental system, seats were reserved for women. The more progressive women have participated actively while the rest of the women candidates have played a nominal part in these Councils. Today, more than 25 percent of women seek election to various state legislatures and have been included in the various levels of government, functioning as ministers at state and central government levels.

As a part of the larger national movement for freedom and social reform, the women's rights movement had the support and encouragement of the leading men of India, including Mahatma Gandhi. An eminent female member of the Indian Parliament, commenting on the independence of political status attained by Indian women, observed that only a little over 30 years after the first agitation for suffrage, women had secured an equality of rights—a shorter time than it took in Western countries. Figures from the general elections in India from 1952 onwards amply demonstrate that women participated almost equally with men in exercising their franchise.

Women in India have gained considerable political status as they have emerged from the comparative seclusion to which they had so long been condemned. Female leadership has developed fairly well since female Indian political leaders have become active in their parties. Women have been represented as President of the General Assembly of U.N.O., President of the Congress party, and as members of the Congress Working Committee as well as of the National Executive Committee of the Socialist party. Lastly, the introduction and implementation of various Five Year Plans have immensely increased the economic and political consciousness of women in India, as they are participating in all kinds of developmental activities.

Legal Status

The concentrated efforts of social reformers and various legislation enacted during British rule have markedly affected the legal status of females in India. Laws enacted to elevate the position of women are related to the marriage laws. As early as 1925, legal distinctions were made between marital and extramarital sexual relations. Subsequently, the famous Sarda Act of 1929, technically known as Child Marriage and Restraint Act of 1929, prohibited, throughout India, marriages of girls under fourteen and boys under eighteen. Because of the closed or rigid social structure of the village, it was impossible at first for any member of the community to lodge complaints in cases of clear-cut violation of this law. More recently, however, the social consensus seems to be in favor of late marriages among the educated urban communities in India. The same trend has also been noticed in rural and semi-educated communities. Nonetheless, polls conducted by the Indian Institute of Public Opinion (1955) have been designed to ascertain the extent to which fundamental rights are actually accepted by the populace. According to the findings, equality of sexes with respect to property rights has remained very much a legal fiction.

In conclusion, it may be pointed out that the broad area of women's rights has been marked by the changes in their relations within the family as well as by alterations in their legal status in the larger society.

Educational Roles

Educational endowments determine to a great extent the role that women may choose to adopt in social life (Narain, 1967). The target set for 1966 regarding elementary education, 62 percent of all girls between six to eleven years and 91 percent for the boys of the same age, has been attained. As late as 1947, the proportion of girls to boys in educational institutions was 30 to 100. However, in regard to primary and even secondary education, this lag now seems to have disappeared. During 1958, out of a total of 51,844 schools, 5,828 were for girls, attended by 4 to 5 million people. Thus, the "teaming millions of India" seem to have hit the targets set for education and, in 1966, approximately 17 percent of girls and 40 percent of boys from eleven to fourteen years of age received secondary education. There is only a lag of 12 percent to 13 percent in girls' secondary education as compared to that of boys. The pupils are prepared at the secondary stage either for the university or for immediate employment after short-term vocational courses. In some of the better public schools, there are special facilities for the study of dancing, music, and fine arts, in order to equip female students culturally for the roles they will have to play as enlightened women in the society.

The expansion of higher or university education since independence in India has been enormous, and today there are more than forty universities with a total of over 1.5 million students. The number of institutions, including the Arts, Science, and Commerce colleges of various universities, is well over a thousand. Nearly 43 percent of the pupils are studying in colleges for women and 57 percent in colleges for males. The institutions for technical and professional education, including medicine, law, and engineering schools, constitute another thousand. More females seem to be receiving medical education than technical or legal education.

Due to the efficacy of education for those seeking marriage, education of girls is gaining wide acceptance in urban areas among middle-class families. Even in rural areas, secondary education for girls does not seem to lag behind that of boys. Expansion programs sponsored by the government of India with the aid of American foundations, (e.g., Wheat Loan) have been set up to develop a realistic spirit of social service and responsible understanding of the problems of rural reconstruction. Socioeconomic improvements have also increased the educational attainments of Indian women inasmuch as they have enabled them to occupy suitable positions in various services and professions.

In the educational system, coeducation is usually postponed until the college level. The students are often so shocked by the novel situation that they either take morbid interest in members of the other sex or remain aloof and detached from them. The gains of coeducation in promoting better understanding between the sexes could be achieved if it were the accepted norm from childhood on. Under such circumstances, some of the artifacts of sex typing among educated males and females might be expected eventually to disappear.

Domestic area

The Samskars

The core of domestic life in India centers around the role relations that emerge from certain *Samskars* (religious sacraments performed during adolescence and adulthood among the Hindus). The male Hindu Brahmin, after the preadolescent period, has to undergo the "Thread Wearing Ceremony," technically called *Yagnopavit Samskar,* which alters the parent-child role relations considerably. Ideally, the dependency relations terminate and a new role relationship, in which the adolescent boy is regarded by his parents as having attained the equal status of "friend," emerges.

There is a clear-cut dichotomy in the roles performed by girls. The first category consists of a simple type of role assumed by daughters in their parental home, while the second category involves the more complex type of roles played by females as wives and mothers in their in-laws' houses. For the most part, adolescent girls stay with their parents when early marriages are not consummated. Although her position is not as favorable as that of a son, the girl is brought up in her family with care and affection and receives formal education. She is expected to help her mother in the performance of her domestic role and to absorb the family and caste traditions.

Chaperonage Customs

In India, the young middle-class girl is still chaperoned. If she goes out alone in the afternoon, she must be back home by 6 P.M. In fact, there are few opportunities for young men and women to meet one another except on the coeducational college campuses. However, in some parts of India, especially northern India and the great metropolitan cities such as Bombay, Calcutta, Delhi and Madras, the strictness of chaperonage has been relaxed by certain modern Hindus, Christians, and Anglo-Indians. Nevertheless, it must be realized that the vast majority of Hindu girls cannot afford to adopt the Western system of courtship because their reputation would be ruined and the main purpose of courtship, which was to seek or choose a partner, would be defeated.

Marriage Patterns

Hindu marriage is essentially a sacrament, a *Samskar,* and not a contract into which both the marriage partners enter, as in the case of Muslims or Christians (Kapadia, 1955). In the case of both adult males and females whose earlier role ascriptions have terminated, after having been brought up as young boys and girls and educated under the parental roof, a new kind of role relationship starts with the negotiations and performance of marriage. In India, marriage brings about a metamorphosis in the roles of young men and women.

For the most part, marriages are arranged in India by the parents or guardians of the prospective bride and bridegroom along the lines of caste,

Varn, and lineage, *Gotra.* Ross (1961) found at least 50 percent of educated Hindus in favor of exercising freedom to choose their marital mate. For the last decade and a half, a compromise formula for arranging marriages has evolved among educated Hindus. In arranging the marriages, the prospective bride and bridegroom are allowed to meet in a semiformal situation, i.e., in a restaurant, movie, or fair. These meetings are arranged by their parents and the young man is allowed to see and talk to his would-be marriage partner in the presence of parents or other close relatives. In cases of arranged marriages, possibilities of rejecting the marriage partner exist on such grounds as appearance, ability, and achievement. The significance of these kinds of arranged marriages lies in the fact that they provide an opportunity for coming to know each other's tastes and talents.

It should be mentioned that caste barriers are losing their hold on choice of marriage partners among educated Indians. The dowry system, a form of bride price, has also been legally abolished since May 1960. Attitudes toward arranged marriage among the upper middle-class Hindus have changed markedly. Nearly 60 percent to 70 percent of the present urban population seem to favor intercaste marriages.

The common cohesive factors in marriage for the Indian couple in the early twenties or even thirties are largely based on the gratification of sexual needs and sacramental duties. Later, when the couple has two or three children, a deep and truly intimate relationship emerges between the partners, irrespective of any sexual or religious bonds. As this more personally meaningful relationship develops, there comes into existence an affectionate dependence on one another. In other words, as the marriage relationship becomes less formalized, the couple begins to feel unity. Divorce is allowed according to the Hindu code but is most likely to take place before the age of thirty or the arrival of children. After this phase, the occurrence of such an idea to either partner seems impossible. Sporadic cases of divorce have been found in certain couples of the later age group who have identified themselves with Western culture.

Childbearing

With the growth of fertility differentials due to social customs inherent in traditional culture, the dynamics of childbearing need to be understood. Childbearing practices are associated with a particular religious sentiment among the Hindus. It is incumbent on a Hindu married woman to bear a male child who, aside from being an asset to the family and the future support of the parents especially in old age, is expected to perform certain religious rights (*Shradh*) after the death of his parents. In the case of the Muslims and Christians, the childbearing process seems to be partly motivated by the desire to increase the membership of their sect.

Contraceptive Practices

In view of what has been said above, it can be logically assumed that the Indian population would find any use of contraceptives distasteful. Today, different types of birth control propaganda and contraceptive techniques are being tried in various areas in an effort to ascertain the optimum system. Vasathani's study (1957) and a number of other related studies reveal that the more educated middle-class Hindus approve the use of contraceptives, although regular use may be lacking. The government of India has been pursuing a vigorous policy of promoting the implementation of family planning programs in urban as well as in rural areas.

Evaluations and Future Directions

Role inequalities imposed by the tradition of centuries cannot be easily eradicated. Women alone cannot bring about equality of role relations in family status, economic, social, and educational fields. Men of India have to be prepared to tolerate changes fostering equality in role relations. They have to give active support to women in equalizing role relations. Radical modifications of the traditional notions of male supremacy are essential to bring about these changes. Ultimately, the men and women of urban areas have to meet the challenges and recognize that rural India's tradition-bound male-dominated system has to be replaced by a more liberal society where role inequalities may be totally eradicated.

The roles found in the Indian family system are not static. Indians are willing to give up, although reluctantly, some of their older family patterns because of their own failure to provide viable alternatives and creative opportunities for the growth and actualization of the individual's potentialities. The real freedom to formulate educational plans, choose genuine work careers, and select intimate and preferred marriage partners would eventually rest on the dissolution of sex stereotyping and radical changes in role definition.

Ultimately, it would seem just to conclude that in agreement with Seward [1946 (1954)], changes in sex roles of men and women in India will be possible only if ". . . each member felt free to follow his particular bent without being branded 'masculine' or 'feminine.' "

References

Benedict, Ruth. "Continuities and Discontinuities in Cultural Conditioning." *Psychiatry,* 1 (1938), 161–67.

Bopegamage, A., and P. V. Veeraraghavan. *Status Images in Changing India.* Unesco Research Center, Delhi; Bombay: Manaktalas, 1967.

Dixit, Ramesh C. "Sex-role Consciousness among Village Children of Upper and Lower Caste Groups." *Journal of the Indian Academy of Applied Psychology.* 5, 1 (1968) 32–36.

Ghurye, G. S. *Caste, Class, and Occupations.* Bombay: Popular Book Depot, 1961.

Indian Institute of Public Opinion. *Monthly Public Opinion Survey,* 1 (October 1955), 11–29.

Kapadia, K. M. "Changing Patterns of Hindu Marriage and Family. III." *Sociological Bulletin,* 4 (1955), 161–63.

Mukherjee, R. *The Sociologist and Social Change in India Today.* New Delhi: Prentice Hall of India, 1965.

Parsons, Talcott. "Age and Sex in the Social Structure of the United States." *American Journal of Sociology,* 42 (1936), 81–94.

Narain, Vatsala. "India." In *Women in the Modern World.* R. Patai, ed. New York: Free Press, 1967, pp. 21–41.

Ross, Aileen D. *The Hindu Family in its Urban Setting.* Toronto: University of Toronto Press, 1961.

Seward, Georgene H. *Sex and the Social Order.* New York: McGraw-Hill, 1946 (o.p.); Harmondsworth, Middlesex: Pelican Books, 1954.

Vasathani, R. "Acceptance of Family Planning in Rural India." *Journal of Family Welfare,* 3 (1957), 14–19.

Veeraraghavan, P. V. *Subjective Assessment of Status in a Rural and Urban Setting. Report II.* Coimbatore, India: The South India Textile Research Association, 1965.

16 STATUS AND ROLE BEHAVIOR IN CHANGING JAPAN

George De Vos and Hiroshi Wagatsuma

One of the basic questions the Japanese ask of themselves today is how and to what degree is rapid industrialization influencing family life and the fundamental conceptions of the roles of men and women. A self-consciously directed technological revolution has transmuted their nation from an isolated and hierarchically organized agrarian country into a highly developed commercial and industrial state with less than 20 percent of the population now engaged in agriculture. These basic economic changes were accelerated by one of the most highly developed systems of mass communication and transportation of any modern country. In less than one hundred years, Japan has moved far from almost total isolation off the coast of Asia to almost the very center of the maelstrom of innovative ideas and experimental values of a twentieth-century technology. Japan's yet uncommitted youth share in the ferment found in the present younger generation everywhere.

And yet, withal, we find Japan continuing to function as an amazingly stable society. There are no major breakdowns of living patterns evident. The divorce rate, shown in Table 1, which is often used as an index of social

TABLE 1 DIVORCE RATES IN JAPAN AND IN VARIOUS WESTERN COUNTRIES:

Per Thousand Population	*1963*	*1964*	*1965*
Japan	0.73	0.75	0.79
U.S.	2.27	2.35	—
Britain	0.67	0.72	—
Australia	0.68	0.71	0.75
Netherlands	0.49	0.51	0.50
West Germany	0.92	0.99	0.93
France	0.63	0.69	0.71

dislocation, although rising in percentage, is as low in Japan as in most Western industrial states (Asahi Nenkan, 1968). This holds true even though the divorce laws in Japan are perhaps the most liberal of any large country in the world. While there has been a postwar increase in delinquency and social deviancy (De Vos, 1962), patterns of anomic behavior among Japanese youth are not as widespread as the newspaper accounts would have them be. Although among intellectuals there is much discussion of feelings of alienation and of confusion about the direction to be taken by Japanese society, one still finds among many ordinary Japanese a fair degree of resignation, if not genuine contentment, with the patterning of their lives. Japanese couples within individual families are most concerned with making a better world for their two or three children by day-by-day concern with hard work, saving for the future, and working out the best possible educational opportunity for their own young. Regardless of misgivings about the past by the nation as a whole, family life in Japan continues to operate with a fairly optimistic view of the future.

Restrictions of space and purpose limit any further discussion here of the complex economic and sociological forces that with increasing pace are changing Japanese life. Let us turn to a more specific examination of changes and continuities in the traditional concepts of the status and role of men and women. We are of the opinion that the overall stability of the Japanese society, in spite of rapid change, is due in no small part to the manner in which role behavior within the family has remained relatively cohesive and relatively satisfying for individual Japanese no matter what the upheavals in recent Japanese political and social history.

It will be our limited task, therefore, to attempt to assess how and to what degree psychocultural continuity within social sex roles has contributed to what appears to be the relatively successful modernization occurring within Japanese culture.

Role dedication in traditional Japan

The concept of social role is central to the understanding of Japanese social life. In Western cultures, the concept of the individual and a goal of individuation have been basic in both religious and social thought since the Renaissance. It has been a generally assumed "good" in Western philosophy that man develops his potentials out of a need for self-realization, whether this self-realization is viewed within the context of a religious ideology or within that of a more materialistic moral philosophy. At the same time, man's sense of social responsibility in Western social ethics has been universalized to include at least the welfare of all the members of his own country if not all of humanity. In this system, tensions can occur between individual religious commitment and the state—as well as between individual ends and the common good.

The particularistic social philosophy of Confucianism, which formed a basis of political and social thought in nineteenth-century Japan, tended to deemphasize the individual as an end in himself and to emphasize instead the network of particularistic obligations and responsibility that the person assumed as a member of his family and of his immediate community. Living in accordance with one's prescribed role within the family as well as within a political and social hierarchy became the ultimate basis of moral values, both subjectively sanctioned by one's own conscience and objectively reinforced by the informal sanctions of the community and the legal codes of the political state. In Japan, no conflict arose between religious ideologies and loyalty to superiors, but conflict could occur between individual passion and role responsibility.

Particularism in moral philosophy is not limited to the traditional cultures influenced by Confucianism. However, the degree of dedication to expected role behavior found in Japan does have a unique cultural emphasis not readily observable elsewhere. From a cultural standpoint, when a Japanese thinks of his "self," self-awareness fuses with some conception of expected role behavior that is often idealized in his mind as a set of internalized standards or directives. Accordingly, his "ego ideal" is conceptualized in terms of some particular form of idealized role behavior. In the past, a Japanese would feel uncomfortable in thinking of his "self" as something separable from his role. When he "actualized" himself he became what in his status and role position he was expected to be, as a member both of a particular family and of a particular community, or as a man with a given occupational position in a particular economic enterprise. For a woman, it was difficult to conceive of herself other than as a wife or mother dedicated to the exacting requirements of these roles. To allow oneself to be a self devoid of any role commitment was to produce in oneself a sense of moral disarray or guilt. In the traditional Japanese mind, to be individualistic in a Western moral sense would be almost equal to being "selfish" in the worst sense of this term. And when a Japanese is "selfish" (thinking only of his self), he fails to be an actualized person. To any ethical traditional Japanese, a person cannot fully exist without playing a proper social role.

Various forms of role dedication can still be observed in the way Japanese carry out prescribed tasks. There is in many Japanese such an intensity of commitment to the occupational role on the part of men and to the marital role on the part of women that their total energy seems to be directed to the end of actualizing their roles. Long-range lifetime goal objectives are pursued from childhood through periods of training in youth and by hard work and endurance until old age. Sacrificing oneself for a cause seems for some to become the meaning of life itself.

Motivational vectors in Japanese intrafamily behavior

To understand better the operation of Japanese role behavior, let us examine the instrumental and expressive role components of the three generational and the two sex-role positions found within the traditional Japanese family. In so doing, it will be possible to show that continuities from the past are still to be found in modern Japanese role behavior. In our forthcoming publication on lower-class Japanese families in Tokyo (De Vos and Wagatsuma, 1971), we discuss in detail a frame of reference for the analysis of role behavior presented by Parsons and Bales in their primary family model (Parsons and Bales, 1955). We find their scheme as presented too oversimplified for descriptive use. Therefore, in our description of Japanese role behavior, we examine social attitudes in role interaction patterns along eight basic motivational vectors. Four of these interactional patterns are primarily instrumental in nature. In instrumental role behavior, action is motivated as a means taken to achieve a goal or to meet a standard by which behavior is judged. Such behavior is performed as a means to an end rather than for the immediate satisfaction inherent in the act itself. The four basic instrumental vectors we considered are: (1) "achievement"—behavior motivated by the desire to attain a future goal, (2) "competence"—behavior related to a concern with actualizing personal adequacy or capacity, or a need to acquire competence, (3) "responsibility"—behavior motivated by a sense of responsibility or obligation to internalized social directives, and (4) "control"—behavior directed toward the actualization of power, authority, or control in social relationships.

We consider expressive behavior to be primarily defined as the attempted resolution of an internal feeling state; there may be an inherent sense of satisfaction gained in the act itself or in the relationship in which the behavior is expressed. The four expressive vectors are: (1) "pleasure-pain"—behavior generally governed by a direct experience of satisfaction or pleasure or their opposites within the self, (2) "harmony-discord"—behavior involving harmony or disharmony, cooperation or discord, or even violence and destructiveness, in human relationships, (3) "affiliation-separation"—behavior directed toward the creation of closeness and intimacy or their opposites, isolation, rejection or avoidance, and (4) "nurturance-deprivation"—behavior involving care, succor, nurture—that is, behavior based on fulfillment of dependent need or its frustration.

Although emphases differ with role position, all family configurations involve instrumental and expressive behavior by all members in at least a three-generation frame of reference. Moreover, there is considerable interpenetration of instrumental and expressive motives in the actual behavior occurring within any given cultural pattern. When one goes beneath the surface appearance of the family in Japan to understand the motivations underlying the observable interaction patterns, one finds a complex network in which various instrumental and expressive motives are inextricably intertwined. There are culturally consistent variations in the strength and direction taken by the particular role interaction variables characteristic for the various role positions. These consistencies can be defined in formulating an ideal normative picture of Japanese family life. Let use examine these normative variables in motivational vectors in some progressive order as they shed light on the nature of traditional Japanese role patterns now being influenced by social change. We shall then be able to delineate the nature of social changes as they are reflected in the way family and occupational roles are actualized by modern Japanese.

Instrumental components of role relationships within the family

Achievement Motivation

Vocational role socialization. In other publications (De Vos, 1960, 1965b; De Vos and Wagatsuma, 1959, 1961) we described the socialization of achievement motivation within Japanese as related to a sense of incurred obligation related to parental sacrifice. We have documented over and over the strong sense of need achievement in Japanese society as it relates to a need to sense personal accomplishment and thereby to "justify" oneself to society. The Japanese are guided by a work ethic every bit as compelling as that demonstrated by Northern European Protestants (cf. Bellah, 1957; Tawney, 1926; and De Vos, 1968a).

The Japanese mother canalizes a culturally structured need to achieve and a desire for competence on the part of her children by fostering in her sons a direct identification with the male familial role as the major goal of life. It must be noted that the identification fostered by the mother (emphasized especially in the case of the first son) is with the *status* and *role of the father* rather than with the father as a particular individual. Traditionally, the father's authority was never challenged, nor did the successfully dedicated mother change her attitude toward this role no matter what might be the behavior of the actual father. Male adult status was never brought into question by any deprecation of the specific individual holding this office. Such deprecation would be considered as unseemly as for an experienced army sergeant to allow his men to know his private attitudes toward a young inexperienced lieutenant who has just been put in charge of his company. For the Japanese mother and the sergeant, duty demands role performance toward the office rather than toward the person.

Conversely, the small girl in Japan learns to identify with the mother's role as a part of her sense of personal achievement. She has ample opportunity to identify with her mother in learning the nurturant, "maternal" behavior to be exercised toward males. If she is an older sister (*nēsan*) she will assume early the role of a sort of secondary mother toward her younger sibs.

It must be stressed that in much of social science and literature the concept of "achievement" as related to social role is too narrowly focused on economic occupational definitions of the male vocational role. It is not recognized that for women in many cultures, achievement motivation is toward the realization of the maternal role and that for a woman this represents as much of a need achievement as any realization of an external instrumental occupational prowess on the part of men. There is in our culture an implicit derogation of the adult maternal role in favor of the more culturally appreciated economic vocational achievement. There has been less emphasis in modern Western societies, especially in the United States, on the female marital role as a specialized counterpart to the adult male vocational role. The woman's role, implicitly at least, is seen as "less worthy" since women simply as housewives are not given the same status as men in an economically oriented society. Arnold Green (1946) states ironically that American middle-class housewives spend half of their time doing what they dislike and the rest of their time thinking of how to get even with their husbands. Such an attitude, even without the exaggeration, is curious when viewed from the perspective of the traditional Japanese woman. She countenances in her mind no confusion either in becoming a dedicated mother or, alternatively, in assuming one of a number of possible career choices that are clearly seen as excluding the maternal role. Marriage means the production of children to insure the successful continuity of a family. This role entails preparatory learning of an exacting nature, both through the observation of her own mother's behavior and through preparatory activities prior to marriage, very often as a maid or servant in another household. Special schools were devoted to preparing the young woman in the graces attendant upon her role as well as in the various more mundane daily skills of running a household. The conduct of a Japanese household was not considered a simple matter but one requiring a great deal of planning and a sense of organization. Moreover, when a woman entered a household as a bride she had to be trained in the particular traditions and values of her husband's lineage, whatever its social function—economic, military, or artistic.

Japanese women could choose an alternative role to that of marriage. There were professional roles for women in Japanese culture but most of these were in the field of entertainment, ranging from the relatively high status afforded a gifted geisha to the pathetic status accorded an ordinary prostitute. There was ample opportunity in the world of entertainment for personally aggressive, dominant, or specially gifted women to exercise both dominance and control, as well as to actualize a sense of competence and achievement as a "business" woman (Yamata, 1956). Success in these various roles outside the marital sphere again demanded special training and a dedication of purpose from a relatively early age. In the past, women felt they gave up more by foregoing the maternal role than they would by assuming it. Becoming a mother was of higher value than becoming a professional outside the home.

The Actualization of Competence

The apprenticeship role, becoming an adult. Although in traditional Japan there was no "adolescent" period that ritually separated childhood from adulthood, each class had its own traditional form of preparation for full adult status, which varied considerably from epoch to epoch in Japanese history. In the use of marriage by samurai to enhance the status of a lineage, parents tended to seek earlier and earlier liaisons so that the age of marriage had been gradually pushed back from that obtaining at the beginning of the Tokugawa period around 1600. The age of adulthood for samurai by the end of the Tokugawa period (circa 1850) was fifteen (Ema, 1925). During this period, the women of the warrior class were considered adult before age fifteen. In the merchant and artisan classes, in contrast, the period of apprenticeship had become increasingly protracted so that some individuals remained in an apprentice relationship with a master even into their middle thirties.

Today, there is throughout Japanese society a recognition of adolescence very similar to that found in the West, with all the attendant problems of psychosexual maladjustment that are prevalent in Western adolescent youth. Similarly, Japanese patterns of transition are somewhat different for middle-class as compared with lower-class youth. However, the differences in this respect are actually less noticeable in adolescents in Japan than in America, since the middle-class type of adolescent reaction is more pervasive. The "acting out" behavior of lower-class Japanese youth is less apparent but not absent. As in the United States, school "dropouts" and so-called delinquent behavior are more prevalent among lower-class youth (De Vos, 1962).

The importance of the apprenticeship of youth during premarital years as an essential part of socialization in traditional Japanese culture has not been given the attention it deserves. To understand adult Japanese it is essential to understand the work mentality as it is developed around an apprenticeship experience. The intensity of the adult role dedication in both men and women receives strong reinforcement during this formative period.

The Japanese, whether samurai, merchant, or artisan, were expected from about age twelve to undergo rigorous training under an adept master as a means of acquiring the technical competence necessary for adult performance. There was no easy acceptance of incompetence or lack of application to the task of learning. Standards were exacting in every field of endeavor. The apprentice was expected to work hard for long hours with little pay. He had no time for "selfish pleasures" and interests but had to put such thoughts out of his mind or limit himself to fantasies about the future day when he would enjoy the pleasures allowed a person of recognized status.

Such an apprenticeship period was not limited to the male vocational role. There were many apprenticelike equivalents for women during their premarital period. Just as many boys were sent out of their own homes to work under someone other than their fathers, girls were frequently sent out of the home to work as maids in the homes of wealthier folk of higher status to learn proper marital-housewife behavior. If not, they were required to perform some service task for their parents to train themselves for future performance.

Boys were very often sent out even when they were to inherit their father's craft or business because it was considered more rigorous, hence better training, to be apprenticed to someone other than the father. The second sons from farm families were encouraged to seek apprenticeships in an urban setting, most often with an artisan but sometimes with a merchant. For the girl from a wealthier family there was required attendance at a special school that was to train her in the polite arts so necessary for a bride marrying into a respectable lineage. A lineage kept its pride by expecting refined behavior of its in-marrying women.

The prewar "discrimination" in patterns of formal education given men and women is still somewhat in evidence today, although all the major universities including the University of Tokyo admit qualified women on an informal quota basis. Any determined woman, if she so chooses, can seriously consider taking on a professional career. Many educated women in Japan, very much as in the United States, will forgo their careers when they marry. Some women choose to follow a professional career after the death of a husband.

One of the real changes in socialization that is occurring in today's Japan is the vocational "imprinting" preceding marriage. The traditional forms of apprenticeship described above are replaced by formal education on the one hand, and the mass communication media on the other. This change is especially evident as it influences the woman's role. Mass media have almost entirely supplanted the direct first-hand experience of the preparatory "maid" period for women as a means of acquiring knowledge concerning the expected role of the housewife. Until recently, most "proper" young women were learning domestic skills through the emulation of the "refined" behavior observed in upper-status households during a period of domestic apprenticeship outside the home. It must be noted therefore, that the traditional Japanese definition of a "maid" has now shifted toward its Western concept of a lifelong occupational role rather than what it was in the past—a learning role by which one acquired desirable adult skills. As a consequence, class-limited role diffusion of domestic patterns from higher-status households into lower-status households no longer occurs through direct experience. Young girls instead turn to popular magazines and television for inspiration and instruction in homemaking. The Westernization of Japanese women is going on at a rapid pace as far as inculcating a mass-media conception of what a home should be.

Apartment-house dwelling is becoming increasingly prevalent in congested urban areas. The young bride learns to make the most of a small living space in which many of the domestic refinements of the old culture no longer have any pertinence. There has been widespread use of the recently developed ready-made foods such as "instant noodles" and soups. The small Japanese home kitchen has become mechanized by the use of such devices as toasters and electric rice cookers. The complicated and time-consuming skills needed for food preparation in the past are rapidly disappearing. For most housewives there remains the necessary daily shopping in neighborhood shops since the buying of large quantities is difficult for those travelling on foot. Increasingly, however, those who can afford cars do stock up refrigerators that are continually growing in size and capacity. More housewives are buying at large food centers and department-store basements. Western cooking is demonstrated on daytime television and is very popular as a home diversion for the housewife who finds herself with increasingly greater periods of leisure.

For men, the apprenticeship pattern still has considerable vitality as a means of vocational socialization in spite of the rapid inroads upon this pattern made by increasingly large-scale factories in the postwar period. Nevertheless, young men are no longer tolerant of the psychological dependence, the hard work, and the harshness experienced in a formal apprenticeship. After graduating from nine years of compulsory school, many prefer to find as quickly as possible some position in a large factory that will afford them both security and wages that increase steadily with seniority. The focus of vocational concern is shifting from acquiring special skills mastered with difficulty to finding positions with shorter hours and higher pay—attitudes that have already been primary for years in Western blue-collar workers.

Japanese youths wish to have time free for after-hours recreation. A variety of such recreation is afforded by the many places of amusement now accessible through the transportation ganglia of modern Japanese urban areas. The virtue of loyalty and the network of associations related to the apprentice-master structure of the past, for urban workers at least, is beginning to disappear. In professional clerical and managerial positions, however, the network of expectations is more apt to endure for some time, since there is still considerable emphasis on loyalty of service in the middle-class segment of the population.

It must of course be pointed out that the ongoing process of change does not terminate the many continuities in Japanese personality configurations and role performance related to the concern with competence and adequacy. The culture continues to be a demanding one in its definition of the adequate performance of adult social roles. Even today, for most Japanese to actualize the adult role, to have a sense of achievement or success, is no mean task. In various studies over the past fifteen years with the Thematic Apperception Test in Japan (Caudill and De Vos, 1956; De Vos, 1960, 1965a, 1965b; Wagatsuma, 1957; Wagatsuma and De Vos, 1962), we have consistently found evidence of very strong achievement motivation related to family responsibility and interdependent nurturant concerns. These achievement concerns are almost invariably expressed in the context of potential incapacity to realize one's own internalized standards. It is interesting to note that concern with adequacy has not diminished as far as Thematic Apperception Test protocols show, whether among adults or fifteen-year-olds (De Vos and Wagatsuma, 1971). High standards pervaded the full range of traditional culture, from the specialized world of art represented by exacting traditions such as the Noh drama, the Kabuki stage, or the various forms of graphic arts, to the everyday world of the lowliest artisan or cook. Everything in Japan is still judged and ranked—the relative position of the major universities, the "belts" worn by judo experts, the ratings of *go* players.

No field of endeavor in Japan has escaped concern with refinement and finesse. During the traditional apprenticeship period, an individual, whether he was treated patiently or harshly, was required to continue until he showed himself to be sufficiently aware of what was expected of him in the way of proper standards. Only then would he be considered worthy of independence.

In marrying an eldest son, the young bride coming into a new household was in a sense entering her second period of apprenticeship under the severe and sometimes jealous tutelage of her new husband's mother. If she failed in any way to meet the exacting requirements, or showed herself to be inept, she could be sent back to her family as a "failure."

It is no wonder, therefore, that the pressures of the past still make becoming "adequate" a difficult and problematical process demanding of the individual a strong endurance and a capacity to maintain himself in submissive and subordinate positions until his society deems him capable of acceptable independent assertion of himself. For the man, ideally achieved social status was that of master merchant or artisan or successful bureaucrat in the premodern samurai hierarchy. Similarly, farmers prided themselves on their proficiency and diligence in producing the maximum crop from very limited soil. For a wife and mother, endurance continued until her children showed to the world their capacities attesting to the mother's years of careful nurturing, training and preparation. Much of what Freud (1955) and Reik (1941) have described as "moral masochism" applies directly to the apprentice mentality maintained by Japanese throughout their preparatory years of training. One must not overlook the fact that present submissiveness was and is related to a sense of the future long-term goal of acquiring competence so as to become independent or dominant in relation to others.

Responsibility and Obligation in Japanese Culture

Ruth Benedict (1946) and Frank Gibney (1953) amply discussed the complicated network of social obligations that are required in fulfilling role expectation in Japanese culture. These social role obligations are the essential component in the Japanese sense of responsibility. The word "responsibility" (*sekīnin*) in Japanese has negative emotional connotations that are not felt quite similarly in the West. Japanese have learned to avoid committing themselves to responsibility unnecessarily since the person who is responsible assumes all the blame when anything goes wrong no matter what his own culpability may have been (De Vos, 1968b). During the Tokugawa period the "responsible" village head, for example, was the one who was punished if any manifestation of rebelliousness among the villagers of his community occurred. Similarly, total families were punished for breach of conduct by any one of their members. The "responsible" person in the family could be required to commit suicide, or in lesser matters, to do public penance, or to give some form of public apology for improper behavior for anyone under his charge. For such cultural-historical reasons, it was highly desirable to retire early, and if one were power oriented, to maintain control from behind the scenes. The ideal, therefore, was to maintain power without having direct responsibility.

This sense of responsibility in Japan is still the residue of the familism of the past, in which the individual ego was not differentiated from an intense sense of social belonging in which each person shared, whatever his particular position was within the family or organization. In the Japanese family, it has been and still is the mother who is "responsible" for bringing up the children. Traditionally, this has meant that when children acted in an unsatisfactory way or committed some delinquent act, it was the mother who made apology to others for the behavior of her child. Often, when the perpetrator of some shocking crime such as murder or bank robbery is apprehended, the mother (much less frequently the father) of the murderer or robber is quoted in the newspaper as saying that she feels very sorry (*moshiwake ga nai*) for her son's behavior. A mother may feel impelled to make a public apology taking full responsibility for her son's behavior. In Japan, if one's dog bites someone, an apology is given, not for one's carelessness in allowing it to happen, but on behalf of the dog, who in a sense "belongs" familially. Therefore, one should feel that the dog's behavior reflects upon his "family."

Conversely, it is implicit knowledge on the part of children that they can cause their mother pain through her sharp sense of responsibility. Such knowledge often leads in consciously explicit terms to the inhibition of improper behavior outside the family.

In the same way, in employment relationships, a worker in a subordinate position in a factory today tends still to identify in a familial sense with his boss, assuming the operation of a reciprocal relationship that goes far beyond that found in Western so-called paternalistic practices. Japanese paternalism derives much of its strength from the traditional expectation that a person playing the role of a boss (literally in Japanese *oyabun*—"father role") would assume almost total responsibility for the health and welfare of his workers (Bennett and Ishino, 1963). The belief that one's boss has such a strong feeling of responsibility allows subordinates the complementary expressive feelings of dependency and loyalty toward authority. Such feelings of responsibility are an internalized part of the code of leadership whether on the part of bureaucrats, businessmen, or warriors.

Now, as in the past, a person cannot function in any Japanese society without explicit interdependency and therefore responsibility to some group in his professional and vocational life. Those who fail to meet obligations soon isolate themselves. A person who seeks to circumvent seniority or becomes too independent finds himself almost totally alienated from Japanese society. An old proverb, "Deru kugi wa utareru" ("The nail that sticks out gets hit"), still seems to express Japanese thought on this matter. This interdependent network makes it very difficult for Japanese to behave individualistically unless they are exceptional artists or other individuals who do not have to give some form of symbolic allegiance to a particular group or competitive segment of the society.

Authority and Control

Distribution of power and decision-making in the Japanese family. Many reading of Japanese authoritarianism assume simply that Japan was traditionally a hierarchical society in which the individual on top made the decisions and took initiative. Both in the external political sphere and within the family or household this is rarely the case. Decisions are very often collective efforts "on behalf of" the family or company head. If a person in such a head position too often counters the collective efforts of his subordinates, who in many circumstances take initiative that would not be acceptable in the West, he may lose his power base entirely by the withdrawal of active support of his subordinates or by some sort of silent resistance that makes it difficult to continue functioning. In actuality, therefore, the distribution of power in the Japanese society is a very complex matter. It is well known that in Japanese political history the person in the official role was very often controlled by his "advisers" or by so-called "retired" individuals who would continue to manipulate events from behind the scenes. Much as in the performance of a drama, direction took place from behind the scenes while the audience observed only the role performances taking place on stage.

It is often thought that Japanese women generally were delegated to servile subordinate roles in which their behavior continually symbolized their inferior social position vis-à-vis men. What is overlooked when only overt behavior is observed is the operation of actual control of the family by women within the family household. No matter what the dynamics of the family, women always carefully deferred to men in accordance with role requirements, just as a powerful regent defers to the royal figurehead on the throne.

Recent trends toward a more overt expression of latent dominance on the part of women are more apt to appear in urban lower-class families, in which women as well as men are less restricted by status considerations than in middle-class families, and therefore are more likely to give freer vent to emotional expressions, whether of a sexual or an aggressive nature. The surface appearance of strong-willed wives and dependent husbands is not, however, totally a product of any postwar "emancipation" of Japanese women or of any such sociological factor as the effects of industrialization on the whole society. One can find in the traditional culture many comic stories and anecdotes (*rakugo*) about the common people's life in the Tokugawa period describing an impulsive and somewhat careless husband as a foil to his more realistic, practical, and dependable wife. It is rather clear in all these anecdotes that the boss, in actuality, was the so-called "dependent" marital partner.

Dominant or submissive role behavior and dominant or submissive personality structure are independent of one another. A sample of 800 records of the Rorschach Tests administered in Japan by De Vos and others (Muramatsu, 1962) taken from both rural and urban communities, revealed no basic, significant, consistent structural differences in personality between Japanese men and women. The general results would indicate that the distribution of personality traits through processes of socialization, including identification, does not lead to very obvious personality differences corresponding to the very obvious Japanese dichotomy in observed social sex-role behavior. Hence, we would assume that in the past, as in the present, there was no significant difference between men and women in Japan in the incidence or distribution of structural traits of personality, basic active or passive attitudes, dominant and submissive needs, and the like. Therefore, while a dominant man can directly assert himself readily within the behavioral prerogatives of the male role, a potentially dominant woman has to find some indirect means of self-expression of dominance within the narrow strictures confining acceptable female role behavior. The means taken come readily to view when one looks beneath the surface and examines the actual distribution of dominant and submissive traits within specific Japanese families. A potentially dominant woman learns to manipulate susceptible men in such a way that they are very often totally unaware they are "deciding" in accordance with the woman's wishes. One's own dependent male child naturally is most susceptible to the exercise of a nurturant control on the part of a mother.

The role of the paternal grandmother is one of the key points of tension in traditional Japanese family life. Tensions arise both out of the harsh dominance with which a mother-in-law very often exercises control over a politically powerless in-marrying daughter-in-law, and out of the way she manipulates the dependent-nurturant ties that are maintained between herself as a mother and her favorite adult son. There is, in essence, a competition for the husband that is only infrequently won by the wife even today in situations where the mother no longer lives with the nuclear family. The defeated wife in turn learns quickly, when she has such propensities in herself, to play the game, and shifts her affective needs and emotional requirements from her husband to her growing children. The inherent power of the role of the mother-in-law, therefore, is such that many major decisions within the family and sometimes even outside the family are subject to her control. It was interesting for us to note in our study of Niike village (Beardsley *et al.*, 1959; De Vos, 1965a) that the strongest sense of household tradition and lineage in a tradition-oriented farm village was found among the older women who, as young brides, had come in as strangers from the outside, but who, through the process of severe hazing and rigorous training over a period of time, themselves became "keepers of the flame" for their adopted households.

The paternal grandfather, conversely, plays a minor, somewhat withdrawn role in many families, or in some he may express an almost maternal kind of nurturance toward the young. If the grandfather is a sufficiently dominant personality, however, he will continue in business matters to exercise control even after his so-called "retirement."

The power that is exercised within the Japanese family was in the past always in the name of the preservation of lineage and the enhancement of family status. Therefore, the family head was never considered to be in a position of true personal power but to be more an inheritor of a role through which power was exercised for family benefit. A family head who was a dominant person, of course, would exercise personal direction of the other members of his family, whereas a more passive person, if not totally inadequate, would heed "suggestions" made directly to him.

Self-control. Sex roles differed to the degree that "self-control" was necessary. As a whole, the role requirements put strong emphasis on maintaining self-control in order not to bring any injury on one's family. In respect to concepts of self-expression of pleasure related to bodily functions, the Japanese concept of self-control differed somewhat from that of the West in that a man could indulge in sexuality, for example, if it in no way interfered with the well-being of his *ie* (house). Unfortunate sexual commitments or possessive feelings toward an inappropriate person, however, could lead to a serious sense of guilt.

That some Japanese men can indulge in relatively uncontrolled, impulsive, "willful" behavior within their families is well documented in our lower-class sample taken from urban Tokyo (De Vos and Wagatsuma, 1971). A few men in our sample can become impulsive to the point of violence with members of their own family. Such internal expression, however prevalent in the traditional culture, was not matched with freedom to behave impulsively in outside relationships. Women particularly were supposed to practice restraint over their impulses to anger or discord vis-à-vis both husband and children.[1]

The practice of self-control in role behavior differs somewhat from that in the West in that Japanese depend very heavily on mechanisms of *suppression* where Western Europeans or Americans tend to practice *repression*. That is to say, Japanese are very often totally aware of their underlying emotional states when they are not appropriate to expected role behavior. In certain circumstances, Westerners express control of emotions by modes of repression buttressed by a strong value placed on the maintenance of "rational," logical behavior. Although Japanese in similar circumstances are often painfully aware of both their own inner feelings and sensitivity to the feelings of others, out of the sense of "self-control" in respect to the expected role they maintain a blandness of surface behavior that Westerners often consider "inscrutable." In a sense, Westerners expect behavior to be more in accord with underlying spontaneous feelings, and to behave otherwise is to be considered insincere. The Japanese concept of sincerity, in contrast, is the maintenance of behavior that is fully in accord with what is required by the person's role. Needless to say, the Japanese understand and are aware of one another's covert attitudes in spite of the surface control, whether the hidden feelings are intense anger or profound sorrow.

Control of family succession and family size. The Japanese corporate *ie,* the "house," has maintained its own achieved status in an intensely competitive achievement-oriented society both in the past and in the present through the careful selection of an appropriate heir. Although primogeniture was officially the prevailing ideal, widespread and flexible use of patterns of adoption allowed for optimal continuity. Adoptions in Japan are remarkably widespread. In our normal controls, more than one-fourth of the families had a *mukoyoshi* in two generations. A *mukoyoshi* is an adopted adult son who marries into the family and takes on the name of his wife. By this means the family selects an appropriate person who shows the necessary vocational aptitude to continue the house. Within the intrafamilial power structure, however, the *mukoyoshi* finds himself relatively powerless so that his position is considered an unenviable one by most Japanese, even though he often comes from a house of far lower status than the one into which he is adopted.

One of the most notable postwar changes in the Japanese family role patterns is the dethronement in many families of the eldest son, the heir to the position of family head. In the past, the eldest brother, very often from a relatively early age, was responsible for making decisions. As a young adult he would be involved in many major decisions, such as the marriage arrangements for his younger sibs, and sometimes he would even make career choices for his younger brothers. Concomitantly, he would assume responsibility for providing educational opportunities for his younger brothers, financing and supporting them until they became established. Younger sons in the past were not given the care and attention accorded to the future house head. Sometimes these younger sons became resentful and tension would often develop between the eldest son and the younger children in a large family.

The eldest sister had no comparable authority but was considered to be an expressively-oriented person who acted in a substitutive sense in performing maternal duties toward her younger sibs. The younger sisters, and especially the youngest or *suekko,* were sometimes given indulgent preferential treatment. The *suekko,* the last child, was expected to stay at home to receive and reciprocate the indulgence of aging parents. It is interesting that William Caudill (1964), in his research on Japan's mental hospitals, found that the incidence of commitment is highest for eldest sons and youngest daughters, who are significantly overrepresented in the schizophrenic patient population in hospitals throughout Japan. This would attest to the psychological tensions inherent in these roles or to the peculiarities of child-rearing practices and the unusual emotional demands that may overburden the psychic structures of these individuals.

In effect, one of the reasons for dethronement of the eldest son is that today most Japanese families have no more than two or three children, and birth order is more important in large families than in small. In small families children tend to be treated more on an individual basis. Moreover, today inheritance is equally distributed by law. In urban areas therefore, one finds no undue emphasis on the role of the eldest son in younger families. In rural communities, however, where families tend to remain larger, one finds *de facto* practice of informal primogeniture still operative.

There is considerable world-wide interest in the fact that the present-day Japanese birth rate insures a stabilization of the Japanese population at about 100 million individuals. The government, with the cooperation of educational organizations, public health agencies, women's organizations, and the mass media, has been more successful than most other governments that are making similar attempts in bringing about population control.

It must be noted that this low birth rate is due to the widespread practice of abortion as well as preventive birth control measures. Postwar liberalization of Japan's legal codes permits therapeutic abortion for economic as well as for mental or physical reasons. The law is so liberal that virtually anyone desiring an abortion in Japan can obtain one (Wagatsuma and Unno, 1958).[2] The result has been estimated at from 2 to 3 million legal and illegal abortions yearly during the early sixties. The rate of abortion seems to be declining somewhat at the present time as technical competence with birth-control measures is becoming more widespread.

One must not interpret the success of population control as due only to recent government measures; traditional attitudes and practices that were already widespread in premodern Japan must be taken into account. For example, among the farmers the practice of infanticide (*mabiki*) was evidently fairly common (Taeuber and Notestein, 1947). (The word *mabiki* derives from the agricultural practice of thinning out plantlings so as to allow the remaining ones to grow better.) The Tokugawa regime was opposed to such practices, which occurred among the samurai as well as among farmers. Edicts were periodically set forth castigating both classes for their selfish indifference to national need. Infanticide was practiced through the connivance of midwives who would "allow" weak infants to die; actually, a piece of wet paper was often put over the baby's face. Gordon Bowles [3] examined birth records in a particular mountain village several years ago and found that until recently, 80 percent of living firstborn children were males, suggesting a continuance of the systematic practice of "thinning out" the first children to assure priority for an eldest son. Today, with contraceptive devices widely available in Japan, families are increasingly being limited by preventive means to the number desired by the parents. A two-child family is preferred although, with the increasing prosperity during the last two or three years, more middle-class families are having a third child.

Artificial insemination is sought fairly frequently in Japan and this offers some interesting insights into Japanese attitudes toward the parental role. The problem leading to the request for medical intervention is often not actual infertility on the part of either spouse, but is seemingly related to the practice of coitus in such a way that the semen does not reach the ova for fertilization. In these cases the husband is the donor. When artificial insemination is sought because the husband is infertile, administering physicians have noted the expression of curiously "Japanese" attitudes. For example, knowing that all donors, who remain anonymous, are supposedly medical students or interns, women come for insemination in the hope they can produce "superior" children, of a higher intelligence than would be possible with their own husbands as fathers. Sometimes, indeed, women whose husbands are not infertile request artificial insemination to insure such superior children. The fact that the donor must remain anonymous often causes concern to the men since it is frequently the husband's wish that some known relative, such as a brother or other near male relative, be used "to keep it in the family."

Expressive components of role relationships within the family

So far we have focused mainly on the instrumental motivations to be found in Japanese role behavior. The same behavior can also be viewed in terms of its expressive motivational components. Only in the abstract can we look at behavior as solely goal-oriented. Sustained goal-directed behavior cannot be maintained for most individuals, whatever their culture, without some continuing sense of expressive gratification, however distantly socialized from the immediate realization of physiological needs. The socialization process within any culture as the shaper of human psychology can be viewed as changing primary needs and gratifications into culturally specific secondary ones.

In this section we examine motivations related to harmony and discord, dependency and nurturance, affiliation and companionship, and the direct seeking of pleasure and gratification or self-expression. Again, one must note how such motives are themselves inextricably intertwined. In examining one type of motivation, we will of necessity have to discuss and relate what we say to instrumental motivational vectors already discussed in the sections above.

One finds in examining Japanese sexual behavior, for example, that not only are self-gratification and physiological need involved, but also, as it can in any culture, sexual congress can be a means of satisfying affiliative needs or feelings of nurturance or dependency. It can even be sublimated from direct expression when such expression comes in conflict with other instrumental or expressive motivations. Consequently, difficulties in a satisfactory sex life can derive from or become the cause of a conscious focus of dissatisfaction. This is especially true in situations where other underlying expressive needs are not fulfilled.

Returning to an examination of social sex roles as expressively motivated, we must again start with the organization of the traditional Japanese family. Both the modern and traditional family in Japan provided and are providing a sense of well-being and security through a sense of "belonging." This sense of belonging today, however, has changed from one that is realized through a quasi-religious reverence for the family as an enduring corporate entity to a more secularized ideal of the establishment of relationships through which one can realize, as the Japanese term has it, *shiawase*—comfort, contentment, and happiness defined in very material terms.

It would be helpful perhaps to point out again that the traditional Japanese word *ie* is not a direct translation of the English word "household," "family," or "house," at least in their most usual connotations. Usage of the English word "house" in special phrases such as "House of Rothschild" is the closest connotative approximation. The implications of this phrase describing the famous banking family that had branches in France, England, and Germany has the same connotation as the Japanese word *ie*. It connotes a corporate entity existing beyond the span of the individual lives of a group closely bound together by intimate ties of blood and kinship. The leadership is passed on. It may be possible that an *ie* develops subsidiary branches such as occurred with the Rothschild "cadet" line. In some regions of Japan, mainly in the Northeast, an extended family structure called the *dozoku* became prominent (Brown, 1966; Cornell, 1964; Kitano, 1962; Nagai, 1953).

The *ie* for Japanese was a framework dealing with clearly divided roles; they derived personal satisfaction from working cooperatively in harmony as part of a larger team encompassing more than just themselves. One could realize nurturant and dependent needs within this framework, not necessarily primarily in the husband and wife relationship. The need to satisfy sharing of one's intimate self in companionship and communion was not considered a reason for marriage. Such sharing was not an institutionalized expectation of the marriage bond; indeed, it could at times be considered detrimental to proper role behavior.

One must note that the Japanese sense of belonging does not derive from any satisfaction in the sense of mutual understanding. Rather, it was related to the diffuseness of oneself in which any painful awareness of an existential separateness could be avoided by the adherence to an awareness of oneself as a family member. Such a loss of self is found satisfying to many members of religious bodies, as Durkheim (1915) discussed in the *Elementary Forms of the Religious Life*. This sense of group identity permits one to gain strength to go beyond one's own personal defects or limitations in the interpenetration that occurs in religious collectivities. Christianity for some of its adherents today basically satisfies such a social need rather than merely offering a particular dogma. In this context, one can point out that the Christian concept of "church" bears some psychodynamic similarities to the Japanese quasi-religious concept of "house;" *kyriakon,* the Greek derivation of the word "church," represents this directly. The church is the "house of the Lord" to which all Christians belong as brethren under God the Father. It offers a sense of transcendental affiliation that supplies the deepest need for dependent security in the Christian sense of self. It is sometimes overlooked that although many so-called psychologically independent Christians may be independent in their human relationship, underlying this independence is some psychodynamic primitive sense of a special dependent relationship with God.

Reciprocal Role Performance: Harmony and Discord in Intra-Family Functioning

The individual in the role vs. the individual measured against the role. Many modern Japanese women who seem to be maritally well-adjusted and satisfied still give evidence of the well-developed capacity manifested in the traditional culture to relate to the *role* of husband rather than to the *person.* This emphasis on role behavior rather than on personal communication is well illustrated in the differences found among the lower-class families in our study of delinquency in Arakawa Ward (De Vos and Wagatsuma, 1971). There are significant differences in the manner in which harmony is maintained and discord avoided among our nineteen normal controls in contrast to those with delinquent children. In respect to achievement and competence, there is no difference in the role behavior of the fathers of these families. Many are obvious economic, vocational, and personal failures. But the mothers of nondelinquents allow themselves far less direct criticism of the manifest inadequacy or shortcomings of their husbands. We were somewhat surprised to find that in six interviews with each mother more than three-fourths of the mothers of the families with problem children expressed a direct and unequivocal dissatisfaction with their marriage partner, and many of them described in graphic terms the types of discord and disharmony that characterized their marital life. Although the mothers of nondelinquent children also criticized their husbands, they did so less frequently and less intensely.

In both groups, we found many women whose basic personality propensities were not at all in accord with the demands of their social sex role. Many of these women felt themselves to be more dominant and aggressive, and even more impulsive than acceptable role behavior warranted. Yet, we felt that the psychologically available techniques of role maintenance, especially dedication to self-controlled behavior within the role, was the critical difference. It must be noted that on a psychodynamic level the integrative mechanisms available to mothers of the normal controls were somewhat better than those of the mothers of delinquents; thus, the mothers of nondelinquents, whatever their propensities, had better psychological means at their disposal to maintain self-control.

Ideally, the Japanese father was never to be treated in any way that was disrespectful to his role position. Whatever the woman's unrealized need for mutual affection or dependency, she was to treat the husband as the symbol of authority and succession in the family. In previous work comparing farming and fishing villages (De Vos and Wagatsuma, 1961) we found in the fantasies elicited by the Thematic Apperception Test that, depending on class and role background, the implicit expectations of women could vary considerably from the self-sacrificing warrior ideal. In the farming village of

Niike, women's fantasy was more clearly in line with traditional normative expectations; successful marriage for love was never depicted, nor were there any instances depicting a woman's aggressive behavior toward a husband in a situation of discord or dissatisfaction. In a fishing village, however, we elicited a number of stories of women who were physically abusive to a drunken or profligate husband. In the farming village, when a woman was depicted in any violent scene, the source of the violence was her deep sense of responsibility for the careful upbringing of her children. Should her children be profligate, the mother could wreak violence upon them.

In the traditional Japanese culture, the terms of address used among the members of the same family further suggest the fact that the relationships are primarily to be in terms of roles rather than individuals. As a general rule, only those with higher status can call those of lower status by their given names with or without affix (such as *san, kun* or *chan*). Accordingly, parents call their children by their given names, and so do the older children addressing their younger sibs. Those of lower status, however, addressing those of higher status must use the words designating the role of the addressee (with affixes such as *sama* or *san*—or *chan* in an exceptionally intimate and informal relationship and/or in the case of a child). Accordingly, children must address their parents as "o-tō-sama" (honorable father) or "o-kā-san" (honorable mother). Unlike American practice, younger children do not call their elder brothers and sisters by their given names unless there is a small age difference and great intimacy. As a rule, a younger child will address the elder brother as "o-ni-san" (honorable elder brother) and the elder sister as "o-ne-sama" (honorable elder sister), or use the combination of name and role such as "Takako-ne-san" (comparable to "Sister Emily"). Particularly different from American practice is the way husband and wife address each other. The husband, as a person of higher status, can and does call his wife by her given name, but this is *not* reciprocated by his wife. In an old tradition, the wife would call her husband by a deferential word like "danna-sama" (honorable master), or more recently by a vague term like "anata" (meaning "you"). In a majority of cases today, both husband and wife, and the wife in particular, call each other by words designating each other's "parental role," the husband calling his wife "mother" (*o-kā-san*) and the wife calling her husband "father" (*o-tō-san*) as soon as they become parents of children. A more recent trend, especially in urban middle-class families, is to use foreign words for father and mother; thus a husband calls his wife "mama" and a wife calls her husband "papa."

Individuals from cultures accustomed to the establishment of more direct spontaneous relationships within the family, particularly between sibs and husband and wife, may find it difficult to understand the emotional implications of the usage of such forms of address. Such usage in Japan puts continual symbolic emphasis on the fact that direct personal relationships would interfere with the performance of duties related to roles.

This is clearly found, for example, in authoritarian structures such as the American Army, which depends for its organization on the fact that orders must be obeyed by unquestioned adherence when given by a superior. The American Army discourages officers and noncommissioned officers from "fraternizing" either by using the same recreational facilities or by addressing one another on a first name basis.

So too in the traditional Japanese family, except in conditions of extreme privacy, it was considered unseemly for families adhering to any sense of status to have the wife call her husband by his given name.

This emphasis on role maintenance, whatever the personal feeling of the man and wife toward each other, had certain expressive advantages as well as the disadvantages of hindering greater intimacy of communication. There was a sense of security attached to the role in that the individual knew that whatever his personal defects, he could maintain himself within the protective armour of his role position. Such use of role maintenance is found especially useful for individuals with an underlying sense of inadequacy. A person, whatever his sense of personal inadequacy (which, given Japanese standards, is a widespread inner experience), could maintain himself within his formal family pattern without a sense of threat. Most vulnerable, of course, is the individual holding the position of family head since this position carried the expectations of family success and the responsibility for failure. Ideally, the individual was placed *in* the role rather than measured *against* the ideal requirements of the role. For the children being socialized within a family, emphasis on role behavior was ideally suited to foster the continuity in vocational identification useful in a lineage system. Observation of the respect accorded the adult male was a continual psychological inducement to the growing male child to take over the privileges of the same vocational-marital position. Identification with the father was fostered at least in respect to the father's role position whatever the deficiency in the father's capacities as a spontaneous individual.

Some Western contrasts bring out more clearly what is implied by this emphasis on the expressive aspects of roles. One can cite numerous instances, especially in lower-class segments of Western society, where the mother's expectations of what a "man" is do not at all coincide with her perception of her husband. In fact, in certain segments of American Negro society or of Irish society, there are almost institutionalized incongruities between what a wife expects of her mate in contrast to the implicit idealized male image. In the Irish family, for example, the role of "father" was often given over in ideal form to the desexualized priest, whereas the actual husband was often depreciated as an inadequate drunkard. Lower-class working men are not given even perfunctory respect by their wives but are continually measured against the role ideals taken from another class. The American Negro boy growing up must cope with the fact that, whether it is consciously acknowledged or not, his mother's picture of an adequate male is very often that of a white middle-class man. When he is being disciplined, his mother will often brutalize him not only physically but psychologically by making it apparent to him that she has no hope for him that he can possibly fulfill.

The traditional Japanese emphasis on role behavior, while deemphasizing intimacy and companionship between man and wife, can also serve as a protective buffer against the appearance of family discord and disharmony in situations where the expressive and emotional gratification is minimal for both spouses. Impressionistically, therefore, one of the reasons for the relative lack of discord in Japanese family life compared with that in other countries is the degree to which women derive personal satisfaction from being competent in their roles rather than from having a mate who meets their personal needs.

Cooperation and competition in Japanese life: status competition between modern families. The deemphasis on overt disharmony within Japanese culture generally should not lead us to assume a lack of intense competition between families or groups. Converse to the sense of loyalty to one's own group is an underlying competitiveness toward others. While there is emphasis on the network of obligations to associates, one is always also continually maneuvering with one's allies against other competitors who are similarly allied in cliques and factions. Partisanship is intense. Loyalties of conglomerates may shift, resulting in the success or failure of certain ventures. Hence, one must insist on the maintenance of harmony within one's own group in order to succeed against others. Competition among factions within the major political parties on the basis of intensely loyal leaders and followers gives a special flavor to Japanese political life.

Kyōiku-mama. The education of children is perhaps the most intense arena for competition observable within Japanese culture today. A phrase one frequently hears in summarizing the behavior of particular women with respect to the education of their children is "Kyōiku-mama," (education-mama). This usage in Japanese refers to the intense nurturant control a particular mother will exercise over her children in direct competition with other mothers in her neighborhood or social circle to see to it that her own children do better in their educational progress. A good majority of middle-class children, for example, are required or encouraged to take extra schooling that is given after regular school hours. Many children are given private tutoring, a service that provides extra income for grade-school or high-school educators, who are highly sought after for this purpose.

Japanese middle-class as well as lower-class mothers will make countless sacrifices, including taking on extra work, to provide the money necessary for tutors and other additional educational expenses so that their children will be in a better competitive position. The reason for the recent widespread increase in the use of tutors is that, whereas mothers previously were able to help their own children, including doing their homework for them, they now find themselves inadequate to help due to the recent changes in curriculum. Attempts to see that the teacher pays special attention to one's own child lead to a great deal of what Americans would consider the tacit bribery of teachers through lavishing on them gifts that go far beyond the legendary apple given an American teacher.

To illustrate, the city of Ashiya between Osaka and Kobe has a large number of upper-middle-class and upper-class residents. School teachers there are known to receive lavish "gifts" including tailored suits. It has been considered quite a plum to become a teacher placed in this area. It was traditional for teachers to receive gifts from the parents of their students and was not considered unethical to do so. Nevertheless, the gift-giving competition in Ashiya had reached such a point that the teachers themselves held a meeting in order to find some means of restraining this practice within acceptable bounds. The parental competition had become so fierce that the teachers became concerned with whether they could maintain any integrity in the face of the implicit obligations incurred.

One of the worst features of this intense preoccupation with the education of one's own child is the tension that arises between neighbors. As indicated, a woman can judge herself a failure unless her children do well at school, and mothers are made to feel a terrible sense of inadequacy to the point of suffering a clinical depression or severe neurotic debilitation in attempting to keep up with the Tanakas. Moreover, the pressure the children feel causes a considerable strain on many of them throughout their childhood and preadulthood (Vogel, 1963).

Status competition between Japanese families in the middle class is not limited to the education of the child but also extends to material possessions. Competition is especially critical nowadays in the realm of household appliances. In the limited space of the small urban apartments that are increasingly used as dwellings for middle-class, so-called "salary men," it has become more important to acquire electric appliances than furniture. When television sets first appeared in large numbers, they immediately became a status symbol that one could not do without. It was reported that families living in apartments would put up a television aerial before they were able to purchase a set so that they would not be seen by their neighbors as deficient. Very recently, the most prized competitive possession has shifted to color television and to the automobile as necessary to the maintenance of proper middle-class status.

For the housewives, status is sometimes defined by such nuances as the richness of the bedding aired over the tiny balcony attached to each apartment. Kiefer (1968), in a study of apartment-house living, reports that one housewife would hang out some rich-looking undergarments to add status to her laundry, although she considered them far too expensive ever to wear. Salesmen visiting apartment-house areas take full advantage of the competitive attitudes in their selling techniques.

The Socialization of Dependency

To understand the emotional patterning underlying Japanese role behavior, it is essential to examine the peculiarities of socialization that lead modern Japanese, as they did those in preceding generations, to emphasize emotional interdependency, whether in the family or in other organizations (Caudill and Scarr, 1962) . Caudill, in his ongoing intensive research on maternal care and infant behavior in Japan compared with that in the United States (Caudill and Weinstein, 1966) , finds that in the socialization of children intensive and continual body contact between the mother and her young children emphasizes certain attitudes. Compared to Westerners, the Japanese remain much more conscious of the satisfaction to be found in skin contact and oral sensuality. This consciousness of the pleasures of the body is further encouraged by customs of bathing and massaging, and, in effect, by the attention to textural details of food, art, and language.

Hovering nurturance, which persists to a far later age in Japanese than in American culture, tends to modify aggressive independence. The child is disciplined by threats of isolation rather than by the inhibition of free movement. The child learns to rely upon ready access to gratifications afforded by his mother. He is not encouraged to distantiate himself from the mother nor to seek independent means of coping with his environment as he is in Western socialization.

The Japanese are extremely conscious in their childrearing of a need to satisfy the feelings of dependency developed within an intense mother-child relationship in order to maintain compliance and obedience. Good will must be maintained so that the child will willingly undertake the increasingly heavy requirements and obligations placed upon him in the school and the home.

On a deeper psychodynamic level, the child serves as an extension of the mother's own ego. Many women have strong achievement needs or desire to express potentials for dominance and other instrumental potentials within their personality by binding the son permanently to herself through the maintenance of nurturant control. The mother in effect uses the son as a masculine extension of her own ego. These underlying psychodynamics help to explain why many mothers become so fiercely competitive with the daughter-in-law who may seek to intrude and break up the hold the mother maintains over the son.

Such emotional undercurrents may be too much for some individuals to bear, and various forms of psychological neurotic debilitation or even psychosis can result. The particular burdens placed by the traditional culture are still evident in the revelation of William Caudill's research that in Japanese mental institutions there is significant overrepresentation of eldest sons (Caudill, 1964).

What is apparent in past patterns of socialization and what seems to be continuing today in intense mother-child relationships is the exercise of seemingly unconscious mechanisms of control by women through the manipulation of the dependent needs of a child.

The converse of such manipulation in this diadic relationship is the manipulation, again either consciously or unconsciously, of the potential giver by the dependent person. This type of manipulation is explicitly recognized by the culture in the well-used word *amae,* which in Western European languages has no direct counterpart. "Amae," as Doi (1962) points out, is an active verb in Japanese, designating an induction of nurturance toward one's self on the part of others. Such passive induction cannot be directly expressed in an active intransitive verb in Western languages. To *amaeru* is to produce passively the state of being loved and indulged by another, a form of emotional judo.

Doi very cogently relates the presence of *amaeru* to a peculiar lack of individuation frequently found in Japanese. He points out that the attitude of *amae* is related to a lack of realization, or even a desire for realization, of an autonomous ego on the part of many Japanese. This is consonant with the emphasis on interdependency noted in Japanese role relationships.

The passivity and dependency of *amae* can be much more egosyntonic for a Japanese than for a Westerner and is without the sense of shame or personal discomfort that a Westerner would feel if, as an adult, he gave himself over to a passive, dependent, yet manipulative role in his social relationships. Such a posture, if conscious, goes counter to the Western ideal of personal autonomy.

For the Japanese male who maintains a lifelong dependent attachment to his mother, there is no feeling of internal conflict, no matter how disappointed his wife is in him when he fails to assert himself in the frequent conflicts between mother and wife. Characteristically, the disappointed wife learns, in turn, to manipulate her husband's passive dependence to her own purposes. She also affectively turns to her own children, insuring the continuation of the pattern into the next generation.

Although Japanese women may be more psychodynamically independent than men in some respects, many of them, through their manipulations, are eliciting *amae* from a grown son. The role requirements for Japanese women wean them from whatever expectations they may have had of remaining dependent on their own mothers. Sometimes, dependent expectations are transferred to the exacting mother-in-law by a young bride, with resultant tensions and unhappiness. In the past, in some sections of Japan, young brides would suffer from "fox possession." Clinically viewed, this behavior was essentially an hysterical psychological disturbance which, while indicative of expressed needs, would also have the unconscious instrumental purpose of bringing forth on one's self the nurturant attendance of others.

The present-day overrepresentation of youngest daughters in Japanese mental hospitals, reported by Caudill (1964), gives evidence that the peculiarities of this role position, which are related to the practice of *amaeru,* can cause serious internal disturbances in psychological integration.

Affiliation

From role commitment to companionship in modern Japan. As indicated, affiliative needs such as intimacy and companionship were not institutionalized as a desideratum of an ideal Japanese marriage. Marriage was a family connection, not an attempted realization of individual needs. A woman became a wife to her husband by means of becoming a member of his family. The objective of marriage was the production of children to continue the *ie.* The serious purpose of marriage was not the forging of a bond between man and wife, but rather the assumption of the parental roles with the appearance of children.

Sex as an expression of mutual affection was not only deemphasized, but even sometimes suppressed, because undue emphasis on affective sexual needs was considered a form of selfish assertion of individuality that could become disruptive to the harmonious functioning of the total household. The important role for a woman was her service function to her children, husband, parents-in-law. Sexual reciprocity and feelings of companionship between spouses might appear but were not to be expected. To make a rather exaggerated comparison, one might almost equate the Japanese housewife in the traditional family to an efficient secretary in an American business company, where any undue emphasis on the sexual aspects of the secretary as an attractive young woman could become disruptive to the smooth functioning of role relationships within the office.

For the man, sexuality, rather than being deemphasized, tended to be deflected as a secondary source of pleasure to be satisfied periodically away from home in the special world of entertainment where women were more explicitly trained to please the sexual needs of men. As has often been indicated, unlike the repressive Christian tradition of the West, sex and bodily feelings were never considered "bad" as defined by Shinto or Confucian ethics. Acceptable sex was, rather, a matter of time and circumstance. A man could easily indulge in outside sexual activities without feelings of guilt as long as he did nothing to disturb the good order and functioning of the *ie.* It was even considered permissible to maintain a mistress on a long-term basis if it did not decrease the financial support of the family. However, should the outside affair become one of such serious financial involvement, everything would be done to apply sanctions to the offending individual.

Such flagrant maintenance of a mistress is no longer readily endured by modern housewives—mistresses have gone underground as has prostitution.

Because of their strong emotional attachment to their own mothers and their basically dependent attitudes toward women, many Japanese men in the traditional culture, as well as today, suffered in varying degrees from a sense of sexual inadequacy or anxiety about their physical prowess as males. Nevertheless, since the man's role vis-à-vis the woman's role in the Japanese culture was clearly defined and prescribed, underlying anxiety about one's sexual prowess could be covered up. As long as a man played the role of a man and husband, supported by his wife's playing her role, he was to some degree protected from facing possible internal sexual problems. In fact, today, when the marriage of companionship has become a recognized ideal and women's magazines emphasize women's right to sexual expressiveness and satisfaction, a type of confrontation often occurs that did not in the past. More explicit resolutions in one way or another become necessary.

The amazing number of bars and places of amusement having bar girls and hostesses in today's Japan attest to the fact that female companionship outside the home still remains highly desirable for many men. But, even in the world of bar hostesses, one must note that the sexuality of the man often could be termed pregenital, that is, not necessarily leading to the completion of the sexual act. The role of the bar girl very often takes the form of a type of ego-boosting, making the man feel important and giving him minor oral gratification. Aggressive male behavior is an ideal realized by relatively few Japanese men. The Turkish bath has become the site for present-day prostitution, and very often the sexual behavior consummated there is a form of passive masturbation, rather than active genital congress in which aggressive as well as sexual needs are satisfied.

One of the major role changes within Japanese culture is the role of the prostitute. In the past, it was a more romanticized role in which the prostitute was often viewed as a basically innocent person who, through the impoverishment of her family, was sold into a house of prostitution, a role she dutifully submitted to on behalf of her family. The modern prostitute or "pan pan" girl is pictured as a more active, aggressive, and "tough" type of person, whose activities are controlled by gangsters, whereas in the past, houses of prostitution were run as businesses by traditional families who passed on their business from one generation to the next. The owners of houses of prostitution would live within the brothel with their entire family, and often the wife would assist in its management.

Sleeping patterns and sexual intimacy. Japanese sleeping patterns tend to limit the opportunity for sexuality between parents. There is a persistence of patterns in which children sleep in the same room as their parents (Caudill and Plath, 1966). There is a usual progression in family sleeping patterns in which the youngest child continues to sleep next to the mother, the second youngest by the father, and the older children sometimes by a grandmother or other adult. A Japanese house lends itself little to privacy, so that the parents must use opportunities when children are absent or asleep for sexual congress. A frequent sexual position, therefore, is that in which the husband approaches his wife from the rear while the couple are lying on their sides. A minimum amount of noise is created in this position. One must note that the amount of sexual play allowed for under these circumstances is minimal. The material from our lower-class working samples substantiates the conclusions drawn by Caudill and Plath that even where separate space is available, child and adult members of the family tend to sleep together. In our sample, there were even mothers who would sleep with the children while the father slept alone. Young children, especially, are never put to sleep by themselves in a room. There is no provision for a crib type of arrangement that would limit the child to the area of his bedding if he should wake up. Therefore, it seems necessary for a mother or some other person always to sleep by an infant or small child.

Postwar changes in premarital sexual communication. During the past five or six years, there has been a notable increase in the practice of "dating." Before World War II, the sexes were segregated beyond the primary schools, but with educational reforms all public schools became coeducational. However, until quite recently one could observe patterns of informal segregation maintained along sex lines. High school boys and girls could not be unduly familiar with one another in any form, and dating by couples in the American sense was considered extremely improper. Informal sanctions were maintained by the students themselves in this respect. But in the last five years, in the very large cities at least, one can observe much more companionship between youths of opposite sexes. Not only is dating taking place, but also one observes couples walking hand in hand; generally speaking, much more direct physical contact occurs among youth in public than did formerly.

The amount of change in this area is documented by Shinozaki (1953), who has compared recent and earlier behavior in a study of colleges and who reports that most students in his sample taken more than ten years ago had never dated. If dating occurred, it usually started after graduation from college. Asayama (1958), comparing Americans and Japanese and referring explicitly to the material in the Kinsey report, found that only 10 percent of eighteen-year-olds in his Japanese sample reported any experiences of kissing, compared with more than 90 percent of American youth. If a similar survey were done today, the dissimilarities between Japanese and American students would be notably less striking.

Nevertheless, even today arranged marriages persist throughout Japan. The principal reason for this, in our opinion, is psychological, and the practice is not due now to any social sanctioning or forces of legal codes, as it was in the past. Marriage for modern Japanese still involves responsibility and obligation to parents, but even more important on a psychodynamic level is the general unwillingness in many Japanese to assume individual responsibility for decision-making either in marriage or, often, in choosing a job career. Many Japanese remain emotionally dependent. Making one's own marriage decision is a frightening prospect that implies the necessity to affirm symbolically one's independence from parents and relatives, an independence that means one can no longer turn to them for assistance or succor in times of need. Although most Japanese consider personal autonomy as highly desirable, it is too frightening a responsibility to assume in making the major decisions of life related to vocation and marriage. Vogel cites a number of forms of marriage arrangement still current in contemporary Japan (Vogel, 1963).

Today, therefore, dating must be considered a form of "playing around" prior to firm commitment to the serious business of life. Similarly, on an intellectual level, youth will espouse political and social causes that they immediately renounce once they commit themselves to some particular business or professional organization. In our interviews with lower-class subjects, we noted that there may be some informal sexual liaisons before marriage, but if a child is born there is usually serious job commitment and the assumption of family responsibility. Such drifting into a marriage bond is not a very frequent occurrence, even in the Japanese lower class. More characteristic is the pattern in which either his boss or a relative will decide for a young man that it is time for him to settle down, and will help him find a suitable mate.

Even when the young couple decide to marry on their own initiative, in order to maintain interdependent ties with their parents and relatives, some form of arrangement will usually be established by an accommodating go-between to give the marriage the proper aura of respectability. We can cite as an example of the continuity of marriage tradition under new guise the recent occurrence in an upper middle-class family known to one of the authors. The son of an American-educated university professor, before leaving for the United States for his graduate work, brought his girl friend home and introduced her to his mother, his purpose being to have her "trained properly" by his mother in the role of a competent Japanese bride. This "responsible" behavior on the part of their son pleased the parents very much. However, psychodynamically what was involved was the son's continuing sense of dependency on his mother, and in actuality what he was seeking was some assurance that he could maintain the maternal tie unbroken.

Problems of companionship in "bed town." One of the chief complaints voiced by modern apartment-house dwellers is the lack of time for companionship between married couples because so many men commute daily to offices sometimes up to an hour and a half distant from home. In fact, however, many husbands do not hurry home in the evening, but stop at bars for an hour or two, or even longer, arriving at home just in time to go to bed. Hence, the nickname "Bed Town" for some of the apartment areas. Men also earn the nickname *Gozensama* (Mr. Earlier Morning) by returning home after midnight most of the week, just making the last midnight train. The prevalence of this practice means that, whatever their ideals of companionship and home life, in many middle-class families the actual time spent together is limited to Sundays, which by new norms are supposedly devoted to wife and children. However, one notes that cartoons, such as one depicting an exhausted husband trailing behind a more energetic wife and children visiting a zoo or some other place of recreation on a weekend, give the impression that what a husband would truly like to do is lie down and sleep through the weekend break.

Danchi, apartment-house wives, interviewed in 1959 by Masuda gave as the three most important traits for an ideal husband, good health, a stable high income, and an understanding attitude toward wife and children (Masuda, 1960). They did not select other possible choices, such as that the husband return home early at a regular time. Implicit in this survey and others like it is that, even today, women's implicit expectations of their husbands' role do not include much sustained companionship or affiliative interest in the wife beyond showing periodic consideration. The chief concern of the wife is that the husband maintain his health and not strain himself unduly so that their income will be assured. In a number of these new "Bed Town" communities, women have taken on most of the concern with the community functions through women's organizations. The PTA, for example, has become more a women's organization, and less time and attention are given by men; people often joke about the PTA as actually being an MTA (Mama-Teacher Association).

Robert Blood (1967) reports a study done among middle-class apartment dwellers in Tokyo approximately ten years ago. His sample was drawn from among the so-called "salary men," that is, husbands employed by large corporations, the majority of whom were college graduates. By and large, the apartment-house dwellers tended to be younger couples with preadolescent children; a fairly large proportion of the women did some sort of part-time work. In this sample of rather progressive people, he compared the nature of the differences in the affectional ties between those who had made a self-initiated love marriage and those who were married through the more traditional forms of marriage arrangement. The differences between these two groups of apartment dwellers in the same apartment area are not so great as some might anticipate. Nevertheless, a few slight trends reach significance on some variables. Comparing marital satisfactions, the affectional attitudes within love marriages are significantly better than those in arranged marriages. But, interestingly enough, women in arranged marriages tend to be a little more satisfied with the husband's vocational ability, decision-making capacity, and actual helpfulness in the home. All differences are extremely slight.

Blood also compared his Tokyo sample with a sample of household residents in the Detroit area. It is interesting to note that there was a striking similarity in the answers to a number of questions asked of couples in Detroit and Tokyo, although there was a differential ranking as to what produces marital satisfaction. Whereas love and affection are cited both by the Tokyo and Detroit sample as the highest source of marital satisfaction, the Tokyo sample ranks "wife as mother" or "husband as father" as a close second in the hierarchy of factors leading to satisfaction. Sex ranks sixth, and companionship ranks tenth for husbands and ninth for wives in Tokyo. Companionship, in contrast, ranks second to love and affection as the principal source of marital satisfaction for the Detroit sample.

In the Tokyo sample, frequency of sexual intercourse has a direct correlation with marital satisfaction: in only 27 percent of those having intercourse less than once a week did both partners see themselves as basically satisfied with their marriage. It should be noted that the emphasis on sexuality and the frequency of sexual intercourse is greater in couples making a love marriage than in those whose marriage was arranged.

Adultery on the part of wives is quite rare in Japan compared to the United States. It is part of the Japanese conception of the woman's role to remain faithful to her husband, ideally even after his death. Although faithfulness is also part of a Western woman's role expectations, the Japanese woman adheres to her role requirements much more strongly than does her Western counterpart. To commit adultery is to give up and to consider one's self a failure as a wife or mother. When adultery occurs in Japan, the wife's motive is most frequently retaliation. Even in the past, when it was the wife's role to admit to a double standard of marital fidelity, many women bore deep feelings of resentment about their husband's mistresses. Although, among successful businessmen of the more conservative type, it is still considered a mark of status and male prowess to be able to maintain a mistress, there is a besetting fear of the potential wrath of the wife. The attitude is sometimes that of a small boy stealing cookies from his mother's kitchen. In episodes in comics or movies of male adultery with women of the entertainment world, much humor is extracted from the man's fear of discovery by his wife. The wife is most often depicted as a fearsome person, more like a mother catching a boy at some indecent activity. The male is seldom depicted as a browbeating tyrant in accord with the Western stereotype of the behavior of a Japanese husband.

Among the favorite Japanese comic strips is that of "Kappa Tengoku" (*kappa*—heaven) in which the latent dominance that men fear in women within their own society is satirized as the manifest form of life in the mythological world of Japanese water sprites. The male *kappa* has a difficult time contending with his formidable spouse.

One of the benefits of belonging to a new religious sect such as *Rissho Koseikai* or *Seīchō-no-Ie* is the individual counseling received by middle-aged wives, who are helped to resign themselves to the fact that after all husbands are really grown-up boys who sometimes consort with women much as children become intrigued by new toys. Women are taught not to take this flighty behavior of their husbands too seriously, but to rely on the fact that maternal behavior binds the man to his wife by dependent ties. The women are reassured in these sessions in which they can share in an institutionalized way in understanding that the maternal nurturant role of marriage puts the wife really in the controlling position within her own household. This emphasis on the maternal aspect of the traditional woman's role rather than on the sexual one reconciles many middle-aged women to the necessity of deemphasizing their own sexual needs or to their incapacity to experience the pleasures of the female orgasm. Increasingly, however, the younger women are taught through the women's magazines to seek some sense of personal adequacy in "a capacity for orgasm." More recently the tone of some of these articles has taken on a more extrapunitive note and husbands are blamed for their lack of finesse and "stamina" (now a Japanese word) in helping women achieve sexual satisfaction. Japanese academicians writing about marriage roles tend to ignore the apparently considerable impact of these women's magazines on the expectations of the younger generation of Japanese couples.

With the postwar legal emancipation of women from their previously inferior position there has been overt recognition of their potential for dominant or assertive traits, always behaviorally latent in the woman's role in the past. One can state that the younger Japanese today is no longer content in a marriage that necessitates the relinquishment of expressive needs for communication or the lapse into a type of proximate living in which one's thoughts remain private and uncommunicated within the family unit. They are seeking, whether they find it or not, some form of companion in marriage as the ideal for themselves. Characterologically, however, there is an impaired capacity in many Japanese to realize this ideal owing to the continuity of emphasis on dependency and its manipulation as basic in interpersonal situations.

Conclusion

In a paean of praise to the role behavior of Japanese women toward the end of the last century, Lafcadio Hearn declared that ". . . the most wonderful 'aesthetic' products of Japan are not its ivories . . . nor any of its marvels in metal or lacquer—but its women," and that, ". . . the Japanese woman is an ethnically different being from the Japanese man. . . ." (Hearn, 1935). Impressions of Japanese women by Westerners have done much until recent times to confirm this stereotyped image of the Japanese woman as a graceful, delicate, quiet wife ready for self-sacrifice in her dedicated subservience to parents-in-law, husband, and children. Her husband, in contrast, is often conceived of as an arrogant despot who does not even hesitate to let his wife pay the bills forwarded to her from the brothels he frequents.

While living examples of these role polarities can still be found, they by no means represent the reality of Japanese social sex roles as they are played in the present day, or as they were played in the past. Japanese marital relationships and patterns of family life in the past, as well as in the present, allowed for considerable mutual satisfaction in some spheres of expressive behavior, in fact considerably more satisfaction than appeared on the surface to Western eyes. Basic traits of character never divided so clearly along sex lines as the more rigid and ritualistic quality of the formalities required in premodern Japan would suggest. Although the range of permitted role behavior has vastly broadened in the present day, one can note that men and women in actualizing their behavior still to a very great degree show continuities with the past in motivational structure. The degree to which one is gratified or not gratified in interpersonal relationships within the family still relates to underlying implicit role expectations that do not differ much from the past in spite of the freer manners of the present day.

Nor are instrumental patterns related to achievement, competence, responsibility, or control greatly dissimilar to those found in the past culture. Changes are occurring in present-day Japanese, especially in those under thirty, but it is not yet possible to determine whether the ultimate direction taken by Japanese culture in the definition of role relationships will be completely congruent with that of Western modernization. To some degree, at least, patterns of instrumental behavior, as well as patterns of self-expression, harmony and discord, affiliation, dependency and nurturance, will continue to be maintained in terms of the interpersonal needs of personality characteristics conditioned or socialized by Japanese culture.

Notes

[1] One of the striking differences between delinquent families and nondelinquent normal controls was relatively unrestrained impulsive behavior and other marks of inadequate maternal supervision, as well as overt expressions of dissatisfaction with the marriage on the part of women.

[2] The Eugenic Protection Law of Japan (Yusei Hogo Ho):

Article XIV, Paragraph 1: A physician, appointed by the prefectural or municipal medical association, upon obtaining an agreement from the person concerned or her husband, can administer an artificial abortion to the person to whom one of the following conditions applies:

(1) The person or her husband has psychosis, feeble-mindedness, psychopathic quality, inheritable physical disease or inheritable physical deformity.
(2) The person or her husband has a kinsman of the fourth degree of consanguinity (or of the closer degree) who has psychosis, feeble-mindedness, psychopathic quality, inheritable physical disease or inheritable physical deformity.
(3) The person or her husband has leprosy.
(4) The person's health will be seriously endangered by the continuation of pregnancy or by the childbirth on the basis of physical or financial reasons.
(5) The person has been impregnated by rape or by threat, or by sexual intercourse that took place during the state in which the person was unable to resist or refuse such an intercourse.

Article XIV, Paragraph 2: In case in which the person's husband is unknown or is unable to express his will or is dead after the pregnancy of the person, the agreement from the person only is sufficient for the administration of an artificial abortion.
(Practically "free" artificial abortion is practiced, if not "illegally" and without registration, on the basis of a liberal interpretation of the meaning of Item 3 of Paragraph 1 of Article XIV of the Japanese Eugenic Protection Law, as cited above.) (Translation by H. W.)

[3] Bowles, Gordon. Personal Communications.

References

Asahi Nenkan (Asahi Almanac). Tokyo: Asahi Press, 1968.

Asayama, Shin-ichi. *Nijusseiki no Sekkusu* (*Sex in The Twentieth Century*). Tokyo: Chuōkoron-Sha, 1958.

Beardsley, Richard K., John W. Hall, and Robert E. Ward. *Village Japan.* Chicago: University of Chicago Press, 1959.

Bellah, Robert. *Tokugawa Religion: The Values of Pre-Industrial Japan.* Glencoe, Illinois: Free Press, 1957.

Benedict, Ruth. *The Chrysanthemum and the Sword: Patterns of Japanese Culture.* Boston: Houghton Mifflin, 1946.

Bennett, J., and I. Ishino. *Paternalism in the Japanese Economy; Anthropological Studies of Oyabun-Kobun Patterns.* Minneapolis: University of Minnesota Press, 1963.

Blood, Robert. *Love Match and Arranged Marriage.* Glencoe, Illinois: Free Press, 1967.

Brown, Keith. "'Dozoku' and the Ideology of Descent in Rural Japan." *American Anthropologist,* 68 (1966), 1129–51.

Caudill, William. "Sibling Rank and Style of Life among Japanese Psychiatric Patients." In *Proceedings of the Joint Meeting of the Japanese Society of Psychiatry and Neurology and the American Psychiatric Association,* Haruo Akimoto, ed. Tokyo: *Folia Psychiatrica et Neurologica,* 7 (1964), 35–40.

——— and George De Vos. "Achievement, Culture and Personality: The Case of the Japanese Americans." *American Anthropologist,* 58, 6 (1956), 1102–26.

——— and David Plath. "Who Sleeps by Whom: Parent-Child Involvement in Urban Japanese Families." *Psychiatry,* 29 (1966), 344–66.

——— and Harry A. Scarr. "Japanese Values Orientation and Culture Change." *Ethnology,* 1 (1962), 53–91.

——— and Helen Weinstein. "Maternal Care and Infant Behavior in Japanese and American Urban Middle-Class Families." In *Yearbook of the International Sociological Association,* Rene Koenig and Reuben Hill, eds. Switzerland: Broz, 1966.

Cornell, John. "Dozoku: An Example of Evolution and Transition in Japanese Village Society." *Comparative Studies in Society and History,* 6 (1964), 449–80.

De Vos, George. "The Relation of Guilt toward Parents to Achievement and Arranged Marriage among the Japanese." *Psychiatry,* 23, 3 (1960), 287–301.

———. "Deviancy and Social Change: A Psychocultural Evaluation of Trends in Japanese Delinquency and Suicide." In *Japanese Culture: Its Development and Characteristics,* Robert J. Smith and Richard K. Beardsley, eds. Chicago: Aldine, 1962, pp. 153–70.

———. "Role Narcissism and the Etiology of Japanese Suicide." Paper read at the *First International Congress of Social Psychiatry.* London, August 1964.

———. "Social Values and Personal Attitudes in Primary Human Relationships in Niike." In *Occasional Papers,* University of Michigan Center for Japanese Studies, 9 (1965a), 53–91.

———. "Achievement Orientation, Social Self-Identity, and Japanese Economic Growth." *Asian Survey,* 5, 12 (1965b), 575–89.

———. "Achievement and Innovation in Culture and Personality." In *The Study of Personality: An Interdisciplinary Appraisal,* Edward Norbeck, ed. Rice University Symposium. New York: Holt, Rinehart & Winston, 1968a.

———. "Suicide in Cross-Cultural Perspective." In *Suicidal Behavior: Diagnosis and Management,* H. L. P. Resnik, ed. Boston: Little, Brown, 1968b.

——— and Hiroshi Wagatsuma. "Psycho-Cultural Significance of Concern over Death and Illness among Rural Japanese." *International Journal of Social Psychiatry,* 5, 1 (1959), 6–19.

———. "Value Attitudes toward Role Behavior of Women in Two Japanese Villages." *American Anthropologist,* 63, 6 (1961), 1204–30.

———. *The Heritage of Endurance.* Berkeley, Calif.: University of California Press, 1971.

Doi, Takeo. "Japanese Language As an Expression of Japanese Psychology." *Western Speech,* 20 (1956), 90–96.

———. "'Amae': A Key Concept for Understanding Japanese Personality Structure." In *Japanese Culture: Its Development and Characteristics,* Robert J. Smith and Richard K. Beardsley, eds. Chicago: Aldine, 1962, 132–39.

Durkheim, Emile. *The Elementary Forms of the Religious Life.* Joseph W. Swain, trans. London: Allen & Unwin, 1915.

Ema, T. *Nihon Fūzoku Zenshi* (*Complete History of Japanese Customs*). Vol. 1. Kyoto: Yamamoto Bunka dō, 1925.

Freud, Sigmund. "The Economic Problem of Masochism." *Collected Papers.* Vol. 2. New York: Basic Books, 1955.

Gibney, Frank. *Five Gentlemen of Japan, the Portrait of a Nation's Character.* New York: Farrar Straus & Young, 1953.

Green, Arnold. "The Middle-Class Male Child and Neurosis." *American Sociological Review,* 11 (1946), 31–41.

Hearn, Lafcadio. *Japan: An Attempt at Interpretation.* Tokyo: Tuttle, 1935.

Kiefer, Christie W. *Social Change and Personality in a White Collar Danchi.* University of California, Berkeley, Department of Anthropology, 1968. Unpublished Ph.D. dissertation.

Kitano, Seiichi. "'Dozoku' and 'Ie' in Japan: The Meaning of Family Genealogical Relationships." In *Japanese Culture: Its Development and Characteristics,* Robert J. Smith and Richard K. Beardsley, eds. Chicago: Aldine, 1962, pp. 42–46.

Masuda, Kōkichi. *Tekkin Apāto-gai no Seikatsu o Saguru (Exploration of Life in Concrete Apartment Houses)*. Nishinomiya: Nishinomiya Educational Commission, 1960.

Muramatsu, Tsuneo, ed. *Nihonjin-Bunka to Pāsonariti no Jisshoteki Kenkyū (The Japanese—An Empirical Study in Culture and Personality)*. Tokyo: Reimei Shobō, 1962.

Nagai, Michio. "Dozoku: A Preliminary Study of the Japanese 'Extended Family' Group and Its Social and Economic Functions (Based on the Research of K. Ariga)." *Ohio State University Research Foundation, Interim Technical Report,* 7 (1953).

Parsons, Talcott, and Robert F. Bales. *Family Socialization and Interaction Process.* Glencoe, Illinois: Free Press, 1955.

Reik, Theodor. *Masochism in Modern Man.* Beigel and Kurth, trans. New York: Grove, 1941.

Shinozaki, Nobuo. *Nihon Jin no Sei Seikatsu (The Sexual Life of the Japanese)*. Tokyo: Bungei Shuppan-Sha, 1953.

Taeuber, I. B., and F. W. Notestein. "The Changing Fertility of the Japanese." *Population Studies,* 1 (1947), 2–28.

Tawney, R. H. *Religion and the Rise of Capitalism.* New York: Harcourt Brace, 1926.

Vogel, Ezra F. "Entrance Examinations and Emotional Disturbances in Japan's 'New Middle Class.'" In *Japanese Culture: Its Development and Characteristics, op. cit.* Chicago: Aldine, 1962, pp. 140–52.

———. *Japan's New Middle Class.* Berkeley: University of California Press, 1963.

Wagatsuma, Hiroshi. "Japanese Values of Achievement: The Study of Japanese Inhabitants of Three Japanese Villages by Means of TAT." Ann Arbor: University of Michigan, 1957. Unpublished master's thesis.

——— and George De Vos. "Attitudes toward Arranged Marriage in Rural Japan." *Human Organization,* 21, 3 (1962), 187–200.

Wagatsuma, Sakae and Shinkichi Unno, eds. *Katei no Hōritau Kyakka (Home Handbook of Law)*. Tokyo: Nihon Hyōron Shinsha, 1958.

Yamata, Kikou. *Three Geisha.* New York: John Day, 1956.

17 SEX ROLES IN THE MODERN FABRIC OF CHINA

Stanley L. M. Fong

When the sound of China is heard, especially in the West, it often strikes a mystical chord. Through the years a lot of strange and fascinating tales have been told by travelers of the sights they have seen. In their wanderings they have come upon many things and observed a different, and somewhat curious, way of life. Sometimes the differences stand out in clear relief, while others are muted. This article will try to unravel and explicate some of the differing and contrasting strands between the East and the West.

The social roles of males and females in the Orient often differ from those in the West. But boys and girls, men and women, in various parts of the world, do share certain similarities, and these universal human aspects should not be overlooked. The two sexes often face the same basic problems of life together and these shared troubles and joys at times overshadow the differences. There is no denying, however, that there are some differences. What is it that makes a man and a woman distinguishable from each other? Beyond the style of clothing, it seems that it is the social fabric that affects the way the sexes behave.

In this chapter, the two sexes will be viewed from the role perspective. People may be looked at in terms of their positions in the social fabric. The places that they have in society will ordinarily define the roles that they will play in life. Every one, of course, will have more than just one role to play in the social system. He or she, for instance, has a number of roles to perform in the family, at work, and so on. On the whole, though, the two sexes are typically given, or assigned to, different social positions in society. Generally, the social roles of the sexes delineate the way they are to relate to one another and to society at large. Individuals are interwoven into the fabric of society primarily by the web of connections between social roles. Thus, it appears that the sexes are shaped by society to a degree, for they have to fit into it.

It is important to know what kind of society the individual has to fit into, for the fabric of one society is not the same as that of another. The contours of a society will be affected, no doubt, by the specifics of the environment, such as whether it is primarily rural or urban. Yet there are some loose ends in the social fabric. If the fabric is ill-fitting or uncomfortable, individuals may try to change the shape of society. Changes are likely to be on a small scale and in the nature of variations on a major theme. Such minor variations seem to be fairly typical of societies that are more or less stable. If, on the other hand, the society is in a state of flux and perhaps moving in a new direction, wide variations from the basic pattern may occur.

When a society changes its contours, some of the patterns inside it will also be altered. A shift in the shape of society often alters the traditional relationships between the sexes. Such transformations are frequently noted in societies that are changing their agrarian forms to more industrialized ones. In the redesigning of a society, changes usually take place gradually, but some sharp breaks may occur, as is true of some social revolutions. The tempo of the times, however, may affect some aspects of the social fabric to a greater extent than others. With regard to sex roles, for example, the role of the Chinese woman of today is different from that of yesterday, but certain basic patterns remain the same. Sex role changes are occurring before our eyes, but to understand the present it is essential to take a look back to the past, as well as forward to the future.

A look back

The vastness of China is awesome. It is a country of great contrasts. On the western border its forbidding mountains separate the country from the rest of the world. Desert wastelands account for the scant population on the west side of China and make it a most difficult area to approach. In the east, however, the great plains are fertile and population density is great. Because of natural barriers, the Chinese have achieved a remarkably high degree of cultural homogeneity.

The Chinese people are ethnically as well as culturally rather homogeneous, but some sharp differences exist in their appearance, temperament, and language. There are two Chinas formed by the gigantic Yangtze River that cuts the country into two halves—the "noodle-eaters" of the north, and the "rice-eaters" of the south. While both strains stemmed from the same Mongoloid stock, the stolid, raw-boned northerner is no more like the sleek, dark-skinned southerner than a Scandinavian is like a Slav. The average northerner is taller than his cousin in the south, and six-footers are common.

Topographically, the differences between North and South China are rather distinct. In the north, the countryside is semiarid, yellow, and dust-blown. The growing season is short, with a cold winter and hot summer, and the fields are checkered mostly with wheat. In the south, however, the country is wet, green, and humid. In the subtropical climate, a year-'round growing season exists, and the fields are decked with rice paddies. These contrasts between North and South China are somewhat overdrawn. Even so, they are so striking and distinct that they suggest two different geographical entities. And yet, there is far more in common between the two halves —socially, politically, and economically—than, say, between neighboring European states, which are quite distinct from one another.

In essence, China is a nation of farmers. About 85 percent of the people at midcentury still lived directly off the land (Forman, 1948). These are the people who have been the backbone of Chinese society. The land has always been the basic foundation of Chinese life and will continue to shape the destiny of the people.

Perhaps the most impressive evidence of China's homogeneity is the universality of the language. On the face of it, this appears to contradict the popular belief that a veritable Babel of tongues exists. This is true along the narrow strip of land stretching from Canton to Shanghai, where the spoken language seems to change from village to village. Outside of this belt the common dialect is Mandarin, the official language. In any case, it may be noted that the written language is uniform throughout China.

One of the oldest surviving civilizations in the world today, China is steeped in the traditions of the past. In the last century its unity was shaken by the West, leaving a deep and lasting impression. This is most dramatically apparent in the political sphere, but deeper and more lasting influences may be discerned in the social and economic patterns of present-day China. But before examining the changes that took place in the fabric of Chinese society, it is important to look at the Chinese family system, the traditional core of Chinese life.

The Traditional Family

The traditional Chinese family system persisted for about two thousand years without any substantial change. It is the root of Chinese society and colors all social life. Confucianism is the social philosophy behind the family system. The principal idea is status, which gives every man and woman a definite place in society. If every man and woman knows his place and acts in accordance with his position, social order is assured. Of the "five cardinal human relationships," three of them are found in the family. They are: the relationship between father and son, the relationship between husband and wife, and the relationship between brother and brother. The remaining two are between emperor and subject, and between friend and friend (Lin, 1935). The family is obviously the starting point of all proper behavior.

In the Chinese family system, males occupy a superior position in relationship to females. The traditional family is patrilineal, where one's origin is traced through a common male ancestor. Thus, males occupy a prominent position in the social order. Because of the extent of kinship ties, the Chinese are able to trace their links to the past by way of ancestor worship, as well as to the future by way of generations to come. The bonds of kinship tie together a large number of people in society and exert a great influence on their social, economic, and political life.

Clan Structure

In traditional China, the family and the clan were the basic social units of organization (Freedman, 1966; Hsu, 1963). Quite often, the clan was the immediate and direct extension of the family. Outside his immediate family, a Chinese was bound by rights and duties to people related to him. A clan comprised people with the same surname, who stemmed from the same common ancestors. Sometimes, in the literature, the clans are referred to as "lineages," but the two terms are the same. Some clans were quite large. In certain parts of the country, especially in the southeast, some clans occupied an entire village or even a town.

In their social design, clans are the same all over the country. Characteristically, the clans assume the following functions: they possess certain forms of property, provide benefits for education and public welfare, care for the ancestral halls and graveyards, set certain rules of behavior, and settle disputes among clansmen.

In the villages, the Chinese were largely involved with their own branch of the lineage. Although individuals were tied together by common bonds, the various links differed in strength. The strongest bonds were based on close blood ties. Other factors affected the closeness or distance of the relationship. Inevitably, some families were rich and others were poor. Some Chinese moved around freely in political circles, and others were simple countrymen without any influence. Thus, even among the clan members, some basis of social distinction emerged.

It would be inaccurate to portray the clan simply as a large family. Its members were too numerous and various for that. It is therefore not surprising to see some unfamily-like behavior among clan members, such as a rich man's squeezing his debtor-kinsman, or a prominent elder's demanding deference from his inferior kinsman. In any case, minimal obligation had to be discharged toward clan members.

In the social structure of old China, a gentry class existed. Going back to the seventh century, any Chinese subject had the right to become an official if he passed an imperial examination (Lang, 1946). Usually, only the well-to-do were able to afford the time and the money needed to master the difficult Chinese script and to meet the high requirements of the examination boards. Traditionally, the gentry formed a link between the local society and the state (Michael, 1955). The local gentry would speak out for the interest of their communities and their clans.

Clans promoted the welfare of their members, thus serving as a mutual benefit society. The same principles applied to the family on an individual basis. This scheme fitted in with the Confucian view of order in which the units at the base of the social pyramid are expected to control themselves in the interest of the state. Thus, some separation of powers existed between the state and the clans. Yet clans were still considered by the state as part of its system of general control over such matters as politics and fiscal spending. In general, a man's obligations to the state were mediated through membership in his kinship group.

Of course, to be useful to the state, the clan had to be well-organized and strong. On the other hand, if the clan grew too strong and prosperous, it might begin to threaten the state. Growing clans occasionally fought one another for power (Freedman, 1962). Sometimes the balance of power swung over, and the powerful clan used its strength to overpower the state. Many a new dynasty came into being in this fashion.

It may be useful, at this juncture, to look at the individual Chinese family. Contrary to popular belief, the average Chinese family was not big; the average size was not more than five or six persons (Freedman, 1962; Lee, 1953). On the other hand, Chinese values encouraged blood relatives to live together under the same roof. Five generations living together was the exalted Chinese ideal of the extended family. But this was rarely realized in practice. Only those who possessed ample wealth were in a position to attain it. Interestingly, the extended family generally began to disintegrate at the moment when there were no longer enough resources for all. At such time, different branches were forced to take what could still be shared from the commonly owned property and go elsewhere. Quite understandably, the Chinese regard the division of a house as a mark of misfortune and the maintenance of a fairly large household as a sign of prosperity and prestige.

After having placed the family in its broader perspective, we may now shift the focus of analysis and look at the individuals comprising the family.

Males in Old Chinese Life

In traditional China, males were the focus of Chinese life while females remained in the background. Chinese males played a key role in the social fabric, for they were the vital ties of the patrilineal clan system. Still, every male had to observe his proper place in the larger design. In the family, a social hierarchy took into consideration generation, age, and sex. The members of the elder generation were superior to those of the younger, and within each generation the eldest had priority over the youngest (Lang, 1946).

The fabric of traditional China was tightly knit, and the steps that individuals took in it were highly circumscribed. The line of authority was clear-cut and remained indelible throughout the course of life. The elders maintained the voice of authority over the younger members. Even after a son was married, for example, he still had to obey his father, just as the father had to obey the grandfather. The Chinese are, as Hsu (1948) puts it, forever "under the ancestors' shadow."

The relationship between father and son is especially stressed, for it is considered the most important one in the family. This relationship, viewed as a link in an unending chain between generations, reaches up to ancestor worship and down to the "sin" of no posterity. Thus, it is said: "There are three things which are unfilial and to have no posterity is the greatest of them." If the family is not perpetuated through the generations, then the branch of the family would be broken.

The father is the symbol of dignity and sternness and is a very powerful figure at home, especially in comparison with Western societies. The power of the head of the household was given to him by the customs and laws of the Chinese empire, which were steeped in the spirit of Confucianism. The father officiated at all of the important ceremonies such as marriage, ancestor worship, and funerals. He also kept the title to all the family property and he alone could dispose of it, as well as of the earnings and savings of all the family members (Lang, 1946). But the father could not disinherit his sons at will, and property had to be equally divided among the sons.

Quite early the son was taught to look up to his father and to the venerable ancestors who came before him. The cult of ancestor worship instilled in him a reverential awe of the past. In terms of a livelihood, the son usually followed in the footsteps of his father. In rural China, the means of securing a livelihood were primarily transmitted within the family. Not only were tangible properties such as land, house, and livestock largely inherited, but also such crafts or skills as brewing, weaving, or painting were acquired through the father-son relationship (Lee, 1953). If a son wanted to be the legal heir to any of these, the first duty he learned as a child was to obey the family's rules. In turn, parents looked to their sons as their insurance against old age.

Because it was important to keep the fiber of the family intact, great care was taken to strengthen it. The web of order between the father and son was carefully spun. According to Hsu (1948), the Chinese male was admonished as soon as he was able to understand:

> . . . to obey his parents, especially his father, to the fullest extent; that it is bad behavior to question his wisdom or decisions; that it is good to do whatever he wants done without the slightest regard for one's own feelings; that it is not desirable to commit oneself to any independent line of action; that it is sinful to do anything which disturbs his father in any way; in other words, that he is to keep himself ready at all times, as long as he lives, to please him, and to be of all possible service to him [pp. 244–45].

Ideally, the younger person had no complaints against this arrangement because his turn would come when others would have to submit to his authority. In Hsu's (1948) words:

> Then the younger man takes the father's place in the great family continuum. In this way the thing of primary importance in shaping personality is the ancestral authority. The more reliance upon this authority the individual shows, the better adjusted he becomes throughout life. This authority over him and prearrangement for him run through every aspect of his life and work, including his marriage and means of livelihood. At every turn the individual is confined within this prearranged framework [p. 258].

The obligations of a daughter were not as great since her ties would be severed when she married into another family. The girls were therefore not as responsible as males for following in the footsteps of their ancestors.

In general, parental authority is a major theme of old Chinese culture. What effect did this type of training have on the Chinese male? As far as social behavior is concerned, the first outstanding quality was an explicitly submissive attitude toward authority. In a typical Chinese village there were very few uncertainties. To quote Hsu (1948) again:

> All routes are, so to speak, barred except one, that which follows the footsteps of his father, his father's father, and the whole line of his more remote ancestors. Along the established path, life is agreeable; all other trails lead to misery and self-destruction . . . He tends to be apprehensive of any departure from the beaten path. . . . [p. 260].

> The son owes to his father absolute obedience, and he must support his parents, mourn for them, bury them according to social station and financial ability, provide for their needs in the other world, and take all necessary steps toward insuring the male line. The younger man is obliged to do these things not only because of his duty to his parents but also because he is indebted to his and his father's common ancestors. Thus, from the point of view of kinship organization as a whole, the father-son identification is merely a necessary link in the great family continuum, with numerous ancestors at one end and innumerable descendents at the other [pp. 236–37].

In regard to the mother, the relationship was an especially affectionate one. The Chinese mother, as is true of all patriarchal families, expressed her love for her children to a greater extent than did the father. In the eyes of the Chinese, the mother was the symbol of kindness. It was quite beyond the mother's role to punish her son except to threaten to report him to the father (Lee, 1953). While the mother might occupy first place in the son's heart, Confucius did not list the mother-son relationship among the five most important ones. The Chinese mother rarely attained a position of real dominance in the family, but the devotion of her children probably brought her deeper gratification than many mothers in other countries (Lang, 1946).

In traditional China, the son honored his parents by his studious observance of filial piety. In dynastic China it was also possible to bring glory to the family by passing the imperial examinations. The entire family would thereby become distinguished. In this way even the poor peasant could make his way up in society. But the number of successful candidates was small. The odds were against the poor peasant because of his disadvantages in education. There are, however, a number of success stories of poor boys who made good. It may be noted in passing that this imperial route was not open to girls, for their place was in the home.

Females in Old Chinese Life

In traditional China, females were seen as inferior to males. The subjection of women was a singular thread running throughout the social fabric of China. It fitted in with the Confucian social philosophy in which a distinction between superiority and inferiority in social interaction was emphasized. Sexual inequality made its appearance at birth. A boy was joyfully received, while a girl was often not. In one of the folk songs in the ancient *Book of Poems,* there is the popular line: ". . . when a baby boy was born, he was laid on the bed, and given jade to play with, when a baby girl was born, she was laid on the floor and given a tile to play with" (Lin, 1935).

As girls grew up they became more aware of the preferential treatment given to their brothers. Their inferior position was regularly impressed upon them as in the "three obediences" required of a woman: when she is a girl, she obeys her father; when she is a wife, she obeys her husband; when she is a widow, she obeys her son. In the family, the social roles played by the sons and daughters were obviously different. The sons were the ones who were to bear the family name and be the legal heirs of the family property. On the other hand, the daughters were raised with an eye toward marrying out of the family. A daughter could only claim a dowry that amounted to a small fraction of the family property.

In times of great hardship, the inferiority of women became almost unbearably painful. The poor, forced by poverty and starvation, sometimes had to resort to the practice of female infanticide, a practice that persisted in China longer than in Europe because of the lower standard of living. In the case of older girls, they might be sold as servants, concubines, or child brides. Even wives were sold occasionally (Lang, 1946). As late as 1919, it was still legal for a man to sell his wife to another man for the purpose of begetting children (Freedman, 1962).

While boys were pampered, girls were often chastened by life's experiences. Superficially, although appearing soft and flower-like, the girls often possessed great inner strength. Chinese women never deceived Pearl S. Buck (1958) who said that they always seem to yield, but they never actually do. "Whence comes this female strength? It is the strength that centuries have given them, the strength of the unwanted" (p. 92). She saw that the son was given privileges, protection, and abundant love, while the daughter had to endure discrimination generation after generation, and had to bear it in silence.

Girls were to play their major role after marriage, but they were trained for this early in life. Young girls were inducted into the house, where they learned to tend to the fire, to cook, to wash, to clean, and to sew. Free play with boys was permitted before the age of ten, but after that they began to be segregated (Levy, 1949). With time, girls were more and more withdrawn from contact with outsiders. At home the girls perfected their skills and waited until a suitable match was arranged for them by their parents.

On this score, there was some difference between peasant and gentry families. The young peasant girls were less withdrawn from outside contact than were the gentry girls. This was due largely to their way of living. In the first place, the houses of the gentry were usually multi-unit affairs, with many interconnected passages surrounded by high outside walls. Gentry women did not have to go outside, for they had servants to run their errands for them. In the case of the peasants, their small living quarters afforded them less seclusion (Levy, 1949). Light inside the house was poor, and peasant girls frequently sat on their doorsteps or along the streets to do sewing and similar chores. They also did their washing along the nearby streams or canals. Since they had no servants, peasant girls often accompanied their mothers to the market. Sometimes they also helped out in the fields, and could not fail to come into contact with the men and women working on neighboring plots of land.

Education was thought unnecessary and even harmful. Girls did not need to read and write and acquire worldly knowledge, for their role was to be an obedient wife and a submissive daughter-in-law. Time and again, old Chinese men repeated: "A woman too well educated is apt to create trouble," or "A woman without talents is virtuous." There were some exceptions in scholarly families. As a rule, however, girls were illiterate, even in the best of families.

When the time for marriage came, a match was arranged for the girl by her parents. The union was arranged through the orders of the parents who enlisted the aid of a go-between, usually a woman. The amateur or professional matchmaker had to be someone whose words could be trusted by both parties concerned. In this enterprise, few decent families would be willing to expose their young daughters to inspection by members of any family other than close relatives. Any reliable information on the girl had to be obtained through a person who was acquainted with the girl and possessed intimate knowledge of her. In this matter the prospective groom's parents always took the initiative, while the bride's parents either accepted or rejected the proposal. After the bride price was agreed upon, and other considerations met, the marriage was settled. On the wedding day, the girl was married to a man she may never have met before. They did not have their own home, but lived with the husband's family. In the new family, the basic role of the wife was to perpetuate the family name by giving birth to male children. A wife was in trouble if she could not fulfill her childbearing role. Of the seven conditions for repudiation, the first is infertility (Lee, 1953). Even if a barren wife was tolerated, the husband was obligated to adopt a son or take a concubine.

In her new life, the first and foremost role of the girl was not that of a wife but of a daughter-in-law. The husband was himself in a subordinate position in a house governed by his father. The young couple had to fit into the grand design (Lee, 1953). As the Chinese idiomatic expression goes, a son does not marry a wife, but a daughter-in-law; when a son is born, the expression is that a grandson is born. So marriage is not just a matter of getting a wife for the son, but taking a new member into the family. It is expressed in the Confucian classics: a marriage is "a union between persons of different families, the object of which is to serve, on the one hand, the ancestors in the temple, and to perpetuate, on the other hand, the coming generation." Since marriage was not considered simply as a matter between two individuals, the personal adjustment between husband and wife was only a minor factor in the selection of a spouse. In practice, the most important factor in selecting a wife is perhaps the likelihood of a girl's getting along with the family members.

Since the two young people did not know each other before the wedding, the problem of adjustment for the newly married couple was a difficult one. The adjustment was made all the more difficult since they did not have their own home, but lived in the husband's family. Moreover, the two were usually fully grown adolescents who had never been alone with any adult member of the opposite sex before (Yang, 1945). In the case of the boy, the role of husband was secondary at best. Since it was, by custom, more important for him to remain a dutiful son and a good brother, the husband had to maintain closer relations with his family than with his wife. If a dispute ever arose between his wife and his mother, the husband would be expected to side with his mother.

Sometimes love and affection bloomed after a brief period of living together. But public demonstration of love toward other family members had priority over the wife. When the husband returned from a trip, for example, he had to greet his parents and his brothers and sisters before he greeted his wife. In fact, it was good taste to affect indifference to his wife, at least in public. In turn, a decent wife avoided sitting with her husband at social gatherings and acted as if she did not know him (Yang, 1945). Should any difficulties arise between the young couple, the bonds of wedlock were so tight that both of them, the wife especially, would have to resign themselves to the situation.

In the new family, the young wife had more duties and fewer rights than in the house of her parents. The training of the daughter-in-law in the new family was left in the hands of the mother-in-law. This was traditionally a point of friction. The harsh treatment of the young wife by the mother-in-law was one of the striking features of the Chinese family. This bitterness stemmed, in part, from the authoritarian character of the Chinese family and from the fact that the young couple stayed in the husband's family home. Lang (1946) commented that perhaps the mother avenged her own unhappy life and bad treatment when she was a daughter-in-law herself.

If the situation was unbearable, occasionally the girl might escape through suicide. If the attempt was unsuccessful, the in-laws would re-evaluate the situation, for if she had succeeded, the event would bring down disgrace on the parents-in-law and perhaps a lawsuit from her irate parents. Usually, attempts were made to alleviate the distress.

When a child was born, the wife was given new recognition immediately, especially if it were a boy. By the act of childbirth, the mother validated her position in the family. It is not surprising that many mothers made their primary emotional investment in their children. In the best spirit of Confucianism, it gave the mother an honored position in the home. In the future when she in turn became a mother-in-law, it would be truly a position of honor and power, well-earned by a life of service.

Traditionally, a Chinese woman did not have a life of her own. Even if her husband died while her sons were still boys, the three obediences required her to obey or to depend upon her sons. Perhaps the most miserable life of all was that of a young, childless widow, whose position was worse than that of a spinster; whatever virtue a widow may have possessed, she was regarded by legend as the most unlucky sign to any male. No bachelor would venture to marry her. On the other hand, it was difficult for her to find the courage to face the traditional stigma of unchastity and the disgrace of remarriage (Lee, 1953).

In upper- and middle-class families, the wife had one more problem to contend with—that of a plural marriage (Lang, 1946). It has been said that concubinage did not bring any disharmony to the old Chinese family, and that the wife and concubines shared their husband without protest. But this is far from the whole story. In a way, the man's desire to have concubines was understandable, for the wife was chosen by his parents, whereas the concubine was selected by him. In the first case, the couple might or might not be compatible, while in the second case, this was more assured. Unlike the attitude in the West, a wife was not humiliated when the husband took a concubine, for it was a culturally accepted practice. In some cases the wife even encouraged the husband to get a concubine. In well-to-do families, potential conflicts could be avoided, since they often lived in many small houses scattered over a wide area. In this way, the wife and concubines were out of reach of each other. Finally, harmony prevailed, for the jealous wife could legally be divorced by her husband according to the seven reasons for divorce.

But the place of the concubine was not as secure as that of the wife, although she was legally a member of the family. A concubine was more easily divorced, or thrown out, for she was protected neither by the "seven grounds for divorce" nor by the "three reasons against it." Furthermore, a concubine's sons were the legal sons of the wife (Forman, 1948) .

While the practice of concubinage existed among the rich, the poor sometimes resorted to the custom of child brides. An infant "daughter" might be taken in by the poor family and brought up as a wife for their son. The underlying motive was to ensure a wife for their son. They were not certain that they would be able to afford the price of the bride when it came time for the son to marry. This form of marriage did not receive the prestige that came from bringing an adult bride into the household. But there were some compensations for the family, for a girl raised in this fashion turned out to be a more willing daughter-in-law. However, there were potential psychological complications in such "sister and brother" marriages.

Footbinding

The custom of footbinding prevailed in old China. It was symbolic of the seclusion and suppression of women. But if it were only a symbol of the suppression of women, mothers would not have been so enthusiastic about binding the feet of their young daughters. It was also considered a sign of beauty, albeit a painfully acquired one, for a pair of small feet could be developed in this fashion.

Footbinding is centuries old and can be traced back to the tenth century (Forman, 1948; Lang, 1946; Lin, 1935) . Bound feet were first fashionable among upper-class ladies, but the practice soon spread to all levels of society. So fixed was the custom in social convention that a woman without bound feet would have difficulty finding a decent husband, even though usefulness in the household and the fields was admittedly restricted by the practice. If a girl had naturally big feet, she would not even be desired as a concubine or prostitute. Only a pauper, forced to preserve the capacity of his daughter to do heavy-duty work, would deprive her of this strange social asset.

Whatever their appeal, the latent intent was clear—bound feet kept women at home and made them safer and less movable property. So says an ancient classic: "Feet are bound, not to make them beautiful as a curved bow, but to restrain the women when they go outdoors" (Lang, 1946).

In some parts of China, however, the practice of footbinding did not catch on. In South China, women with "natural" feet could be found. Such traces may have been left over from the spirit of the original matriarchal system of old China. In her travels, Pearl S. Buck (1954) commented on these women:

> They were beautiful strong women . . . they were not ladies of leisure. Instead they did all the work of the family, very much as though they were maids, and the whole family depended upon them and they were always stronger than their husbands [p. 166].

In the last century, when China was governed by the foreign Manchu rulers, their non-Chinese aboriginal women did not bind their feet. Curiously, the Manchu emperor issued a decree to stop footbinding among the Chinese, but had to rescind it within a few years because of the strong outcry by the Chinese. The custom had become a deeply rooted aesthetic ideal, but its preservation was also a symbol of Chinese opposition to foreign rule (Lang, 1946). Footbinding was still popular at the turn of the century, both in the rural areas and in the cities.

As the Western trend progressed in the cities, the practice of footbinding slowly decreased. Lin (1935) noted that Christian missionaries first led the crusade to abolish this custom, although circumstances were also favorable, since Chinese women had found a suitable substitute in the modern high-heeled shoes. On the way to a new China, fewer Chinese were binding the feet of their daughters. The practice did not seem altogether fitting in a new society where the bondage of the past was being removed.

Winds of change

About the middle of the last century, Chinese society was affected by the impact of the West on its shores. Before that time, China had closed its ports to foreign trade because it enjoyed a self-sufficient economy and valued its conservatism. In 1842, a new era was ushered in with the "opening" of China by the British (Feuerwerker, 1964), followed by other Western powers including the United States (Lang, 1946). After failing to stem the Western tide, the Manchu dynasty was forced to open its major ports (Fairbank, 1958).

A series of defeats shook the complacency of the Chinese Empire, which reluctantly admitted that the West had a superior culture and decided to imitate some of its ways. As a step in this direction, the classical examination system was relegated to the past, and Chinese students were sent abroad to learn the skills and knowledge of the West. The students who went overseas were to play a great role in changing the fabric of Chinese society.

When the last dynasty was overthrown, a new type of government was instituted to replace it. China was proclaimed a republic in 1912. Thus, the monarchy was replaced by a democratic overlay, but the long years ahead were difficult ones.

There were two parties with contrasting plans to remake Chinese society. One was the Nationalist Party (Kuomintang), and the other the Communist Party of China. The former grew out of the original revolutionary party and was a middle-class democratic national party; the latter was principally a peasant-based group, founded in 1921. The two parties joined together briefly to redesign society, but their differences finally erupted in a civil war that was to tear China apart for a quarter of a century. Interestingly, the two borrowed their divergent political blueprints from the West (Feuerwerker, 1964; Schurmann & Schell, 1967; Snow, 1968).

In this brief overview, the events covered are important in that they led to the alteration of the traditional Chinese fabric. The composition of Chinese society was affected at various points, including the political and economic system, the family, and the place of the individual in it. These subunits of society can be conceptualized as a system of hierarchies, each stratum nested in the one above, like a set of Chinese boxes. In this set, the members are constantly changing. The sex roles of male and female in changing society are examples of such ongoing developments.

Some Urban Trends

Due to the influence of the West, China became a transitional society. The Western tide swept into the large seaports first, and slowly spread to the adjacent areas. While signs of Westernization began to appear in the seaports and cities, the people in the more remote inland areas were scarcely touched at all. The great bulk of the Chinese population inhabited inland areas, and they continued to live much the same as they had for centuries.

In the China of old, it was difficult to draw a clean line between rural and urban areas. Even within the walls of the ancient Chinese cities, a rural atmosphere permeated the ways of the people. The city was a place where the wealthy landlords often came to live and where the peasants and artisans came to trade and work. But the atmosphere began to change with the impact of industrialization.

Western modes of production were first adopted by the government, and Chinese private enterprises soon followed suit. Modern factories began to spring up. Some of the cities established enough factories to deserve the name of industrial centers that opened up new opportunities, drawing youths from the country to seek a new way of life. Some of them returned home after a few years, but they brought with them new habits, tastes, and ideas. With improvements in transportation, country and town were brought closer together. However, as industrialization progressed, it speeded up the deterioration of the self-sufficient peasant economy. The introduction of inexpensive Western goods replaced some of the handicraft products of the Chinese. Industrial development in China was limited, however, and the rural population still made up the bulk of the population. As late as the thirties, about 75 to 85 percent of the Chinese population were peasants (Lang, 1946).

Western influences began to appear, to a greater extent, in China's cultural life. Foreign missionaries opened churches, schools, and hospitals throughout the country. Translations of Western literature were popular. New Westernized services were introduced by individuals and the government. In the cities there were new places to go and new things to do. Aside from coeducation, young couples could be seen together dining in restaurants, attending movies, and dancing.

Disintegration of the Traditional Fabric

The old form of the Chinese family was incompatible with the tempo of modern life. The dominance over youths by the older generation, over women by men; and over the individual by the family seemed out of place. In breaking away from the past, the old no longer represented wisdom and virtue, but out-moded traditions. The future of the country now lay more in the hands of the young people. They were needed everywhere to fill leading as well as subordinate positions, whether in industry, in government, or in the professions.

As industrialization progressed, it accelerated the disintegration of the peasant economy. The family was gradually deprived of its role as a productive unit, and consequently the family head lost his status as leader of the work of the family. With better transportation, the young were able to get work away from home. The increased mobility of the population weakened the control of the family and encouraged new family units to come into being.

The rise of industrialization provided a vast market for female labor that was not utilized in the old economy. Women were especially desired in the textile industry and related fields. As they became accepted as factory workers, old barriers in other lines of work began to be lowered.

Women with bound feet were obviously unsuitable for work, and the movement against this practice, weak before industrialization, became more widespread. After the Chinese Revolution, the Republic endorsed this action. There was relatively little resistance to this new trend. In places where women could get work, the men soon agreed that footbinding was objectionable. But in the more backward regions, even in the late thirties, one could still find the old practice.

Coupled with their acceptance in modern industry, the doors of education were opened to women. The private schools first admitted only upper-class women. It may be noted that there were a few missionary schools for girls at the turn of the century, but they were generally mistrusted by the imperial government and the people (Lang, 1946). The need to educate women was soon recognized by the new Chinese government, and public schools were opened for girls. At first their education was limited to elementary schools and teachers' seminaries, but they were later admitted to the top of the educational system; girls were admitted for the first time to the Peking National University in 1919, followed by coeducation in almost all colleges (Lin, 1935).

With their modern education and training, women entered the world of work. In the professions, they often competed equally with men. Some of these women became quite distinguished in their fields. Others went into business, especially after the government recognized women's property rights. Women also participated actively in political pursuits. In the Revolution of 1911, a number of the wives and daughters of the upper class were noted for their part in it. Similarly, working-class and peasant women also streamed into political work, participating in the trade-unions, the Kuomintang and Communist parties, and even in the army. In the army, the women soldiers were treated with great respect by their male comrades and enemies.

The status of women was greatly changed with the acquisition of their new roles in society. In the eyes of society, a higher evaluation was placed on female life (Levy, 1949). Her new occupational role especially elevated her status in the family. The young daughters were now employable in factories, and child labor grew by leaps and bounds, despite laws pretending to regulate it. Women were now a definite economic asset, more than able to earn their keep. If they did not live at home, but in the cities, they would usually send their wages home. In turn, women received a greater voice in family affairs.

The education of women, no doubt, added to their prestige. It opened a new world, bringing them into contact with a whole sphere of life previously closed to them. It expanded their contact with nonfamily members and gave them a new perspective on family life. In comparison, the traditional Chinese girl had little or no alternative to the old way of life, and her seclusion and confinement in the home precluded the possibility of discovering an alternative, if one existed.

The emancipation of the Chinese woman was thus under way, paved by growing economic independence and education. But the rate of social change was still slow, for the old Chinese system did not give in without a struggle, and industrialization did not proceed as rapidly as hoped. Women, even the educated ones, were far from having attained complete equality. In the forties, Lang (1946) reported that there were few women in the professions or in the civil service, and their number at school was still small. The forces of Westernization have been at work, however, and have affected the country. The Chinese family has undergone deep changes, and the government has welcomed and tried to accelerate these changes.

In creating a new social order, the leaders of China were faced with the grave task of revamping the old Chinese society and building a new ideology suitable to changing times. The old values had to be altered before new ones could be created. In this light, Confucian philosophy, classical education, the old administrative system, and traditional forms of social organization were subjected to criticism. The old family system was not spared either.

In the past, protests never attacked the foundations of the family system, filial piety, or subordination to male and paternal authority. Although some contradictions existed between the interests of the state and those of the family, the Confucian family was basically adjusted to the Confucian state—economically, politically, and ideologically. But with the sweep of industrialization, the old Chinese family system became a serious obstacle to progress.

Chinese Renaissance

With the launching of the "Chinese Renaissance Movement" in 1916, the old family system came under powerful attack (Lang, 1946). The rule of the family patriarch was openly challenged. The youth movement rallied the most progressive elements and focused their aims on radical changes in Chinese social and political life, demanding real democracy and popularization of the culture. It proclaimed the right of the individual to find happiness through self-fulfillment. In this respect, the aims of the youth movement were similar to those put forward by the advocates of the Italian Renaissance.

The youths desired a more powerful voice in the political life of the country. Confucianism was seen as being incompatible with freedom and a constitutional regime. The Confucian rules of obedience—of subject to his sovereign, of son to his father, of wife to her husband—had to be eradicated. As citizens of the Chinese Republic, it was out of line to behave like the obedient sons and grandsons of the Confucian age.

It was natural that the movement tried to enlist and appeal to Chinese women, the so-called "unhappiest creatures in the world" (Lang, 1946). The leaders advocated a family life based on mutual love and respect of husband and wife as well as a program for woman's emancipation, stressing their right to enjoy economic independence, to choose their own mates, and to remarry if they were widowed.

The young Chinese of the movement proceeded, at times, to translate their words into deeds. Educated youths assumed a powerful role in the political life of the country for the first time on May 4, 1919, with their historical demonstration against Japan and the Versailles Treaty. In China the movement is known as the May Fourth Movement, and some Communist students played a major role (Snow, 1968).

Leaders of the Nationalist government were influenced by the movement. They felt the contradiction between the old type of family loyalty and the patriotism desired by the new citizen. It was realized that the idea of family and clan unity had to be replaced by the idea of national unity. They also stressed the desire for the equality of women and the need to enlist them in the fight for freedom. In this regard, the government repeatedly passed resolutions urging the reform of the family.

Propaganda against the old family system was vociferous. Criticism was based on the idea that people who were not related did not assist each other and cared only for their kinsmen, not for their country. It was also felt that family loyalty imposed the obligation to find employment for incompetent relatives and impeded national liberation and progress (Lang, 1946; Lin, 1935).

The critics and reformers of the old Chinese family system were, no doubt, influenced by Western thought. Resentment against foreign domination did not stop the Chinese from borrowing Western ideas and techniques. This borrowing has been useful in the refashioning of a new society.

Demands for change grew stronger. In 1931, a new civil code was issued regarding the family. The provisions of the code left no doubt that the leaders were inspired by the desire to remold the Chinese family along Western lines, preserving little of the old Confucian patterns. The code completely disregarded ancestor worship, thus breaking the pillar of the old family and kinship system. It did away with the idea that a male heir was a vital necessity. Among some of the provisions, the code granted equal inheritance rights to both sexes, entitled children to choose their own mates, eased the traditional restriction on the range of relatives eligible to be married, outlawed polygamy, and sanctioned divorce by mutual consent (Freedman, 1964).

But the enforcement of this liberal code has proved difficult. The new law is a great step forward, but the question remains whether the people will make use of it. Except for the families living in large cities, the new laws are at variance with the actual social conditions. The majority of peasants are ignorant of the new law and violations presumably continue in many parts of the country (Lang, 1946; Levy, 1949; Lin, 1935).

At this juncture it may be useful to illustrate the changes that took place in the sex role of females, and how the old and new intersected in the life of a Chinese girl. Such a shift has been documented by Pearl S. Buck (1954). With her perceptive eye, she relates the change in a girl from a traditional, well-to-do family with the lovely name of Hsu Pao-ying. The girl came by to pay a visit one day:

I have known her since she was a mite, with a fat solemn dumpling of a face, with no nose to speak of. At that time, her feast-day garb was a pair of ridiculously small red-cotton trousers with a little coat to match; a pair of shoes made to resemble improbable tigers, and a cap like an embroidered doughnut, with a tiny pigtail done up in cerise yarn sticking through a hole. Her parents are of the good old conservative type, not believing in overmuch book-knowledge for a girl, and with an eye to a good husband and mother-in-law for the child. An older married sister, advanced in views through a five years' residence in Shanghai, had teased them into sending Pao-ying to a boarding-school in the nearest city. When the child left last for school, last autumn, she was a tractable, meek, sweet-faced little thing, rather frightened at the prospect of leaving home. She had the patient air which all little Chinese girls have who are enduring footbinding. I have never heard her volunteer a remark, and in my presence she had always been particularly awed and reverential—an attitude I have ever found very pleasing in the young.

Yesterday she came in a delicate blue satin of a more fashionable cut than I had ever seen; her feet were unbound and in little clumping, square black leather foreign shoes. She was evidently very proud of them; they looked like shoes for a very rough little American boy, and had steel taps on the heels. They stuck out most oddly from her exquisite brocaded skirt.

After we had exchanged polite remarks, and had taken our first sip of tea, she was so evidently conscious of her feet that I could not but comment on her unusual footgear.

"It is the very latest fashion," she replied with great satisfaction. "You know that, of course, in the big cities like Peking and Shanghai, the really fashionable girls do not bind their feet anymore. At the boarding-school they don't either; and so, when I came home, I cried for three days, without food, until for peace they unbound my feet so that I might wear these beautiful American shoes. My feet are still too small, but I stuff cotton in the toes" [pp. 186–87].

New Styles in Marriage and Courtship

The Western type of conjugal family, consisting only of parents and children, has been adopted to a great extent by the modern Chinese. The old Chinese ideal of the large family has fallen out of favor. Even in old China, the joint family of three or more generations persisted only in the upper classes, for it was out of reach of the lower classes primarily because of social and economic considerations.

In industrialized cities, the upper classes that had more intimate and sustained contacts with the sources of Western culture were able to assimilate the conjugal type family. In the country, however, where families of the upper, or landlord, class were still relatively big, they were managed more or less along traditional lines. Their educated sons or daughters, however, after completing their schooling, often stayed in the cities and set up their own small families (Lee, 1953).

On the other hand, in the villages, the poor peasants might be living in *nominally* conjugal families, but the way their wives and children were treated and brought up was fundamentally traditional. They did not live together in the spirit and form of the conjugal family. Typically, they would revert back to the larger family type whenever economic conditions improved.

There were social forces in the city favoring the development of the conjugal family. The cost of living in the city often prevented young industrial workers from inviting their parents and elderly relatives to stay with them. On the other hand, workers' wives and children often found jobs in the factories and thus were able to stay with their husbands and fathers. Sometimes, cultural discrepancies between the generations contributed to the separation.

Young Chinese couples might leave their parents' home to find work in a distant city. Their temporary absence often turned out to be a permanent separation, with no idea that they were about to establish a new family unit. Eventually, there were more conjugal families and fewer joint families in the cities than in the country (Lang, 1946).

Although the joint family system was becoming less popular, the prospect of leaving old parents to live alone bothered some people. In such cases, children permitted their parents to move in with them, perpetuating the "double family" or stem family, a form common even in old China.

In the cities, the life style of the people was often altered. The old rigid separation between the sexes began to be relaxed. Youths in the coeducational colleges often studied and spent their leisure time together. But social intercourse was not confined to the upper class alone, for the girls in modern factories sometimes came into contact with their fellow workers and got acquainted. This social climate was conducive to the appearance of new dating and courtship patterns (Lang, 1946; Lin, 1935). When girls realized their new companion role, young men began to see them in a new light. Chinese men no longer settled for the old traditional division of their emotional life: a wife for the home, a concubine for sexual satisfaction, and a friend to share one's hopes, ideas, and dreams (Lang, 1946; Levy, 1949). They wanted a girl who would combine all these roles. Such a girl could be chosen only by the boy himself. As the relationship between the sexes became more personalized, romantic love was considered an essential prelude to marriage. A girl could no longer be seen simply as a childbearer, her primary role in the old society.

Nevertheless, side by side with the new, the old way still persisted in love as elsewhere (Lang, 1946). Even in their own circles, students still saw marriages arranged in the old style. In spite of the new civil code, many people did not marry mates of their own choosing. Parents, backed by tradition, did not give up their power without a struggle, and few children insisted on their new rights. In the villages, free choice was almost unheard of. Some parents clung to the conviction that it was absolutely impossible and even dangerous to permit children to choose their own mates, especially if the parents had already picked one out for them.

In the cities, however, parents were generally less tradition-bound than those in the country. They were more favorable toward the new trend. Three variations from the old pattern emerged in the cities: (1) the parents arranged a marriage for the youth with his consent, (2) the youth selected his own mate and asked for his parents' approval, and (3) the couple married without consulting their parents. The first two are compromises, but the last represents a complete break with the past.

Social trends developed in which there were greater opportunities for young people to meet, but some social constraints still existed (Lang, 1946). The upper classes usually enjoyed greater freedom. Students in the coeducational colleges enjoyed a favored position. In upper-class homes, house parties were given often. But in the middle and lower classes, the sexes were still generally segregated and mixed parties, infrequent. As for public entertainment, there was not much in the way of dances, concerts, sporting events, or demonstrations. Working-class people were therefore disadvantaged to some extent.

In all levels of society, the matchmaker still held a useful position. Among the moderns, the shy ones relied heavily on friends and relatives to assume this role. The old rule of forbidding prospective mates to see each other, of course, was overlooked. Some of the traditional matchmakers not only introduced young people to each other, but also carried out negotiations between families, in the style of Jewish and East European matchmakers.

After the boy and girl had found each other, the bride price presented a financial hurdle to marriage that continued in spite of widespread public sentiment against it (Lang, 1946). In the upper and middle classes expensive trousseaus replaced a literal payment, but were considered essential for the reputation of the girl and her parents. The traditional wedding was elaborate, culminating with a feast for relatives and friends. In the thirties, as part of the New Life Movement, the government provided "collective weddings" for the purpose of reducing the usual great expenses involved in marriage. Couples were gathered together and married simultaneously by city authorities. The whole procedure was so inexpensive that even the poorest of the poor could afford to get married. This practice, however, was not adopted by the bulk of the people because of their traditional regard for the importance of the wedding day (Huang, 1961; Yang, 1959).

In the conjugal families, the web of social relationships was rearranged. The traditional tie between the generations was loosened. With respect to the father-son relationship, strict submission to the father no longer carried with it the same imperative. The potential conflict between mother-in-law and daughter-in-law usually could be avoided. As a consequence of these changes in family pattern, the tie between husband and wife became stronger.

The roles of the couple as father and mother were also modified. Their childrearing practices were often different from those of their parents. They took a less authoritarian posture and became more companionable. The traditional belief that it is unmanly to help with the housework and child-caring activities also started to disappear, and if the wife were a working mother, the role assignment of the couple tended to overlap to a greater extent.

In a transitional society moving from the old to the new, some social dislocations are inevitable. The most dramatic examples are afforded by the marriages between old-fashioned girls and modern young men, arranged by anxious parents in the vain hope of bringing their errant sons back to the fold. On the other side of the coin are the cases of country husbands in love with girls whom they met in the cities where they went to find jobs. The most obvious solution to such a dilemma is divorce which, however, is extraordinarily hard on the traditional Chinese wife. Lang (1946) depicts the situation as follows:

> For a woman in old China to be divorced was to be disgraced. And these old-fashioned wives live in old China! Worst of all, they cannot understand why they are abandoned! They know that they have been married like their mothers and grandmothers, according to the rules of propriety. They know they have been dutiful wives and obedient daughters-in-law, they have done everything to please their husbands, even borne them sons. If their husbands were not satisfied, why did they not take a concubine? Neither are the parents of the husband pleased by divorce. They pity their daughters-in-law, or value their services which they know modern daughters-in-law would never perform. But modern girls refuse to be concubines, they insist on clear-cut decisions. They demand that the first wives be divorced [p. 203].

In some tragic cases, the wife commits suicide. In others, the man compromises by marrying again without divorcing the first wife.

Educational discrepancy between partners may sometimes be a source of difficulty. If the career of an educated man takes him to the city, he may sometimes want his wife for companionship and participation in social events. But the country wife may not be able to cope with the situation, especially if the city women are also educated.

In regard to the old, their place in modern Chinese society has declined. In modern society, the accent is on youth. The elders once enjoyed a secure and honorable place in Chinese society, with the observance of filial piety as their insurance against old age. There is a growing tendency for children to assume less responsibility for their parents. There are more and more instances of old parents who have married sons and yet live alone (Lang, 1946). As is fairly typical of industrial societies, the problem of old age looms greater with time and tends to be a neglected issue.

These trends are also occurring in such places as Hong Kong and Taiwan. They are part of the Chinese fabric, at least historically. The progress of Westernization may vary from place to place, but the conflict between the traditional and modern way of life is felt in all these places. The clash between the two cultures engenders similar conflict in sex roles throughout the Chinese scene (Fong & Peskin, 1969; Freedman, 1966; Wolf, 1968; Wright, 1964).

While modern trends in sex roles are developing on the urban scene, traditional patterns are still strongly rooted in the more remote villages. The differences between the two areas have been growing more apparent. On the whole, China is still largely agricultural, but it is generally agreed that the progressive industrialization of the country holds the key to its future. In transitional China, all the major political parties spoke out early for industrialization, but they differed in the means they proposed to use in achieving this objective.

Red flags over China

The fabric of Chinese society was altered rapidly with the triumph of Communism in 1949. Chinese leaders started immediately to replace the chaos of war with a Soviet-type of order: a new administration was established, businesses were nationalized, and the poor were mobilized. The present regime maintains that the Chinese Revolution has not yet ended, that vestiges remain to be swept away, that new organizations need to be strengthened, and that new citizens must be trained. The end may not be in sight, but the design of the new society is clearly beginning to emerge.

The Chinese government has embarked on a reconstruction program and, despite failures and setbacks, a number of goals have been attained. The country is now unified and organized, and a powerful but flexible political system governs the remotest parts of the country and the smallest units of society. Foundations have been laid for modern industry, science, and technology, and China is becoming one of the world's major industrial nations (Hobbs, 1966; Schurmann & Schell, 1967).

The fact remains that China is still one of the world's poorest nations, and this is readily admitted. Although China's 100 million city-dwellers may be moving fast into the modern era, it may be some time before her 600 million peasants turn into modern producers. The Communists are determined to remedy this state of affairs.

The progress of Chinese Communism has been marked by long periods of careful, practical development interspersed with short bursts of intense ideological mobilization. Before invoking visionary ideology for mobilization purposes, the Chinese Communists always wait until they have control over the people they want to mobilize. In developing a new society, there have been some attempts to refashion the traditional attitudes of the Chinese people. The easy-going Chinese of yesteryear are being taught that suffering, hard work, self-control, constant study, and unswerving compliance with the decisions of the state and Party are needed for the cause of building a new country (Schurmann & Schell, 1967). Thought reform has been initiated to tear the Chinese out of his traditional ways in order to create a "new man" in the new society. These sessions attempt to cut the individual's emotional and cultural ties to the past and, as a step in this direction, an effort is made to destroy the individual's traditional identity as a filial son—denouncing the old order in the form of his father—in order to make way for a new identity, that of a zealous citizen of the Communist regime.

The question may be asked as to how well thought reform has succeeded. There is evidence that individuals range from completely zealous converts to resisters, the great majority of the people falling in between. The program is currently less active than during the first five years of the regime. As years go by, the young people will be exposed only to Communist teaching. Thus, the emphasis will inevitably shift from reform to continuing indoctrination in the form of "the correction of ideological errors" (Lifton, 1957).

Redesign of the family

The forces of social change sweeping the country have also affected the traditional family system. In the cities, the Chinese family has been altered during the past decades. But the change came about spontaneously and not as a result of coordination and conscious planning by an organized political power (Yang, 1959). The present regime is concerned with remaking the entire fabric of China's political, economic, and social life, and the family is part of this scheme.

The movement to alter the family on a national scale began formally with the proclamation of the Marriage Law in 1950. With the implementation of its policies, alterations in the traditional family have been occurring in all parts of the country. The importance attached to remaking the family stems from the realization of the central role the institution plays in shaping the lives of individuals. Traditionally, the family is one of the most important units of production, and there is hardly any aspect of traditional social life that is not affected by the ties and influence of the family.

The Chinese family system is largely responsible for the stability of the traditional social order and the long continuity of Chinese culture. In the old order, the traditional family could operate effectively in spite of the numerous dissatisfactions of women and the young arising out of its authoritarian character, but it prevailed since the surrounding society was also set up along similar lines.

The State as Father

In a changing world, however, the traditional family system seemed out of place. There was a popular demand from educated youths for a "family revolution" in the second decade of this century. The needs of a modern industrial and national state are different from those of the old order. Some of the original functions of the family system are being displaced by new economic and political endeavors. In a modern economy, the job market is based more on the objective qualifications of the individual than on kinship ties. Furthermore, the family or clan system divided the population into numerous self-contained groups, while the organization of a modern industrialized nation requires a greater degree of integration and coordination among the constituents. In building their socialist state, the Communists recognized a contradiction between the kinship organization and the new society. Traditional loyalty to the family conflicted with loyalty to the state. When the Communists came to power and initiated their program of family reform, they were essentially promoting with greater vigor a slower process of change already under way. The family and clan system had been undermined with the land reform program. In the process, the possibility of being confronted with politically dangerous clans was removed. By enforcing its rule, the present government took away the property of the clans (land and ancestral temples) and prohibited ancestor worship as part of its general ban on superstitious practices (Freedman, 1964, 1966).

New sanctions were brought to bear on the traditional family system. The brunt of family reform fell on the rural areas where the old system was strongly rooted. In trying to break the hold of tradition, the Party, as a first step, encouraged children to report their fathers for any infraction of Party principles. By freeing the young person from established authority, he became more amenable to indoctrination by the new order. The thrust that broke the hold of the past turned out to be a two-edged sword. Once encouraged to defy the authority of their parents, youths displayed a similar disrespect for the authority of the state. Some second thoughts began to occur, and it was officially recognized that the propaganda campaign against the control of elders might lead to misunderstanding. Some of the social pressure was removed so that a new balance resulted between parents and children, without returning to the past.

The Communists called for drastic reform of the traditional family system that they retained as a basic social unit, but with markedly reduced functions. In a fashion, the paternalism of elders has been displaced by the authority of the state (Schurmann & Schell, 1967).

New Marriage Law

In the days before Communism, the family law drawn up by the Kuomintang government in 1931 was never applied in any general way. After a review of the old law, the Communist government announced the new marriage law of the People's Republic in 1950, according to which marriage is based on free choice of partners, on monogamy, on equal rights for both sexes, and on the protection of the lawful interests of women and children (Freedman, 1964; Yang, 1959).

When the marriage law came out, there was some fear that it would herald the death of the Chinese family. At first there was an epidemic of broken marriages. After 1953, however, things quieted down, at least until the communes were created in 1958 when there was talk of introducing mess halls, nurseries, kindergartens, old peoples' homes, and enforced separation of husbands and wives. These threats to the continuation of the family proved to be ineffective because the institution has survived, although cut down in size to conjugal units. In general, the rights of women and children have been recognized. Filial piety has been eradicated, but children can be exhorted as responsible Communists to respect and support their aged parents.

The greatest change in family form is to be found in the peasant family, which is no longer a self-contained economic group with total control over its resources and work. The only private property the family can own is the house and a small plot of land allocated to it. The rest is collectivized. The family is now part of a larger organization that determines the economic rights and duties of individual members, male or female. This system has affected the social roles of both sexes, but females especially. Women can participate equally in production and are thus on equal footing with their husbands. But women still retain part of their traditional sex role, for they have to find time for their domestic chores.

Young men and women now enjoy greater freedom and equality in marriage and divorce. In contemporary Chinese life, getting married is a private decision between the two interested parties. In general, girls are out and about more than they used to be. In fact, the officialdom tries to encourage their association with young men and to this end sponsors chaste dances and other decent types of activities (Freedman, 1964; Yang, 1959).

By what criteria do young people choose their future mates? This is no easy question, and there may be as many answers as there are people. Freedman (1964) hazards the guess that traditional Chinese values and the asexual puritanism of Chinese Communism would dispel erotic love. Youths who are more old fashioned, may still request their parents to arrange a marriage for them, or rely on their friends to play this role.

The commune

In the early years, the tempo of family reform was rapid, but, as indicated above, after 1953 the mass organized campaign has noticeably slowed down (Yang, 1959). Even in the rural communes, the family is still a unit. Robinson (1964) reports that it is not unusual for three generations to share a vacated gentry house and pool their earnings. It is legal for everyone to reclaim a fraction of his original land. Seen from one angle, the communes are a means of imposing government policy, and from another, they are highly democratic (Robinson, 1964). Elections are held for the director of the commune and for the leaders of the brigades and teams. But formal democracy is overruled by the Party from the outside.

The forward movement of the new society has been held back, however, by the growing population. In the face of this swell, later ages for marrying, and birth control are being encouraged (Myrdal, 1965; Robinson, 1964; Yang, 1959).

Strain Between Generations

Some of the changes in the social life of the peasants in the commune have been documented by Myrdal (1965). The changing roles of the sexes are interesting and have resulted in no small amount of stress and strain between the sexes and between the generations. Old women can still recall the days when they were "worthless," when the call to unbind their feet was first heard, and when they began to work side by side with men in the fields. The peasants interviewed by Myrdal often sound like voices from the past. For example, a young woman who taught grown-ups to read and write recalls a discussion on the topic of the woman of today:

> We discussed whether women are men's equals or not, and most said: "Within the family, man and woman are equal. We help the men when they work in the fields and they should help us in the house." But many of the older women said: "Women are born to attend to the household. A woman cannot work in the fields. That can't be helped. It is just that men and women are born different. A person is born either a man or a woman. To work in the fields or in the house." We had long discussions. The young ones were all on the side of equality and freedom. It had now become quite usual with our generation for husband and wife to discuss the family's problems and decide about them together. Women now no longer work in the house, they also work in the fields and earn their own

> money. But the men of the older generation still say: "What does a woman know? Women are worth nothing!" In such families the men decide everything and their wives say: "We are just women. We are not allowed to say anything" [p. 252].

The changing pattern of social interaction between the sexes has also caused some uneasiness. The views of older women are colored, of course, by the old custom of segregation between the sexes. The young teacher continues:

> Another thing we have to deal with now and again is that the old women find it difficult to understand that nowadays women laugh and joke with men. They scold their daughters and daughters-in-law and granddaughters for not observing decent behavior. When that happens, we have to speak with the old women about the equality of the sexes. We tell them that, now, a woman is the equal of a man in the family and in society. She does not just look after the home, she also works in the fields. She has to vote and she can be elected. It is obvious that she also talks with men and jokes with them as comrades. We remind the old people about their own bitter youth and keep telling them that as women now are equal, they also have the right to chat and joke. The old people say that they agree we are right. But in their heart of hearts they always feel uneasy and uncertain when they see girls joking with men. But we are patient with the old people. They can't help their attitude. Perhaps not all old women are like that, but most, I'm sure, think it indecent and immoral and shocking that young people talk with each other. The young people, of course, are all agreed. None of the young people think like the old ones on this question. So it will solve itself in time [pp. 256–57].

Coupled with the freedom of socializing with the opposite sex, free choice in marriage is a further source of conflict. The wide publicity given to the Marriage Law produced many new marriages based on free choice, but was later followed by a general rise in arranged marriages in some of the rural communities (Yang, 1959). Some stubborn peasants still favor the old rural practice of purchase marriage. For example, Myrdal (1965) tells of a father whose daughter wanted to marry a "poor" boy, but he objected, saying:

> I had to pay dearly for my wife. Now I have been giving this girl food and clothes. I have brought her up and she just goes off. It isn't right. I just lose and lose all the time. I must get back something of all the money I have laid out on her. If she can't fall in love with a man who can pay back what she's cost, then it isn't right for her to marry [p. 256].

The New Sex Roles

The traditional Chinese family has been affected by the tempo of the times. In the last few decades, the Chinese family in the city has been changing in the direction of the family in the West, i.e. of life in a developed economy. The change sponsored by the Communists, but only partially brought about by them, has carried the movement into the rural areas. The Chinese family does not control the lives of its members as effectively as it once did. The young are no longer subjugated by their parents, and women enjoy greater freedom from the restraints of a male-dominated society.

The type of family that is popular in the West has never been typical of peasant societies. It is rather interesting that modernization should have progressed so far with the Chinese peasant family. It is generally thought that industrialization is the crucial variable for changing the form of the family (breaking it down to simpler form and enabling women and children to break away from traditional ties). It may be that the forces operating on the rural and urban family are quite different, but they may produce similar outcomes. In both cases, the power of the traditional family has been undermined. The changing conditions of society have provided youth with alternatives to following in the footsteps of their parents. The increased independence and self-reliance of young people today have changed their relationship to their parents. We have already seen that as the traditional ties between the generations weaken, those between man and wife become stronger. It seems likely that this trend will continue and eventually permeate all Chinese life in the future.

In a new society where the trend is toward a greater degree of freedom of association between the sexes, the style of interaction is often changed. The sexes may be exposed to social situations that they, or their parents, have never faced before. The young people may then begin to develop new social techniques. An old-fashioned girl who has been properly secluded at home may never have the opportunity to develop such social skills. Such a Chinese girl would be astonished and embarrassed if she were told that she must find her own mate now (Buck, 1954). In the past, there was little opportunity to mix with the opposite sex. In Communist China, some young people do not seem to know what to do with their new freedom now that they have it. There are reports of couples getting married after having known each other for only a week or two (Huang, 1961). Such unions often end in divorce a short time afterward. The government is trying to discourage such instant marriages and to educate the public against it.

In a society that is undergoing a transition, there may be some conflict between the old and the new sex roles. For example, the traditional Chinese frown on the show of affection in public. It is even indecent, in their eyes, to hold hands in public (Lang, 1946). In regard to what behavior is appropriate for the sexes, the attitudes of the parents are likely to be fixed, while those of the younger generation are more open. Conflict between old and new social roles has been beautifully described by Pearl S. Buck (1962), in *Hearts Come Home*. It is a story about two young people who are trying to conform, outwardly, to the Western style of the boy-girl relationship, but in their hearts they are truly old-fashioned.

On the whole, with the modernization of the social fabric of China, the people have altered their life styles in such a way as to approach those in other developed countries. The spread of industrialization may create a greater bond of social similarity between the different peoples of the world. Perhaps a universal community will one day emerge.

References

Buck, P. S. *My Several Worlds*. New York: John Day, 1954. (Paperback edition, Pocket Books, 1956.)

———. *Letter from Peking*. New York: Pocket Books, 1958.

———. *Hearts Come Home and Other Stories*. New York: Pocket Books, 1962.

Fairbank, J. K. *The United States and China*. Rev. ed. Cambridge, Mass.: Harvard University Press, 1958.

Feuerwerker, A., ed. *Modern China*. Englewood Cliffs, N.J.: Prentice-Hall, 1964.

Fong, S. L. M., and H. Peskin. Sex-role Strain and Personality Adjustment of China-born Students in America: A Pilot Study. *Journal of Abnormal Psychology*, 74, 5 (1969), 563–67.

Forman, H. *Changing China*. New York: Crown, 1948.

Freedman, M. "The Family in China, Past and Present." *Pacific Affairs*, 34 (1962), 323–36.

———. "The Family under Chinese Communism." *Political Quarterly*, 35 (1964), 342–50.

———. *Chinese Lineage and Society: Fukien and Kwangtung*. New York: Humanities Press, 1966.

Hobbs, L. *I Saw Red China*. New York: McGraw-Hill, 1966.

Hsu, F. L. K. *Under the Ancestors' Shadow*. New York: Columbia University Press, 1948.

———. *Clan, Caste and Club*. Princeton, N.J.: Van Nostrand, 1963.

Huang, L. J. "Some Changing Patterns in the Communist Chinese Family." *Marriage and Family Living*, 23 (1961), 137–46.

Lang, O. *Chinese Family and Society*. New Haven: Yale University Press, 1946. (Republished by Archon Books, 1968.)

Lee, S. C. "China's Traditional Family, Its Characteristics and Disintegration." *American Sociological Review*, 18 (1953), 272–80.

Levy, M. J. *The Family Revolution in Modern China*. Cambridge, Mass.: Harvard University Press, 1949.

Lifton, R. J. "Brainwashing in Perspective." *New Republic*, May 13, 1957.

Lin, Y. T. *My Country and My People*. New York: Reynal & Hitchcock, 1935.

Michael, F. "State and Society in Nineteenth-century China." *World Politics*, 7 (1955), 419–33.

Myrdal, J. *Report from a Chinese Village*. New York: Signet, 1965.

Robinson, J. "The Chinese Communes." *Political Quarterly*, 35 (1964), 285–97.

Schurmann, F., and O. Schell, eds. *Communist China*. New York: Vintage, 1967.

Snow, E. *Red Star over China*. Rev. ed. New York: Grove, 1968.

Wolf, M. *The House of Lim: A Study of a Chinese Farm Family*. New York: Appleton-Century-Crofts, 1968.

Wright, B. R. "Social Aspects of Change in the Chinese Family Pattern in Hong Kong." *Journal of Social Psychology*, 63 (1964), 31–39.

Yang, C. K. *The Chinese Family in the Communist Revolution*. Cambridge, Mass.: M. I. T Press, 1959.

Yang, M. C. *A Chinese Village*. New York: Columbia University Press, 1945.

EPILOGUE

SOCIAL CHANGE AND CULTURAL SURROGATES

To point up certain general implications of the present volume, we had originally chosen as our final selection an article by Margaret Mead published in 1940 which, in spite of the date, is not "dated." This paper reflects, with surprising timeliness, recent thinking in the areas of age and sex roles. In the perspective of relatively stable preliterate societies, the author clarifies for the more complex, rapidly changing cultures the current generation struggle as well as that of the previous generation when the essay was written. Mead sees the basic dynamics of socialization not in the Freudian terms of the child's identification with the parent but, rather, in relation to the peer group. In periods of accelerated social change, this is necessarily so because ". . . the child will never be, as an adult a member of the same culture of which his father stands as the representative during his early years." In other words, the old role models failed to provide solutions for the problems unique to each generation. New models for different patterns of living had to be worked out. The socializing function of the age peers and sex-role partners took on crucial significance.

Since 1960, we have seen a new kind of generation conflict, worldwide in scope. Today's youth do not live in the world in which their parents were reared, and this experience is shared by all young people, who now can no longer find adult models anywhere.

This new generation gap was the subject of the series of *Man and Nature Lectures* that Margaret Mead delivered at the American Museum of Natural History in 1969, and we reprint here an editorial from *Science* (Vol. 164, No. 3876, April 11, 1969) that summarizes these conclusions. The whole series is published as *Culture and Commitment* (the Natural History Press, 1970).

THE GENERATION GAP[1]

Margaret Mead

The young people who are rebelling all around the world, rebelling against whatever form the governmental and educational systems take, are like the first generation born in a new country listening to their parents' tales of the old country and watching their parents grapple, often clumsily, often unsuccessfully, with the new conditions. They have no firsthand knowledge of the way their parents lived far across the seas, of how differently wood responded to tools, or land to the hoe. They see the tasks which their unaccustomed elders are performing as poorly done; they feel that there must be a better way, and that they must find it.

For now, nowhere in the whole world are there any elders who know what the children know, no matter how remote and simple the societies in which the children live. In the past there were always some elders who knew more—in terms of experience, of having grown up within a system—than any children. Today there are none. It is not only that parents are no longer a guide, but that there are no guides, in the older sense of the term, whether one seeks them in one's own country, or in China, or in India. There are no elders who know what those who have been reared in the last 20 years know about what the next 20 years will be.

All of us who grew up before the war are immigrants in time, immigrants from an earlier world, living in an age essentially different from anything we knew before. We still hold the seats of power and command the resources and the skills which have been used in the past to keep order and organize large societies. We control the educational systems, the apprenticeship systems, the career ladders up which the young are required to climb, step by step.

The elders are separated from the young by the fact that they too are a strangely isolated generation. No generation has ever known, experienced, and incorporated such rapid changes, watched the sources of power, the means of communication, the definition of humanity, the limits of their explorable universe, the certainties of a known and limited world, the fundamental imperatives of life and death—all change before their eyes. They know more about change than any generation has ever known and so stand, over, against, and vastly alienated from the young, who, by the very nature of their position, have had to reject their elders' past. Just as the early Americans had to teach themselves not to daydream of the past but to concentrate on the present, and so in turn taught their children not daydream but to act, so today's elders have treated their own pasts as incommunicable, and teach their children, even in the midst of lamenting that it is so, not to ask, because they can never understand. We have to realize that no other generation will ever experience what we have experienced. In this sense we have no descendants. At this breaking point between two radically different and closely related groups, both are inevitably very lonely, as we face each other knowing that they will never experience what we have experienced and that we can never experience what they have experienced.

As long as any adult thinks that he, like the parents and teachers of old, can become introspective, invoke his own youth to understand the youth before him, he is lost. But once the fact of a deep, new, unprecedented, worldwide generation gap is firmly established, in the minds of both the young and the old, communication can be established again.

[1] Adapted from lecture III, "Culture and Commitment," of the American Museum of Natural History's "Man and Nature Lectures Series V."

Recent books for further reading

Aries, Phillipe. *Centuries of Childhood: A Social History of Family Life,* Robert Baldick, trans. New York: Alfred A. Knopf, 1962.

Bernard, Jessie. *The Sex Game.* Englewood Cliffs, N.J.: Prentice-Hall, 1968.

Blitsten, Dorothy R. *The World of the Family.* New York: Random House, 1963.

Blood, Robert O., Jr., and Donald M. Wolfe, *Husbands and Wives: The Dynamics of Married Living.* New York: Free Press, 1960.

Brenton, Myron. *The American Male.* New York: Coward-McCann, 1960.

Broderick, Carlfred B. and Jessie Bernard, eds. *The Individual, Sex, and Society.* Baltimore: Johns Hopkins Press, 1969.

Buck, Pearl. *Hearts Come Home and Other Stories.* New York: Pocket Books, 1962.

Campbell, John. *Honour, Family and Patronage.* Oxford: Clarendon Press, 1964.

Chombart de Lauwe, Paul, ed. *Images de la Femme dans le Société.* Paris: UNESCO, 1962.

Cohen, Yehudi A. *The Transition from Childhood to Adolescence.* Chicago: Aldine, 1964.

Dahlström, Edmund, ed. *Kvinnors Liv och Arbete (The Life and Work of Women).* Stockholm: Studieförbundet Näringsliv & Samhälle, 1962.

De Vos, George A. and Wagatsuma, Hiroshi. *The Legacy of Endurance.* Berkeley, Calif.: University of California Press, 1971.

Dodge, Norton T. *Women in the Soviet Economy: Their Role in Economic, Scientific, and Technical Development.* Baltimore: Johns Hopkins Press, 1966.

Erikson, Erik H. *Childhood and Society.* 2nd ed. New York: Norton, 1963.

———. *Identity: Youth and Crisis.* New York: Norton, 1968.

Feuerwerker, A., ed. *Modern China.* Englewood Cliffs, N.J.: Prentice-Hall, 1964.

Foster, P. J. *Education and Social Change in Ghana.* London: Routledge & Kegan Paul, 1965.

Friedan, Betty. *The Feminine Mystique.* New York: Norton, 1963.

Friedl, Ernestine. *Vasilika.* New York: Holt, Rinehart & Winston, 1962.

Geiger, Kent H. *The Family in Soviet Russia.* Cambridge, Mass.: Harvard University Press, 1968.

Goode, William J. *World Revolution and Family Patterns.* New York: Free Press, 1963.

Herskovits, Melville J. *The Human Factor in Changing Africa.* London: Routledge & Kegan Paul, 1963.

Hsu, Francis L. K., ed. *Psychological Anthropology: Approaches to Culture and Personality.* Homewood, Ill.: Dorsey Press, 1961.

Hunt, Morton M. *Her Infinite Variety: The American Woman as Love Mate and Rival.* New York: Harper and Row, 1962.

Kaplan, Bert, ed. *Studying Personality Cross-Culturally.* New York: Harper and Row, 1961.

Kenkel, William. *The Family in Perspective.* New York: Appleton-Century-Crofts, 1960.

Kirkpatrick, Clifford. *The Family As Process and Institution,* rev. ed. New York: Ronald Press, 1963.

Klerner, Richard H. *Marriage and Family Relationships.* New York: Harper & Row, 1970.

Komarovsky, Mirra. *Blue-collar Marriage.* New York: Random House, 1962.

Lacey, W. K. *The Family in Classical Greece.* London: Camelot Press, 1968.

Lamson, Peggy. *Few Are Chosen: American Women in Political Life Today.* Boston: Houghton Mifflin, 1968.

Lewis, Edwin C. *Developing Woman's Potential.* Ames, Iowa: Iowa State University Press, 1968.

Lewis, Oscar. *La Vida.* New York: Random House, 1966.

Makarenko, A. S. *The Collective Family: A Handbook for Russian Parents,* R. Daglish, trans. New York: Doubleday, 1967.

Marmor, Judd, ed. *Sexual Inversion: The Multiple Roots of Homosexuality.* New York: Basic Books, 1965.

Mead, Margaret. *Culture and Commitment.* New York: The Natural History Press, 1970.

Norbeck, Edward. *Changing Japan.* New York: Holt, Rinehart & Winston, 1965.

Nye, F. Ivan, and Lois W. Hoffman, eds. *The Employed Mother in America.* Chicago: Rand McNally, 1963.

Patai, Raphael. *Sex and the Family in the Bible and the Middle East.* Garden City, New York: Doubleday, 1959.

———, ed. *Women in the Modern World.* New York: Free Press, 1967.

Paulme, Denise, ed. *Women of Tropical Africa,* H. M. Wright, trans. Berkeley: University of California Press, 1963.

Paz, Octavio. *The Labyrinth of Solitude: Life and Thought in Mexico.* New York: Grove Press, 1961.

Queen, Stuart, Robert W. Habenstein, and John B. Adams. *The Family in Various Cultures,* rev. ed. Philadelphia: J. P. Lippincott, 1961.

Rabin, A. I. *Growing Up in the Kibbutz.* New York: Springer, 1965.

Ruitenbeek, H. M., ed. *The Problem of Homosexuality in Modern Society.* New York: Dutton, 1963.

Seltman, C. *Women in Antiquity.* New York: Collier, 1962.

Silberman, Bernard S., ed. *Japanese Character and Culture: Book of Selected Readings.* Tucson: University of Arizona Press, 1962.

Stephens, William N. *The Family in Cross-Cultural Perspective.* New York: Holt, Rinehart & Winston, 1963.

Stephens, William N. *The Oedipus Complex: Cross-Cultural Evidence.* New York: Free Press, 1962.

Theobald, Robert *et al. Dialogue on Women.* Indianapolis: Bobbs-Merrill, 1967.

Toman, Walter. *Family Constellation: The Effects on Personality and Social Behavior.* New York: Springer Publishing Co., 1969.

Udry, J. Richard. *The Social Context of Marriage.* Philadelphia: Lippincott, 1966.

van den Berghe, Pierre L., ed. *Africa: Social Problems of Change and Conflict.* San Francisco: Chandler, 1965.

Vogel, Ezra. *Japan's New Middle Class.* Berkeley: University of California Press, 1963.

Ward, Barbara E., ed. *Women in the New Asia.* Paris: UNESCO, 1963.

Wagley, Charles. *The Latin American Tradition.* New York: Columbia University Press, 1968.

Williamson, Robert C. *Marriage and Family Relations.* New York: Wiley, 1966.

Winch, Robert F. *The Modern Family,* rev. ed. New York: Holt, Rinehart & Winston, 1963.

——— and Louis W. Goodman, eds. *Selected Studies in Marriage and the Family.* 3rd ed. New York: Holt, Rinehart & Winston, 1968.

NAME INDEX

SUBJECT INDEX